The Unpast

This series of publications on Africa, Latin America, Southeast Asia, and Global and Comparative Studies is designed to present significant research, translation, and opinion to area specialists and to a wide community of persons interested in world affairs. The editor seeks manuscripts of quality on any subject and can usually make a decision regarding publication within three months of receipt of the original work. Production methods generally permit a work to appear within one year of acceptance. The editor works closely with authors to produce a high-quality book. The series appears in a paperback format and is distributed worldwide. For more information, contact the executive editor at Ohio University Press, 19 Circle Drive, The Ridges, Athens, Ohio 45701.

The Unpast

Elite Violence and Social Control in Brazil,

1954–2000

R. S. Rose

Ohio University Research in International Studies
Latin America Series No. 44
Ohio University Press
Athens

12 11 10 09 08 07 06 05 5 4 3 2 1

The books in the Ohio University Research in International Studies series
are printed on acid-free paper ♾™

Library of Congress Cataloging-in-Publication Data

Rose, R. S., 1943–
The unpast : elite violence and social control in Brazil, 1954–2000 / R.S. Rose.
p. cm. — (Ohio University research in international studies. Latin America series ; no. 44)
Includes bibliographical references and index.
ISBN 0-89680-243-4 (pbk. : alk. paper)
1. Violence—Brazil—History—20th century. 2. Political violence—Brazil—History—20th century. 3. Elite (Social sciences)—Brazil—History—20th century. 4. Social control—Brazil—History—20th century. I. Title: Elite violence and social control in Brazil, 1954–2000. II. Title. III. Research in international studies. Latin America series ; no. 44.

HN290.Z9V564 2005
303.6'0981—dc22 2005002778

"The past is never dead. It's not even past."

—William Faulkner

Contents

Preface

For my teacher and friend, Knut Sveri: *Jeg håper at Britt skulle har synest om den har siste avsnittet.* Best wishes, as well, go out to Wally Dean Couch for providing me with five months of quiet respite in Sweden. Thanks to you, "Dutch," I found the time to complete the manuscript and punch in the final years of data that make up part of chapter 6. The job of interpreting that mountain of figures, once it was ready to be analyzed, was made easier by the generosity of J. Barry Gurdin.

I never forgot that the numbers I was entering into my computer were all that was left of once-living human beings. People with lives, bills to pay, with lovers, spouses, children, and parents who cared for them. These persons were the victims of elite violence in a culture that downplayed and continues to deny their importance. Few individuals have ever protested their murders. One of the first was Hélio Bicudo. His courage in the face of evil, his ideas for a more just Brazil, and his refinement of the final chapter of this, my twenty-two-year effort at understanding why death squads happened first in the Americas in his country, moved my intellect and captured my soul.

Deputado Estadual Paulo Melo and his staff, especially Lina Paula, are two additional persons who bucked the tide. If for nothing else they deserve mention for providing me with an early copy of their valiant work, "Relatório e conclusão da comissão parlamentar de inquérito para apuração de responsabilidades pelo extermínio de crianças e dolescentes no estado do Rio de Janeiro." Why can't there be more people like these in this unfulfilled paradise that has cried out for justice for so long?

John W. F. Dulles sent me many valuable items from his own files and put up with my pestering phone calls and e-mails over the years. I am happy and grateful that he could review part of this manuscript. He was always there to lend a hand and cheer me on—even when he knew I was taking a philosophical road different from his own. He remains my favorite *brasilianista.* Richard Quinney likewise looked at a later version of my efforts and not only approved it but encouraged me beyond words alone. Thank you, Richard.

Also supportive in their own ways were Gail Abbott, Nilo Batista, Jan Knippers Black, Douglas Corbishley, Marcio Luiz Donnici, Branca Eloysa Pedreira Ferreira, Paulo Apulcro Fonseca, Edu and Grasiella Freire and their friends in São Paulo, Paul Friday, Fernando Gabeira, João Vicente Goulart, Stuart Henry, Crister Kågéll, Ester Kosovski, Solomão Malina, Luis Cláudio and Cecilia Marigo, Togo Meirelles, Eliana Furtado de Mendonça, João Pinheiro Neto, Rosa del Omo, Mike Ormsby, Waldecy Catharina Magalhães Pederia, Eliane Perez, Paulo Sérgio Pinheiro, Tony Platt, Anita Leocadia Prestes, Luís Carlos Prestes, Lygia Prestes, Peter Wickman, and Per-Olaf Wickström.

To those at the various archives and private collections who so kindly assisted me, I would like to add my recognition. Without their professional and dedicated assistance, none of my hard work would have come to fruition. The list includes the Arquivo Nacional, Arquivo Público do Estado do Rio de Janeiro, Benson Latin American Collection, Biblioteca da Fundação Getúlio Vargas, Biblioteca Nacional, Comissão Pastoral da Terra-Acre, Comissão Pastoral da Terra-Goiânia, Fundação Casa Rui Barbosa, Fundação Getúlio Vargas/CPDOC, Instituto Brasileiro de Geografia e Estatística, Instituto Histórico e Geográfico Brasileiro, Lyndon Baines Johnson Presidential Library, Movimento dos Trabalhadores Rurais sem Terra, National Archives, Notícias Populares Archives, O Dia Archives, Ordem dos Advogados do Brasil, and the records of Tortura Nunca Mais.

Then there were all those I lied to in Brazil. With such a topic as elite violence and its connection to extermination groups, I had to develop a justification for being in the country. I hope these people understand why I could not tell them the truth. There was a real danger of losing my life. This was underlined early on in the research, when Anonymous-3 discovered that a Brazilian sociologist had been murdered for her inquires into the activities of the death squads. The cover story we quickly concocted was that I was in Rio doing a study on race relations for the University of Stockholm. Later, as I kept returning to Brazil, we said that I was writing a book on my own about social control during the Getúlio Vargas governments—which actually became volume two of this project.

I would likewise be remiss if I did not acknowledge all the work done on my behalf through the diligent effort of each person offering evidence in confidence. Since this narrative is not aimed at injuring the innocent, individuals who felt uncomfortable at having their names revealed are listed on an incognito basis. All of these persons feared either real physical harm or that something negative would happen to their careers should they be connected to the information they provided. Bear in mind that mere gossip was not accepted. In all situations, anonymous informants were in a position to give expert or actual eyewitness accounts of the events in question. Finally, a word of thanks to my editors and anonymous reviewers at Ohio University Press for getting me to focus my ideas in ways that cut to the essence of this undertaking.

Abbreviations Used in Text and Notes

ABC	Santo André, São Bernado do Campo, and São Caetano do Sul, the working-class industrial districts south of the city of São Paulo
ACB	Arquivo Castelo Branco (Castelo Branco Archive)
ACC	Anti-Communist Crusade
ADEP	Ação Democrática Popular (the Organization for Popular Democratic Action)
AGV	Arquivo Getúlio Vargas (Getúlio Vargas Archive)
AI-1	Ato Institucional No. 1 (Institutional Act No. 1)
AI-2	Ato Institucional No. 2 (Institutional Act No. 2)
AI-5	Ato Institucional No. 5 (Institutional Act No. 5)
AJB	Arquivo Jornal do Brasil (Jornal do Brasil Archive)
AMFORP	American Foreign Power Company
ALN	Ação Libertadora Nacional (National Liberation Action)
APERJ	Arquivo Público do Estado do Rio de Janeiro (Public Archive of the State of Rio de Janeiro)
ARENA	Aliança de Renovação Nacional (National Renovation Alliance). The post-1964 military governments' political party.
CCC	Comando de Caça aos Comunistas (Communist Chasing Commandos)
CENIMAR	Centro de Informações da Marinha (Naval Intelligence Center)
CGT	Comando Geral dos Trabalhadores (General Workers Command)

CIA	Central Intelligence Agency
CISA	Centro de Informações e Segurança da Aeronáutica (Air Force Intelligence and Security Center)
CIE	Centro de Informações do Exército (Army Intelligence Center)
CNBB	Conferência Nacional dos Bispos do Brasil (National Conference of the Brazilian Bishops)
CPDOC	Centro de Pesquisa e Documentação de História Contemporânea do Brasil (Center for Research and Documentation of Contemporary Brazil)
CPT	Comissão Pastoral da Terra (Pastoral Land Commission)
CPTAA	CPT–Acre Archives
DEOPS	Departamento Estadual de Ordem Política e Social (State Department of Political and Social Order). The political police in some states. The political police in São Paulo changed their official designation to DEOPS in 1969.
DOI-Codi	Destacamento de Operações de Informações (Operation and Information Detachment). Slightly refined versions of OBAN units that were established throughout the country in 1970. Each DOI component worked out of a Codi (Centros de Operações da Defensa Interna, or Centers for Internal Defense Operations) facility.
DOPS	Departamento de Ordem Politica e Social (Department of Political and Social Order). The political police in several Brazilian states, including the state of Rio de Janeiro from 1938 until 1975. Also the generic term applied to all forms of the political police by Brazilians from the late 1920s until 1983.
ESG	Escola Superior de Guerra (Superior War College)
FA	*Foreign Affairs*

FEB	Força Expeditionaria Brasileira (Brazilian Expeditionary Force). The Brazilian military contribution to the Allied effort during World War II. It was American equipped and fought in Italy.
FUEC	Frente Unida dos Estudantes do Calabouço (United Front of Calabouço Students)
G-11	Grupos de Onze (Groups of Eleven)
GDE	Grupo de Diligências Especiais (Special Diligence Group)
IBAD	Instituto Brasileiro de Ação Democrática (Brazilian Institute of Democratic Action)
IBGE	Instituto Brasileiro de Geografia e Estatística (Brazilian Institute of Geography and Statistics)
IMF	International Monetary Fund
IPÊS	Instituto de Pesquisas e Estudos Sociais (Institute of Research and Social Studies)
IPM	Inqueritos Polícia Militar (Military Police Inquiries)
JLAS	*Journal of Latin American Studies*
LBJPL	Lyndon Baines Johnson Presidential Library
LBR	*Luso-Brazilian Review*
MAM	Museu de Arte Moderna (Modern Art Museum)
MDB	Movimento Democrático Brasileiro (Brazilian Democratic Movement). The effectively powerless post-1964 opposition party.
MR-8	Movimento Revolucionário 8 de Outubro (8th of October Revolutionary Momement)
MST	Movimento dos Trabalhadores Rurais Sem-Terra (Movement of Landless Rural Workers)
OBAN	Operação Bandeirantes (Operation Bandeirantes). Formed on July 1, 1969, OBAN was the centralized in-

	telligence service in the state of São Paulo made up of the army, air force, navy, DEOPS, Polícia Federal, Polícia Civil, Força Pública, and Guarda Civil intelligence services.
OPS	Office of Public Safety program
PARASAR	Páraquedistas de Salvamento Aéro Resgate (Air Force Parachute, Safety, and Rescue Unit)
PCB	Partido Comunista do Brasil (Communist Party of Brasil) until September 1960, Partido Comunista Brasileiro (Brazilian Communist Party) after September 1960
PPARJ	Political Police Archives, Rio de Janeiro *See the explanatory note at the start of the bibliography.
PSD	Partido Social Democrático (Social Democratic Party)
PSP	Partido Social Progressista (Social Progress Party)
PTB	Partido Trabalhista Brasileiro (Brazilian Workers' Party)
ROTA	Rondas Ostensivas Tobias de Aguiar (Tobias de Aguiar Proactive Patrol)
SDLC	Scuderie Detetive Le Cocq (Shield of Detective Le Cocq)
SNI	Serviço Nacional de Informações (National Information Service)
SOMOC	Superintendência da Moeda e do Crédito (Office of Money and Credit)
SRB	Sociedade Rural Brasileira (Rural Brazilian Society)
SUPRA	Superintendência da Política Agrária (Office of Agrarian Politics)
IT&T	International Telephone and Telegraph
UDN	União Democrática Nacional (National Democratic Union)
UDR	União Democrática Ruralista (Rural Democratic Union)

UKPRO	United Kingdom, Public Record Office
UNE	União Nacional de Estudantes (National Union of Students)
USAID	United States Agency for International Development
USP	Universidade de São Paulo
VPR	Vanguarda Popular Revolutionária (Popular Revolutionary Vanguard)

Note on Racial Terms

In 1976, the respected conductors of Brazil's censuses, the Brazilian Institute of Geography and Statistics (Instituto Brasileiro de Geografia e Estatistica, or IBGE), asked Brazilians to identify their own skin color. This was, of course, an attempt to ask them their racial type. There were 134 terms given by the respondents.

In the United States, we often use terms such as African American, Asian American, and Native American. In Brazil, color terms are the accepted praxis for all racial groupings (except that "indigenous" is used for native peoples). Therefore, following for the most part the IBGE classification from the 2000 census but replacing color terms that might be offensive to some readers, the following five main terms will be used in this work: Asian (for *amarela,* lit., yellow), black (*preta*), indigenous (*indígena*), mulatto (for *parda,* lit., brown), and white (*branca*).

Introduction

THE TRAIL OF elite violence in Brazil really did not begin with the events on the following pages. In an earlier monograph, I hypothesized that this road winds its way back to Portugal, the mother country.[1] Violence by the country's elites has, sadly, always been a part of the social fabric in Brazil. Granted, violence is present in all societies. It is a cultural universal. This begs the question then, at least in the Brazilian context, of violence by whom against whom? One consequently arrives rather quickly at the need for definitions of what is meant by *elites, violence,* and *social control,* as such concepts manifest themselves in South America's largest country.

Using wealth and power as indexes, it is easy to construct a continuum with those possessing large amounts of one or both variables at one end and those without much of either at the other. By elites, then, we mean those able to command wealth and power. This could be the result of inheritance, social position, business acumen, or all three. Those in the center of the continuum, the so-called middle class, had their numbers dramatically reduced by the policies of the minister of the economy, Antônio Delfim Neto, in the 1960s and '70s. Still, middle-class citizens should rightly be included alongside members of the upper classes when the interest of their class, or what was left of it, coincided with those of the more elevated stratum. This fluid way of conceiving the middle class allows it to be either a circumstantial ally or a foe of those really in control.

The lower classes were/are excluded from this process with two exceptions. First, when members of that group enjoy some kind of celebrity status. Observe that this position is often fleeting and is available to few persons. Second, when lower-class Brazilians become members of what I have earlier termed the *subelite*.[2] This category is composed of both situational and transitory muscle providers, examples of which include the police, conscripted members of the military, guards, and bodyguards, plus various kinds of bullies in the employ of some higher authority.[3] Richard Quinney has stated that such individuals are

> "repressive workers" in that they engage in the actual or threatened use of physical force and legal punishment. While they do not produce surplus value, they do secure the social order (through the apparatus of the capitalist state) so that capitalists can privately accumulate capital. The concrete use-value of their work is to maintain domestic order, to make the society safe for capitalist accumulation and to protect class relations. Although these workers occupy a fraction within the working class, and are not therefore members of the "ruling class," in terms of the use-value of their labor they act against their own working-class interests.[4]

Quinney was writing primarily about the United States. In spite of this, witness that in Brazil, and indeed in other so-called developing countries, that is, nations with large numbers of poor people, those who come to occupy these subelite roles are, in reality, surrogate enforcers for those who employ them and whose goals they have internalized. This internalization process has to be at least outwardly unambiguous and unequivocal or the individual will be replaced from the pool of reserve laborers clamoring for work. To insure their own safety, the elite purposefully fill the lesser ranks of such bastions with persons from the lower classes but watch over them with officers from or near their own echelon.

The type of violence to be focused on here then falls within the downwardly directed intercaste and especially interclass varieties. Of all the brutalities in the human repertoire, these two variations have been responsible over time for genocide on a mass scale. One need look no farther than Nazi atrocities to recognize this in its most extreme form. But just as anti-Semitism had been around for centuries in Europe before the advent of Nazism, so too had intercaste/interclass violence long been a fact of the Portuguese social experience. Colonists naturally brought it with them aboard the first galleons to the new country following Brazil's discovery by Pedro Alvares Cabral on April 22, 1500. It was a brutality that was employed on a huge scale based upon the economic necessities of the institution of enslavement.

Slavery

Just as England had an early monopoly on slavery above the equator, the Portuguese had the market practically to themselves in the southern hemisphere. Not only did the Portuguese enjoy supremacy, they used it with abandon to import substantially larger numbers of slaves to Brazil than those which the English succeeded in bringing to their Caribbean and American colonies. Moreover, the Portuguese from at least these early colonial days were adequately suited to control their cargo. It is said that they had mystical imaginations, harsh temperaments, and frequently possessed a cruel vindictiveness matched only by a thorough lack of mercy.[5]

Herein lie the two roots of elite violence and its application in Portuguese America. It was a synergistic relationship between the violent temperament of many Portuguese and the large number of persons to be controlled. That is, it has been estimated that English vessels brought about five hundred thousand Africans just to what would become the United States of America. The Portuguese, and later the independent Brazilians, in contrast, transported some four million Africans to their possession in the Brazil.[6] This created a situation in which persons of Luso-European heritage became a white minority in a sea of black faces.[7] Bondsmen became such an integral part of daily life in Brazil that they could be found everywhere—from the plantations to almost all trades where muscles and strong backs were required. In addition to working at animal husbandry and agricultural chores, they occupied the entire gamut of domestic responsibilities. Any job that was filthy or dangerous or both was sure to be done by the enslaved. They could even be found walking the streets as slave-prostitutes earning money for white pimps. It seemed, moreover, that everyone except the poorest whites owned someone to do their dirty work.[8]

With such a sizeable number of people held in servitude, keeping them in check was of the highest importance.[9] The social control techniques used by slavers and the owners of slaves almost defied description. Beginning in

Africa, individuals entering slavery were frequently branded like cattle with the identifying mark of the initial purchaser responsible for their passage to Brazil. This flesh-burning ordeal took place before setting sail from Africa or after arrival in Brazil. It was also common when slaves were sold between masters and could even be seen on the cheeks of slaves as a sign of owner displeasure. Some bondservants had the letter "F," which stood for *fujão,* or escapee, seared onto one shoulder. It was a living notice to everyone. When so marked slaves tried to flee again, their ears were cropped off. A third attempt usually resulted in the malcontent's execution. There was even the suggestion in 1755, later turned down in Lisbon, that recaptured slaves should have their Achilles tendon severed in one foot. This would prevent them from further attempts to escape since it would dramatically reduce their mobility. It would not, however, keep them from hobbling to work.[10]

If they lived long enough to reach the land across the Atlantic, conditions were so bad and treatment was so severe that the average life span for fresh captives was two to seven years. By 1603 any bondsman who rebelled and killed his master or one of his master's family had his hands cut off before being lynched. In outlying provinces, particularly in the north, the enslaved were habitually treated worse than in Rio de Janeiro. It was noted in Bahia in the 1750s that it was not unusual to have an assistant tie a slave's feet together, then hoist the slave up, upside-down at the ankles, with a rope thrown over the limb of a tree and beat him almost to death.[11] The priest who made these remarks added that

> although flogging with the *chicote* (rawhide knout or whip) was limited to a maximum of forty lashes under Portuguese law, . . . Brazilian slave-owners thought nothing of inflicting two-, three-, or even four-hundred lashes. He also states that there were some slave-owners who, whenever they bought a new slave, had him soundly flogged straightaway, simply out of a sadistic determination to show that they would stand no nonsense. He advocates the abolition of such barbarous punishments as flogging with the *chicote,* pricking the victim's buttocks with a pointed knife, cauterizing the wounds with drops of hot wax. . . . [and or] . . . with salt, lemon juice, and urine.[12]

The cleric's recommendations were ignored. Shortly before abolition in 1888—making Brazil the last country in the new world to officially outlaw slavery—it was noted that the custom of thrashing the enslaved with whips soaked in solutions like vinegar and sand, to cause infections and extra pain, was still being practiced.[13] Lashes were often administered by a *feitor* (overseer) or by one of his assistants. In several situations, the bondsman was simply whipped to death. Other problem-causing slaves were hung or thrown into furnaces or boiled alive. Sometimes pregnant slaves were kicked and beaten to death if they could not produce the required amount of work. This kind of eventuality, coupled with the demands made upon them, meant that slave suicides were high, reaching 70 percent of all suicides in Rio de Janeiro in 1865 and 80 percent up the coast in Sergipe.[14]

All things must end, however, or so it would seem. The formal conclusion to servitude in Brazil was carried out in a slow state-by-state arrangement. This gradual procession had a fifty-five-year history beginning in 1833, when England granted freedom to slaves in her worldwide possessions. In the Caribbean, one result of this change of heart was an increase in the price of sugar. Accordingly, the British were soon adamant that Brazil also end the ignoble institution since sugar produced in slave-labor economies was cheaper. At one point legislators in Rio de Janeiro tried to make London think Brazil was fulfilling the recently signed Palmerston Act of 1839 banning the traffic in human flesh. But it was all window dressing, and the corresponding saying, *"Só para inglês ver,"* entered the vocabulary. The expression means "Only for the English to see,"[15] and it is used to this day to signify something is a bluff.

After more haggling with Britain, which included in the 1850s the stationing of English warships along the Brazilian coast to stop the flow of slaves from Africa, the Brazilian bonds of slavery finally began to unravel. In 1865, whipping the enslaved sentenced to labor gangs was outlawed. The following year, using them in government works was stopped, and freedom began to be granted to the government's own slaves serving in the Paraguayan War (1864–70). In 1868, the state of Ceará conceded liberty to a hundred freshly baptized slave children. Most were females as, evidently, male offspring were still too highly valued as future laborers to be released. Three years later the Lei do Ventre Livre, or "Law of the Free Womb," was promulgated. This statute mandated that children of slave parents in all parts of Brazil were free after reaching eight years of age. At that point masters could release them in exchange for compensation from the state, or the children could continue to work for their masters until reaching twenty-one. Most owners opted for the second choice. In the 1880s both Ceará and the Amazon Territory endeavored to mitigate slavery within their borders. To the south, Rio Grande do Sul next permitted slaves their freedom if they agreed to an arbitrarily decided number of additional years in servitude. In 1885, slaves more than sixty years of age, nationwide, were given their liberty. The next year, public whippings of all bondsmen and women were made illegal. São Paulo also joined the abolitionist movement in 1886. *Paulistas* (persons from the state of São Paulo) adopted the plan being used in Rio Grande do Sul, though by that time the enslaved were deserting their owners in large numbers. The emperor, Dom Pedro II, was likewise ailing and abroad. Realizing the unavoidable and acting as regent, Princess Isabel signed the Lei Áurea or "Golden Law" in 1888, bringing an official end to Brazilian slavery.[16]

Caste into Class

In the meantime, specially selected teams of white males were sent to Europe to compete with groups from Canada, the United States, and Argentina to attract white immigrants. Estate owners wanted more white workers to supplant departing black laborers. They also wanted to whiten the country's gene pool. Free transportation and jobs were the watchwords. Dirt-poor Italians became the largest contingent of immigrants to avail themselves of the Brazilian offer. They landed by the boatload, and many wound up in the coffee plantations, particularly in the state of São Paulo.[17] There the duties once performed by slaves were turned over to them. The trouble in this was that former masters and their hired assistants failed to make the mental adjustments necessary to treat the newcomers as free individuals. Since they did the work once done by the enslaved, they were largely treated as slaves. This was exacerbated by the fact that race mixing had gone on for years. The result was that Brazil became much more of a class-based than a caste-based society. Whereas in the United States animosity was/is often directed toward blacks, irrespective of their class, in Brazil ill feeling was/is aimed at the poor, irrespective of their color.

Subelites

As the number of immigrants increased in São Paulo, elites expanded the police forces assigned the job of keeping the immigrants passive and obedient. Representatives of the law were empowered to use all the might at their disposal in this task. With little constraining them, violence by constables became so widespread that a representative of the Italian parliament, after a visit to São Paulo in 1899, returned home to complain to his colleagues about the savagery of the paulista police. The members of the Parlamento Italiano became so infuriated that a bill was introduced to prohibit all future emigration of Italians to Brazil.[18] The measure failed to be ratified, but had the delegates made the arduous sea journey to the port of Santos and then up to São Paulo, they might well have voted differently. From at least 1892 to 1904, arrest rates in the city were roughly double those of London. Perhaps even more revealing is the curious detail that fewer than ten percent of those picked up were ever charged with an offense.[19]

From those times to our own, violence by the representatives of the elite has only increased. New techniques to torture and disfigure were developed or imported. It did not matter if the scene was rural or urban. It did not matter if there were laws passed or constitutions in effect. The poor made up a *régime d'exception* largely left outside the de facto protections afforded under simple words on paper. Note that one can turn this upside down and say that the Brazilian elite, being protected by their laws, could do as they wished to the unprotected classes. Laws were never meant in the first instance for the lower strata except as guides to social control.[20] Persons in positions of power and influence used and continue to use the implied threat of immediate and exaggerated violence to maintain a precious order—order defined by them and conducive to them, and order often defiled by them.

Those who react to this analysis might call attention to "elite disunity," which is really a misnomer, in Brazil. In so doing, these advocates ignore one moré that has fused elites together more than any other. One of the bonds within this group that united it more frequently than did anything else was the constant clash it waged when need be against the lower classes or those with lower-class interests. This skirmish—at times hidden, at times open—was fought in the name of money, power, or both. Occasionally individuals on society's bottom resisted and even fought back as in the case up to 1940 of rural banditry (the *cangaço*).[21] At other times there were manifestations of proletarian displeasure, as in the failed socialist revolution of 1935 or the events preceding and subsequent to the Golpe (coup d'état) of 1964. Despite the epoch, each attempt to fight back was met with the brute force of an elite definition of order via appointed subelite enforcers of that definition. The norms used to support this structure produced citizens who wallowed in a kind of culturally deterministic belief that such was normal, that such was the Brazilian way. Actually, many moral definitions were and are cultural artifacts of the class in power learned in one's family, the educational system, and via the mass media—then reinforced through the continual process of socialization—and, as Foucault would quickly point out, through the practice of mutual observation to spot any transgressors veering off the chosen path.[22]

Excuses

If the violent domination of one class by another is a crime, then this chain of events is best viewed and understood from the perspective of critical criminology. Other approaches seem either empty of analytical power or like mere folly. One need only consider the argument of the so-called social biologists to see the pathological school of deviance, complete with instincts, lurking in the background. Whatever the name, there are those who refuse to give up on the idea of instincts causing human behavior, particularly criminal behavior. When one approach is disproved, another with a different twist and a different name seems to pop up later. This instinctual explanation is not without its champions in Brazil. During twenty-two years of research in the country, this researcher heard Brazilians repeatedly insist that the behavior of the lower classes had some kind of nameless genetic component. Often their commentary had racist and sexist overtones. This being so, the orators pontificated a universal treatment for the *povão* (or Brazilian masses) by individuals who know what is best for them. Naturally these messiahs of right and wrong should come from the better-off sectors of the nation.

This biological argument in Brazil reaches up to the top echelons of government. Consider the position of Oswaldo Aranhã, who was foreign minister during the authoritarian Estado Novo (New State; 1937–45). On her way north in 1938 to conduct research, American anthropologist Ruth Landes stopped off in Rio de Janeiro to visit Aranhã and was informed by him, "Since you are going to study Negroes, I must tell you that our political backwardness, which made this dictatorship necessary, is due entirely to our Negro blood. Unfortunately. So we are trying to breed the blood out, making one nation of all the people, 'whitening the Brazilian race.'"[23] Aranhã was, of course, referring to the program to attract persons of European heritage to immigrate to Brazil, as long as they were not penniless Jews.[24] His opinions continue to manifest themselves in the general adoration of light-skinned, blond whites. This dovetails into the class-based nature of Brazilian social reality when one learns that anyone with money is even more popular.

Such views are part of a culture that is already in place for all new arrivals, whether they come to the country by birth or by plane. It is empty rhetoric tempered by time but believed by some in all classes and waiting as part of the cultural makeup created at key points by elites of another era. With the artificial eloquence of Aranhã and those before him came the institutions to safeguard the elite and assign an ascribed status to everyone—especially those on the bottom. As part of this motif, dire social situations, complete with their regulations and vile treatment, have been considered natural for generations. All this has been accomplished to lionize those in power and keep them safe. Many Brazilians believe that contemporary offenses such as trafficking in narcotics or assault and robbery almost always involve poor nonwhites. Layers of lies keep them from seeing that there is nothing racial to any of this. These positions fail to encompass the larger reality. It is the system that keeps the lower classes unemployed or underemployed. It is the system that keeps them involved with fast-way schemes out of poverty.

Critical Historical Criminology

On the pages you are about to read, the road from the origins of downwardly directed intraclass violence in Brazil continues. It began with the first volume in this series, *Beyond the Pale of Pity,* which was set before the discovery of Portuguese America. Why a starting date to a sociological journey so far in the past? The answer lies in the fact that much of standard sociology and criminology is devoid of the histories that incorporate folkways into cultural patterns. If one were to consider the crimes of elites, for example, would it not be more complete to view their offenses via their cultural antecedents? Or is it enough to simply plug numbers from modern-day events into cells and then grind them up in correlations and linear regressions? The answer is self-evident. The second methodology is locked in "illusions of the present."[25] It lacks a connection to the *why*. This project is thus not just one of critical criminology but also one of critical historical criminology. It proceeds from a fervent criticalist conviction that the violent domination of one class by another is *indeed* a crime. Through an appreciation and application of historical processes, it is hoped that we can paint a more compelling canvas of those crimes in their relation to current social events.

Our tools will be those of primary and secondary historical, criminological, and sociological evidence. Whenever possible, reserves of information, like good lawyers presenting a case, will be corroborated by additional resources and parenthetical commentary. The historian's hierarchy of sources—archival materials at the top and internet sources at the bottom—will be used. In between will be interviews, scientific journals, government studies and reports, books, and articles from representative sectors of the mass media. This is a pathway to insight that plain numbers can never provide. It is the study of causes. Indeed, Quinney has said, "What is importance in the study of crime is everything that happens before crime occurs. Thus, the elementary ontological question of the nature of reality remains a pressing one for us."[26]

A somewhat humorous instance might emphasize the argument: Why do today's *cariocas* (residents of the city of Rio de Janeiro) almost always insist that males wear long pants when entering downtown public buildings even in the heat of a sticky tropical summer? One need look no farther than the Belle Époque (Beautiful Epoch). This was the time of elite dandyism that began around the end of the nineteenth century and lasted until World War I in some of the major cities of South America. In Rio, along with a facelift of the business district, there was an effort during the Belle Époque to move the lower classes out of the city. Since the government could not just order these individuals to move and maintain their pretense at fairness, a haughty legislative attempt was one of the options considered. Representatives of the upper classes, duly elected to represent everyone, wanted to make it a crime to walk about inadequately dressed in the capital.

Aimed directly at poorer males, this legislation stipulated that all men in the center of town had to wear proper shoes, a shirt, and at least a sport-coat. The proposed regulation, called "The Sanitary Project Bill," can be translated as follows:

1907—Project No. 82
Prohibition against Persons in Shirts without Sport Coats and without Shoes from Using the Streets and Parks in the Urban Part of the Federal District

The Municipal Council resolves:

> Art. 1. No one will be allowed to pass through the streets and parks of the urban part of the Federal District in a shirt without a sport coat and shoes, and be free from a fine of five réis for the first offense or double thereafter.
> Art. 2. All laws to the contrary are revoked.[27]

The bill made it all the way to its third reading in the governing body before being discarded. Nonetheless it gives us a glimpse of attitudes regarding what males should wear when in downtown Rio that still exist, albeit in a mitigated form. The fine of five réis, by the way, was equal to about forty hours' work for an average employee from the lower classes. It is likewise remarkable these days to watch carioca men return home from the city center and immediately change from their more formal attire into shorts, some kind of shirt, and sandals.

Focus

The underlying question then must be, Whose reality matters? Did Quinney mean everyone's reality? Perhaps, but he was certainly not considering upper-class actuality as the focus of his attention, unless it was to understand how this minority has controlled the reality of the majority. Be they slaves subject to the parasitic actions of owners attempting to squeeze the last drop of labor out of them or snobs using the law to rid a particular section of town of plebian presence, the reality of the great bulk of the Brazilian people will be, and rightly should be, the focus of *The Unpast.* We will carry on this dialogue on two levels. First we will look at the power behind the throne from the perspective of what elites wanted and how they used enforcers and laws in the second half of the twentieth century just as they always had. Our discourse will also consider the way this state of affairs has affected ordinary men and women just as it always has. Only at this later juncture will numbers be employed to enable us to view who it is that is being victimized.

Be warned: the country Brazilian elites inherited and added to was not/is not blissful for the povão. At one point in chapter 6, there is a passage where several members of a *paulistano* (persons from the city of São Paulo) death squad are drinking in a bar following a killing. Blood is dripping out of the trunk of one member's parked car onto the asphalt outside the tavern. Someone was just eliminated and stuffed in the trunk. Unconcerned about the attention-getting mess, the owner of the vehicle shows his colleagues a hacked off earlobe, now part of his personal key chain. The men laugh and continue drinking. No one is really worried. No one really cares. The logical conclusion was reached in 1957, when death squads became a fact of life. They were the *first* extermination groups in the modern era in the Americas.[28] Before these killers were turned loose, however, our saga begins anew with the events set in motion early one morning in 1954.

Last Hope

Gegê and Jango, 1954–64

Chapter 1

The Muscler of Governments

By midmorning Brazil was overrun with grief. Cars stopped in the streets, and their occupants got out and walked around asking each other if what they had just heard on the radio was true. Businesses already functioning quickly closed for the day; others never opened. Schools sent their students home. The tears began—and gave way to mayhem in some parts of the country when infuriated citizens went after the suspected causes of it all.[1]

In São Paulo, thousands of workers declared themselves on strike, and a gathering estimated at twenty thousand had to be kept from gutting the building housing Assis Chateaubriand's Diários Associados (Associated Newspapers). The wounded there reached one hundred. Chateaubriand's holding company and his tabloids had been on the wrong side of the political fence. So too had been two newspapers in Porto Alegre, *Estado do Rio Grande do Sul* and *Diário de Notícias.* They were burned to the ground, as was the radio station Farroupilha. Also attacked were the American Consulate, Citibank, the offices of the Partido Libertador (Liberator Party), Partido Social Democrático (Social Democratic Party), Partido Social Progressita (Social Progress Party), União Democrática Nacional (National Democratic Union), Souza Cruz of the British American Tobacco Corporation, and the local Coca-Cola subsidiary. Four people lost their lives. At least twenty-six were injured. In Belo Horizonte the office of the

United States Information Agency was partially damaged. The army and police calvary had to be called out to disperse the crowds. In Recife, too, there were demonstrations.

Another display of rage erupted in the former Brazilian capital, Rio de Janeiro. When the distraught there tried to storm the American embassy and the headquarters of Standard Oil, the police opened fire, wounding as many as six people. One protester was killed, but the authorities quickly removed his body. The throng that gathered at Cinelândia, one of Rio's main downtown squares, as did crowds everywhere in the city, slowly began to boil because of the ingenious words broadcast on the radio every ten minutes. With each new transmission the scene became tenser. Portraits of the author could be seen everywhere. Finally, people started to shout "Down with the Americans!" "Death to Lacerda!" and "Death to Marinho!" Three different mobs then sacked newsstands, set fire to two delivery trucks of the Rio de Janeiro daily *O Globo*, and roamed from one place to another with sticks, ripping down election banners and pictures of opposition candidates. The offices of the Movimento Nacional Popular (National Movement) were torn up. Canadian-owned Light & Power and the telephone company also suffered damage. The police took a large number of Communists into custody for trying to start a sympathy strike with the one in São Paulo—but not before the leftists effectively launched a rumor that newspaper owner and commentator Carlos Lacerda had taken refuge inside the American embassy.

Frantic, Lacerda was actually at Rio's Santo Dumont Airport asking former police inquisitor Cecil Borer for protection for his own daily, *Tribuna da Imprensa*. Over the telephone, Borer, who was chief of the Political Section of DOPS (Departamento de Ordem Politica e Social, or the Department of Political and Social Order—the dreaded political police), said that he would send some men around to protect the publisher's newspaper. Lacerda then allowed himself to be transported by helicopter to the air force's base at Galeão. Setting his feet back on solid ground, the journalist went into hiding for four days at the home of a friend on Ilha do Governador.

Meanwhile, the police that Borer sent to the *Tribuna da Imprensa* managed to restore order. When they arrived, they found that the Polícia Especial (Special Police) or "Tomato Heads," so called in the parlance of the times for their khaki uniforms and red caps, had only made things worse by joining with an unruly swarm wanting entry into *Tribuna*'s offices. In fact, the "Heads" succeeded in getting inside the building through an adjoining structure, then they grabbed a Brazilian flag from the hands of *Tribuna* employees after cocking and pointing their machine guns at the reporters.[2] The Polícia Especial was created in the 1930s out of the Polícia Civil (Detective Bureau), expressly on the orders of the supreme commander to create an offensive police unit. Each member was chosen from the most physically fit specimens available and was led by Lt. Euzébio de Queiroz Filho. The Polícia Especial's main facility was at the top of Rio's Santo Antônio Hill, which has since been removed. At its zenith the structure was not a popular place to think about, as it had an inquisitional aura. Several kinds of unimaginable, indeed unmentionable, events happened within its guarded walls during the entire span of its existence. Euzébio was reputed to be a sadist.[3]

While the Polícia Especial would last only another six years before being disbanded,[4] DOPS had been around in one form or another since 1907.[5] Initially formed to keep a watchful eye on the laboring classes, it would live on under different names until 1983.[6] During most of the 1930s and into the 1940s, the political police too had been a part of the Polícia Civil, which in turn was run by one of the most detested police chiefs in Brazilian history—Filinto Müller. Borer and many of his officer colleagues at DOPS had previously been either Tomato Heads or Polícia Civil functionaries or both. Some had been involved in information extraction. All had been taught the art of police science during the heyday of Queiroz Filho and Müller. Heinous forms of torture were still utilized, and their use and sophistication would only grow. The povão, plus those without influence, were still disappearing in the black of night. The only person who might have stopped it all was now dead. He had taken his own life rather than relinquish power. Near riotous conditions continued for days, and the ill feeling over his sudden departure would continue for years. It was August 24, 1954.

Changing Course

Even before the corpse of President Getúlio Vargas was carried from the official mansion in Catete, there was effectively a new group of men in control. They had actually been the final arbitrators and the ultimate deciders for some time. The individuals in question—the military elite—had continually regarded professional politicians with suspicion and contempt. Led by commanders blinded by their own professionalism and positivist traditions, Brazil's soldiers watched nervously from the wings, believing that only they knew what was ultimately best for the country. Several of the officers in ribbon and braid were former *tenentes* (lieutenants). As a group of conspirators, the tenentes were behind the 1922 and 1924 revolts against the government of the much-hated head of state Artur Bernardes. They were interested in obtaining more influence within the Old Republic (1889–1930) for an officer corps of soldier-intellectuals. These potential fighters had been taught that only a pure and unbiased military could lead Brazil to its destiny among the world's great nations. In their opinion, their calling was not merely to provide for the nation's external security.[7] No, since the days of the Constitution of 1891,[8] they had felt that their overriding duty was to be the last guardians of its internal tranquility as well.

Vargas had been aware of these developments. Since 1947 he had been witness to the swaying views of the officers in the army's Military Club. In this contest, the faction that was pro-American and for foreign investment and which ultimately had a hand in Vargas's downfall, came to be called the Democratic Crusade. In opposition were the nationalists, who generally favored guarding Brazil's resources, clamping down on her remittances abroad, and pulling the country into an independent stance on questions of foreign policy. Since the first of these groups was openly in favor of the United States, the other gravitated in the opposite direction and was falsely accused of being Communist oriented. Yet which side an individual chose, even in a world ablaze with Cold War rhetoric, was actually academic since what many of these officers really wanted exceeded the very essence of their raison d'être.

Particularly with the end of World War II, Brazil's military leaders had grown into nothing more than a semiautonomous group of know-it-alls with weapons. Because of their endless internal politicking, they were far from being the force behind the government's wishes. Rather, they understood their duty as being the judges, the juries, and the executioners of their own interpretations of those wishes. Instead of being the government's muscle, by the end of the oppressive Estado Novo the Brazilian military had come into its own more than ever as the muscler of governments.

The New Team and the "Democratic Lie"

Taking over for Vargas was Vice-President João Café Filho. Taking over the job of minister of war for the soon-to-leave Gen. Góis Monteiro was General Henrique Lott.[9] On August 5, 1955, in commemoration of the year-old murder of former air force major Rubens Vaz, the catalyst to Vargas's finale, the individual who helped Café Filho choose Lott decided to offer a few solemn comments to an assembly of air force officers. When General Canrobert Pereira da Costa, an outspoken anti-Communist who enjoyed more prestige than anyone else in the army, finally rose to speak, he warned his audience over and over again about the corruption in high places that worried him and all good patriots. "The country," he said, "was passing through a . . . democratic lie . . . that was based on . . . an immoral and corrupt pseudo-legality. . . . [The only thing that would salvage the situation, the general concluded, would be a] . . . rigorous and austere improvement in political practices."[10]

These comments so insulted a number of legislators that they called for Canrobert's immediate arrest. But the general was president of the Military Club, and he was also known to be mortally ill. So nothing was actually done to refute his remarks. They were not intended for the general body of lawmakers anyway. Canrobert's oratory was aimed essentially at the ticket detested by many of the men in uniform in the upcoming presidential elections: the governor of the state of Minas Gerais, Jucelino Kubitschek, and his running mate, João Goulart.

As the campaign of 1955 unfolded, the military and one of the opposition parties, the conservative UDN (União Democrática Nacional), claimed that Goulart wanted to build a *república sindicalista,* or a country run by the unions. To this was added a forged letter that quickly appeared on the pages of *O Globo* and in Carlos Lacerda's *Tribuna da Imprensa.* Lacerda read the document on a September 16, 1955, television program before publishing it the following day. Called the "Brandi Letter," it alleged that Goulart conspired with Argentina's Juan Perón to arm Brazilian "worker-shock brigades." These armed laborers would then be the forefront of a movement to bring about the unionized republic. The real purpose of the correspondence, however, was to create more enemies for Goulart within the armed forces. It was not until December of that year—after the election had been held—that the Brandi Letter was proven a fake.

It has been alleged that the CIA was involved in the affair, along with the Crusada Brasileira Anticomunista, or Anti-Communist Crusade. Nonetheless, Lacerda used the illicit document to hound away incessantly at Juscelino and "Jango," as Goulart had been called since childhood.[11]

Even with these tactics, the results of the election on October 3, 1955, gave the victory to Kubitschek and Goulart, much to the consternation of the military, the UDN, and Carlos "The Crow" Lacerda. Lacerda was occasionally referred to with this interesting title after May 25, 1954. This came about after a cartoon in that day's issue of the pro-government tabloid *Última Hora* ridiculed him. The drawing depicted him "hovering" (i.e., not letting go of the story in his own paper) over the body of Nestor Moreira. Moreira had been a correspondent with the carioca daily *A Noite*. One day he got into a disagreement with a taxi driver over his fare, and both men ended up going to a Polícia Civil station in Copacabana to settle the issue. Moreira never walked out alive.[12] Lacerda used the episode in his newspaper to intermittently harass Vargas. The implication was that the editor was tenacious about all subjects dear to him.

The period immediately following the vote was filled with simmering allegations of the return of the *getúlistas* (followers of Vargas), of Communist links to Goulart, and, to be sure, of the election support given to Juscelino and Jango by the Brazilian Communist Party (Partido Comunista do Brasil), or PCB. One of the defeated presidential candidates was Plínio Salgado. He kept enough votes from going to northeastern hero Juarez Távora to insure Kubitschek's victory. Salgado had been the leader of the Integralist, Brazil's Fascist movement during the 1930s and beyond. After the election he made peace with Kubitschek, but not Goulart, on the condition that Juscelino not establish diplomatic relations with the Soviet Union or allow the Brazilian Communist Party to function openly.[13] When Canrobert died at the end of that October, all the pieces for a dramatic graveside confrontation fell chaotically into place.

CANROBERT'S ECHO

When the day of the funeral arrived, there was nothing really out of the ordinary until the fourth officer to speak stood to give his eulogy. Then, in war minister Lott's presence, Col. Jurandir Mamede scathingly used some of the criticisms expressed by his recently departed brother-in-arms. In the name of the Military Club, Mamede repeated Canrobert's charge that the "democratic lie" was based on an "immoral and corrupt pseudo-legality."[14] Mamede was one of the leaders of the army's section of the Brazilian Anti-Communist Crusade. Paraphrasing Canrobert, the colonel demanded to know how the most important political post in the republic could be given to a candidate who had not won a majority of votes. And, in direct reference to one of Goulart's long-held goals, would it not also be a mockery of the law for this minority government to legitimize itself by granting the vote to Brazil's illiterates?[15]

In 1955, approximately 40 percent of the population over fifteen years of age was illiterate. For many years a literacy qualification had been the most commonly used method to disenfranchise the poor and nonwhites. In the maneuverings preceding the election of 1945, Vargas had tried to get around the literacy qualification in the cities for his own benefit. Nonetheless, the eligibility requirement remained a feature of Brazilian election law, and it was not done away with until July 1, 1985.[16] All of this was mere conjecture, however, as independent-minded Henrique Lott was determined to abide by the results of the election. Moreover, having others publicly taunt his authority was intolerable to him. Lott was just as resolved to end public outbursts by junior officers who felt it was their duty to speak out. The minister of war made up his mind then and there that Mamede would be disciplined despite the apparent endorsement of his ideas by many of their colleagues.

The ESG

On August 20, 1949, then-president Eurico Gaspar Dutra formed the Escola Superior de Guerra (ESG; Superior War College), long a dream of Brazil's armed forces. The ESG had an interesting history that dovetailed into the Brazilian army's association with the United States in World War II. From the American viewpoint the relationship had very clear, long-range goals:

> Until the early 1960s the preponderant influence of the U.S. military was largely concentrated in a single clique or faction within the Brazilian military. It was the faction that, as the Brazilian Expeditionary Force [FEB] . . . , had fought alongside the U.S. Army Fourth Corps in Italy. The primary objectives of the U.S. armed forces involving the . . . [FEB] in the Italian campaign were reportedly the establishment of close ties with the Brazilian military elite and the exposure of that group to the modus operandi of the

> U.S. military so that it could go back and build up a "first class" military organization in Brazil.
>
> The . . . [FEB], under U.S. tutelage, established and staffed Brazil's Superior War College.[17]

Although the school offered courses on standard military subjects, many items in its curriculum were new and reflected an increased preoccupation with the larger Cold War picture of national security. This new concern within the broader context of Brazil's security was evident in the seven academic sections of the school. They were: 1) Political Affairs, 2) Psychological-Social Affairs, 3) Economic Affairs, 4) Military Affairs, 5) Logistical and Mobilization Affairs, 6) Intelligence and Counter-intelligence, and 7) Doctrine and Coordination. To meet the challenge of world Communist expansion, a Doctrine of National Security was developed and stressed in lectures. It emphasized that Brazil's power must become an "integrated expression of all national resources and the will to use those resources to attain and support, internally and externally, Brazilian [elite] objectives."[18] Furthermore, "because the ESG was to be concerned with all phases of development and national security, it was felt that the Brazilian military needed to socialize civilians from such fields as education, industry, communications, and banking into the correct national security perspective."[19] Hence nonmilitary personnel went through the Superior War College in large numbers. Along with military officers they formed a group with common class interests. Finally, "the tradition gradually grew that each class toured the United States as a guest of the U.S. government, visiting major military and industrial complexes. Visits normally included a short meeting with the president of the United States."[20]

Café Filho's Health Problems

Lott's desire to punish Col. Mamede was one thing. The ability to do it was quite another. As an officer on the staff of the ESG, he was out of Lott's chain of command and under direct orders of the president. But before Lott could settle on a course of action to get Mamede, a new event unfolded. On November 5, 1955, Café Filho was taken to the hospital, reportedly with heart problems.[21] On November 8 the president's physicians said that he was still too sick to leave the hospital. As a consequence, the government was temporarily turned over to Carlos Coimbra da Luz, president of the Chamber of Deputies and next in the line of presidential succession. In and of itself, this should not have caused Lott problems except for the fact that Luz had warmly praised Mamede's words. With such views, Luz flatly refused to do anything to rebuke the colonel. The provisional head of the country and the nation's leading general were about to make the fate of Mamede a test of wills.

THE SHOWDOWN

Summoned to Catete at 5 P.M. on November 10 and made to wait for an hour and a half, Gen. Lott soon had his confrontation with the transitory chief of state. The meeting had no effect on Luz's decision, and thus Lott tendered his resignation. The interim president accepted the war minister's offer to resign and even named his replacement, Álvaro Fiuza de Castro, on the spot. The matter should have ended there, but Lott was evasive. Instead of turning his office over to his successor immediately, he pointed out that there were a few loose ends to clear up and that he would hand over his post the next afternoon. Lott belonged to no real faction within the army. For this reason, several reactionary officers felt that his removal as minister of war would be possible and would benefit their cause. It is possible that these men staged the Mamede Affair to achieve this end. One of the officers involved was Lt. Col. Golbery do Couto e Silva.[22]

Meanwhile, led by Carlos Lacerda, Rio de Janeiro was ablaze with chatter of a coalition among officers allied with Mamede, acting president Luz, and those planning a coup d'état against the assumption of Kubitschek and Goulart. For his part, the vice-president elect was not totally uninformed about the designs of the men who would keep him and Juscelino from office. A month before the election the political police had been informed in a letter they stamped "SECRETO" that Jango and political ally João Batista Luzardo had smuggled weapons from neighboring Uruguay and Argentina to two Brazilian *fazendas,* or farms.[23]

The larger conspiracies against the democratic process infuriated Lott. As a result, in the early morning hours of November 11, he joined an opposition group within the army calling for an armed insurrection to insure that Kubitschek and Goulart came to power. This faction also wanted

Lott to remain as war minister, or at least to prevent the unpopular Fiuza from taking his place.

THE SPECTACLE IN THE BAY

The drama that was played out in the next few days was something to behold. Shortly after 4 A.M. on November 11, 1955, Lott's soldiers arrived to take control of the presidential palace in Catete, only to discover that it was empty. Carlos Luz had been warned and had fled to the naval cruiser *Tamandaré* moored in Guanabara Bay. With Luz on board the *Tamandaré* were the ship's captain, Sílvio Heck, a host of lesser officials, Mamede, Lacerda, as well as president of the Brazilian Anti-Communist Crusade and commander-in-chief of the fleet Admiral Carlos Pena Boto. Because the navy and air force remained loyal to his caretaker government, Luz decided to travel by sea, within territorial waters, to Santos. Paulistas were thought to be friendlier to his administration.[24]

Originally at anchor in the capital for maintenance on her boilers, the *Tamandaré* was hastily put back into service. Once Luz and his party came aboard, she steamed toward the mouth of Guanabara Bay at greatly reduced speed due to the uncompleted repair work. The forces under Lott's command were ordered to halt the ship dead in the water, but Luz was unwavering about reaching São Paulo. This created a call to battle stations at two of the forts guarding Rio's harbor; the installation at Leme and the one at the west end of Copacabana. They began to lob live rounds at the *Tamandaré* as she squeezed out of the bay, shielded part of the time by an Italian freighter.

LOTT TAKES CHARGE

Although the warship dodged all of the incoming rounds, Carlos Luz was not so lucky. At Lott's insistence the Congress deposed him. The wording used was that the acting president was physically impeded from governing the country since he was out to sea. This legal interpretation of Luz's status was upheld two days later when he returned to Rio, humiliated and still sequestered in the *Tamandaré*. Jânio da Silva Quadros, the governor of São Paulo, had helped defuse the affair by informing Luz that he was unwelcome in his state. After the *Tamandaré* dropped anchor and everyone left the vessel, Col. Mamede was posted to an out-of-the-way billet in the interior of São Paulo.

Languishing away in the hospital, Café Filho learned that Nereu Ramos, the leader of the Senate, was the new acting president, and that Lott, very much in the driver's seat, had had himself reinstated as the minister of war on November 12. Shortly thereafter some of Lott's men approached Café Filho and asked him whether on his return to the presidency he would retain his former ministers. Lott's thinking was that he did not want Eduardo Gomes and Amorim do Vale back in the cabinet since they had supported Carlos Luz. Café Filho answered that he would make no concessions, essentially admitting that he was with those plotting against Kubitschek and Goulart.

When informed of Café Filho's response, the minister of war called a meeting with key subordinates and amplified the already nagging issue of the sick president's health. He let Congress know that he wanted Café Filho out since his heart problem interfered with his duties as president. At first the body of lawmakers stalled. But following a determined show of force, they meekly backed down and removed João Café Filho from office on November 22, 1955, by a vote of 179 to 94. The Senate confirmed everything later in the day, 35 to 16.[25]

The Sidelines

Right on schedule, on January 31, 1956, Juscelino Kubitschek and João Goulart were sworn in as Brazil's new president and vice-president. Though Lott and the ministers of the navy and air force continued at their posts, there was in no way a closing of ranks and healing of wounds in the military. Juscelino wanted peace so that he could carry out his programs. Weighing against this, many of the losers in the October election and the November incidents saw the nation's two new leaders as a clear return to the Vargas era. These would-be shapers of Brazil's destiny were nonetheless forced by the recent events to pensively wait on the sidelines.

One of the places in which members of the unsuccessful segments of the military hierarchy could rethink plans and strategies was the Escola Superior de Guerra. Particularly important in this clique was the man who came to be called "Dr. Go," Golbery do Couto e Silva. His influence on events would be enormous for the following three decades as, among other things, the brain behind the Doctrine of National Security.

Golbery received advanced training in 1944 at Ft. Leavenworth, Kansas, and served with the FEB in Italy as an intelligence officer. In 1954 he drafted the Manifesto dos Coronéis, or Declaration of the Colonels, signed by eighty-two colonels and lieutenant colonels opposed to the plan of João Goulart to raise the minimum wage by 100 percent for some city workers. This resulted in the exit of Goulart from his post as the minister of labor. The military felt that Jango's idea would be inflationary. They also disagreed with the amount of money that was budgeted for the army and the idea of an average worker making as much as an army second lieutenant. It has also been contended that the Manifesto dos Coronéis was merely a pretext on the part of dissatisfied entrepreneurs who viewed the minister of labor as someone more in favor of the workingman than the businessman.[26]

While it is true that much of the officer corps was or came to be anti-Goulart, it has been pointed out that the reason offered by them in their opposition to Jango as a bearer of the red menace was perhaps incomplete. The main organ of the landowning establishment, the Rural Brazilian Confederation, was aghast at Goulart's interest in unionizing rural labor. A report it submitted to the National Security Council contributed to the broadside by the colonels. In 1988 the army and the military chiefs of staff were the first and second largest landowners in Brazil, which had been the case since the mid-1950s, albeit with some variations in the order.[27] Note that this does not include land owned privately by men in uniform. Golbery's job was made easier by Carlos Lacerda's commentary on the pages of his *Tribuna da Imprensa,* which began as soon as Jango became the minister of labor. There is the suggestion that the CIA financed this editorial clamor on the part of the *Tribuna*'s editor.[28]

JACAREACANGA, ARAGARÇAS, *BARROSO*, AND BRASÍLIA

While the more conservative segment of the armed forces bided its time, there were those who could no longer endure what they felt was happening, despite not having a majority of the army's strength behind them. This was the crucial variable, as a handful of rebelling air force officers soon discovered. Their anger erupted into the Jacareacanga and Aragarças Revolts of 1956 and 1959, flare-ups that were put out almost before the rest of Brazil knew they had begun. Another attempt, led by a small group within the navy, to capture Kubitschek while he was on the cruiser *Barroso* in 1957, likewise fizzled for the same reason. The real issue in the Jacareacanga incident was the premature opposition in the air force to Jango's, and not Juscelino's, taking office. The Aragarças affair was a bid at coercing Jânio Quadros to run for president in 1960. It was also a reaction to the mythical leftist uprising that was to be led by the governor of Rio Grande do Sul, Leonel Brizola, supposedly to take place in December 1959. The naval arrest of Kubitschek was to be a lesson to the government by a still fuming navy for opening fire on the *Tamandaré*.[29]

But the real fire was far from out. Pockets of discontent within the military continued to disobey orders and to scheme—some individuals even refused promotions—all through these volatile years. Aside from their admonitions, President Kubitschek was left to run up the public debt, building his Brasília and setting up his program of "fifty years' progress in five." These were words that had a nice patriotic ring to them without naming just who would progress and just who would pay.

Enter Jânio the Eccentric

Henrique Lott stepped down from his post as minister of war to be one of the three presidential candidates in 1960. Ademar de Barros also ran, as did Jânio Quadros. Using a broom as a campaign symbol for cleaning up government, Quadros beat his nearest competitor, Lott, by a comfortable margin of 15.3 percent. The new vice-president was the old vice-president and running mate of Gen. Lott, João Goulart. Brazilian elections at the time were really two contests: one for president and the other for vice-president. The victors did not have to be from the same side.

During the campaigning, Jango seemed to shift more to the left after anti-Communists at the Third Congress of Brazilian Trade Unions doused plans put forward by PCB (now renamed the Partido Comunista Brasileiro) leader Luís Carlos Prestes to create a single national union of workers. The event served to fuel the suspicions of an already nervous military. If this were not enough, once he moved into the Alvorada, the freshly constructed presidential palace in Brasília, Jânio added to these apprehensions by forming a military-led commission to look into allegations of corruption in the former Kubitschek-Goulart administration. The assertions against Kubitschek would be used to cancel his political rights by the post-1964 military dictators. One might argue that in giving the green light to this investigation in the first place the new president was really laying the groundwork for what he was planning as a later option—a grab at more power.

The problem with Jânio Quadros, besides his drinking, was that he possessed an odd personality. Illustrations of this include edicts early in his presidency that raised a few eyebrows. Among these were ordinances prohibiting horse races on weekdays, commercial advertising in theaters and cinemas, card playing in private clubs, soccer players' participating in more than one game a week, and bikinis in beauty contests or on the beaches in general. That Quadros's plans for Brazil occasionally went to even more bizarre extremes can be seen in his July 1961 directive to the military to prepare plans for the invasion and occupation of the three Guianas.[30]

Stubborn and vain, Jânio had a near mania for defining himself as an outsider, in a niche above political factions. Once he took office on January 31, 1961, he became a father figure—the only man who could put order back in the disobedient Brazilian household—if only in his own mind. One of the first areas that he attacked was the inflation problem. His administration began a program of financial cutbacks, retrenchments, and subsidy withdrawals that were much more drastic than anything ever attempted by Kubitschek. Yet all of this was nothing more than a successful put-on to obtain further loans from European and North American banks in as short a time as possible. Then again, these loans were not to compromise Brazil's new autonomous foreign policy. This may well have been the main reason behind Quadros's refusal to accept a $300 million foreign assistance package from American special envoy Adolf Berle. Arriving in the country shortly after Jânio took office, Berle apparently offered the money in return for Brasília's cooperation in the planned Bay of Pigs affair on April 17, 1961. Despite Jânio's refusal of the American package, Berle was able to arrange the go-ahead from the International Monetary Fund (IMF) and other foreign creditors on a loan of more than $2 billion.[31]

A man who prided himself on his individuality, Quadros decided that he should begin pulling the country out of the United States' orbit. He planned to establish firmer contacts with the world's nonaligned nations in a move that actually was an attempt to increase exports. Some of the new targets for

Brazilian goods, however, were not exactly the best Cold War friends of the hemisphere's "northern neighbor." As Jânio was later to write,

> Brazil, either through misinterpretation or distortion of its better political judgment, spent many years without regular contacts with the countries of the Communist bloc, even to the point of having only roundabout and insufficient trade relations with them. As a part of my government's program, I decided to examine the possibility of renewing relations with Rumania, Hungary, Bulgaria and Albania; these have now been established. Negotiations for the reopening of relations with the Soviet Union are in progress and an official Brazilian mission is going to China to study exchange possibilities.[32]

Following the American boycott of Cuba at the Alliance for Progress meetings in Punta del Este, Uruguay, in August 1961, Quadros granted the Cuban delegate, Ernesto "Ché" Guevara, a personal request for an audience in Brasília. There were several reasons why the president agreed to see Guevara. The immediate aims centered around the possibility of increasing trade between the two countries; on resolving the unsettled question of political refugees in the Brazilian embassy in Havana; and on Jânio's naïve wish to be the driving force behind Cuba's readmission to the Latin American Free Trade Association.

All this was well enough, but no sooner had the celebrated revolutionary reached Brasília than Quadros outdid himself by presenting Guevara with Brazil's highest award for foreigners, the Order of the Cruzeiro do Sul. This unexpected gesture was evidently made to underline Jânio's initial hope of strengthening economic ties and to convince Castro to suspend the shooting of a group of Spanish priests. One might also include that it was an attempt to discourage Cuban support of Francisco Julião's Peasant Leagues, then the largest and most politically troublesome group of organized rural laborers. In so doing, Quadros hoped to keep support of the Left despite economic decisions disliked by them.[33] The gesture also had latent outcomes. Ché's new medal kept the Brazilian military agitated.[34] It focused as well the attention of Carlos Lacerda, a man whose abilities for the peculiar might be considered in a league with those of Jânio Quadros.

Once the capital had been moved to Brasília, the old Federal District became the state of Guanabara. Lacerda was elected its first governor on December 5, 1960, largely through support of the middle class. No longer simply a powerful journalist but a powerful journalist and an influential governor, Lacerda immediately set to work berating Quadros's foreign policy on his radio programs and in his newspaper. In the aftermath of the Ché Guevara affair, the Guanabara governor lashed out in a biting media broadcast on the evening of Thursday, August 24, 1961. It was a speech in which Lacerda accused Quadros of taking the country where it did not want to go and filling Brazil with leftist ideas that it did not want to hear. Topping this off, Lacerda, who was privy to inside information, charged that the president was planning to close Congress through new institutional changes that would concentrate more control in the hands of the chief executive.[35]

The Card Games

Quadros had been looking for a way to augment his power. He wanted to be a strong president, something on the order of Charles de Gaulle. If he was thinking of using a ruse to pull this off, he no doubt felt he chose the time well. Everything was set to occur on Friday the twenty-fifth after the legislators in Brasília left the capital and were flying home for the weekend. Goulart was in Asia leading a commercial delegation.

Jânio listened to Lacerda's radio harangue (the pretext) and knew that the military would never allow João Goulart to succeed him, so he abruptly quit (the bluff) the morning after Lacerda's broadcast. Most probably, Quadros reasoned that since his threat of renouncing office had worked so well before—up until then he had used it four times in his political career—he might as well try the poker move one more time. Convinced that the armed forces' hatred of Jango would prevail over their final approval of his resignation, he pressed on, banking that he could blackmail his way to increased authority. It was something the job, and most certainly the man, required. Attributing his decision to "occult forces," Jânio took the step that was to haunt him the rest of his life; he relinquished the presidency and flew off to São Paulo. In a dispatch back to London, R. S. Isaacson of the British embassy speculated later that Quadros's love of whisky might have influenced what was essentially an impetuous act.[36]

Drunk, sober, or somewhere in between, Jânio was in for the surprise of his life. Once his plane touched down at São Paulo's Cumbica air force base, he waited in a building just off the tarmac to be victoriously called home by the military. Yet when news from Brasília came, Quadros learned that his resignation had been accepted. Whereas the professional politicians and the professional soldiers felt unable to control the cranky outsider, they ultimately decided that they could manipulate Goulart and perhaps even keep him from taking power.

Being physically out of Brazil may have actually hampered Quadros and saved Goulart. If the vice-president could be kept from assuming the job that was legally his, new elections would have to be called within sixty days.[37] With such an election in mind, the presidency was passed to Ranieri Mazzilli, head of the Chamber of Deputies. It all looked fine on paper and might have worked except for one snag: Congress refused to go along with the charade.

The legislative roadblock came as a bomb to the military. On August 30, 1961, one day after the elected representatives made their decision known, Odílio Denis, the minister of war, Gabriel Grün Moss, the minister of the air force, and Sílvio Heck, the minister of the navy, issued a thunderous joint statement.[38] Written by the chief of the National Security Council, Golbery do Couto e Silva, it proposed in no uncertain terms that João Goulart not be allowed to re-enter the country.[39] The ministers (Golbery) added that during

> the time he held the post of Minister of Labor, Sr. João Goulart demonstrated very clearly his ideological tendencies, . . . with objectives evidently political, actually injurious to the real interests of our working classes. And not any less true was the extensive penetration . . . of that office, even including key positions in his administration and in the unions, *by active and known agents of international communism* as well as by an uncountable number of leftists.

The officers went on to add that Jango would bring with him

> a period of turbulence . . . followed by agitations, outbursts, and even bloody clashes in the cities and in the country, [all a product] of armed subversion. Ultimately, . . . [this process] would end in the ruination of democratic institutions and with them justice, liberty, and peace—all the highest measures of our Christian culture.
>
> *As president of the republic, in a regime that gives wide authority and personal power to the chief of the government, Sr. João Goulart will consti-*

tute, without any doubt, to give the clearest incentives to all those who wish to see the nation sink into chaos, into anarchy, [and] into civil strife. The armed forces, infiltrated and domesticated, would transform themselves, as has happened in other countries, into simple Communist militias.[40]

The latter was a clear reference to the serviceman's role in Cuba, and the generals may also have been thinking of Jango's pro-Communist union support.[41] It is debatable, however, if this is the entire story. A case could also be made that the leaders of Brazil's military were aghast at the thought of having to lose some of their power to a government run by a populist. In other words, that they might have to obey instead of being obeyed. João Goulart presented the greatest challenge to the military in this regard since 1889, and most of the colonels, generals, and admirals would eventually vow to break him. Dr. Go led the first salvo in this campaign in 1954. Now he was putting words in the mouths of Denis, Moss, and Heck to keep Goulart from returning to Brazil.

The men in braid and ribbon might have succeeded had there never been a Leonel Brizola. Brizola was not only the governor of Rio Grande do Sul but also Jango's brother-in-law. More of a firebrand in those days than in later years, Brizola commandeered the transmitters of Rádio Guaíba and began to stir up his state from the basement of the governor's palace with his "Rede da Legalidade" (Legality Network). From August 27 to September 5, the programming featured the feisty commentary of the governor. A hastily composed patriotic song kicked things off when the show went on and off the air and during intermissions. The ditty, repeated over and over again, had but three lines:

Avante, brasileiros
De pé
Unidos pela liberdade[42]

Forward, Brazilians
On your feet
United for liberty

But Brizola was too smart to depend on just the support of *gaúchos* (persons from the state of Rio Grande do Sul). Behind the scenes, he convinced General José Machado Lopes, commander of Brazil's 3rd Army, stationed in Rio Grando do Sul, to come out in favor of Goulart's return.

Quadros's sudden exit made it impossible for the soldiers calling the shots in Brasília to insure that all of their colleagues were with them. The 3rd Army was one of four Brazilian armies maintained in the country. It was also one of the better equipped and larger fighting forces due to its proximity to Argentina, Brazil's traditional adversary. A conservative but a follower of the law, Gen. Lopes sided with Goulart. A thirteen-day stalemate ensued. Unless someone gave in, the prospects were good for civil war. Then, on August 30, 1961, former American vice-president Richard Nixon remarked that the "acceptance of Goulart's leadership in America's largest Latin neighbor would be a disaster for the United States." He urged the U.S. government to take action. Nixon's provocative commentary was made available to the Brazilian embassy in Washington, D.C., by a news agency. It was apparently never published in Brazil or even in the United States. Ten months later, following Jango's Washington, D.C., visit, John F. Kennedy had an Oval Office conference with American ambassador to Brazil Lincoln Gordon and presidential assistant Richard Goodwin. They discussed the embryonic conspiracy moves by Brazil's military, the conditions under which this should be encouraged, and what it might cost to support Brazilian political parties opposed to Goulart. According to one report, it was at this meeting that JFK gave the "green light for the military overthrow."[43]

Homecoming

As Jango began traveling a winding route back to Brazil—he even went via the United States to try to placate Washington—a solution to the crisis began to be hammered out. A parliamentary system was suggested and mulled over. The military did not like the idea but resentfully agreed. Goulart would be shoved upstairs as president in the arrangement, or so many of the officers believed. Other disgruntled military men plotted to kidnap or somehow harm Jango after he arrived.

"Operation Mosquito" was the initial attempt to assassinate the new leader as he returned to Porto Alegre via Montevideo. Concocted by the air force, the plan was to shoot down or abduct the aircraft carrying Jango from Rio Grande do Sul to Brasília. Another group of armed conspirators was waiting on the tarmac at the new Federal District airport just in case Jango's plane got through. For two days Goulart waited at Porto Alegre while the military ministers negotiated and complained. Among other things, they claimed they could not guarantee Jango's safety if he took to the air. But it was all happening too fast. Time was against the generals, and their last-ditch maneuverings came to naught. The men waiting at the Brasília airport were chased off by a group of sergeants led by Antônio Prestes de Paula. Unorganized, the military brass had been outflanked again.[44]

On September 7, 1961, Brazilian Independence Day, João Goulart was sworn in as the republic's next president.[45] Tancredo Neves became prime minister. In spite of their fresh victory, the two men did not wait around relishing the limelight of their new offices. Almost at once, Goulart and Neves started laying the groundwork for a plebiscite. The object of the special election would be to return the country once more to a presidential form of government.

OTHER ATTEMPTS TO KILL GOULART

Operation Mosquito was not a singular event. There were numerous attempts on the life of João Goulart. Next time around, the idea was for agents of the state of Guanabara to assassinate him when he traveled to Chile in April 1963. Subsequently, elements friendly to Governor Carlos Lacerda endeavored to liquidate Jango, his family, and political allies when they visited one of his properties in Jacarepaguá, near Rio de Janeiro. Among the persons incriminated when the murder weapons were discovered was Charles Borer, brother of Cecil Borer. Also implicated were the head of public security in Guanabara, Gustavo Borges, and Sandra Cavalcanti, Lacerda's secretary for social services. The weapons, ten .45-caliber machine guns, ample ammunition, grenades, radio transmitters, and other items, were all American made. Then there was the bomb that actually went off too soon under the speaker's platform at the March 13, 1964, rally in Rio de Janeiro. This was followed by a plot to drop dynamite by plane on Jango and his party while he was speaking in Belo Horizonte on April 21, 1964, at one of the planned but never carried out mass meetings. Following the dynamite, two or three individuals in the crowd were to machine-gun the survivors, and failing this, snipers using rifles with telescopic sights were to open up on anyone left alive. After he was deposed and residing in Uruguay, Jango learned that Brazilian commandos were going to kill him. Another report suggested that Uruguayan officials had learned of a proposal to kidnap Goulart and Brizola. Once Jango moved to Argentina, his wife, Maria Tereza Goulart, stated that there were warnings that his office would be bombed and that a gang from Mar del Plata was going to slay her husband or abduct their children. During the same period, the United States had Jango on a hit list of important South American opposition figures that were to be assassinated. This was part of the plan dreamed up by Chilean dictator Augusto Pinochet and called "Operation Condor." It was an effort to coordinate the security and intelligence forces in Southern Cone countries to combat leftists and eliminate suspect leaders. The Americans may well have been involved in this effort. In Goulart's case, he was telephoned and warned in Spanish to get ready because he would be next.

Despite his usually unflappable exterior, Jango was bothered enough by all these threats that he sent his two children to live in London and was planning to move there himself. In the meantime, he constantly went around with a sidearm, even while president. But Operation Condor operatives never really eased up. Two months before Jango's mysterious death, his son, João Vicente Goulart, reported that an attempt was made to kidnap the elder Goulart from his offices at the Monte Cooper Business Center on Avenida Corrientes in downtown Buenos Aires. Jango was saved only by not being there. Two days before his death, it has also been alleged, a trio of individuals connected to the Uruguayan intelligence service followed Goulart to his fazenda in Argentina.[46]

"GENERAL" GO AND IPÊS

Despite the settlement that established a parliament, there were those who were still not satisfied. One of these was Golbery do Couto e Silva, who was so upset over Jango's compromise victory that he retired from active duty. Because Dr. Go decided to take his pension early—he had just celebrated his fiftieth birthday—he was promoted two ranks to that of a lieutenant general, in accordance with the standard policy with officer ranks of the day. "General" Golbery, as he was thereafter called, lived on his retirement income for only two months before being hired by a group of prominent businessmen. His new employers needed someone of Golbery's stature for their recently formed IPÊS (Instituto de Pesquisas e Estudos Sociais, or Institute of Research and Social Studies).

IPÊS was a virulently anti-leftist state within a state founded early in 1962. Offices were established in Rio de Janeiro, São Paulo, Belo Horizonte, Porto Alegre, Curitiba, Recife, and Belém. With Golbery as the main intellect, the group set up its headquarters in thirteen rooms on the twenty-seventh floor of a downtown Rio skyscraper. Funded with several million dollars for research, the people at IPÊS began compiling dossiers on what would one day number forty thousand persons. They undertook and maintained a network of domestic spies and purchased a number of large, supersensitive recording devices, which they put to use bugging some three thousand Rio de Janeiro–area telephones.[47] Each week Dr. Go would circulate a report with "the results of the *contacts* that he had made" (italics mine).[48] Likewise important were the analyses. "To create intellectual barriers against the spreading of Marxist ideas, IPÊS issued more and more 'democratically oriented' studies about economic and social problems. It furnished articles to the press. It even reached the masses by issuing pamphlets that had the well-known earmarks of cheap paper and poor typography."[49] The cheap paper and printing mimicked the *cordel,* a kind of cultural-comic book usually displayed on a line or cord.

In fact IPÊS worked at several projects all at once. With the help of associates and graduates from the Escola Superior de Guerra, it tried to convert key officers, such as Amauri Kruel, Olímpio Mourão Filho, and others, who were thought to be on the fence . Mourão Filho was the Integralist who first dreamed up the "Cohen Plan," the excuse used by Vargas to usher in the Estado Novo back in 1937.[50] The Ação Integralista Brasileira were prominent Fascists in pre–World War II Brazil.

The military part of IPÊS's ESG group made up an informal cadre headed by General Humberto de Alencar Castelo Branco (Branco took the Ft. Leavenworth course in 1943 and fought with the FEB) and composed of generals Ernesto Geisel (Ft. Leavenworth course), Ademar de Queiros (served with the Allies in North Africa and with the FEB in Italy), Cordeiro de Farias (Ft. Leavenworth and FEB), Heitor Herrera, José Ulhoa Cintra, Riograndino Kruel (following the leftist uprising of November 1935, Riograndino was the torture-ignoring inspector general of police), and rounded out by Golbery and Mamede. There was also participation by Admiral Otávio Medeiros (the Brazilian naval attaché in Washington, D.C.), the chief of the Brazilian delegation to the Brazil–United States Military Commission and later Riocentro bomb-ignoring head of

SNI (Serviço Nacional de Informações; National Information Service), and by a number of other officers, such as Danilo Venturini, Heitor de Aquino Ferreira, and João Batista Figueiredo. Col. Murilo Ferreira, as well as Lt. Cols. Muniz de Aragão and Ivan Mendes, eventually joined. General Agostinho Cortes led the São Paulo affiliate.

The nonmilitary side to things was made up of right-wing businessmen and intellectuals such as Hélio Beltrão, Roberto Campos, Delfim Neto, João Batista Leopoldo Figueiredo, Glycon de Paiva, Paulo Aires Filho, Antônio Luís Gallotti, José Garrido Torres, Rubem Fonseca, Mário Henrique Simonsen, Luís Antônio da Gama e Silva, and Miguel Real, the former head of the National Department of Doctrine of the Integralist movement.[51]

Besides publishing numerous books, pamphlets, and comic strips, the institute produced fourteen films on democracy that were shown all over Brazil—even in *favelas* (shantytowns) from the back of a truck. Trusted students were sent on trips to the United States. Other funds were made available to assist anti-leftist organizations. IPÊS subsidized and trained red-baiting union leaders, too, both in the city and in the countryside.[52]

As for Brazilian women, they too were educated on the meaning of democracy. Classes were given to ladies "who had decided to organize actively after coming to feel that children were falling under the control of Communist student leaders."[53] Just which of these women's groups IPÊS helped to establish or contributed to remains a mystery. Nevertheless, throngs of conservative women soon became a part of the events in Rio de Janeiro, São Paulo, Belo Horizonte, Recife, and Porto Alegre.

FOLLOW THE MONEY

Not to be forgotten was the Instituto Brasileiro de Ação Democrática (Brazilian Institute of Democratic Action), or IBAD. IBAD specialized in funneling foreign funds—much of which came from the CIA—to IPÊS and to right-of-center peasant organizations. It has been stated that the CIA's Rio operation established IBAD in 1959 to cover U.S. interference in the 1960 presidential campaign. Eventually, many foreign firms were huge contributors to IBAD. As but a glimpse at this financial side of the picture, during just the six months from May to October 1962, IBAD received Cr$1.3 billion, or $3,299,492, from the Royal Bank of Canada and the Bank of Boston alone. At least 297 American companies contributed something. Various international firms added their own donations. In alphabetical order, not by the size of their gift, the list included: AEG, Bayer, Belgo-Mineira, Bethlehem Steel, Ciba, Coca-Cola, Cross, Enila, Esso, General Electric, General Motors, Gulf Oil, Hanna Mining, Herm Stoltz and Coty, IBEC, IBM, Remington Rand, Schering, Shell, Souza Cruz, Standard Brands, Standard Oil of New Jersey, Texaco, Texas Oil, U.S. Steel, and Willys Overland. Other foreign funding was obtained through a wheat-fund operation run by the U.S. embassy. Both in overall strategy and financially, the CIA, IPÊS, and IBAD were three closely linked partners.[54]

IBAD likewise coordinated campaign contributions, through its subsidiary ADEP (Ação Democrática Popular—the Organization for Popular Democratic Action), to help defeat political candidates friendly with Goulart, as well as to sidetrack government initiatives in the legislative area. The latter function was usually carried out by a coalition that called itself the Ação Democrática Parlamentar (Democratic Parliamentary Action). It was composed of right-wing elements from the UDN, Partido Social Democrático (PSD—Social Democratic Party), the Partido Social Progressista (PSP—Social Progress Party), and by other smaller political entities.

São Paulo was home to the second largest office of IPÊS and also to the Fundo de Ação Social (Social Action Foundation), which often tried to imitate IPÊS's main organization in Rio. There were additional, sometimes less effective, networks all over the country, many of which had an economic connection with the industrial colossus up north. One of these was the Anti-Communist Crusade of Carlos Pena Boto. The ACC ran a gnawing campaign of criticism in the press. They also claimed they had sixty-five hundred members, whose contributions paid for everything. From under this canopy of antigovernment forces, the slighted comments, misrepresentations, and outright slander against Jango, and what he wanted to do, became daily affairs. Pena Boto had a hard time holding back his feelings, and on this score he perhaps summed up the opposition's opinion best when he stated point blank that President Goulart was nothing more than a crypto-Communist.[55]

Chapter 2

The Excuse

João Belchoir Marques Goulart was many things. One thing he was not was a closet Communist. His politics were more attuned to the mixed-economy ideas of European social democracy. He was merely ahead of his time. In his own words, Jango believed that "honest capitalism, which is of the healthy nationalistic type and a friend of progress, always deserves my applause and support. There is another kind of capitalism, however, that will never be free of my formal repulsion. I am referring to inhuman capitalism that is so obsessive in form and essence, characteristically anti-Brazilian, that it generates trusts and creates privileges, and that, knowing no homeland, doesn't hesitate to exploit and dance for joy on the misery of the people."[1]

Goulart was born on March 1, 1918, on a fazenda in São Borja, Rio Grande do Sul, not far from the estate owned by the Vargas family. His father was a rich gaúcho *coronel*[2] who had made a fortune in the cattle and sheep business on two huge ranches. In his youth, Jango was an outstanding soccer star and almost turned professional. At five feet seven, with brown eyes and hair combed straight back, he was shy and something of a bohemian.

By age sixteen he had sired a son with the family maid. That same year he came down with a gonorrheal infection that left him permanently lame in his left leg. The result was a slight limp that only endeared him years later to many people, especially those from the lower classes, who could not afford adequate medical attention. His physical disability did not keep him from attending law school in Porto Alegre, although he usually showed up just to take the examinations. This method of attending school was not uncommon among rich Brazilians. Following graduation in 1939, João began to manage the family's properties. When the elder Goulart died in 1943, Jango was already wealthier than his father through his own investments in ranching. Another 34,580 acres of choice land and thirty thousand head of cattle became his through inheritance.[3]

Corruption and Goulart

The more prominent Jango became, the more his critics accused him of fraud in or near the reins of office. His admirers said that he was just gifted at knowing how to make cash grow. It is thus best to consider the allegations at this point. A good many of these charges came from questionable sources, from personalities who could have been accused of corruption themselves, from people who had connections with or received funding from the CIA, or from those who eventually turned against him. The veracity of the following material is therefore yet to be shown and is in need of further research.

The dean of America's Brazil scholars, John W. F. Dulles, asserts that while he was justice and interior secretary for the state of Rio Grande do Sul from 1951 to 1952, Jango "profited from the sale of contraband trucks" along with Gregório Fortunato, the presidential bodyguard who was charged with plotting to kill Lacerda in 1954.[4] The source of this information was Getúlio's and Jango's archenemy, Carlos Lacerda's *Tribuna da Imprensa.* Lacerda's views on such matters in respect to Vargas, Goulart, and even Kubitschek should of course be weighed against his own fixation on becoming president. In addition, it has been said that during his strident public life Lacerda made a fortune out of corruption himself.[5]

Ivan Hasslocher, general director of the money laundering IBAD, provided a variation on the contraband theme. He stated that Fortunato and Goulart smuggled cars, perfume, and other items after Goulart became the national minister of labor on June 15, 1953. Hasslocher went on to claim that Jango's father was relatively poor and that his famous son acquired his wealth through illegal commissions, which Goulart then invested in land. It was Hasslocher's view that Jango did not keep his money in overseas bank accounts. The former director of IBAD said that Aguinaldo Boulitreau Fragoso, who died in 1978, and Manuel Pio Corrêa gave him this information.[6] Corrêa later denied knowing anything about corruption and João Goulart.[7] Corrêa himself was a diplomat assigned by the 1964–85 military dictators to be Brazil's ambassador in Montevideo. One of his main jobs was to keep an eye on Jango's activities in the Uruguayan capital. Another person who spied on Goulart and Brizola in Montevideo was Saulo Gomes. After the truck smuggling charges, in August 1956, the *Tribuna da Imprensa* began to accuse Vice-President Goulart of having arranged for a lumber deal with Argentina's Juan Perón. While business with Argentina itself was not unlawful, a bribe of one million Argentine pesos, together with sixty thousand dollars for Jango and an associate, Carlos Maura Ronchetti, certainly were. This was what Lacerda, then leader of the UDN, and the rest of his party loudly proclaimed had taken place. A commission was set up to investigate the affair, and another hearing was established at the urging of the PTB (Partido Trabalhista Brasileiro—Brazilian Worker's Party) and PSD to determine whether or not Lacerda had violated national security laws by revealing a document from the Itamarati, or Brazilian Foreign Office, during his exposé. Goulart denied the charges, and a stacked commission found him innocent. The committee looking into Lacerda's use of restricted material found him guilty but lacked enough votes to press charges. One could argue, however, that Congressman Lacerda was saved by his colleagues in the lower house who were afraid of any kind of limitation being placed on their freedom of speech in that legislative body.[8]

The former president of the American Chamber of Commerce in Rio de Janeiro, wealthy businessman William Sweet, has his own charges against João Goulart. In his unpublished autobiography, he remarked that

> The President, Jango Goulart, was not communist. He was one of the biggest landholders in Brasil. Before his election he was one of the biggest contraband operators in the country. I knew him personally, and knew that he was not adverse to capitalist delicacies such as corruption. I was part of a group that prepared a large project for the State of Maranhão, involving land redistribution and the industrialization of Babaçu [nut]. U.S. financing had been approved by the U.S. government agencies, but the signature

> of the Brazilian President was necessary. I had a number of conferences with him on this, and finally received his verbal approval. Then I was invited for a cocktail by the President's spokesman, and told that the President wanted US$5 million off the top. The project was dropped.[9]

Asked by this author for corroboration of his comments and an explanation of what he was doing in the early 1960s in Brazil, Sweet responded, "I was not surprised when I went for cocktails with this man (I forgot his name) because I was emotionally very involved with the group that made the revolution [the 1964 military takeover]."[10] Sweet's admission was an understatement. Besides his entrepreneurial interests in the country, he states elsewhere in his autobiography that he "was used by the [Brazilian] military to carry messages back and forth between them and the American Ambassador [Lincoln Gordon]."[11] It seems peculiar as well that the nut deal Sweet describes would involve the president of Brazil rather than someone at the ministerial level.

Professor Dulles is also in possession of a 1963 interview he had with Rio businessman Otakar Svacina (reprinted below). Svacina's main entrepreneurial activity during the 1950s and '60s was the importation of raw copper from Chile and Peru into Brazil. An immigrant from Czechoslovakia, Otakar passed away in 1992. However, Svacina's son, Otti, remarked that his father was a bitter anti-Communist who felt that the Goulart government was "linked with the Soviet regime as well as with the Chinese popular republic."[12] In defense of his father, João Vicente Goulart refutes the substance of Svacina's remarks by stating the obvious—his father was already one of the richest men in Brazil. Why would he want to compromise his political effectiveness with any inkling of dishonesty?[13]

INTERVIEW NO. 28 JULY 8, 1963

Lunch with Otakar Svacina

a) The amount which Ricardo Jafet is generally recognized to have loaned his own enterprises from the Bank of Brazil (when he was its president) is two billion cruzeiros.

Svacina says that Ademar de Barros was reasonable in the cut he took on São Paulo government business contracts. The people around him seem to step in and get more, more even than Ademar thinks they do.

> In the deal providing busses to São Paulo, Vice-President Goulart asked for 15%. With something for Svacina this would make the price of the busses much too high. (Svacina had been asked by Ademar and Jango to make up a tender, which it was understood would get the business). Svacina pointed this out. Ademar, a reasonable man, left it up to Svacina who suggested 5% for each. (Later, after Jango had left for Rio, Ademar asked for 8% so as to do better than Jango!). Monthly payment papers for 200 busses over 5 years had to be made in a hurry as Quadros was coming in. Anyway this was a genuine deal, not just a paper one, and São Paulo got the busses. Ademar left for 'exile,' instructing Svacina to pay to someone else. The someone else used the money from Svacina to buy a gas station, and so Ademar did not get his share.
>
> (Quadros took bigger cuts than Ademar.)
>
> Ademar, back from 'exile,' said he had no funds and needed his 'cuts.' But Svacina finds it difficult to deal directly with Ademar, because the people around Ademar, all out for their own percentages, create a sort of wall around Ademar.
>
> Recently President Goulart sent a message to Svacina saying he would like ten million dollars and wondering if a deal can be arranged to provide such a cut for him. If the ten million were 10% this would have to be a 100 million dollar deal and that kind of money for investing in Brazil does not seem to be around. Too big.
>
> Ademar is direct, pleasant, nice to deal with.[14]

During the discussions with Professor Dulles about the Svacina interview, he indicated that Jango wanted the ten million dollars transferred to his Swiss bank account. He likewise mentioned that the military put together an archive on Jango's illegal intercession in a Banco do Brasil loan to Amuri Kruel. Kruel wanted the loan to make improvements to his fazenda in Espírito Santo. This dossier was said to be among the documents stored in the Archivo Castelo Branco at the Escola de Comando e Estado-Maior do Exército in Rio. Unfortunately, the file in question contains only a reference to Kruel and the bank loan. There is no mention of Goulart having been involved.[15] Some of what the military said it uncovered, mainly concerning Jango's dealings in land and cattle, was published in *O Cruzeiro*. Goulart attacked this *O Cruzeiro* report as a "tissue of lies" through his lawyer, Waldyr Borges, in a later issue of the same weekly magazine.[16] The military never published a rebuttal. To be fair to John W. F. Dulles, the subject of one of his own books, Heráclito Sobral Pinto, remarked that Jango was not corrupt in a letter written prior to the November 1955 government crisis.[17]

Then there was the time when President Jânio Quadros attempted to blemish his political opponents, demoralize Congress, and increase his own chances of being given stronger powers. While he was Quadros's vice-president, João Goulart was among those targeted through the use of special presidential investigative councils to look into corruption during Kubitschek's administration. One of the charges, for example, was that Goulart had stolen government silverware while in office. And despite his vehement denial, a more serious claim placed him in the center of a scheme that bilked labor-pension funds. No matter how hard they tried, however, the committee could never prove anything. Finally, there is the charge by Jango's former friend, Samuel Wainer, that he handled the "bribe box" for Goulart. Fellow journalist Rivadavia de Souza, on the other hand, discounts this accusation.[18]

Vargas and Goulart

Subsequent to Getúlio Vargas's downfall on October 29, 1945, the deposed ruler returned to his fazenda, Itú, near São Borja to rethink his political options. One of Vargas's regular visitors during this time of introspection was his longtime neighbor and the man who would talk him into another try at the presidency, João Goulart. The two men got along extremely well even if there were noticeable differences. Besides the thirty-six-year gap in their ages there was the question of style. "Gegê" (Vargas) was a man obsessed with power; Jango could have cared less about such things.

Aside from Vargas, Jango developed a distinct distaste for hobnobbing with the upper classes. In fact, his personality sometimes irritated other leading Brazilians. Different from many of them, he had simple tastes. Goulart was a soft-spoken gaúcho who loved ordinary Brazilians. Unlike Vargas, he did not have a reputation for stretching the truth, nor for doing things out of spite. Getúlio knew this, just as he knew that Jango tried to treat most people, including his employees, as equals. Toping everything off were his opinions—views that were totally out of line for someone from the landed elite. He favored the reduction of social inequalities and a limited agrarian reform.

While it is true that Getúlio initiated a number of needed public programs for the urban worker, most were empty of real substance. They nonetheless won him the diminutive "Pai dos Pobres" (Father of the Poor). But Vargas began flirting legislatively in a similar way with rural labor only[19] when he was convinced that the workingman was his final option to stay in office. This is where Goulart fit in nicely. For without being a radical, Jango's interests and connections were in and to this very proletarian sphere that Gegê so coveted.

It is also correct that Jango obtained much of his political schooling at Getúlio's side and used his teacher's name to justify numerous policies. It is incomplete, however, to view him simply as the heir to the old master's mantle because Getúlio snuck a copy of his "last testament" into Goulart's coat pocket before committing suicide. Those who see Jango as a continuation of Gegê's populism, but with a penchant for social legislation, are somewhat off the mark as well. This is because it is debatable how many of the ideas behind the social programs of Getúlio's second administration were his own and how many were Goulart's.

Many comments on and studies of João Goulart are built on the work of his enemies. These efforts usually find him timid and irresolute. In actuality, in the very essence of this most controversial of Brazilian presidents could be found an adroit spirit determined to help the povão. Yet he was not a man free of defects. One of his best qualities was really a political liability and part of his undoing. Concisely put, almost all his life Jango maintained a fierce personal loyalty to those who helped him. The characteristic of being overly loyal to someone considered a friend is a trait particularly noticeable among gaúchos. It was a noteworthy flaw in João Goulart.[20] Despite that limitation he was to become, in the CIA's words, "a shrewd political manipulator who . . . skillfully presided over a political scene of great complexity and diversity."[21]

THE POLITICAL NOVICE

Goulart's first contact with voters came through his growing relationship with Vargas and the national elections of December 2, 1945. His job was to be Getúlio's spokesman for the endorsement of Dutra. Then followed the period of learning at the side of the expresident. Jango was given the directorship of Porto Alegre's PTB. The PTB was Vargas's political machine specifically created to rob support from Luís Carlos Prestes's PCB.[22]

In 1947, with Getulio's backing, Jango was elected to the state assembly. He spoke only once in front of the gaúcho policymakers, and that was in defense of the small farmer. Goulart preferred instead to build up the strength of the PTB in Rio Grande do Sul's interior. As the next presidential election approached—this time it was scheduled for October 3, 1950—Vargas virtually turned Jango's São Vicente ranch into his political headquarters. Getúlio Vargas had decided to run again for the nation's top job.

Out on the campaign trail, Goulart was constantly at Getúlio's side, confiding, discussing strategy, or receiving visitors. When the ballots were tallied, Getúlio had won by more than a million and a half votes. Jango took over the national directorship of the PTB before the election and was himself elected to a seat in Congress in the Vargas sweep. But Goulart thought there was more opportunity for him in Rio Grande do Sul. He thus took leave of the federal post in 1951 and accepted a position arranged by one of Getúlio's cousins as the new secretary of justice and the interior for the state of Rio Grande do Sul.

Time passed and João Goulart moved ever upward. He strengthened the PTB, prospered in his other duties, and was called by Vargas to the capital in June 1952 to attempt to resolve a dispute within the party's executive branch. Jango dealt with the obstacle so effectively that he ended up becoming the national president of the PTB. Next on his résumé was organized labor as he began arbitrating union problems for the president. Again his efforts were successful. There was, however, a cost. The new triumphs brought cries from the opposition that the old master was at it again, preparing another coup d'état, this time with working-class help. It likewise opened a file on Goulart in the office of military intelligence, where records were kept on potential enemies. It was the second dossier. DOPS had been looking at João Goulart since June 16, 1947.[23]

MINISTER OF LABOR

Jango's influence and prestige within union circles grew. They increased to such an extent that in 1953, "when Getúlio needed to exchange the winks with the working classes for promises, Jango left the shadows [and was made] the Minister of Labor."[24] At thirty-five, Goulart already enjoyed the reputation of being one of the country's most important workforce allies. In opposition, some saw his nomination to this key government job as an indication that Vargas was trying to stifle conflicts with workers—conflicts that were due to low wages and the high cost of living—by appointing politicians who were willing to collaborate with the unions and the Communists. What the reactionary sectors missed was that Jango consulted with Communists in the trade-union movement just as he consulted with conservatives and moderates and everyone else in the trade-union movement. Even after he became president, he continued to do so.[25]

As Jango eased into his new role, one of his first concerns was the economic ground that was being lost by the urban worker. In the last month of 1951, Vargas allowed the Minimum Salary (Brazil's monthly adjusted minimum monthly wage) to be increased to a point about 14 percent higher than the first Minimum Salary in 1943. Most city workers were paid in an employer-determined number of minimum salaries. This might have been a nice Christmas present if it not for the fact that the consumer price index had gone up 100 percent during the same period. Workers were fuming. There were large strikes in March 1953 in São Paulo and in June down on the leftist-run docks in Rio de Janeiro, Santos, and Belém. Jango was given the jobs of cleaning up this mess and of winning for his boss the title of defender of workers' rights.

The dock strikes were soon resolved in favor of the stevedores, but in October the same men were once more out on the picket line. Contrary to the charges that he was a Communist and that he tolerated Communists, Goulart did not give in to the dockworkers this second time. The new strike was put down with government force. Jango maintained that he was willing to negotiate only within the realm of what was possible. The lesson was well taken because in his final months at the helm of the labor ministry the soldiers never had to be called out again. Goulart much preferred the bargaining table, and he settled a number of additional labor disputes this way. Often he came out on the side of proletarian interests and was even referred to by his conservative critics, in their typical sarcastic style, as the "Minister of Laborers."[26]

In January 1954, Goulart began to prepare legislation that would double the monthly Minimum Salary and freeze prices in the process. The

Minimum Salary was not the same in all parts of Brazil. It was higher in urban areas due to the cost of living in cities. Jango's augmentation would take workers in the Federal District from twelve hundred to twenty-four hundred cruzeiros per month. He would later write that the Minimum Salary at the time kept a good number of Brazilians in hunger and misery.[27] Goulart's plan was designed to stave off Carlos Lacerda's campaign to remove Vargas by building sympathy among upper-level employees. The minister of labor advised the president that in case of a loud oppositional outcry over his scheme, he would allow himself to be thrown to the wolves so as to avoid any loss of face to Vargas. Once Goulart's legislation neared its final stages, and the business community, landowners, Lacerda, and eighty-two colonels and lieutenant colonels were up in arms, this of course is exactly what happened.

Getúlio accepted Jango's resignation on February 22, 1954, the day he presented his proposals.[28] Yet just over two months later, on May 1, against the advise of his cabinet, Getúlio put his former labor minister's suggested wage hike into effect and gained all the credit and part of the muddle. He did not freeze prices as part of the package as Jango had originally urged. The new Minimum Salary continued the variation by region. It was highest in the Federal District, at Cr$2,400, and lowest in rural areas of Rio Grande do Norte, where workers had their monthly salaries raised to at least Cr$555. This last sum was worth US$29.49 on May 1, 1954.

At this point in his term as the nation's elected president, Vargas was gambling, floundering, and thrashing about for increased support from the urban wage earner.[29] Vargas was not after parity in wages between urban and rural workers. What parity there was was his biggest wager, and he lost. The wage hike fueled an already worrisome inflation, and the former dictator should have known that traditionalist domestic and foreign elites, accompanied by the military, would never allow any real income changes to benefit labor that were to be offset from their pockets, even if only briefly.

On His Own

Jango was deeply moved by Vargas's suicide and returned to São Borja to start over. He ran for the Federal Senate as the PTB candidate from Rio

Grande do Sul on October 3, 1954, but was defeated. Despite this loss, Goulart was still seen as the legitimate heir to and spokesman for much of Getúlio's last lurch at staying in office. For this reason, and because of his voice in the labor sphere, Jango's PTB and Kubitschek's PSD joined forces in the presidential elections that were held exactly one year later.

As the two men were out searching for votes, an event took place that dramatically changed João Goulart's life. With his brother standing in for him, he got married by proxy on May 17, 1955. The bride was Maria Tereza Fontela, and she was the seventeen-year-old niece of Spartaco Vargas, one of Getúlio's two younger brothers.[30] Their marriage was evidently happy enough at first to produce two children. The relationship, however, became problematic, as Jango was never completely faithful. Maria Tereza then followed in kind with a vengeance. Loud arguments became part of the routine. She would ultimately say that her husband "was not a prince or a king; he had only money."[31] As their relationship floundered, Jango continued to see other women once in a while if for no other reason than to keep up the facade of Brazilian machismo.[32]

Return of the Presidency

Years later, on January 6, 1963, the plebiscite that Goulart pushed for to end Brazil's parliamentary experiment was resolved at the ballot box. Of the country's eighteen million voters, over eleven and a half million went to the polls. The results revealed that nearly nine and a half million Brazilians wanted a return to presidential government. Just over two million (or about 18 percent of the total) wanted things kept the way they were. Jango, flush with victory, was proclaimed president, this time a real one, at 6 P.M. on January 23, 1963.[33]

Tancredo Neves would later remark, "Never has a Brazilian president initiated his government under such adverse conditions as did João Goulart."[34] Neves's observation could not have been more precise. The euphoria of the plebiscite's victory faded with the opposition's blockade of nearly anything of significance that Goulart tried to accomplish in the months to come. Besides the high-ranking military and homegrown conservatives, antagonism was centered in two additional sectors. The foreign business community, led by the Americans and their government in Washington,

D.C., plus Brazil's own *latifundiários* (or large landed estate owners) now more than ever counted themselves in the opposition's camp. The combined power of these four bastions of reactionism to block legislation and refuse crucial loans would change Goulart—as it might change anyone—into a man who, at times, appeared inconsistent.

UNREASONABLE NEIGHBORS TO THE NORTH

Jango's plan of action for his new administration, his proposal to bring the country into the twentieth century, revolved around the Reformas de Base, or package of Basic Reforms. The problem, however, was that some of the items in the Reformas did not sit well with Brazil's North American friends. The displeasure had begun brewing at least by September 1962, when a new law governing the remittance abroad of profits earned in Brazil by foreign firms passed through parliament. Goulart delayed his signing of the measure, using it partially as a bargaining chip with Washington. The move was not well received by the Kennedy administration.

Kennedy's concern was based on the fact that the United States had become the largest single investor in Brazil. American businesses had poured in nearly half of the total foreign capital in the country. By 1960 American entrepreneurs had invested around $1.5 billion in Brazil, on which they extracted about $3.5 billion. Any actions, laws, or protests against foreign capital, or against taking earnings out of the country would quickly incur the ire of any administration in Washington, D.C.[35]

There was also the matter of Brazilian intransigence at the Punta del Este Conference in Uruguay (January 22–31, 1963). At issue was a continuation of the independent Brazilian foreign policy, started under Quadros, that defied the United States' wish to drum Cuba out of the Organization of American States and to impose economic sanctions against Castro. Goulart instructed his foreign minister, Francisco San Tiago Dantas, to oppose these anti-Cuban moves. Jango had already refused an apparent $80 million U.S. bribe to come out against Fidel,[36] and San Tiago Dantas was still apparently a team player. When his turn came to speak at Punta del Este, San Tiago eagerly complied with Goulart's instructions and criticized Dean Rusk's anti-Cuban stance. The American delegation responded by letting it be known that under the Alliance for Progress program, aid for noncooperative nations could well be held up. Perhaps the blackmailing worked because the final vote was fourteen against the Cubans, none in favor, and one country, Brazil, abstaining.

There were other things that the Americans did not like about Brazil, and one of them was the governor of the state of Rio Grande do Sul, Leonel Brizola. The early 1960s were years of growing Cold War anxiety in many parts of the globe. Brazil witnessed a period of increased nationalism and spiraling bipolarization. Brizola was a man to make his reputation in such times. He likewise came to savor political power during these years, after becoming identified with the poorly thought out positions of the nationalistic Left.[37]

The United States of America and the governor first locked horns over the one cruzeiro ($.05) "sale" of the U.S.-owned Companhia de Energia Eléctrica Rio-Grandense in May 1959. Some fourteen months later, Brizola alleged that he had uncovered a plot by U.S. Ambassador John Moors Cabot, the CIA, and the FBI to photograph select files from his state's DOPS branch. For the right to copy what they wanted, the Americans offered to re-equip gaúcho police forces to the tune of one million dollars. Similar deals were mentioned as having already been signed with São Paulo and Pernambuco. Brizola, however, vehemently refused the *ianque* (Yankee) proposal. When the Cuban Missile Crisis erupted in October 1962, Leonel had been one of the louder Brazilian voices objecting to U.S. policy.[38]

Two and a half weeks after the Punta del Este meetings he was at it again, expropriating the gaúcho subsidiary of International Telephone and Telegraph. The subsidiary, the Companhia Telephônica Rio-Grandense, had owned the telephone concession in Brazil's southernmost state since 1927 and was officially valued at 1.35 billion cruzeiros, or nearly 4.4 million U.S. dollars. A purchase price just over US$483,000 was offered to the conglomerate, but only part of this amount, $64,516, was deposited with the arbitration court handling the case. Rio Grande do Sul's judges then decided that IT&T's asking price minus depreciation should have been a paltry eight thousand or so dollars. No further money was paid out as Governor Brizola claimed that the difference of $56,516 should be returned by the IT&T subsidiary. Even after a blitz visit to Brasília by Robert Kennedy, Goulart, in a move that lost face with the American government, eventually supported Brizola's performance.[39]

THE PROVINCIAL ELITE

By the time Jango took office in 1961, half of Brazil's arable land was owned by less than 2 percent of its population. For those rural laborers—the group as a whole made up an estimated 24.4 percent of the economically active population at the time—who could take a break from their chores and follow the new president's inauguration, little had changed.[40] Indeed, little had changed since the 1880s, when boatloads of mostly poor Italians were imported to replace the slaves.[41] Working conditions, proper housing, education for their children, and medical facilities were abominable. Justice was still a nearly nonexistent commodity. Malnutrition was rampant. The foreman's whip routinely tore into flesh. Troublemakers were branded as bandits or killed.[42]

Getúlio Vargas had succeeded in blocking the power of other coronéis, but the rural counterparts of these men ruled largely as they had for centuries. On fazendas, and more and more often on multinational agrabusiness installations in the country's interior, they continued to command their realms as if they were the sovereigns of old. João Goulart was the first Brazilian president to seriously confront these power brokers. What he attempted was an overall transformation through improvements for rural labor combined with an equitable land-reform package.

To be implemented largely through SUPRA, or the Office of Agrarian Politics, the president's proposals were designed to provide change through government acquisition of land, much of which would be set aside to establish small- to medium-sized cooperatives. This new expanse of territory was to come into the government's hands four ways: 1) by confiscation for the public's well-being, 2) by donation, 3) by abandonment, and 4) through purchase.

From the landowners' point of view, the most controversial of these four means was the first: confiscation for the public's well-being. Among the justifications that allowed the administration to seize property were: the land was not being used; it was underused, it was used for socially nonproductive ends, it had been obtained with public monies, and that confiscation was necessary for environmental protection. Also included were lands that did not produce enough revenue to allow their owners to pay all employees at least one regional Minimum Salary and those near centers of population that were necessary for the production of goods and food products.

If these ways to lose one's possessions were not enough, Article 8 of the measure stated that compensation for all expropriated properties was to be made in twenty-year bonds equivalent to the declared tax value of the land. This was a move to save revenues since many owners of rural real estate dishonestly listed the value of their holdings as zero. The interest on the bonds was 6 percent per year with inflationary correction fixed at 10 percent annually on the face value of the bonds. This was hardly popular with investors as it was designed to stifle land speculation and help fight high inflation. Cash payments could have been made through negotiation.[43] But the administration would have come out a winner here too as they could have offered lower purchase prices in place of the unpopular bonds. There was one snag in the government's intentions, however, as a constitutional amendment was needed to substitute the bonds for the cash.

Aside from legal changes to help the functioning of the entire project, Jango's scheme of Basic Reforms included a massive literacy campaign; tax changes that were aimed at increasing government funds and improving investments, providing more income equilibrium; eliminating the public debt; as well as several organizational improvements in Brasília. A new centralized structure was planned to control money and banking policies and inflation in the process.

The cost of importing products to be used in the local manufacturing of medicines, which were sometimes marked up as much as 2,000 percent, was to be controlled. Likewise, Goulart envisioned a revamping of the university system to do away with lifetime professorships. Diplomatic relations were to be started with the Soviet Union and the People's Republic of China. And, not to be left out, the election process was to be expanded to give the vote to enlisted military personnel and the nonliterate—much to the chagrin of the country's elites, both those in uniform and those in coat and tie.[44]

João and John

President Goulart visited President Kennedy in Washington, D.C., during the first week of April in 1962. Among the topics the two leaders discussed was an arrangement to check further confiscation moves by Brizola or anyone else who might be willing to follow his example. Jango suggested that his country purchase U.S.-owned public utilities in Brazil, specifically those under the control of the American Foreign Power Company, or AMFORP. The U.S. firm's Brazilian assets were in excess of $100 million. Kennedy agreed, and a commission was established to study the details and work out a price. Later that month, when the amount to be paid to AMFORP—$135 million, 75 percent of which was to be released to the concern in dollars—was announced, many persons on the left felt uncomfortable. One of these distressed personalities was none other than Leonel Brizola. Unable to control himself, the governor of Rio Grande do Sul went into a tantrum.[45]

The Governor of Rio Grando do Sul

Mercurial at this stage in his life, Leonel was not above resorting to fisticuffs in the hallowed halls of Congress or in an airport departure lounge, provided several armed bodyguards accompanied him. The waiting room incident took place at Rio de Janeiro's Galeão Airport on December 26, 1963. There, Brizola saw journalist David Nasser walking through the terminal and attacked him from behind. He is reported to have had twelve bodyguards. Irritated over the story "Centauro dos Pampas" (Centurion of the Pampas), in which Nasser made fun of him, Brizola screamed that he was going to shove the story down Nasser's throat. He then delivered a blow to the side of Nasser's head. Before the writer could pick himself up, the crowd and members of the air force separated the two men. As they were being pushed apart, the governor yelled that he was still not satisfied. Later, on TV, Leonel stated that he would like to whip Nasser. Brizola may not have been aware of it, but at the time of this episode David Nasser was suffering from Parkinson's disease. Brizola's distrust of the press, and of some of his political colleagues, went back many years. So too did his melodramatic behavior. In 1954 he had challenged a state senator to a duel for having said that he kept the *caixinha* (payoff box) for the state of Rio Grande do Sul. Brizola then offered the same option to the director of the newspaper *Diário de Notícias* for printing a narrative about the incident.[46]

Luís Carlos Prestes felt that Brizola was foolish during these years.[47] And the president knew that Brizola's temper required a special patience. In Jango's view, it had a tragic origin. When Brizola was but five years old, he, his mother, brothers, and sister were bound to chairs and forced to watch the beheading of José de Oliveira Brizola, Leonel's father. The elder Brizola was said to have run off with someone else's livestock. When the tied-up family was found, the feet of the children were soaked with their father's blood. The experience, in Goulart's opinion, made Brizola rebellious. As he grew to adulthood, Leonel was noted for choosing vehement solutions in circumstances where there were such options. Years later no one knew to what degree he had really changed. Goulart recounted this story to explain the enormous tolerance he had for his brother-in-law. Jango occasionally put this patience to use in front of other people when Leonel, calmly and rudely, accused him of being a coward, complaisant, or for making too many concessions.[48]

There were at least two other reasons why Goulart attempted to keep his feelings under wraps concerning Leonel Brizola. Even though he disliked the man more and more, he felt obligated to him for being the deciding factor in his safe return to Brazil and ascent to the presidency. But at the top of the list was the fact that Brizola was Goulart's brother-in-law. Jango consistently worried about hurting his sister Neuza Brizola's feelings if he reacted too harshly against her husband.

Leonel Brizola obviously realized the triple effect he had on the president and by early 1963 had shifted his political position to egotistically challenge Goulart at nearly every turn. Instead of uniting himself behind the country's elected leader and behind policies that had a chance of being tolerated by Brazil's foreign and domestic leaders, Brizola tried to steal Goulart's political thunder. This he did by upping the ante again and again, promising more to the workingman than the ruling classes were willing to swallow. Many times this forced Jango to follow suit. What Brizola was after was not, in the first instance, an improvement for the Brazilian proletariat. Leonel Brizola was concerned only with Leonel Brizola. He wanted to change the election law that prohibited officeholders or their relatives from immediate succession. Leonel Brizola wanted to be the next president of Brazil.[49]

The Governor of Pernambuco

In Pernambuco there was another politician who also wanted to live in the Alvorada. Miguel Arraes, the sometime leftist governor of the state, had earned Goulart's respect and unwavering loyalty. When Arraes was Recife's mayor he backed Jango's bid to take office in 1961. The following year, Arraes was elected governor and rapidly set about to improve the standard of living afforded Pernambuco's rural workers. He saw to it that the Minimum Salary and unions were applied more evenly or made available. Legal aid and state-run stores were established to provide less expensive legal protection, goods, and medicines.[50] All of this was needed and welcomed by the agrarian laborer. But there is, nevertheless, the possibility that the governor did what he did out of fear of losing part of his political base to the Socialist lawyer Francisco Julião of the Peasant Leagues.[51]

Plano Trienal

In the governmental sphere, Jango's administration embarked on an economic program to combat a 52-percent inflation rate while at the same time ambitiously promoting high internal growth. Backed by a cabinet of eminent center-to-left jurists, professors, and other notables, Goulart's Plano Trienal de Desenvolvimento Econômico (Three-Year Economic Development Plan) was to be the centerpiece in his Basic Reform efforts. The endeavor called for the creation of a strong cruzeiro, the reduction of inflation through a decrease in state spending, a limit on credit, and the unfortunate need to augment the yearly revenue taken in by the government. (This final item could have been done by a tax increase and/or by getting Brazilians to pay their taxes in the first place.) On the advice of the IMF, wheat and petroleum subsidies were to be ended. To help bring about growth, new loans and investments were included in the Plano Trienal.

This first attempt by Goulart at modest changes within a stacked system was bound to fail owing to the building clamor against it in traditionalist Brazilian circles and because Washington was playing cat-and-mouse with Brasília. San Tiago Dantas may well have suspected this American reaction. Newly shifted to the post of minister of finance and complete with his ever-present rabbit's foot good-luck charm, he jetted off to the United States to try to mollify Washington in March 1963.

Unbeknownst to Goulart, San Tiago Dantas had already been corrupted by the honoraria he was receiving from big business and by his own dreams of one day becoming the nation's leader. He secretly aided those forces conspiring against Jango. During the trip to the United States, he attempted to persuade large American companies, such as IT&T, to come out against Goulart, in addition to obtaining any aid that could be of assistance to Brazil. At first unaware of San Tiago's betrayal, Jango had him lead a special project to evaluate all groups near the reins of power that could harm his presidency. Being a political turncoat was really nothing new to San Tiago. In 1932 he took a fancy to integralism after leaving law school. Soon Dantas rose to one of the highest posts within the Brazilian Fascist movement, becoming responsible for the AIB section on justice. He quit the organization just prior to the ill-fated Integralist coup, the so-called pajama-*Putsch* of May 1938.[52]

San Tiago Dantas needed 1.8 billion dollars in aid, loans, and assistance. He hoped that much of this would come from the United States. After long, drawn-out negotiations, however, San Tiago was offered only $84 million. Another $398.5 million would be released if Brazil did what it was told. Not only were anti-inflation and austerity measures part of the deal but, between the lines, the Americans suggested some type of action against the Profits Remittance Bill. They advocated as well that Jango rein in the confiscations and verbiage of brother-in-law Brizola. Finally, they demanded that $30 million go toward the purchase of the IT&T holdings.[53]

Returning home at the end of March, San Tiago found the Plano Trienal losing many of the allies necessary to satisfy the Americans. It was a foregone conclusion that Brizola and Arraes would be livid. Joining them this time were Luís Carlos Prestes and the PCB, the powerful leftist union Comando Geral dos Trabalhadores (CGT, or General Workers Command), progressive Catholic groups, the União Nacional de Estudantes (UNE, or National Union of Students), not to mention a good deal of Congress. Without more of the sought-after foreign (American) funding, however, the reactions of all these people and groups, together with the plans of the government, were largely political castles built on empty promises.

Inflation continued to increase over the coming months, and so too did the number of paralyzing strikes by workers demanding economic viability. It must have seemed to the president that the country was headed down a cul-de-sac. Not ready for radical solutions and lacking the foreign capital, Jango had little recourse except to let the Plano Trienal die in a total cabinet reshuffle that June. AMFORP was not far behind; it passed into oblivion on July 1, 1963. The United States then decided that the

Brazilian government had failed to live up to its end of the austerity agreements and canceled the conditional $398.5 million loan in addition to all Alliance for Progress funding.

American Duplicity

Washington did continue, however, to provide money, more than $100 million, to what it termed "Islands of Administrative Sanity." These were nothing less than inducements to governors who were either on good terms with the Kennedy Administration or openly hostile to Goulart. Among those singled out to receive this aid were Minas Gerais's Magalhães Pinto, São Paulo's Ademar de Barros, and Guanabara's Carlos Lacerda.[54]

It was at about this time too that the number of carioca, *mineiro* (from the state of Minas Gerais), and paulista policemen being educated in the United States began to increase dramatically. Under USAID's (United States Agency for International Development) Office of Public Safety (OPS) program, twenty-six Brazilian police personnel were transported, at U.S. taxpayer expense, to the American mainland in 1962 for further training. The following year, this figure jumped to sixty-two members of the law enforcement community, of whom forty-three (69.3 percent) were from Minas Gerais, São Paulo, and Guanabara. This was more than twice the number of police brought to U.S. professional schools from these three states at any time prior to the 1964 military overthrow. The apparent objective of the Brazilian government since 1959, under the Office of Public Safety program, had been to establish a federal police force. Although the Polícia Federal was not formed until 1969, the Americans flew police personnel to the United States for more instruction anyway and poured money into the police education programs already operating within the Islands of Administrative Sanity.

Brazil would come to be the largest Latin American recipient of aid from the OPS. In 1964 alone, $1,159,000 of assistance was provided. Numerous U.S. Public Safety Advisors, averaging nearly twenty per year between 1961 and 1970, were also a part of the deal. Many, if not most, of these new on-site helpers were FBI or CIA agents. Others were Vietnam veterans and U.S. prison guards. A smaller number were funneled into

Brazil as "English teachers," supposedly to work at BRASIS (Brasil America Sociedade Inglês—Brazil American English Society).

The United States, through its Brazilian ambassador, Lincoln Gordon, was out to shore up its southern flank from Cuban communism. Since men in blue, and indeed language instructors, are the first physical contact between a foreign public and the American government, Washington was keenly interested in an educational format in each setting that expounded its own goals. Both in the United States and at home in Brazil, police cadets patiently listened while their American advisor-teachers led classes on the latest techniques to combat the red peril, or indeed any movement, at the street level. There were courses in internal security, urban patrolling, crowd and riot control, refined administrative methods, weapons, public relations and, of course, torture. Over at BRASIS, coming generations of Brazilians were slowly indoctrinated into America worship.[55]

Land Reform

Along with San Tiago Dantas's trip to Washington, D.C., on March 9, 1963, the Brazilian government submitted its much-anticipated Agrarian Reform Bill that month. The measure ran into enormous resistance in Congress by the members of the Ação Democrática Parlamentar, a group indirectly backed by the CIA.[56] Carlos Lacerda was evidently a key personality in convincing various fellow lawmakers in the UDN to vote against an amendment to the constitution that the proposal required. As for the PSD, another component of the Ação, it was a party made up of landowners that included an especially powerful segment of archconservative (read: less than honest in declaring their property values) *fazendeiros* (farm owners) from Minas Gerais. Faced with this joint force, Goulart's chances of passing agrarian reform were practically zero in light of the fact that two-thirds of Congress had to agree to any change to the constitution. Failing such a modification, no expropriated property could be paid for in bonds. Reimbursements had to be made in cash—and money was the one thing that was lacking.

The administration's resolution struggled in committee until October, when it was finally defeated by a vote of 176 to 121. This setback for the president marked a turning point in Goulart's thinking. Together with the demise of the Plano Trienal, the amendment's defeat made the president feel more than ever that he would have to go outside the legislative system to get things done.[57] This is precisely what Jango attempted to do next in respect to land reform.

The new vehicle in his efforts at rural change was to rework the proposal that Vargas had sent Congress in April 1954. After nearly nine years of debates, Goulart was finally able to sign the Rural Laborer Statute into law on March 2, 1963.[58] To fight against debt peonage, the enactment stipulated that all rural workers be paid in money or in goods. Persons under sixteen were to receive half the pay of an adult. The new statute shortened the workday to eight hours, guaranteed Sundays off, and provided for paid vacations. Belonging to a rural union was also permitted.

It was on this solidarity with worders issue, what is more, that the president decided to concentrate his energies.[59] To help create a power base and wrestle land from obstinate fazendeiros, Brazil's rural labor would be unionized. The objective was to increase the two hundred or so rural unions that existed in January 1963 to eighteen hundred or more as quickly as possible. Political groups from all over the political spectrum vied for the attention of agricultural workers during this activity. In the end, at a December meeting of factions from all sides, CONTAG (Confederação Nacional dos Trabalhadores na Agricultura—the Confederation of Workers in Agriculture) was formed, accords were reached, and CONTAG's top positions went to the Communists. Aghast, the latifundiários lost little time in organizing themselves into CONCLAP (Conferência Nacional das Classes Produtoras—the Council of the Producing Classes).[60]

The End of IBAD/ADEP and the Sergeants' Revolt

Goulart was partially aware of what some of his political enemies were up to, and at the end of August he decided that he had had enough of IBAD and ADEP. They were closed for three months by presidential decree, accused of illegal electoral activities. In November the edict was extended, and the following month they were formally dissolved through the courts. An investigative body set up to look into the affairs of IBAD and ADEP had uncovered a CIA try, through these two organizations, to buy the 1963 plebiscite.[61]

> The CIA had spent as much as $20 million, and everyone involved at the U.S. embassy, from Lincoln Gordon down, was worried about the incriminating evidence that might be made public.
>
> A scandal was averted only by three lucky developments: five of the nine members of the investigating committee had themselves received CIA funds; three of the banks involved—First National City Bank, the Bank of Boston, and the Royal Bank of Canada—refused to reveal the foreign sources of money deposited in the IBAD and ADEP accounts; and best of all, President Goulart, still hoping to get along with Washington, saw to it that the final report was laundered.[62]

Twelve days after the initial IBAD and ADEP shutdowns, and coinciding with a nationwide bank strike, 650 air force and naval sergeants mutinied at 4 A.M. in their barracks near Brasília. Perhaps triggered by anti-Communists colleagues, the non-coms were up in arms over the fact that no enlisted man could vote or hold elected office anywhere in Brazil. In the general elections of 1962, the sergeants decided to challenge the law by running candidates from the ranks for posts in several states. In Guanabara, São Paulo, and Rio Grande do Sul they won under the banner of Jango's PTB. Nonetheless only a single victor, Antônio Garcia Filho, ever took his seat in the state assembly. One of the other two men appealed the decision by a lower court declaring that he was ineligible, but his petition was turned down. With the aftertaste of judicial defeat still in their mouths and following a speech by their leader, Antônio Prestes de Paula, the enlisted men picked up their weapons.[63]

The sergeants quickly took over part of the capital and arrested several government officials. But without any real plans for what to do next, they proceeded to meander around the streets in disorganized bunches. Army units loyal to Goulart, who was in Rio Grande do Sul, were called in to quell things. By 4 P.M. it was all over, but not before two persons had been killed. Over the next few days, 536 rebels were arrested. The prisoners, 284 from the air force and 252 from the navy, were brought to Rio de Janeiro and put aboard the onetime steamer but longtime prison ship *Raul Soares,* which was anchored in Guanabara Bay. In São Paulo, an additional 11 sergeants plus the president and secretary of the machinists union were also taken into custody. Months later, on the eve of dramatic changes in Brazil, 19 sergeants were sentenced to four years' incarceration. The generals and admirals, however, were unimpressed. They were impervious to the changing times and could think only of keeping order within the ranks. They demanded stiffer penalties along with mass expulsions.[64]

Hidden from view, several members of the military elite were already plotting against their constitutionally elected leader. Their first meeting was held in Petrópolis on March 13, 1963, the same day as the huge rally down in Rio de Janeiro. General Nélson de Melo, Minister of War Amauri Kruel, Field Marshal Odílio Denis, field marshal and former president Eurico Dutra, Admiral Sílvio Heck, plus one additional admiral and two air force generals, attended the Petrópolis gathering. By early May, they had let their American contacts know that one of the most important aspects of U.S. help would be a rapid recognition of the new regime, should the planned overthrow of Goulart be successful. With this request, the conspirators were in fact asking for a green light from the U.S. government.[65]

Lacerda Goes Public

Near the end of September 1963, the *Los Angeles Times* published an interview with Carlos Lacerda that had near instant repercussions in Brazil. His scathing anti-Goulart harangue was reprinted in Rio's English-language *Brazil Herald* on October 1 and found an audience in government and military circles. Claiming that his remarks were directed specifically to the American people, the governor of Guanabara affirmed that while Goulart was not a Communist, there were Communists in his administration and insinuated that these "Reds" were involved in a concerted attempt to bring to bring the country to a standstill.[66] He stated that the military ministers were deliberating what to do with Jango. One option was "to choke him off right now." In the next breath Lacerda began campaigning for Jango's job. He talked about what he would do if he were president. Land reform, strikes, and cost-of-living wage increases were not in the governor's program. The governor-journalist went on to urge that the United States withhold additional economic support to Goulart and to hint, between the lines, that some kind of American intervention might be necessary.[67]

The warlords whom Goulart had chosen to head the nation's armed forces were perhaps most irritated by this last possibility. They advised Jango that Lacerda should be arrested.[68] Together with what some of them saw as a lack of presidential spine in the Sergeants' Revolt, several of these ministers were jittery over reports that the Americans had already landed some military hardware for the opposition in the northeast. In an accompanying commentary, they accordingly berated Lacerda, boiling it all down to the fact that he was simply just a "bad Brazilian" and "bad citizen."[69]

As for the weapons, they were largely of Czech origin and had been smuggled into Brazil by a U.S. navy submarine. They were intended to be discovered and thereby provide the justification for an American military intervention. There was likewise a CIA base in the state of Piauí large enough to handle helicopters. Also, in nearby British Guiana, unknown to the authorities there, the United States maintained an airfield as an observation post with fifteen jets ready for emergencies. On no less than two occasions in April and May 1963, General Olímpio Mourão Filho, representing the plotters, requested U.S. arms. He even went so far as to state that when the coup got underway, "The following weapons will be required within 10 days after [the] action starts: ammunition for rocket launchers, 15,000 submachine guns, mortars, and flame throwers."[70]

The Advancing Storm

Along the corridors of power in Washington, D.C., there was no ill will against the Guanabara governor, at least not yet. Besides his Island of Administrative Sanity funding, they helped to secure Lacerda's position with a number of new firearms brought in illegally from Bolivia or Paraguay. Although the Americans provided Lacerda with aid, they were coming to view him as a less-than-stable element. In early April 1964 the CIA stated that Lacerda's "hotheadedness and emotional approach have frequently tended to decrease his effectiveness."[71]

Another recipient of U.S. interventionism and military criticism, according to the *Brazil Herald* on October 1, 1963, was the governor of São Paulo. Via the resources at his disposal, Ademar de Barros had his agents visit Stroessner's Paraguay, buy weapons, and slip them back into Brazil. Both he and Lacerda were busy preparing for a direct confrontation with

Goulart, in part through a plan to support various opposition paramilitary groups, including a growing number of fazendeiros. The paulista governor alone had increased the size of his state's Força Pública (Public Force) to sixty thousand troops, and he had no qualms about not keeping it a secret. The Força Pública, called the Polícia Militar (Military Police) in most states, had nothing to do with the police of the Brazilian armed forces. Still in existence, they live in military-style barracks and wear uniforms and are supposed to provide the services of an identifiable police force protecting the civilian population. In the 1960s, however, they were largely loyal to and directed by their respective states' governors.[72]

A civil war was clearly in the making, and on October 4, 1963, Jango acted to remove Lacerda and Ademar in one stroke. It was Goulart's minister of war, General Jair Dantas Ribeiro, who suggested the action taken. After mindfully considering the other legal alternatives, the president decided to ask Congress for a state of siege. Carlos Lacerda and Ademar de Barros were to be apprehended on charges of exceeding their authority. Jango banked on the support of the leftist CGT labor union, his own PTB, Leonel Brizola, Miguel Arraes, and the promises of the army to enact the measure. They all let him down. But the army played the key role, as in so many situations in Brazil. The leading generals were willing to topple Lacerda and Ademar in exchange for Goulart's concurrence in the removal of Miguel Arraes. This stipulation, before the army would act, was made *after* the request for the state of siege was delivered to a waiting Congress. There had been hints that the armed forces might do something like this as far back as the time of their rebuttal to Lacerda's *Los Angeles Times* interview. While the military chiefs were still friendly to the president on the pages of the *Brazil Herald*, they warned that the country's economic and social problems were "aggravated by the maneuvers of extremist minorities. On one side are the preachers of revolution who try to intensify the class struggle. On the other side are groups interested . . . [in] stop[ping] Brazil's development and turn[ing] back its social evolution and economic emancipation."[73]

Goulart rejected the new condition, saying that he could not go against an old comrade-in-arms, particularly since the Pernambuco governor had helped him become president against the wishes of the military. The CGT and Brizola were of the opinion that the powers allowed the president under marshal law would or could also be used against them. Arraes had evidently felt this way all along, and the PTB was never really rallied *en masse* behind the proposition. Without the soldiers' display of force to maintain order, all of Jango's natural allies were lining up to vote against the passage of the measure. Fooled on the one hand by his military command for refusing to reconsider his loyalty to Arraes and let down on the other by his civilian colleagues, Jango withdrew the state of siege request on October 7. His embarrassment was difficult to hide.[74]

Perhaps this is why the president did nothing in the face of new information that the 3rd Military Region was planning a coup. The tip was provided by a reporter and a photographer who traveled all over the south of Brazil on a suspicion furnished by Goulart to Samuel Wainer, the editor of allegedly friendly *Última Hora.* In all there were 178 pages of comments and some 500 photographs depicting a branch of the Caixa Econômica Federal bank in Porto Alegre being used as a weapons depository, conservative clergymen training reactionaries in the art of guerrilla warfare, and various officers in the act of putting together some sort of scheme.[75]

G-11

Goulart's government finally countered with a number of reassignments and changes of command in the armed forces. There also followed a partially successful general strike in São Paulo. Leonel Brizola too was in the thick of things. On October 25 he called on all progressive Brazilians to organize themselves into "Groups of Eleven." Speaking in Rio on Radio Mayrink Veiga, Brizola said that the people needed to form these units so as to avoid being defeated in the coming conflict. They must be ready to take up arms to fight for Basic Reforms, thereby saving Brazil from homegrown elites and foreign plunderers. Using soccer, with its eleven players on a side, as a model, the Brazilian G-11s were to have units with 11 members, districts of 11 units (121 members), provinces of 22 districts (2,662 members), and regions of 11 provinces (29,282 members). Radio Mayrink Veiga was dubbed the voice of Brizola and his followers on the left. It has been stated that his urging to form Groups of Eleven was the straw that broke the conservative part of society's back. If traditionalists were not against Goulart before, they most assuredly were after this event.[76]

No longer the governor of Rio Grande do Sul but a federal congressman representing Guanabara, Brizola, in a coded message to his followers over the airwaves, remarked that the hour had arrived to "distribute the *books* [guns] with which we shall liberate Brazil."[77] In case the pending upheaval failed, all-important hostages such as judges, mayors, sheriffs, councilmen, influential politicians, and other personalities were to be summarily shot. Known as "Raul" and "Otavio" in G-11 code, Leonel had clearly given himself the largest slice of responsibility. According to the political police, the Groups of Eleven hierarchy was set up with the following personalities:

Chief	Leonel Brizola
Communications	Col. Dagoberto and Paulo Schilling
Material	Adm. Câdido Aragão
Organizing in the unions	Paulo Schilling and Antônia Batista de Almeida
Organizing in rural environments	Padre Alipio
Organizing in the north	Lamartine Nogueira Leal
Organizing in the northeast	Neiva Moreira
Organizing in São Paulo	Almino Affonso
Organizing in Guanabara, Paraná, Rio Grande do Sul, and Santa Catarina	Leonel Brizola

The eleven-person squads attracted only a few thousand individuals, and despite being allied with the PCB they remained unorganized, unarmed, and therefore ineffective as a potential fighting force. In reality, the only force the G-11 truly represented was the one behind Leonel Brizola.[78]

NOVEMBER 22, 1963

The assassination of John F. Kennedy marked the end of America's indecisiveness with João Goulart. With the arrival of Lyndon B. Johnson in the White House, U.S. policy toward Brasília hardened.[79] LBJ did not see a reason to talk any longer. To the new American president Brazil could not, Brazil would not, become another Cuba or anything in between. In those days of the fear of creeping communism, Jango had become a political liability to the free world. He would have to go, one way or another.

As the United States government was deciding how best to achieve this aim, Goulart concluded that the only way to achieve his Basic Reforms, even if in a modest way, was through presidential mandate. The final straw was the failure of the proposal by his new finance minister and the former governor of São Paulo, Carvalho Pinto, to improve the federal deficit and bring down an inflation rate that would hit 75.4 percent in 1963. Worked out carefully in advance, the project had been enacted in October through the Office of Money and Credit, or SUMOC, as Instruction No. 255. The measure made it mandatory for all private banks that went beyond a stipulated credit limit to buy government bonds. SUMOC 255 immediately ran into flak from the banking and entrepreneurial communities, which saw it as a law that was meant to stifle investment and capture personal savings. What these institutions were really saying, however, was that a large external debt and high inflation are good for the banking and entrepreneurial communities.

Adding to the controversy was the fact that the Americans refused to reschedule Brazil's foreign debt or provide any new loans. Carvalho Pinto resigned on December 19 amid pressure from Brizola and complaints about the ineffectiveness of his domestic economic policies. A specially nominated *minister extraordinarie* later alleged to the press that SUMOC 255 would result in a loss of 500 million cruzeiros ($833,333) in unpaid taxes in 1963.[80] Yet this was really beside the point among the paulista entrepreneurs because Carvalho Pinto's dismissal convinced whatever lingering loyalists there were that they too should conspire against the president.

New Tactics

With Brizola hounding away for the job, Goulart next attempted to soothe the PSD by selecting one of its members, Nei Galvão, to take Pinto's post with orders to shelve SUMOC 255. But no amount of coaxing could revitalize what had once been a PTB-PSD coalition in Congress as the PSD moved ever farther to the right. Owing to the CGT's refusal to cooperate with his state of siege request, Goulart had begun supporting the more moderate União Sindical dos Trabalhadores (UST—the Union of Syndicated Workers). Nonetheless, strong pressure from the Communists and CGT persuaded him to reconsider his break with the more radical union.[81] The die was thus cast. Since Jango would not back down from his avowed plans to reform the country, many of his subsequent moves would be by decree. Each would be aimed at regaining the confidence of unions, agricultural workers, students, and the political parties on the left.

Rule by decree translated in rapid-fire succession into medical benefits, sick leave, and pensions for rural workers. All businesses with more than one hundred employees were ordered to offer free elementary education to their staffs. Jango adjusted his own popular 13th Salary, an extra paycheck given out just before Christmas, to make it more effective. A review was ordered of each of the foreign-owned mining concerns, and the president indicated that all concessions that were not used for more than twenty years could be canceled.[82] Non-Brazilian petroleum companies such as Esso, Gulf, Shell, Sinclair, Standard, and others were put on notice that henceforth they would have to use products manufactured in the country by state-owned Petrobrás or products imported into Brazil by the government. Someone apparently got to Samuel Wainer with a bribe of three hundred thousand dollars. Supposedly a longtime PTB ally, the newspaperman thereupon began attacking the administration's plans for expanding Petrobrás at the expense of foreign firms.[83] Petrobrás had come into being during Vargas's last administration.

But by far the thorniest item on Goulart's agenda was finally signed into law on January 17, 1964, much to the consternation of Lyndon Baines Johnson. Fought tooth and nail by American ambassador Lincoln Gordon, the Lei de Remessas de Lucros, or the Remission of Profits Law, went into effect without any changes. It limited the amount of profit that a person or company could transfer out of the country each year to 10 percent of the value of the original investment without correction for any subsequent inflation. The improved benefits for workers and, particularly, the Remittance of Profits Law caused an illicit exodus of hard currency in the first three months of 1964. More than $2 billion may have left Brazil during this period.[84]

January through March saw a different kind of Goulart administration and an equally different kind of reaction by the opposition. Things reached a high point with the announcement of a massive government-sponsored rally at Rio's Praça Cristiano Ottoni (Cristiano Ottoni Square). The March 13 event was scheduled to help promote the administration's Basic Reforms package. Adversaries worried that if the president wanted to arouse the crowd about their common tragedies on March 13, "he did not have to search for evidence. Every day the newspapers had fresh examples. The minimum wage was $23 a month; the old and disabled had to get by on even less. One pensioner who had lost his leg in a railroad accident won a slight increase when Rio's zoo director testified that it cost five times the man's monthly pension to feed an adult chimpanzee."[85]

The air, likewise, became thick with rumors by both the opposition and the government of respective golpes. Paulo de Tarso, the minister of education, João Pinheiro Neto, the head of SUPRA, and Miguel Arraes had all been rebuffed or heckled, or soon would be, when they tried to speak in São Paulo. At two gatherings, the agitators were Ademar's police disguised as students. The IPÊS-supported UCF (União Cívica Feminina—Women's Civic Union) disrupted another meeting being held to promote the legalization of the PCB and then attempted to stop the governor of Pernambuco from taking part in a television interview. Not to be outdone, more fazendeiros, more conservative women, and more angry mobs did much the same thing in Minas Gerais. At a leftist Latin American union convention held in Belo Horizonte in February, which included a few delegates from Eastern Europe, João Pinheiro Neto and Leonel Brizola were both kept from speaking. Only Arraes successfully completed his discourse behind a barricade of unenthusiastic mineiro police.[86]

FRIDAY THE THIRTEENTH

Still, it was the main course—the March 13 rally—that brought everything to a head. Arranged in part by the CGT, the spectacle in Praça Ottoni was but the first of several such assemblies that the leftists around Goulart convinced him to hold.[87] Jango would sign some of the reforms into law at each rally. His advisors hoped that in so doing he could gather enough popular support to force the lawmakers to make constitutional changes allowing for more significant improvements. It was a tricky affair, and Jango did not want his brother-in-law to rock the boat by saying too much. Confronted with this wish and agreeing to soften up his commentary, Brizola was allowed to be one of the sixteen speakers. The platform from which they would give their remarks was the same one Vargas used for several of his addresses.

Trains and buses from all over the area brought workers to two railroad stations, one of which is downtown, adjacent to Praça Ottoni. By the time the orators began at 5 P.M., the plaza, surrounded on one side by the towering headquarters of the army and on the other by the rail depot itself, was filled with a sea of banners, placards, and close to two hundred thousand faces stretched out before the speakers' platform onto Avenida Presidente Vargas. The more outrageous slogans, such as "Down with the Gorillas" (that is, the enemies of the people), "Hang Lacerda," and others, may have been the work of small groups who wanted to give the rally a radical look. Even the numerous hammers and sickles were said to be the work of some people from Petróbras who managed to squeeze their way into positions in which they would be filmed and photographed.[88]

The Right tried to diminish the turnout through an anonymous telephone campaign in which startled listeners were told not to go to the Communist meeting. An effort was also made to force Jango to reflect on those opposed to him by having anti-Goulart sympathizers who lived along his route to Cristiano Otoni Square burn candles in their apartment windows.[89] Guarding the politicians was the largest group of army police and marines that had ever been assembled for such duty. Some three thousand soldiers stood ready with machine-guns, tanks, and high-powered search lights.[90]

Arraes and Brizola both gave animated speeches. Arraes said that there would be an end to governing Brazil without the people and that the country had "come to the streets to resolutely defend the liberties that a Fascist minority is trying to destroy."[91] Brizola, either by design[92] or because of the chants and applause, lapsed into a monologue that was not far from asking the faithful to take up arms. He called on Goulart to stop compromising and to organize a government that was in accord with the wishes of the masses. Congress was not about to give the people anything since the rural and urban elite dominated that institution. If a referendum were held, he reasoned that the povão would overwhelmingly vote to have the current congress replaced with one that represented the views of "workers, peasants, sergeants, nationalist officers, and authentic men of the people."[93] Parading a Group of Eleven before the gathering, he thundered, "Our path is peaceful, but in the face of violence we will respond with violence!"[94]

A bomb started a brief fire under the speaker's platform that afternoon,[95] although that was not why the president delayed his departure from Laranjeiras Palace again and again. Finally leaving in an armored car at 7:32 P.M., Jango put things off so that he would not have to hear Brizola speak. But he still arrived too soon and took a seat on the rostrum only to witness part of his brother-in-law's emotional appeal to revamp Congress. A number of other orators followed. Then, as the searchlights cut eerie columns across the humid night sky, Jango rose to face the crowd.[96] With

Maria Tereza Goulart at one side and Communist union leader Oswaldo Pacheco da Silva on the other,[97] the president began by thanking those who had arranged the gigantic function and the brave carioca people in particular. Then he said that because his thoughts were being broadcast on both radio and television he would be able to talk to all Brazilians and "not just to those who've succeeded in obtaining an education at school. But also to the millions of our brothers who pay with suffering, with misery[, and] privation for the right to be Brazilians working from sunrise to sunset for the glory of this country."[98]

So that everyone could understand, he went on in simplified Portuguese, explaining that Brazil had become an anti-people democracy of the privileged. The clique on top wanted to dismantle Petrobrás and increase its iron grip on business through national and international cartels. This group (although it was not true) drove Getúlio Vargas to the supreme sacrifice.[99] Those trying to constrain reforms, and above all else changes to the agricultural system, threatened everyone. Improvement in this one area would be a complement to the end of slavery for millions of Brazilians who were rotting away in the countryside.

His administration, Jango said, was trying to realize a democracy based on the desires of the common people that also tried to make the common people see that their aspirations could be realized only through law, understanding, and social harmony. The powerful were against this. But no matter, Goulart went on, because he was inspired in his quest by the words of Pope John XXIII, "who taught us that the dignity of the human spirit normally demands, as a natural basis of life, the right to use the riches of the land. [This in turn] . . . corresponds to the fundamental obligation to award private property to everyone. It is within this authentic Christian doctrine that the government has attempted to place its social policies, especially in respect to our agrarian situation."[100]

Continuing, he mentioned that he was not afraid of being called a subversive for proclaiming that much of the problem was a fault of the constitution. This document needed to be revised so as to end the privileges of a minority, to make land available to all, and to allow everyone a voice in political life through their vote. Jango next thrilled the crowd by announcing that he had just signed the SUPRA land reform decree. The SUPRA decree was a watered-down version of what Goulart really wanted. This was to make it more acceptable to conservatives. While in the proposal stage, it called for the expropriation of abandoned or nonproductive properties larger than 1,235.5 acres (500 hectares) that were within 18.6 miles (30 km) of public or private dams, railways, and major roads. The confiscation of properties above 1,235.5 acres was a result of a personal request by Luís Carlos Prestes. Jango's original plan set the limit at 247.1 acres (100 hectares). Prestes evidently convinced the president that the larger figure would touch only latifundiários and not medium-size landholders. The communist leader knew whom they should be going after.

By the time the decree was signed, the 18.6-mile strip had been reduced to 6.2 miles (10 km). The government planned to use the confiscated properties to establish small- to medium-size cooperatives in the vicinity of larger metropolitan areas, where the ebb and flow of jobs and produce were greatest. Although the original legislation did not use the tactic of the strip, it too would have been felt most near the big cities as the government was out to provide work and increase agricultural production in the process. Land seizures in remote sections of the country, where manpower was scarce and transportation expensive, were of secondary importance. Payment to former owners was to be made in bonds on the declared tax value. Between March 13, 1964, and the end of the month, a number of expropriations were made. Before he left the rostrum, João Pinheiro Neto was informed by the president that two of Goulart's own holdings, one in Goías and the other in Rio Grande do Sul, would be the first properties confiscated.[101]

Jango continued by saying that the decree should not be considered the end of the line because constitutional modifications were needed in order to allow the government to pay former landowners in bonds or other noncash forms of remuneration. Japan under Douglas MacArthur, Italy, Mexico, and India were all cited as examples of nations where land reforms were enacted without money.

"All nations on earth, regardless of their political regimes, battle against the curse of the unproductive *latifúndio* [large landed estate]. Capitalistic nations, socialistic nations, nations in the West and in the East have all come to the conclusion that it is not possible to advance and live together with massive rural plantations. . . . What we are intending to do in Brazil by means of agrarian reform is no different from what has been done in all developed countries on this planet. It is a progressive step that we need to take and that we have to take."[102]

Cheered throughout his speech, Jango wiped the sweat from his brow and went on. He told the crowd that he had also signed into law the nationalization of all private oil refineries. If Getúlio Vargas had been alive, the president knew that it would have been an emotional moment for him to see the refineries of Capuava, Ipiranga, Manguinhos, Amazonas, and Destilaria Rio-Grandense pass into the hands of Petrobrás.[103]

Goulart was nearing the end of his address. He had already discarded the prepared text to speak extemporaneously. Jango always sounded better off the cuff, and the multitude adored it when he did so. And they especially liked what he was saying now. Rent controls were next on his list of reforms. He promised that within a few hours he would be issuing a decree aimed at the extortion-like prices charged by some landlords. Public servants and physicians were likewise promised that their needs would be looked into soon.[104]

In conclusion, the president added that nothing would stop him from safeguarding the liberty of the people. To do this, he said, he would "depend on the understanding and patriotism of the brave and glorious armed forces of this nation."[105] Jango ended by emphasizing that his administration would "fight with all of its strength for the reform of Brazilian society. Not just for agrarian reform, but [also] for tax reform, for election reform—by increasing the size of the electorate by giving the vote to illiterate citizens and enfranchising all Brazilians—for improving democratic life, for economic emancipation, for social justice, and for the progress of Brazil."[106]

REACTIONS

It was a moving presentation. Nevertheless, because Brizola, Arraes, various groups from the Left, and fifth columnists from the Right were all at work, and some of them delivered remarks as well, Jango's speech came off in a more radical light than it actually deserved. The money that had been made available to educate the public against the fear of a spreading Red pestilence gave those who would depose Goulart their chance.[107] Much of the middle class, if they had not done so previously, and virtually all of the elite painted the president a vibrant shade of crimson after March 13. Besides the cries that he was a bad remake of the old professor, a large landowner himself, an apparent *petite bourgeoisie* from the upper class, and full of vacillations in the face of the enormous pressures he faced, this one night sealed his fate. The military in all its conspiring pomp could now point to a growing opinion against Goulart, wash its hands of the guilt, and put its plans into a preoperational stage. It would be just nineteen days before the generals took action.

Even as all the speech making was going on in Rio, at the Praça da Sé, or Holy See Square, in the very heart of São Paulo, a number of women gathered, praying for God to save Brazil from communism. In Belo Horizonte, Magalhães Pinto was not beseeching any higher authority. The governor of Minas Gerais practically broke with the government, stating that he failed to recognize the authenticity of those who presented themselves as the champions of reform while using their suggestions as a pretext for agitation aimed at disturbing groups or individuals. His remarks were a reaction, couched in political double-speak, to the reforms in the SUPRA decree just enacted. On a more direct level it was likewise reported that various fazendeiros in Minas had vowed to kill or be killed defending what was theirs when and if the measure was signed and Communists (anyone) began invading their lands.[108]

The Last Try

On the sixteenth, Jango asked Congress to approve seven items: 1) a reform of the constitution so that confiscated land did not have to be paid for in currency, 2) the vote for illiterate Brazilians, 3) the vote for sergeants and enlisted men and the right for them to hold office, 4) the legalization of the PCB, 5) the relegation of legislative power to the executive, 6) the elimination of lifetime university professorships, and 7) the option for the legislative and executive branches of government to hold plebiscites in respect to constitutional reform.[109]

Many of these proposals were in actuality long-sought Goulart objectives. All had been rebuffed earlier, and the expanded list would meet with the same fate in Congress. Perhaps Jango suspected such a result since he did not trust the promised rent-control bill to his enemies in Congress. Instead he decreed it into law one day after the Praça Ottoni rally. Landlords were forthwith obligated to advertise the monthly rent of their apartments or houses in cruzeiros according to the size of the dwelling. Rents were set by the government and were tied to the minimum wage in each area. Goulart later decreed a 100-percent wage boost, retroactive to March 1, 1964, for all members of the armed forces as well as public functionaries.[110]

On the other side of the picture, the antigovernment forces knew little rest. To offset the rally of March 13, IPÊS mustered all the women's groups it could and put them to work organizing huge counter rallies of concerned citizens. Turning out under the banner of "The March of the Family with God for Liberty," the largest of these events took place in the center of São Paulo on March 19. An estimated five hundred thousand persons gathered that day to chant anti-Goulart and anti-Brizola slogans. They were urged on by the speeches of several right-wing congressmen, as well as by Guanabara governor Carlos Lacerda, although he arrived late and took part in only some of the proceedings.[111] Also sharing the oratory spotlight was Plínio Salgado,[112] former chief of the "Green Chickens,"[113] as his ultrarightist Integralists were called behind their backs.

Waiting for the Right Moment

Brazil's disgruntled military leaders watched cautiously what was unfolding on the streets of São Paulo, just as they had peeked discreetly at the March 13 rally from behind the curtains of the War Ministry, adjoining Praça Ottoni. On the day following the São Paulo march, army chief of staff Humberto "Tamanco" Castelo Branco,[114] the second-highest four-star general in the army, leader of the impending coup, and soon-to-be first dictator of the March 31–April 1 "revolution," circulated his thoughts on what was unfolding.[115] To help recruit the officers who would command actual troops, Castelo Branco mentioned two threats facing the nation: a constitutional assembly to enact Goulart's Basic Reforms and the agitation of the leftist CGT. He then reiterated the armed forces' self-ordained role of constitutional guardian, that is, the ultimate judges of what was and what was not legal. Their job, he claimed, was not to defend the government's programs but to guarantee constituted power. A proposed assembly with the authority to reform the constitution was viewed as a move to promote the closing of Congress. It was likewise seen as an attempt to impose despotism through violence. The army chief of staff next observed that "insurrection is a legitimate resource of the people. [But] it could then be asked; do the Brazilian people want a civilian or military dictatorship or a Constitutional Assembly? It appears that the answer is no."[116]

Castelo Branco went on about the pseudo–trade union movement wanting to turn the country over to Soviet-style communism. He finished by noting that the armed forces could not betray Brazil and that they would "continue to respect their superiors and the authority of the president of the republic."[117] This bizarre pledge, on the other hand, was immediately qualified by that hallowed *sanctum sanctorum* of the Brazilian military, that is, "Within the limits of the law."[118]

Jango's initial reaction was to sit tight, thinking that perhaps a majority of officers under his command would maintain a strictly legalistic posture. The reality of the predicament was that anti-leftist sentiments within the military were already winning the day. When this finally became obvious, Jango decided to arrest Castelo Branco. The error here was that Goulart waited too long to see which way the wind was blowing before issuing his order. The officer finally sent to do the job, 1st Army chief General Armando de Moraes Âncora, was not happy with the assignment and balked at carrying it out. Coupled with this was the fact that Castelo Branco threatened suicide if he was taken into custody.[119] Jango did not want to transform the chief of staff into a sacrificial victim, so he momentarily backed off and flew to his fazenda in Rio Grande do Sul on the twenty-fifth to reflect on strategy in friendly surroundings. He would not have to contemplate long.

SEDITION

Besides the bombs exploding now and again in larger Rio, the military *golpistas* (plotters of a golpe) stumbled across a fresh way to goad the government and bring many undecided officers into line at the same time. Even as Jango was flying south on the twenty-sixth, the Association of Sailors and Marines, an enlisted men's group, was meeting at the CGT machinist union building in the former national capital. The maritime organization met to celebrate its second anniversary and to congratulate Petrobrás on the newly acquired foreign refineries. The seamen were also mulling over petitioning the government for improvements in their branch of the armed forces. Some changes to a sailor's lot had come in the wake of the Naval Revolt of 1910—but not many.[120] During the meeting at the

CGT, the men voted to support Goulart's call for Basic Reforms. The navy minister, Sílvio Mota, then warned that politics was not the business of enlisted men. When the seamen persisted, he had several of the leaders arrested and placed in the brig for ten days. This provoked the 3,647 sailors and marines encamped at the union hall to up their demands.

The assembly was led by Cabo (Petty Officer Third Class) José Anselmo dos Santos, who may have been a CENIMAR-CIA plant. The possibility that Anselmo was a CENIMAR (Centro de Informações da Marinha, or Naval Intelligence Center) agent and steered by the CIA was reputedly passed on to Goulart, who did nothing about it. In opposition to this version, or perhaps to camouflage his trail, Anselmo was arrested after the takeover and claims to have been tortured. There are those, however, who say that he was not a CENIMAR or CIA operative at the time of the seaman's meeting but that he was probably converted in 1971 after joining VPR (Vanguarda Popular Revolutionária, or Popular Revolutionary Vanguard), traveling to Cuba for training, and being arrested following his return to São Paulo. Anselmo was in Chile at the behest of São Paulo detective Sérgio Fleury, attempting to discover what he could there on leftist Brazilians in exile. He is also reported to have worked for the Chilean intelligence service DINA (Dirección Nacional de Inteligencia, or National Directorate of Intelligence). Both men participated in Operation Condor on the side of Brazil's military governments. Anselmo later had his facial features altered through plastic surgery (Fleury's idea) and was given a new identity and a new life. Still protected by the military as of this writing, he lives unknown to the rest of the country in the urban sprawl that makes up the city of São Paulo.[121]

All of that was still to come. Back at the union hall Cabo Anselmo saw to it that several new requirements were added to the Association of Sailors and Marines' list. These included the stipulation that the association be officially recognized. An overhaul of disciplinary practices within the navy was also called for, as were demands that sailors be able to reenlist after ten years of service and have the right to marry. The men wanted to be able to wear civilian clothes when off duty, to eat the same food as officers, to be enfranchised along with nonliterate Brazilians, and for amnesties to be declared both for those involved in the Sergeant's Revolt and for a select number of colleagues imprisoned on other charges. Topping everything off, the man who had led the rebels in 1910, João Cândido, was carried into the meeting to thunderous applause. That night the ecstatic seamen watched Soviet director Sergei Eisenstein's film *The Battleship Potemkin.*[122]

These orchestrated displays of insubordination, heightened by scathing speeches from Anselmo, prompted the navy minister to send a unit of forty marines to the union hall to arrest everyone. Vice Admiral Câdido Aragão, the apparently semi-educated head of the marines, had already been to the CGT building. He was a man totally in Brizola's corner. He had been appointed by Jango to lead the marines in a move made to pacify Goulart's brother-in-law. Aragão was not popular among his more traditionally minded military peers. This was not simply because of his radical politics but because he was one of the highest-ranking mixed-race officers that the Brazilian navy ever had.[123] All he did at the union hall was have a friendly chat with the seamen inside.[124]

Once the detachment of sailors sent to make the arrests pulled up and turned off their vehicles, they put down their weapons and joined the mutineers. Disgusted at this new insubordination, Sílvio Mota fired Aragão and sentenced him to ten days in the brig. He then had the army move in with five hundred troops supported by twelve tanks. A standoff of nearly twenty-four hours ensued while Communist and non-Communist union officials, government aides, officers, and sailors all discussed what to do.

When Goulart broke off his trip to Rio Grande do Sul and hurriedly returned to take charge, a solution to the crises seemed to be at hand. Sílvio Mota resigned, and the rebels were virtually allowed to choose his replacement. The man selected, retired admiral Paulo Mário da Cunha Rodrigues, was unpopular with navy conservatives for, among other things, having a black wife.[125] On March 27, he re-installed Aragão and with Goulart's blessing let the rebels be trucked to the 1st Army's headquarters. They were held briefly and then released. Delirious, many of them then paraded, singing and shouting, from one end of Rio to the other. All of their demands were to be met.[126]

Yet the joy on the faces of the sailors was also to be short lived. Their euphoria represented a breakdown of order and discipline at the most profound level. This was what the admirals had been loathe to see in 1910, and it was the same thing in 1964. It was the last straw. The very next day, the naval commanders drew up a manifesto condemning what had gone on and in ultimatum-like terms reiterated that a mutiny had taken place and that something would have to be done. While they did not lower themselves to refute the demands of the men under their commands, the thirty-five admirals who signed this landmark of Brazilian naval thinking were quick to point out several things that they found particularly impertinent. Among these was the fact that some sailors had been out of uniform both at the union hall and during the revelry that followed and that others had even flashed the "V" for victory sign with their fingers.[127] Meeting at Rio's Naval Club on Avenida Rio Branco, they symbolically lowered the nation's flag in front of the building to half-mast. The gesture was indicative of deeper displeasures. A number of officers even set about working on a plot to capture the ministry of navy, a radio station, and an ammunition dump. Earlier they had contacted trusted counterparts in the army but found them cool to the idea. The men in soldier green were already weaving their own web to depose the president but the plan was not to be put into motion until April 2.[128]

THE AUTOMOBILE CLUB

For some time, Goulart had been informed of rumors of an impending coup. He may well have been convinced that it was only speculation, owing to the assurances of military support given him by General Assis Brasil, the head of his presidential military staff.[129] Jango consequently opted to go ahead with plans for another rally. It was not the outdoor type as on March 13 but a smaller assembly to pay honor to the Military Police Sergeant's Benevolent Association on the night of March 30. Noncommissioned officers in the Polícia Militar were of course not the only persons invited to hear Goulart speak. All noncoms in the military, the Polícia Civil, and the fire department in the state of Guanabara were urged to attend the affair, which was to be held at Rio de Janeiro's Automobile Club. It was hoped that the turnout might reach twenty thousand or more as free transportation was offered to and from the event.

As he was preparing his speech, Jango was told that the Military and Naval Clubs just agreed in principle to stand together. Visibly irritated, Goulart felt that the only way to meet the challenge was through a direct confrontation. He decided to alter his statement, giving it more fire.

The Automobile Club was packed, but with nowhere near the hoped-for number. Perhaps there were two thousand in addition to civilians and family members. Conspicuously absent, a majority of top-ranking military men were among those who decided they had other things to do. No one with the rank of general bothered to attend.[130] The significance of these truancies would become apparent soon enough.

Preceded by speakers of varying importance and in the presence of Cabo Anselmo and all of his civilian ministers, Jango began his televised comments by immediately pointing out that

> a minority who live with their eyes focused on the past provoked the crisis in which the country presently finds itself. [Such people are] afraid to confront the bright future that will be opened [through a democracy that integrates] millions of our countrymen into the economic, political, and social life of the nation. . . .
>
> The forces and the persons who provoked the suicide of [our] immortal president, Getúlio Vargas, and who were responsible for the renouncement of my predecessor, those who tried to stop three elected presidents from taking office, in 1950, 1955, and in 1961, are the same who have now united against reform; fighting against each with weapons, slander, bribery, and lies.
>
> [As] in the crisis of 1961, these same buffoons who today exhibit a false zeal for the constitution would like to tear it up and bury it in the cold earth of a Fascist dictatorship.[131]

Goulart then affirmed, "The nation is witness to my pledge to always speak with absolute frankness to the Brazilian nation." "Last year," he went on, "I noticed that a wave of crises were about to threaten the stability of the country. We determined their causes and set about to resolve them. Soon, however, we observed repeated attempts to subvert these efforts. This sabotage campaign, besides distorting government directives, even resorted to using the religious sentiments of the people."[132]

Referring to the recent marches of the Family with God for Liberty in São Paulo and demonstrations of women in Minas, Jango added that the best answer for these impostors was given by the cardinal of São Paulo when he discussed the fact that in Latin America the rich talk a lot about basic reforms while those who decide to put them into practice are called Communists. In the opinion of the prelate, Goulart said, "The fanatical egoism of many wealthy people is a problem much more serious and urgent than that of Communism." To all of those who are involved with political rallies for religious reasons, the president urged that they ponder whether or not they were "defending the doctrine of he who through his death on the cross was the salvation of humanity, or only the interests of a few financial groups, or of those allowed to vote?"[133]

Answering his own question, Jango assured his audience that "there do not exist sentiments more Christian and democratic than those devoted to improving the situation of the people, and to reformulating old structures that only maintain Brazil in stagnation, underdevelopment, and destitution. There are no greater enemies of these wishes . . . than those of injustice, hunger, misery, and suffering."[134]

After explaining why the government had shut down IBAD, Goulart made a plea to the sergeants and corporals present. He told them that they should faithfully follow the orders of their officers but that they should never accept the dictates of those wishing to tread on the feelings of Brazilian citizens. Additionally, they should be on guard against individuals in positions of command who were trying to divide the patriotic armed forces over the issue of discipline. "Who is it that is speaking of discipline? Who is flaunting discipline [this time]? Who is trying to plot against the president of the republic in the name of discipline? They are the same ones who in 1961, in the name of a false discipline, in the name of the supposed order and sham legality they were defending, arrested scores of Brazilian officers and sergeants."[135]

Following an observation that these weavers of intrigues had even briefly jailed Marshal Henrique Lott when he supported Jango's assumption of the presidency in September 1961, Goulart directed his attention to the newly ended Sailor's Rebellion. He said that his first reaction on returning from the south was to categorically prohibit the use of any kind of violence against unarmed men in a union building. Evidently, there had been some unnamed persons who had advocated its use. "No one more than I," Jango proceeded, "desires the strengthening of the armed forces. No one more than I desires glory for the Navy. No one more than I desires that [our sailors] live in a climate of comprehension and understanding, of respect and discipline. But discipline is not forged through hate and exaltation. Discipline is built through mutual respect among commanders and those they command."[136]

The president was not finished with his speech, but he had run out of time in the minds of several of his generals. He had said enough, and particularly damaging was his insult to their autocratic conceptions of authority and obedience. The tanks would be rolling within minutes.

The Golpe of 1964

At the end of March, Brazil had four standing armies. All of them played a role in the drama that had begun to unfold, but only two had the main parts: the 1st Army, centered in Guanabara, Rio de Janeiro, and Minas Gerais, and the 2nd Army in São Paulo. At 2:00 P.M. on March 30,[137] Carlos Luís Guedes, one of the 1st Army's generals in Belo Horizonte, went down in history. Having been assured of arms if he needed them by the assistant military attaché at the American embassy, Lieutenant Colonel Vernon Walters,[138] Guedes took it upon himself to begin the golpe "by requisitioning all gasoline and by arresting ninety-three 'pro-communists,' including three state legislators. 'Someone has to start [it],' he remarked."[139]

Guedes had been scheming for months with mineiro governor Magalhães Pinto and another still-active Green Chicken, Lieutenant General Olimpio Mourão Filho.[140] Minas was chosen by the larger group of conspiring officers to start the fireworks since São Paulo had done so first in 1932. That, of course, had been the attempt by the paulistas to wrestle the country from the Vargas dictatorship and return it to rule dominated by local elites.

Now Guedes was on the phone to Mourão Filho, who had gone to Ouro Preto with his wife to celebrate Catholic Holy Week. At first Olimpio said he could not leave his spouse, who was very involved with the religious festivities. "If you don't immediately take command [of the operation], I will do it at Juiz de Fora," Guedes barked.[141] Mourão Filho hesitated, but later that night as he listened to Jango's speech over the radio he decided to take charge of an immediate march on Rio de Janeiro. The Communists had to be stopped!

These were the watchwords by which a legal government was overthrown. Mourão Filho hurried back to his detachment at Juiz de Fora and waited for Guedes's reinforcements to arrive. Large numbers of mineiro Polícia Militar were pressed into service. Even as some of the units began showing up, Mourão Filho's armor clanked south to the border with Guanabara and waited. Martial law, which included the death penalty, was declared in Minas Gerais by the ex-Integralist.[142] Mourão Filho next got down to the public-relations business of reading manifestos to the nation over the radio. In between broadcasts he contacted other conspirators by telephone. Some, like General Amauri Kruel, the commander of the powerful

2nd Army, had been called earlier in the day. Kruel was the hinge on which the entire conspiracy rested. He wavered, listened to pleas by both sides, but remained uncommitted. A gaucho and staunch anti-Communist, Kruel was also a longtime personal friend of João Goulart.

Jango was hampered by the disorganization caused by his minister of war, Jair Dantas Ribeiro, being in the hospital for surgery.[143] Despite his condition, Dantas Ribeiro managed to order a large contingent of men and weapons to head north and deal with Mourão Filho. Then again, what Olimpio was doing was more than promoting just a local uprising. His act of armed defiance compelled many other generals to decide whether the time was right for their long-awaited coup. Still it all depended on Kruel, who was telephoned time and again by both sides in frantic attempts to gain his support.[144] During his last conversation with the president, Gen. Kruel ended up urging Jango to rid himself of his left-of-center advisors. When Goulart steadfastly refused, Amauri had his excuse. He would forsake his companion.[145]

Goulart's house of cards was giving way. The final blow came when the group sent to do battle with Mourão Filho switched sides. This occurred after former DOPS special agent and now army marshal Odílio Denis convinced the leader of the government force, Colonel Raimundo Ferria de Souza, that by backing the administration he would be supporting Communism. Col. de Souza had been Denis's secretary for fourteen years. It was not difficult for Denis to browbeat him.[146] All that was then really left to do was to continue on to Rio and mop up. Matters had gone smoothly; only a few shots had beeen fired, resulting in a minimum loss of life. The traitors were aided by the knowledge that the United States and France had both offered to help. But perhaps some of the golpistas were unaware that the Americans had tons of arms and ammunition ready to be airlifted to Brazil, plus a naval task force steaming south from the Caribbean—just in case. The warships, led by the aircraft carrier USS *Forrestal,* were part of what the Pentagon named "Operation Brother Sam." The U.S. government was preparing to send, in addition, the following equipment in the fight against the democratically elected government of João Goulart: 250 twelve-gauge shotguns; 110 small arms, including ammunition; 7 C-135 aircraft (6 for ammo transport and one for support); 8 fighter aircraft; 1 talking-bird aircraft; 1 airborne command post; and up to 8 tankers, deemed necessary for rescue and support.[147]

Lincoln Gordon confided some years later to *Folha de São Paulo* reporters that the American military contribution had three objectives: 1) to scare the forces loyal to Goulart and support those trying to depose him, 2) to supply logistics and logistics only, especially petroleum products, to the golpistas, and 3) if necessary, to evacuate U.S. citizens. Gordon, however, was not entirely candid with the journalists. This was because he was the one who decided which, if any, of the military hardware (planes, guns, and ships) being assembled for use in Brazil would actually reach the hands of the anti-Goulart forces.[148] The actual purpose of the American weapons and men, as in so many other instances in Latin America's past, was to protect American interests. In the case of João Goulart, the United States' interests were to get rid of him. Had the battle gone the other way, or if the pro- and anti-government soldiers became locked in a stalemate, the Americans, including their planes and their firepower, would have been just offshore, standing by. U.S. support may well have been larger than this single naval task force. One report states that the Americans were ready to fly in paratroopers from the Panama Canal Zone. And it was all up to Lincoln Gordon. He could pull the trigger.[149]

THE COWARDS

With their own lack of resources, with wavering colleagues defecting in quick succession, and with the American armada on the way, one might have expected the conspiring officers to be out in front of their troops yelling, "Onward Men!" Many of the generals and colonels were, but then again, some were not. For a time, the largest concentration of land forces that Goulart controlled were those situated at the army base in the northern part of Guanabara called Vila Militar. Adjacent to the fortified complex is the working-class suburb of Marechal Hermes. Crouched on the floor of an apartment in Marechal Hermes during the entire conflict were approximately thirty cowardly army officers and the brainpower from IPÊS, all too afraid to even look out the windows. The people who lived in the apartment had to go about their business, stepping over the stooping bodies. Among these leaders of men were "General" Golbery, Lieutenant Colonel João Figueiredo, and possibly General Ernesto Geisel. So grateful was Figueiredo that years later, when he was dictator, he invited himself to be one of the pallbearers at the funeral of the apartment's owner.[150]

The Escape of Jango and Brizola

As the military situation began to go against Jango, another curious event took place. Lacerda's chief of public security, Col. Gustavo Borges—not one of those gripped with fear—began to place his men in strategic positions throughout the city. The government's own security in Rio de Janeiro was rapidly coming to a standstill. Realizing this, on Wednesday, April 1, Goulart decided to leave Rio and fly to Brasília, where he hoped to rouse support. His departure was not a moment too soon. By 3 P.M. four tanks commanded by a young lieutenant, Freddie Perdigão Pereira, took up positions for the golpistas around the presidential mansion in Laranjeiras. They had just missed capturing their quarry.[151]

Leaving Santo Dumont Airport in the early afternoon, the British-built Vickers Viscount carrying the president and his party headed out of Guanabara Bay past Sugar Loaf and turned right, swooping down to fly low over Copacabana.[152] On reaching Brasília, Jango had a number of hurried conferences and awaited the results of a meeting between Gens. Armando Âncora and Amauri Kruel. Âncora had taken over the war minister's post for the recovering Dantas Ribeiro. He had also traveled to the border with the state of São Paulo to see Kruel under a flag of truce. His assignment was to try and talk some sense into the president's former confidant. But Âncora too bent under the pressure of the moment, telling Kruel that Jango had gone to Rio Grande do Sul. His mission, he said, was therefore ended and he returned to Rio de Janeiro to surrender his command to General Arthur da Costa e Silva. Because of this turn of events, and because unfriendly forces were on their way to Brasília, Goulart left the nation's capital, again by plane, during the evening of the first. This time he really was flying to his native state, where the 3rd Army, under General Ladário Pereira Teles, remained staunchly anti-golpe.[153]

Arriving in Porto Alegre at 4:30 A.M., Jango entered into another round of conferences. Brizola, who was initially in Rio Grande do Sul on other business, made a number of suggestions at the last of these all-night meetings. Because justice minister Abelardo Jurema was now prisoner back in Rio, Brizola volunteered to take over that job. The other ministers accompanying the president, Oswald Lima Filch (agriculture), Amauri Silva (labor), and Wilson Fadul (health), would all remain at their posts. Gen. Ladário would assume the minister of war position and begin to beef up the protection around Porto Alegre. Goulart's brother-in-law went on to say, "Mr. President, if we win, we will take you back to the palace, to Brasília, to return to power. If we are defeated, you won't have a problem, you can enter Uruguay."[154]

Although Leonel Brizola wanted to fight, Jango was not about to sacrifice the blood of his fellow citizens in such a lopsided cause. He was woefully outnumbered. There were just over a thousand men and one motorized regiment under Ladário. They would have to contend with fifty thousand soldiers in Rio Grande do Sul, plus the army that Kruel was leading south from São Paulo.[155]

Jango decided to voluntarily leave Brazil for exile in Uruguay, which he did on April 4, 1964. Manoel Soares Leães flew him to safety in a single-engine Cessna. Days before, Leães had flown Maria Tereza and the couple's two children to Montevideo. On April 7 the Cessna returned. It came in low over the waves to avoid the air force's radar before landing on a deserted stretch of beach at Cidreira on the Rio Grande do Sul coast. Dressed in a military uniform and waiting for Leães was Leonel Brizola. The plane took off without incident and the two men landed later in Punta del Este.[156]

No guns were fired and no lives were lost as a result of Goulart's directives during the golpe. In June he was visited in Montevideo by then Chilean senator Salvador Allende, who brought a newspaper with him from Rio de Janeiro. The tabloid published remarks by Lincoln Gordon calling Goulart's overthrow "the most important event since the Berlin Wall and the Cuban Missile Crisis."[157] Hearing this, Jango said, "He's an imbecile." "No," Allende replied, "he's probably right. After your downfall, I will also be deposed. Had your government remained, we could have liberated Latin America. Without it, things will be much more difficult."[158]

It is reported, but unlikely, that Jango re-entered Brazil alive. The weekly magazine *Manchete* claimed that he made one quick incognito visit to Rio Grande do Sul. His son denies the story.[159] Goulart always hoped that Brazil's new dictators would allow him to return as a simple private citizen. No offer ever came in time. Prematurely old at fifty-eight, he died at his Argentine ranch, La Villa, near the town of Mercedes on December 6, 1976. The immediate cause of death was listed as a heart attack. Even so, there have been unsubstantiated murmurings over the years that Jango was poisoned.

Jango had been known to have a bad heart for years. He suffered a series of heart attacks; one may have occurred in Mexico City while he was on his way back to Brazil from the visit with Kennedy. Another even came to the attention of those shadowing him while he was in exile. For the rest of his life, however, Leonel Brizola believed that Jango died of poisoning. He came to this conclusion through firsthand knowledge of the threats made and attempts carried out against potential political rivals to the military governments in neighboring countries during Operation Condor. There is also the fact that an autopsy was never performed on Goulart's body. Brizola found it highly irregular for the Argentines not to have done so when a foreign dignitary, in this case an ex-president, died on their soil unless some powerful sector of the foreign government involved requested that an autopsy not be conducted. It was the same story on the Brazilian side of the border. No autopsy was carried out on the body of João Goulart before interment. Enrique Foch Días Vásquez, a Montevideo lawyer, put forward a poisoning theory. A former member of the Uruguayan security service, Días said that the medication Goulart took on the eve of his death was altered so as to provoke a heart attack. The culprits, according to Días, were ex–federal representative Cláudio Braga and the former mayor of Brasília, Ivo Magalhães. Both men had economic reasons for killing Jango, among which were the stealing of stock from one of Goulart's business operations in Paraguay that were hidden in a mattress at one of his fazendas. Jango's family, as well, now feels that something other than the assumed cause of death could have ended Jango's life. A legislative commission was formally established on May 2, 2000, to investigate the connection between Goulart's death and Operation Condor.[160]

Soon after his passing, and with the approval of Ernesto Geisel, the former president's body was brought back across the border in the back of an ambulance and hastily driven to a funeral in his hometown of São Borja. SNI agents were there waiting, ready to watch the mourners and report anything out of the ordinary to the generals up in the Federal District. Among the things the SNI noted were that the sermon was brief and that the presiding priest, Wiro Rauber, said nothing of a political nature. All was fairly calm until the procession to the cemetery, when many of those lining the streets cried out, "Jango! Jango! Jango!" Even more audaciously, these pleas for the man who had so provoked their imagination were now and again broken by anonymous shouts of "Liberty! Liberty! Liberty!"[161]

Indeed, with all of his qualities and all of his foibles, the ouster of João Goulart represented an end to an era of optimism, particularly for the country's lower classes. Maria Tereza later stated that the fall of her husband "was a fall for all of us; for a Brazil that believed in its present and knew that better times were not an eternally unobtainable goal."[162] The next twenty-one years of military rulers would slowly generate a different breed of Brazilian, whose goal of the larger good was supplanted by the greed of individualism. It was a transformation that produced increased migration to the larger urban areas with the revocation of Goulart's plans for agrarian reform. With too many people, Brazil's major cities would witness staggering increases in poverty and crime. They would become metropolitan cesspools that were nearly ungovernable. The people who lived in them would grow to be pessimistic about their nation and their fate. Without knowing it at first, they would be merely products of the insidious governments that nurtured them. Without knowing it, they were no longer and maybe never would be "The country of the future."[163]

Anti-Revolution

The Golpe of 1964 and Its Aftermath

Chapter 3

In Shining Armor

As the plane transporting Jango and his advisors descended in altitude over Copacabana, those who had binoculars witnessed an incredible sight stretching out below. Carnival had ended seven weeks before, but again the streets were beginning to fill with merrymakers. Many of the revelers were so independent minded that they never would have accepted the Basic Reforms Goulart fought so hard to create.[1] Probably a larger number were full of enthusiasm for what they saw as the defeat—once again—of communism in Brazil. The shouting, dancing, and laughter went on until April 2, when roughly two hundred thousand persons took part in a huge rally in Rio de Janeiro that was led by the March of the Family with God for Liberty. U.S. ambassador Lincoln Gordon noted in a communication back to the persons in charge at the state department that the only sad detail was the limited participation of the lower classes.[2]

The Americans

Gordon and Vernon Walters were busy at many things both before and after the coup. The U.S. diplomat talked President Johnson into recognizing the new regime, also on April 2, before Jango had even left the country. This was followed by a U.S. government telegram that both Gordon and Walters are supposed to have delivered to self-proclaimed war minister

Costa e Silva, urging that their be no executions. Yet after pumping millions into Goulart's downfall, it seems dubious indeed that the Americans would be averse to a little bloodletting to make sure that the Communist, Socialist, and progressive agitators did not return.

Later it was announced that two members of the post-golpe junta, Admiral Augusto Rademaker and General Francisco Correia de Melo, were planning to summarily execute all officers who remained loyal to the ousted regime.[3] Lincoln Gordon's "presence on the Brazilian political scene was so obtrusive that some irreverent students painted a slogan on the walls: 'Enough of middlemen—Lincoln Gordon for president!'"[4] As for Walters, the PCB contended that he had had a hand in deposing al-Awwal Farouk in Egypt, Arturo Frondizi in Argentina, and Manuel Prado in Peru. Further, it is said that he had compelled a number of Arab leaders to sign beneficial petroleum contracts with American companies or face being removed. Walters comically sloughed off these charges with the comment to his superiors that "on the seventh day I rested."[5] But it has been stated that in Brazil he became "the linchpin, the one person all the officers would talk to while they were still afraid to talk with one another."[6]

Already the confidant of Gen. Castelo Branco—Walters had been the U.S. army's liaison with the Brazilian forces in Italy, and the two men had shared the same quarters there while fighting for the Allies—the American encouraged Branco "to take power. A week before the coup, Walters wired full details of its organization to Washington."[7] Years later, even during the darkest days of the dictatorship, Walters could find only praise for his Brazilian colleagues: "A regime basically unfriendly to the United States has been replaced by another one much more friendly. Some may regard this as bad. I do not. I am convinced that if the revolution had not occurred, Brazil would have had another Gulag archipelago."[8]

In the 1970s Gen. Walters became deputy director of the CIA. There are unconfirmed reports that in this position he had connections with Chile's secret police, DINA, and with the murder of Orlando Letelier, Salvador Allende's foreign minister.[9]

Operation Salami

Gustavo Borges's police had already taken up their positions as the presidential Viscount passed overhead. They were well into the battle plan known as "Operation Salami," which was just another way of saying a housecleaning. The pro-PTB *Última Hora* and the headquarters of the National Union of Students were both sacked and put to the torch. *Novos Rumos* was a little luckier. Objectionable books, literature, and idealistic propaganda were burned in front of the UNE edifice in what must have reminded many of a similar scene concocted by the Nazis. It was not the first time that the building had been attacked. The structure had been shot up and decorated with the wording "House of the Moscow Lackeys" by paramilitary rightists at 3 A.M. on January 6, 1962. Things were different this time. There was no longer a need for hit-and-run tactics. Across town, soldiers tore down placards that had been put up around Cristiano Ottoni Square for the rally of March 13. Officers of the law—Governor Lacerda had beefed up through the reinstatement of several police ruffians—made arrests all over Guanabara in the early hours of the golpe. Among those policemen given their jobs back were several former members of the force who had been reprimanded as a result of a 1962–63 case in which a number of Guanabara *mendigos* (beggars) were murdered. Homes were broken into and pillaged. Beatings took place. There were shootings, injuries, and killings.[10]

AI-1 and the First Cassações

On April 9, Costa e Silva and his festooned contemporaries in the navy and air force issued the first of several commands: Ato Institucional No. 1 (Institutional Act No. 1), or as it quickly came to be called, AI-1. Those who were still dancing in the streets must have thought that the band had missed a beat. Already on April 2 the military had been letting out hints in the press that they did not feel the country was ready yet for general elections.[11] Now, with AI-1, it became clear. There were no misplayed notes. In fact, there was to be no more music. The positivist officers had been looking for a justification for decades to return to absolute power. No more of this behind-the-scenes catering to incompetent civilian politicians. This was their chance to do things right—the military way. The men in uniform were staying in power and would govern as they saw fit with only a show of public involvement.

The edict started out with two and a half paragraphs of backslapping before giving the first clue of what was to come. But then, there it was:

"The victorious revolution . . . legitimizes itself."[12] The generals then added that

> to demonstrate that we do not intend to radicalize the revolutionary process, we have decided to maintain the *Constitution of 1946* [and have limited] ourselves to modifying it only in respect to the powers of the president of the republic. [We have done this so that he] can complete his mission of restoring economic and financial order within Brazil and take the urgent measures appropriate to drain off the hostile and isolated groups of Communists whose pus has already seeped not only into the higher levels of government but into its administrative subsections as well. In order to further reduce the absolute powers that are part of the victorious revolution, we equally resolve to maintain Congress, with relative restrictions on its powers, [as are] consistent with the present Institutional Act.[13]

The new rulers of Brazil next got down to real cases in the eleven articles that made up AI-1. Article 1, as promised, retained Congress but imposed limitations on its authority that were to be outlined. Article 2 set the terms of office for the president and vice president. They were to expire on January 31, 1966. Article 3 allowed the president to amend the constitution if he received a simple majority vote within Congress on two occasions. Article 4 gave the president the right to send urgent legislation to Congress, legislation that became law automatically if Congress did not vote otherwise within thirty days.[14] A filibuster on the part of the government's supporters could thus insure the passage of nearly any bill. Article 5 took all budgetary power out of congressional hands and placed it with the president. Article 6 gave the president the right to declare a state of siege. Article 7 suspended constitutional guarantees in respect to job security and tenure. All levels of civil servants and members of the military were the targets of this measure. It meant that anyone who had been pro-Goulart or to the left of the political center should start packing his bags. This article also limited the way evidence could be presented by a defendant.

Article 8 declared that investigations could be brought against persons or groups who acted illegally in relation to the state. Individuals committing mutinous offenses would thus be liable for their conduct. This stipulation laid the foundation for the massive witch-hunts that were already landing thousands of Brazilians in jail and subjecting an unknown number to the horrors of the torturer's fist.[15] Article 9 set the date for the next presidential election for October 3, 1965. Article 10 gave the chiefs of the army, navy, and air force the prerogative "in the interests of national honor and peace," to *cassar,* or suspend the political rights (i.e., to vote, to run for office, to hold office, to belong to a political party, and so forth) of selected citizens for ten years.[16] Moreover, Article 10 gave the generals the power to remove any elected federal legislator from office. Article 11 stated that AI-1 would expire on January 31, 1966.[17] The new government and the military would have until then to get things in order.

Brazil's authoritarian Renascence started off with a bang one day later, when the leaders of the armed forces, using Article 10 of AI-1, canceled the political rights of one hundred individuals. To add insult to injury, and to build up the angle of the Communist threat, they placed the name of Luís Carlos Prestes first on the list and that of João Goulart second. Jânio Quadros landed in the number three position, although with all of his oddities the seriousness of his ranking might be called into question. Miguel Arraes and, way down in the tenth slot, Leonel Brizola, followed him. There were other top figures there too, besides those who were just bystanders or in some cases commentators to what had gone on, like journalist Samuel Wainer and engineer and PTB activist Rubens Paiva. Paiva made the list for being in the parliamentary commission set up during the Goulart government to investigate IBAD.[18] Finally, rounding out everything, forty members of Congress had their mandates terminated in a second section of the measure.[19]

One of the twin pillars of opposition to the way João Goulart did things had his demands dealt with next. Ranieri Mazzilli was declared acting president in the early morning hours following Jango's April 1–2 flight from Brasília to Rio Grande do Sul. During the coming two weeks, while the generals were maneuvering to decide which of them would be the new chief of state, Mazzilli revoked Goulart's month-old land-reform decree.[20] This decision to keep the country in the agrarian Dark Ages was enthusiastically received by the landed elite and all those loyal to unadventurous thinking.

Among the various meetings taking place behind closed doors during this fortnight hiatus was one at Guanabara Palace. Several governors attended, and foremost among them was Carlos Lacerda. After some discussion, the state administrators decided to submit a single name to the military as their choice for president. Lacerda had a name in mind when he was called to the telephone to speak with U.S. ambassador Lincoln

Gordon. Later, the American called a second time. Then Lacerda started to get calls from New York and from various Brazilian military personalities. Finally the governor caved in and put aside his original recommendation. Unable to stand the pressure, he submitted a different candidate to the gathering, the candidate whom the telephone urgings had been about all along. It was the name of the man who would shortly become Brazil's first military dictator in the twentieth century, General Humberto de Alencar Castelo Branco.[21]

Operation Cleanup

Castelo Branco was sworn in on April 15, 1964. On April 16 Vernon Walters had a private lunch with the new leader. Forever afterward, as if to deny the obvious, Walters refused to admit to any complicity in the golpe, including that he had prepared an emergency plan for President Johnson's staff in case the events of March 31–April 1 turned into a full-blown civil war.[22] Less than a year after the military assumed power, Colonel Walters became Brigadier General Walters. When his tour of duty was up, Castelo Branco went to see him off and to personally thank him "for the services he gave to Brazil."[23]

From the moderate camp, Castelo Branco represented a split between the so-called hard liners and the so-called moderates. But, considering the man just from the human rights issue, if Castelo Branco could be labeled a moderate, it was a description bordering on exaggeration. Twelve days into his term of office, Brazil's new ruler showed his teeth. The nation was to be dredged of any and all left-of-center elements in order to conform to the Doctrine of National Security, as already envisioned by the soldiers over at the Superior War College.[24] This meant a continuation of the dragnet by the authorities that had been going on since April 1. The targets were the politically left of center and the enemies of those with secure power bases in an affair called "Operation Cleanup."[25] Laws were put into effect on April 27 that excused everything in the name of the newly created Military Police Inquiries.[26] Called Inquéritos das Polícias Militares, or IPMs, these virtual inquisitions often came to be controlled by hard-line colonels who put pressure on Castelo Branco to turn up the heat. With summary powers,[27] the IPMs snooped into "the activities of employees—

civilian and military—at municipal, state, and federal levels, to identify those engaged in subversive activities. The IPMs constituted the legal mechanism for the systematic search for absolute security and elimination of the enemy within. [Theoretically,] once an inquiry was complete, the chief of the department to which the suspect was connected examined the alleged involvement of the accused person or persons. The final decision concerning punishment was up to the president, the state governors, or the mayors [depending on the importance of the violator]."[28]

Operation Overhaul

On the same day Castelo Branco was sworn in, April 15, up in Washington, D.C., J. Edgar Hoover may have written a letter to a Mr. Brady in Brazil. While the authenticity of this communiqué cannot be verified from its place of discovery—the DOPS Archive in Rio de Janeiro—if true, it indicates that the Americans were much more involved with the overthrow of João Goulart than has been previously assumed. Written on FBI stationery, Hoover virtually admits the involvement of the Bureau, an entity that is supposed to focus its attention solely on domestic issues within the United States. The director began by saying,

> I want to take this means to express my personal appreciation to each agent stationed in Brazil for the services rendered in the accomplishment of "Overhaul."
>
> Admiration for the dynamic and efficient manner in which this large[-]scale operation was carried out in a foreign land and under difficult conditions, has prompted me to express my gratitude. The CIA people did their part well and accomplished a great deal; however, the efforts of our agents were especially valuable. I am particularly pleased that our participation in the affair was kept secret and that the Administration did not have to make any public denials. We can all be proud of the vital part the FBI is playing in protecting the security of the Nation, even beyond its borders.
>
> I am quite aware that our agents often make personal sacrifices while fulfilling their duties. Living conditions in Brazil may not be of the best but it is indeed encouraging to know that because of loyalty and a realization that you are contributing a vital if not always a glamorous service to your

country you stick to the job. It is this spirit which today is enabling our Bureau to successfully discharge its very grave responsibilities.[29]

The Continuing Cassações

All through the last nine months of 1964, elected representatives were waking up to find their names included on the latest list of *cassações,* or individuals who had had their terms of office annulled via Article 10 of AI-1. On the national level, the roster was composed of fifty federal deputies, five alternates, and one senator, and former president Juscelino Kubitschek. The armed forces did not like Kubitschek, especially his plans to run again for the presidency in 1965. So they established a military commission, presided over by Lt. Col. João Figueiredo, to try to pin something on him. The dossier eventually submitted to Castelo Branco was thick with allegations that Figueiredo and his team had pieced together. Chief among the charges was that Juscelino had let Communists organize and infiltrate the unions. He had also permitted the PTB to deal illegally with the Banco do Brasil. This was done, the report alleged, in order to get João Goulart's support in the 1955 presidential elections. Figueiredo's narrative continued, stating that Juscelino and Jango had paid the PCB Cr$20 million for its members' votes, that Kubitschek had agreed to pay the Communists an additional two hundred thousand dollars for their support in 1965 (he was supposed to have already paid them fifty thousand dollars), and that in general Juscelino was involved in just too many shady business deals and other corrupt activities.[30]

At the state level, forty-three assemblymen and eleven surrogates lost their seats. In municipal government, ten aldermen were likewise removed from the decision-making processes. The majority of these ex-lawmakers were from Goulart's PTB, followed in second place by the PTB's sometime ally, the PSD. Besides checking the power of these two parties, the cassações also served as a point-blank warning to all politicians who were not reactionaries, like most of those in the UDN, which lost not a single representative.[31]

Purges within the civilian bureaucracy were another feature of 1964, which was by far the most prominent year for these firings and forced retirements. Using figures that the military kept of such civilian axings, it was reported that 1,408 government employees had been terminated by the end of the year. The ministries of public works, finance, and labor led the list by handing out exactly 999 pink slips. These bureaus were highly accountable in the military's opinion for implementing Goulart's social and economic programs. There were, additionally, 205 police firings after the golpe until the end of 1973, including 66 from the Polícia Militar and 131 from the Polícia Civil. And naturally the public servants were not alone. Numerous union officials, students, writers, journalists, artists, scientists, editors, professors, members of religious orders, businesspeople, intellectuals, and soldiers in the armed forces were all told that their services would no longer be needed.[32] As for those from Brazil's defense establishment, the number removed reached at least 1,164 commissioned and noncommissioned officers, together with 50 air force and 1,509 naval enlisted men. In a preposterous ceremony, each serviceman to be discharged was declared *legally dead* while standing at attention and being drummed out of the service. The "widows" of the chastised officers were then given a pension proportionate to their husband's former rank and number of years of active service. Most of those women who had the misfortune to have been married to one of the enlisted men, however, received nothing in 1964, never received anything, and will not receive a farthing under Brazil's Constitution of 1988.[33]

There were, as well, some 5,000 investigations begun against more than 40,000 people. Many of these inquiries resulted, either before or after the fact, in an apprehension. Over 500 Brazilians were taken into custody in São Paulo during the week following the golpe. The number of detained hit 3,000 three days later in Guanabara. From April 1 to July 30, 1964, DOPS calculated that 314 arrests were made just to the north in Belo Horizonte. In Recife, along with the detentions, the political police confiscated 10,000 "Communist coveralls" that Miguel Arraes and his leftist associates were supposed to be planning to issue to a peasant militia before making a grab at power. No mention was made of the fact that this attire might have been the first complete set of clothes that some of these workers had ever had. In Rio, nine Chinese nationals from a trading mission to Brazil were picked up, beaten, and presented to the mass media as proof that dangerous foreign Communists—the real coverall-wearing kind—were trying to subvert the country. The police appropriated roughly a hundred thousand dollars in their possession. The paranoia over a Chinese connection continued among the authorities at least until mid-1968.[34]

One estimate put the grand total of captured persons at close to 50,000 nationwide. Such sweeping seizures were carried out mainly as propaganda. The new powers that be had to show that they were on top of a planned Communist takeover. In most cases those brought in for closer scrutiny were questioned, warned, and then quietly let go. In other instances the manhandling of prisoners to dig out information, to intimidate, or to settle old scores was applied in generous doses. No small number of suspects fell into police hands by way of denouncements. César de Alencar was one energetic example of those who named names. He turned in 140 of his coworkers at the national radio station. While perhaps as few as 36 people were fired, two extra informants helped Alencar out: Hamilton Frazão and Celso Teixeira.[35]

Where did the victims come from? The nation's political police and other organs of the security apparatus had *fichas,* or cards, on thousands of people. In addition, there were the *dedo-duros* (lit., hard fingers; finger pointers or stool pigeons). These people seemed to be everywhere. Their presence promoted an atmosphere of innuendo and paranoia in the workplace. Take the case of IBGE. The agency that takes Brazil's census and reports on other important national statistics was overrun with snitches ready to turn in fellow employees and anyone suspicious who walked in off the street. DOPS in Rio de Janeiro reportedly received tips from the following IBGE personnel:[36]

Natalina Neves de Assis
Laura Craveiro Barbosa
Pericles Santos Cruz
Ernesto Doria
Alberto Raja Gabaglia
Eva Werneck Maciel
Clovis de Magalhães
Yolanda Leão Camaz Magalhães
Rivadavia Galves de Mello
Orlando Aurélio da Rocha
Alvaro Silveira Filho
Virmar Ribeiro Soares

Passing the Torch of Torture

Since the times of Filinto Müller in the 1930s and 40s, the knack of making someone suffer physically had undergone a revolution of its own in Brazil. Müller was known as a hater of leftists, organized labor, nonwhites, and Jews. His school years at Rio's prestigious Realengo Military Academy were filled with cheating without being caught. Later he joined the famous Coluna Prestes (Prestes Column) but was kicked out by its de facto leader, Luís Carlos Prestes, while the rebels were camped at Foz do Iguaçu in 1925. The reason for this disgrace was that Filinto wrote a letter to his superiors stating that he wanted to visit his family, then exiled in Paraguay, and promised that he would rejoin the column later in Mato Grosso. He had really planned to desert, however, after earlier turning coward at a two-and-a-half-mile crossing of the Paraná River. The mighty tributary was just too turbulent for Müller's liking. Talking a number of soldiers under his command into deserting with him, Filinto snuck into Argentina along with one hundred contos de réis (Brazilian currency then worth over US$10,500) of the Coluna's money. Filinto's story continued in Buenos Aires, where he worked as a car washer, taxi driver, and then as a real estate agent. Returning to Brazil in 1927, he was apprehended and sentenced to two years in prison. Müller conspired in a minor way in the 1930 movement that brought Vargas to power, and he ended up on the staff of Getúlio's first minister of war, General José Fernandes Leite de Castro. In 1931 he became the secretary to João Alberto in São Paulo. Moving to Rio with his boss in July of that year, Filinto's duties included those of an inspector of the Guarda Civil (Civil Guards), traffic division, a subsection of the Polícia Civil. In January 1933 he was made the head of Vargas's restructured and renamed political police, the Delegacia Especial de Segurança Politica e Social (Special Police for Political and Social Security, or DESPS). Two months later, on the recommendation of João Alberto, whom he was replacing, Müller was anointed chief of the Polícia Civil. His appointment carried cabinet-level status. Pro-Nazi, Filinto was the only member of this inner circle to have free access to the leader of the country. While police chief, he is supposed to have invented a head-and-testicle-crushing apparatus.[37]

In 1944, when Vargas realized the Allies would win the war, he sacked Filinto. But many of the police under Müller's command continued in law enforcement for decades. Into the 1960s, they employed largely home-grown techniques of torture. America had been sending a limited number of police advisors to the country since Vargas's day. Following the golpe, however, U.S. reticence was swept away as its security specialists came to the country in droves. One such individual was Dan Mitrione. Daniel Anthony Mitrione became world infamous through the 1973 Costa-Gavras film *State of Siege*.[38] As might have been predicted, *State of Siege* was cancelled for political reasons the night of its premiere at the American Film Theater in Washington, D.C. The movie was unpopular with the Nixon administration, and it was banned for several years in Brazil, probably because there is a Brazilian flag in one scene.

Once the generals secured their flanks, Mitrione became a U.S. public safety advisor in Belo Horizonte. His assignment: to give formal classroom demonstrations to his Brazilian counterparts on the latest types of torture using common and political prisoners as well as beggars freshly plucked off the streets. One detainee who was used as a guinea pig later remarked that when he finally saw *State of Siege,* he wondered why Costa-Gavras had left out the laughing. This individual remembered that when he was tortured, those sitting in front of him were not diligently taking down notes as in the film but laughing and having a really great time. During his Brazilian tour of duty, which lasted from September 1960 to mid-1967, Mitrione claimed, both before and after the coup, that he had instructed who knows what to some one hundred thousand Brazilian policemen, or at that time about a sixth of the nation's police force. Officer Dan was later sent to Uruguay to continue his work before being captured and executed by the MLN (Movimento de Liberación Nacional—National Liberation Movement), more commonly known as the Tupamaros. On his wrist at the time of death was a watch engraved with thanks from the Brazilian army's torture and death division, DOI-Codi.[39]

> [Mitrione's] advice resulted in cell members being shot to death while they were in the act of surrendering with their hands up. Those who were taken prisoner were tortured and women prisoners were raped as well as otherwise tortured. Many innocent persons were tortured and in many instances killed, while being held suspect. His thirst for brutality reached such a height that the former chief of police in Montevideo, Alejandro Otero, was fired from his position in 1968 when he told Mitrione that he could no longer comply with Mitrione's sophisticated and brutal methods of police torture. Inspector Otero later told Brazilian journalists of torture methods utilized under the orders of Mitrione that left some of the most hardened journalists with tears in their eyes.[40]

One of these techniques even bore Mitrione's name, although hard evidence on its use and that Mitrione actually invented it are lacking. The device, the Mitrione Vest, was inflatable and was used during interrogation to put extreme pressure on the chest, sometimes fracturing the rib cage. It is unknown whether the Mitrione Vest had a connection to the contrivance thought up by Filinto Müller. Nonetheless, it is important to remember that the United States, and some of its allies—Portugal and England, along with South Africa, South Korea, and Israel—did not export what they knew about torture solely to Brazil. Techniques were made available via Operation Condor to support friendly regimes all over Latin America and in several parts of the capitalistic world. The battle plan was to root out and destroy creeping Communism. Brazil, for its part, helped in this undertaking by sending torturers to question, maim, and kill Brazilian exiles in Bolivia in 1972, Chile in 1973, and Argentina in 1976, following the respective military golpes in those countries. In the Chilean instance, the Brazilian torture squads worked over some of the local opposition after the fall of Salvador Allende. The Brazilian security machine visited Uruguay as well, to aid in tracking down Tupamaros. The job was given to a team sent by São Paulo detective Sérgio Fleury. Fleury was also an instructor in torture with OBAN (Operation Bandeirantes). He had no qualms about torturing anyone—not even nuns. Fleury was one of the police who briefly questioned Fernando Gabeira after the machine-gunned but still alive idealist was captured. Gabeira's impression of Fleury was that he was deceitful, vain, and not the brightest of people. Sérgio Fleury was offended at having to sit through the presentations by Mitrione. He evidently felt that the American could show him little that he did not already know.[41]

The generals in Brasília could not have disagreed more. They christened one of the streets in Belo Horizonte in Dan Mitrione's honor. This was a tribute never bestowed on Fleury by those in charge. Not to be outdone, following Mitrione's death, Frank Sinatra and Jerry Lewis gave a performance in Mitrione's hometown of Richmond, Indiana. The two entertainers donated the evening's receipts to Henrietta, Mitrione's widow. On arriving in Richmond, Sinatra told a TV reporter, "We owe a debt of gratitude for men like these who work for our country."[42] Mr. Sinatra also gave a short speech following the performance. Among his comments was the observation, "You sit back and think of Dan Mitrione, and you know that things ain't all that bad."[43]

The Brazilians watching Mitrione's lectures were far from what might be called uninformed novices. Above and beyond the beatings, rapes, and burnings with cigars and cigarettes, which were almost de rigueur for common criminals, the 1964 golpistas had come by a host of new ingredients to deal out pain, deformity, and death all over the country. There was even a Naziesque gas chamber at an army barrack in Goiânia where the exhaust of a diesel engine was pumped into a prisoner-filled room. The number of persons who died or sustained serious brain damage from this one device is not available.

By the end of October 1966, all police stations in Guanabara are reported to have had a place to carry out torture *(sala de torturas)* where prisoners could be scientifically abused. At one station house, the men on duty bragged that they could raise a person from the dead and make him confess to all the crimes of the last hundred years. One cop stated that he had served two decades on the force and that in his view—as well as those of 99 percent of his colleagues—a thief confesses only while dangling and under the club. Three instances out of hundreds were typical of the treatment one could expect. It did not matter if a single person, a group, or a multitude was accused of the offense.

In São João de Meriti, a working-class municipality north of Rio, a policeman had a relative whose store was losing several cans of consumer goods a night due to theft. After having the problem explained to him, the lawman turned his *cachorrinhos* (lit., little dogs; criminals who pass information to the police in exchange for money and protection) loose, and within thirty minutes a suspect was produced. The individual was vigorously questioned but refused to confess. So the constable in charge of the interrogation let a case of beer (twenty-four 19.38-oz. [.57 liter] bottles) fall on the man. This broke his legs and a number of ribs. But still the man would not confess. Finally, beaten into a coma, he was thrown into a humid cell. The stool pigeons then returned, saying they had turned in the wrong person. The man who had been beaten was only the owner of a hole-in-the-wall bar (a *birosqueiro*), that is to say, not a socially important individual. So the police simply turned him over to his wife, who had waited outside the jail for a week. The couple never pressed charges.

In a South Zone murder case, still unresolved as of October 30, 1966, numerous persons were brought in for questioning. A number were then sent to the same São João de Meriti police station, where they were immersed for long periods in tubs full of pure salt. From there they had to be taken directly to the hospital. Last, in a police district in Rio's South Zone, the Peg-Pag supermarket case resulted in the arrests of more than two hundred persons. Some were roughed up and tortured during the seven months it took the police to solve the crime (December 11, 1965, to July 15, 1966).[44]

Indeed, Rio de Janiero held a continuum of surprises for those taken into custody. Just being roughed up was nothing. At the other end of possibilities were special cases receiving special attention. Some of these latter individuals came to know the peaks that make up the world-renowned carioca landscape in a way different from those who view these granite mounds as tourists. This was because more than one political prisoner was subjected to the *proceso corcovado* ("Corcovado Process"). Corcovado is a finger of granite, 2,309 feet 7 inches (704 m) above sea level in the South Zone of the former capital. One side of Corcovado has a spectacular ninety-degree plunge, straight down. Christ the redeemer, a mammoth statue and symbol of the city, was inaugurated on the pinnacle in 1931.

Following the overthrow of Goulart, leftists and leftist sympathizers were included in the parade of prisoners taken up to the summit and, below the opened arms of the King of Kings, made to stand for hours on top of the low protective wall at the edge of the cliff surrounding the monument. They were placed with their backs facing the oblivion below and tormented by rifles and bayonets that were jabbed ever so tauntingly into their flesh. Police in other areas simply used high walls or barriers for less melodramatic but equally effective results.

If prisoners came down off the mountain alive, they might then be made to stretch out their arms and have telephone books plopped into each hand. This oxymoronic process was called the "Christ the Redeemer" torture. There was a variation named *ginástica* ("Gymnastics"), wherein detainees were compelled to do deep knee bends while holding the telephone books. One slight modification—raising an arm—and you were doing the "Statue of Liberty," which involved standing while holding some heavy object aloft in one hand. When utter exhaustion set in, any prisoner who dropped the phone book was beaten.

Brazil's post-1964 torturers had a near obsessive fascination with naming their pain-producing techniques after the life or sufferings of Jesus Christ. There was the "Crown of Christ," for example, which was a steel band that could be wound tight, crushing the skull and literally popping out one's eyeballs.[45] Another, perhaps more melodramatic, method went by the simple name *Cristo* ("Christ"). In this procedure, the subject was lashed to a suspended cross. The bulky crucifix was then lowered until the victim's feet were impaled on two open cans. Too sickening? Then forget the religious element. Other individuals were tied up and hoisted into the air where they could be used as convenient punching bags. There was a twist to this, too, in that one could be raised into the air upside down. The flicking of cigarette ashes into the eyes completed this particular torture, known as *pisca-pisca* ("Blink-Blink").

Policemen sat on other suspects in an ordeal known as *pêso* ("Weight"). Threats, shouts, and prods were added until the sufferers agreed to begin lifting a heavy object once the constables got off. Ether was dripped onto the scrotum of some of these prisoners, especially the ones unwilling to talk. The chemical is said to have produced fast results.

Snakes!? Why not? One anaconda regularly found its way into the cells at Rio's Division of Robbery and Larceny. No doubt the reptile slithered into the cages occupied by political prisoners too. The creature measured nine feet eight inches and was taken out of service only following a newspaper exposé. At least one political detainee had another serpent, a boa constrictor named Miriam, placed in his cell to keep him company.[46]

Algemas (manacles or handcuffs) were employed to fasten suspects to a tabletop or into a chair and left for several days at a time. Another kind of device to sit in went by the appropriate name "Dragon's Chair." It was an old barber's chair, covered with metal strips, that was plugged into an electrical outlet. In 1972, a microphone was hooked up to the machine that controlled the amount of current that could be zapped into each victim; the louder the voice of the interrogator, the more electricity. Some models had a hole cut out of the seat so the victim's testicles could drop through and be securely fastened. The urge to jump out of the chair with each new jolt was offset, obviously to the roaring delight of the guards, by the tearing possibility of self-mutilation. But then, the very act of sitting might even be a torture, as victims could be fitted with a bracelike arrangement to keep them from resting in this most natural of ways. Such devices were direct descendants of the *libambo,* which was used during the formal days of slavery and probably during the informal ones as well. The libambo was a metal collar that had any number of outwardly projecting iron bars attached to it. The bars were often one foot (30 cm) or more in length. When in place around the neck, the apparatus made running away difficult and proper rest nearly impossible.

An even more grim and relatively simple course of action—still in use in Brazil—was the *pau-de-arara* ("Parrot's Perch"). Captives to be skewered in the pau-de-arara are forced to sit on the floor, often naked, with their legs curled up in front of them. They then have their wrists bound together, such as by handcuffs, on each side of their legs. An iron pole is next slid through the gap just behind the bent knees and on top of the individual's arms at the elbows. Thus constrained, the iron pole and attached victim are lifted off the ground and placed in some kind of secure position. Two stacks of tires a few feet in the air often serve this purpose. One end of the pole is flopped onto each stack with the wailing torturee suspended between them like a piece of beef on a spit. While dangling, sufferers are raped, beaten, burned with cigarettes, dunked, or shocked. In the period after the golpe the direct-current alternative was carried out with U.S.-supplied hand-cranked military field telephones. Then as now the anus, genitals, teeth, and ears were all targets of electrical attention.[47] So widespread did the combination of the pau-de-arara and electric shock become that in the late 1980s it was reported that "most precinct houses in Brazil still have electric-shock machines and that many have parrot's perches that can be set up or struck down virtually at a moment's notice."[48]

Really tough prisoners and those destined to know the extremes of sadism were literally charbroiled on a *churrasquinho* ("Little Barbecue"). The little barbecue consisted of the usual pau-de-arara plus one extra feature. Pure alcohol was placed in a large pan below the subject, or a piece of twisted paper or cardboard was inserted into his or her rectal cavity. In both cases, the alcohol and the paper were set ablaze. A variation on all this did not bother with the pan or the alcohol. Old newspapers were the only combustibles used in a torture known as *quentura* ("Hot").

Some prisoners, both common and no doubt those of conscience, were taken to the Guandu River, where they were bound and then thrown from the bridge. Their heads were pulled from the rushing current over and over, just often and long enough to keep them from drowning. This was the abominable *banho* ("Bath"). Though one did not have to be driven all the way out to this river on the western flank of the earlier capital. Back at police headquarters there was always the *banho chinês* ("Chinese Bath").

Not really a way to cleanse oneself, the Chinese bath consisted of a pail filled with oil or sewage. Into this debris a victim's head was crammed and held until an instant before the individual passed out. The coughing and choking prisoner might then be approached from behind and hit simultaneously with cupped hands over the ears. Called the *telefone* ("Telephone"), this torture does not sound very sophisticated, but it frequently caused rupturing of the eardrums. The telefone became very trendy with the men responsible for fishing out information and confessions. It left no marks on the outer body, unlike the various tongs and pliers. Historically very popular, these last two tools have long been a part of the working equipment of the bone-crushing, fingernail-yanking Brazilian police.

The navy also had its own specially selected group intimidators over at CENIMAR in Guanabara. These men were second to no one in sadism. The installation they worked out of consisted of a group of three facilities in which some of the most horrible torture of all took place following the military's seizure of power in 1964. What is more, the navy's professionals used an array of techniques to bring about pain that were apparently their own inventions. In a particularly efficient example, prisoners reported that they were strapped into a chair and then ordinary powdered soap would be ground into their eyes. A bright light was then turned on in front of their faces while their heads were confined in a stationary position facing the glare.

Just as had been done in the times of Artur Bernardes and Getúlio Vargas, no less than one prisoner, Communist Célio Augusto Guedes, was almost certainly tortured to death and then thrown out the window of a government detention facility. The only difference this time was that Guedes's lifeless body was dumped from the ninth floor of the CENIMAR edifice in Rio de Janeiro and not from the second floor of the Polícia Central (Central Police Station). But exactly like the cases of Conrado Niemeyer in 1925, Victor Allen Barron in 1936, and others throughout the years, the authorities declared that Célio Guedes had committed suicide.

Then there were the *geladeiras* ("ice boxes"). The geladeiras employed by the students of Filinto Müller were no longer the large common cells stuffed sardine can full with prisoners. The new geladeiras, also mockingly called "Music Boxes" by the sentries, were actually small refrigerated cubbyholes. There were several different sizes of geladeiras. The smallest were 18" × 4' 9" (47 cm × 1.45 m) while the largest were 6' 5½" square (nearly 1.97 m^2). At first captives were placed in them for a few minutes at a time, dressed only in their underwear or completely naked. Then they were taken out for questioning, tortured, or doused with water and thrown back in for a more thorough deep freeze. The temperature in these chambers dipped as low as −7.6° Fahrenheit (−22 Celsius). It was also possible to increase or decrease the intensity of light or to have no light at all. Loudspeakers completed the package.

Located high on the wall opposite the door, the geladeiras' sound boxes emitted all kinds of noise—including the moans of other victims. This went on around the clock. Sleep was impossible because of the clamor. The stench was another feature designed to weaken the spirit; food was laced with fast-acting laxatives. Toilets were not available. Prisoners were starved for their first five days, then the spiked provisions began arriving at unexpected hours. By the end of the fifth day, meals consisted of three spoonfuls of rice with beans. From the fifteenth day on, these already paltry rations were dished up every third day. Water was provided, but only when the guards felt like it, not when the detainee asked for some. The entire routine was referred to as *o sistema inglês* ("the English System"). Its goal was to psychologically break suspects so that their cooperation could be obtained with as little physical violence as possible. The English system came to Brazil at the end of 1970, when a group of army officers returned home after studying British attempts to break captured members, suspects, and sympathizers of the Irish Republican Army.[49]

Back at the Vila Militar army base in Rio, Lt. Ailton Guimarães of the Polícia do Exército (Army Police), like Dan Mitrione, gave torture lessons on live political prisoners. Other experts, like Col. Ary Pereira de Carvalho, Capt. Lacerda (possibly Enio Albuquerque Lacerda or Jofre Fernandes Lacerda), and Sgts. Alvaro Barbosa Silva, Pevelari (probably Mario Antonio Polvorelli), and Juvenal Antunes Pereira, sometimes assisted Lt. Ailton. Juvenal busied himself over in Tijuca, too, at the Army Police garrison.[50]

Miguel Arraes, Francisco Julião, and Gregório Bezerra

In Pernambuco, the downfall of Vargas in 1945 brought few operational changes in the undertakings of the state's police. In 1948, DOPS agents apprehended thirty-one members of the editorial staff of the Recife newspaper *Folha do Povo*. They were taken to the Casa de Detenção and placed in a cramped cell. Then, under the direction of officers like Eudes Costa, all of the journalists were beaten for being suspected Communists. There were cases of food poisoning. It was said that a prisoner who had raped a teenage girl was given better treatment. A week later, Governor Alexandre Lima Sobrinho turned DOPS, the police, and a number of *capangas* (private bodyguards who intimidate and murder) loose in Jaboatão and Recife. Scores of persons were punched and battered. Some sixteen were kidnapped.[51] This legacy of elite violence lived on into the 1960s.

After the golpe, a number of idealists did not wait around to be manhandled. Their exits from the country were either winked at or went unnoticed. Others were bigger prizes. Such was the case with Pernambuco's governor, Miguel Arraes, who was apprehended on the afternoon of April 1, 1964. While on their way to make the arrest, the army units sent to capture the governor's palace and its occupant killed two high-school students for chanting anti-military slogans. The governor was spared a similar end. Arraes was never tortured, but he was stripped of power and whisked off to the penal facilities on Fernando de Noronha Island. Evidently, important personalities who went untouched did so for one reason only. The military did not want to turn these individuals into martyrs. This was no doubt the logic behind the fact that Luís Carlos Prestes was never physically tortured following his arrest in 1936. Note that family members—Olga Benário (companion) for Prestes and Valdyr Ximenes (brother-in-law) for Arraes—were fair game.[52]

In addition to his leftist inclinations, Governor Arraes was disliked by the armed forces for disbanding a notoriously savage group of police thugs in Pernambuco called the "Esquadrão de Cavalaria da Polícia Militar" (Military Police Cavalry Squad). He also greatly reduced the use of violence and torture by the police in general in his state. Although with the victory of the rightists from the barracks, the billy club and other devices quickly reappeared.[53]

Francisco Julião, leader of the Peasant Leagues and a federal deputy, was not as lucky as Miguel Arraes. Escaping to Minas Gerais, Julião was taken into custody near Brasília on June 3, 1964. He went through three torture-free weeks in the jails of the Federal District. This was not to be the case once orders came through to transfer him to Pernambuco. Arriving at the command center of the 4th Army in Recife, Julião was beaten with truncheons and thrown into a cell that measured eleven spans of the hands in length by four in width. He was kept there for two months. For fifteen days he was not permitted to take a bath. During the entire time his only bed was the concrete floor of his cell.[54] Then again, the treatment dished out to the leader of Brazil's landless peasants was almost tame in comparison to what was done to Pernambuco's most renowned Communist.

Sixty-four-year-old former army sergeant Gregório Bezerra and eighty other militants originally tried to get weapons from the Miguel Arraes administration in 1962. Their goal was to help agricultural workers ward off expected blows from the landed elite. Later, as the golpe unfolded, Bezerra again asked Recife for guns. The aim this time was to paralyze sugar mills and factories in the southern part of the state. When the weapons failed to materialize, Bezerra began moving among safe houses in Recife and several outlying areas trying to decide what to do. Soon a group was chasing him. It was organized by sugar mill owner José Lopes de Siqueira Santos, who was well known for being behind the massacre of a number of defenseless rural workers. Falling into the hands of the Força Pública in the municipality of Cortês soon after the coup, Bezerra was violently taken from the police by Santos's capangas and delivered in chains to the 4th Army in the *pernambucano* capital.

His first interrogators, already becoming known for their torturing of political prisoners, were two lieutenant colonels, Hélio Ibiapina Lima of the IPM process in Pernambuco and Antônio Bandeira, chief of the intelligence section within the 4th Army. Lt. Col. Ibiapina remarked that Bezerra had been his physical education teacher at the military academy in Ceará. Ibiapina felt that Bezerra had been the best instructor of the subject at the school and said that he had been very popular with the students. Ibiapina, on the other hand, had not been popular with his colleagues in Ceará or later, when as a result of an investigation at the Rezende Military Academy he was fired from the faculty. He was let go for a reason that could not be disclosed, but may have had to do with the fact that Ibiapina was a religious fanatic.[55] "He thought Brazil could only be purified by a bloodbath and he devoted his energies and considerable power to eradicating the two great sins that he believed were threatening the country's soul: Communism and progressive Catholics, the latter [was in his view] a devil inspired stain that had contaminated the Church's body and was threatening Western Christian civilization."[56]

As soon as they had Bezerra in their hands, the two officers began showering him with insults: "Sergeant Gregório Bezerra! Bandit! Murdering coward! Traitor of the country and the army! You want to hand Brazil over to Soviet Russia! Thief! [But] now you're firmly in our grip and won't escape! This time you'll receive the punishment you deserve for your crimes against the nation since 1935! You're going to pay a high price! Criminal! You'll never again have the chance to betray the country [and make it] the servant of Moscow!"[57]

To defend himself against this onslaught, Bezerra began to speak but was stopped in midsentence by a solid blow to the face. His nose was bloodied and several teeth were knocked out. With his wrists bleeding from handcuffs that were too tight, he was then taken to the Cinco Pontas army fortress. After being questioned by General Justino Alves Bastos, he was turned over to one of the most fanatical torturers of the post-golpe period, Lieutenant Colonel Darci Ursmar Villocq Viana, head of Pernambuco's company of mechanized infantry.[58]

Villocq immediately set to work on Bezerra, beating him with an iron bar about the head. The colonel then had some of his men punch and kick the Communist in the stomach, intestines, and testicles. A physician who attempted to talk some sense into these uniformed torturers was himself smacked in the face. Villocq put Bezerra in a cell for a short time; then he returned with the iron bar for several more swings. At this juncture, the mechanized infantry commander used pornographic terms and descriptions as he attempted to force the metal rod into Bezerra's anus. Gregório squirmed enough to avoid this, but lost a few more teeth in the shuffle. Three sergeants then grabbed Bezerra and held him for their superior. Taking his victim by the hair, Villocq proceeded to drag the sixty-four-year-old through a vat of battery acid. The discomfort must have been excruciating. There was no time to recover, however, because a length of rope was next placed around Bezerra's neck, and he was made to walk across coarsely crushed gravel. Villocq got a laugh from those helping him when he explained that this was to "alleviate the pain in his feet."[59]

Finally, an army jeep pulled Gregório through the surrounding streets by the rope still chokingly in place. Several women—including Villocq's own wife—watching on the sidewalks cried openly. The little procession was filmed and later shown on evening television.[60] Villocq yanked on and cursed at Bezerra until they reached the camp's school for reserve officers. Then he invited the students, teachers, and other soldiers who were quickly gathering to "Lynch this bandit!"[61] When no one seemed so inclined, Villocq began to plead. "He's a monster! An agitator! He has a plan to set fire to the [neighborhood] . . . and burn up all of the children! Let's kill this outlaw! Come on! Hit him until he's dead!"[62]

Still, no one appeared willing to help the actual villain. Enough people, on the other hand, became so repulsed by what they were witnessing—Villocq even wanted to hang Bezerra in the public square—that phone calls were made to the commander of the 4th Army, the same Justino Alves Bastos. The callers apparently failed to realize that the general had questioned Bezerra and then turned him over to Villocq.

Following the golpe in the northeast, Gen. Alves "transformed himself into a [kind of] viceroy of a captaincy that extended from the Amazon to Bahia."[63] His word was law even for the likes of Villocq. For whatever reason, Alves had a change of heart and decided that an alive Bezerra was better than a dead Bezerra. An end to the torturing was ordered, and the prisoner was returned to his cell. Bezerra had a fractured skull in two places, broken and missing teeth, a deformed face full of hematomas, two swollen hip joints, and feet that looked like a mixture of hamburger and burnt skin. His cellmates picked off the blackened flesh so that he would have to be sent to the base hospital to save his life. Yet even with the medical help, at his advanced age, he never really got well again. Until his death in 1983, Bezerra suffered from insomnia; from prostate, heart, kidney, intestinal problems; and from ears that had been "telephoned" once too often. Citing a line from Jean-Paul Sartre's *Morts sans sépulture,* he later remarked, "In a world of such malice, life has no significance."[64]

More Fatalities in the Northeast

The 4th Army did not limit its attentions to Miguel Arraes, Francisco Julião, and Gregório Bezerra. Col. Bandeira's intelligence forces created a general climate of apprehension in Recife through the bugging of phones. Fear about whether it was safe to talk was well founded. Many of those brought in for questioning because of something that had been overheard came to know the persuasive talents of Ibiapina, Villocq, and two holdover torturers from the horrors of the Estado Novo of Getúlio Vargas, assistant policeman Álvaro da Costa Lima and ultimately Francisco de Assis Lima. These four men came to be known as "The Quartet of Death."[65]

Of all of the victims in the state, farm laborers suffered most. The propertied elite and their capangas showed agricultural workers and organizers what it meant to have spoken up while Jango was in office. The retributions and beatings took place over several months. Those who failed to commit suicide or turn up murdered were sent off to Recife to face the Quartet's music.[66] Costa Lima was described as "the most violent civilian torturer in Pernambuco."[67] He became so busy with his new duties that he hired Francisco de Assis Lima, who was known as "Chico Pinote" ("Chico Jump").

Francisco ("Chico" is the common nickname for Francisco in Portuguese) had been a police hit man and torturer during the Vargas dictatorship. At some stage in the Estado Novo, he worked for Pernambuco's secretary of security and the Polícia Civil chief, Malvino Reis Neto. One of the things he and the other torturers liked to do at the time was to soften up prisoners by cramming fifty captives into cells originally built to hold two inmates. In the mornings they were let out only if they were to be tortured. A crackdown by army general Manuel Rabelo Mendes stopped some of this for a while. During the interlude, however, numerous cadavers began to be discovered in Recife's outskirts. Curiously, their faces were always smashed in so as to make identification nearly impossible. Chico is also said to have forged a number of documents so that he could retire early. He did not want to work as a policeman for the administration of Cid Sampaio, the governor of Pernambuco before Miguel Arraes. Chico then obtained a position as a police chief in the south of the country and lasted in that capacity until the end of April 1964, when he was fired for irregularities.[68] He would later work with CENIMAR in Rio de Janeiro. But reunited again in the Recife jails of the Secretaria de Segurança Pública (or State Department of Public Safety), Costa Lima and Chico Pinote made a bitter team indeed.

In a scene reminiscent of Josef Mengle on the platform at Auschwitz, as each group of new detainees arrived, Costa Lima and Chico Pinote ordered all the workers, the Communists, the poor, and the blacks to be shoved to one side. Everybody else was taken to Pernambuco's Casa de Detenção. Conditions at the Detenção were abominable; some cells measured a mere 5' 7" × 2' 11" (1.70 m × 90 cm). After the group bound for the Detenção had left, Costa Lima turned his attention to the collection of singled-out prisoners. Cramped for space, he was probably not above an immediate summary execution or two to lighten the load.[69] The case of a single Trotskyite, Sônia Montarroyos, or "Tatiana," perhaps exemplifies what was waiting when Costa Lima and his staff took charge.[70]

Under age twenty-one when she was apprehended in a Recife suburb, Tatiana fell into police hands at the start of November 1964 on direct orders from Col. Ibiapina. She was taken to the offices of the Secretary for Public Security. There she spent the night listening to the whine of whips, the split second of silence, followed by the piercing shrieks of sufferers. Owing to some kind of mix-up, the next morning she walked out scot-free, through the front door. Taking cover at the home of friends in a working-class district, Tatiana was left alone on the third night after her escape. Perhaps it was the returning isolation, perhaps it was something else, but she began hearing the haunting voices from her hours in captivity. Hysterical, Tatiana rushed wildly into the streets and started screaming. The police were soon called and she was re-arrested.[71]

Brought once again to the Secretaria de Segurança Pública, Tatiana was questioned by several men, among whom were Capt. Bismarck Baracui Amancio Ramalho, Maj. Dynaldo Domingos de Souza, and Álvaro Costa Lima.[72] They wanted to know about the Trotskyites: who were the members, where they met, and what arms they had in their possession. When she refused to give them this information, Costa Lima burned her repeatedly with a cigar. Then her Uruguayan fiancé was led into the interrogation room and in his presence three men raped her. Sônia's boyfriend panicked while this was going on and told everything. His disclosures, however, did not stop the attack, nor did they win the couple's freedom. Later, after spitting in Costa Lima's face during the filming of a TV program, Tatiana had her head shaven as punishment. She was then hurried into the array of military and civilian confines in Recife's less-accessible outskirts.

Torture was evidently commonplace at many stops along the Recife *gulag*. The testimony of one witness about an ordinary criminal attests to this feature of life in Recife's jails.

> One of the times I was imprisoned at DOPS, I saw a common delinquent brought in from Caxangá. The individual's body [had been] eaten by a *virola*—a type of whip made from strips of inner tubes. His hands [were] extremely swollen balls after being hit with a *palmatória* [a holed wooden paddle or ferule]. The open wounds on his back descended in parallel trenches from his neck to his waist [leaving a] pallid, spongy flesh with withering edges. In all my experience as a leftist activist, with various police arrests, I never saw a case of such impressive torture. The victim was a good-looking, white youth who moaned, unabated, without saying

> anything. He could barely stand [as] the weight of his edematous hands kept his weary arms from being lifted.[73]

In the meantime, and some four stops later, Sônia landed at the army installations in Tijipió, where she was immediately stripped and placed nude into a 3' 3" square (99.5 cm^2) cage called "Little Fernando." The device was located in a basement or some other dark room. Sleeping proved impossible not only because of the position of her body—she was constantly bent over—but also due to the fact that a spotlight was turned on in front of her face every thirty minutes. She found herself anticipating each flash of light. Her food consisted of pieces of bread and half a cup of water twice a day. Sometimes, when her starvation rations were brought in, the guards would push her head into Little Fernando's bars. After about fifteen days, she was moved, still naked and still in Little Fernando, to a wooded area at the rear of the army base. She was left there at the mercy of the sun, rain, and insects. A soldier who took pity on her by giving her his raincoat was thrown in the stockade for four days.

Slowly, Tatiana began to have more hallucinations. She thought she was her own mother, that she was a prostitute, and that her daughter had died. One day, when told that her brother had been taken in, she replied that her mother was an only child. Finally she was transferred to the Tamarineira Mental Hospital, where she was subjected to shock treatments and repeatedly threatened with strangulation by one of the eight patients in her cell. Following a series of releases, one at the behest of liberationist archbishop Dom Hélder Câmara,[74] Sônia ended up fleeing Pernambuco for Rio de Janeiro, and ultimately Uruguay, when her preventive arrest was ordered one more time.

While Sônia Montarroyos needed psychiatric help, some healthy people were also sent to Recife's mental hospitals. A number of these political "patients" were tortured. A psychiatrist from Rio de Janeiro, Rosita Teixeira de Mendonça, decided to investigate the rumors of torture in Pernambuco's mental institutions. The fact that once she arrived in Recife, she was shadowed by the police, warned of imminent arrest, afraid of having an accident should she leave her hotel room, and rushed to take an early morning flight out of town all lend support to the validity of her suspicions. Perhaps Dr. Mendonça remembered that down in Rio de Janeiro, Filinto Müller had also been accused of having sent some torture victims to local mental hospitals back in the last half of the 1930s—regardless of their sanity or guilt.[75]

The destiny of other northeastern Brazilians three decades later was just as humiliating if not just as painful. Thousands were apprehended, according to one estimate.[76] As these numbers grew into another clean-up-the-cities campaign, workers, students, bums, the politically active, prostitutes, women and children, journalists, crooks, union officials, enemies of the powerful, and even a few priests were all swept up and freighted off to Villocq, to the 4th Army, to DOPS, or to the various police agencies. Some passed through the *buque,* or "Bunker," at the headquarters of the secretary for public security.[77] The term was a euphemism for several different cubicle-like containers. Each was murky, humid, and without bathing facilities. They ranged in size from one-person crypts to those a bit larger and packed with up to fifteen suspects. The toilet consisted of a simple hole in the floor. In the reeking air produced by this arrangement, individuals used their hands, which they then wiped on the walls in crude attempts at hygiene, as toilet paper. Prisoners of all stripes, from robbers to radicals, were mixed together in the buque.[78]

Ordinary offenders, it should be pointed out, were grateful for the presence of political prisoners since it meant that the attention of the guards was occasionally focused on other individuals. Some from this group of common lawbreakers, like many of their activist counterparts, were tortured, murdered, and subjected to situations that played havoc with the male mind-set. For instance, one run-of-the-mill wrongdoer recounted to a prisoner being held on political charges in Recife's bunker that he had been "forced by a known policeman and later federal legislator to place his mouth on the genital organs of a menstruating prostitute. He and ten other criminals were made to perform this depraved sexual act while the officer roared in laughter, insisting that the *spectacle* continue as he was in the throes of an orgasm."[79]

In Rio Grande do Sul

Recife was certainly not the only state where the patrons of power and authority permitted the use of torture or worse after April 1, 1964. There were beatings of newly arrested leftists and leftist suspects by the army in

Natal, plus kidnappings and an increase in the number of carcasses of rural workers being pecked at by vultures on the roads of Ceará, Goiás, Minas Gerais, Paraíba, São Paulo, and Rio Grande do Sul, if nowhere else.

Army colonel Washington Bermudez, the secretary for public security in the gaúcho state, ordered the torture and murder practiced by DOPS in 1966. The squad of torturers on the Ilha do Presídio (or Island of the Prison) adjacent to Porto Alegre was made up of DOPS agents like Itamar Fernandes de Sousa, José Morsch, [Luís Carlos?] Nunes, and the usual group of men who were addressed by only one of their names or by a synonym in front of the prisoners. In this latter assembly, there were Renato, Carbone, Osvaldo, Ivã, Ribeiro, Correia Lima, Sgt. Pedroso, and Régis. One witness, who spent fifty-nine days in this DOPS dungeon, reported that Régis was a sadist who consistently volunteered to mistreat the prisoners. Years later, at a congressional investigation into what happened to DOPS's archives in the state, Pedro Carlos Seeling, one of the best-known gaúcho DOPS agents—he was awarded the "Pacification medal" by his superiors—cried while testifying that DOPS operatives in Porto Alegre never tortured anyone during the military dictatorship. Besides Washington Bermudez, the army also detached others to Rio Grande do Sul. One of the most feared figures was Major Átila Rorsetzer. Rorsetzer liked the effects of electricity on those he questioned. He was likewise connected to army intelligence—CIEx (Centro de Informação do Exercito—Army Information Center)—and to SNI.[80]

And in the Cidade Maravilhosa

The men involved in blood-and-guts confessions in Recife said that they did what they did in order to avoid executing suspects. In Guanabara, Carlos Lacerda offered no such twisted logic, despite the temptation, and despite his ability to do so. No, at first the governor/journalist simply denied that such practices were taking place.[81] There was a higher power, though, which told the faithful that they were absolved from the straightjacket of the fifth commandment. Temporal adherents and, for that matter, anyone else who listened must have felt relieved when his holiness the archbishop of Rio de Janeiro, Dom Jaime de Barros Câmara, informed parishioners that to "to kill a Communist is like killing a thief; it is not a crime."[82]

The archbishop's remarks merely served to legitimize what was already occurring in larger Rio de Janeiro. As the first days of April unfolded, Gustavo Borges's men, competing police units, and the armed forces made many arrests. A few of those taken into custody were executed at once. Others mysteriously disappeared forever.[83] An unknowable number were tortured to death in the most extensive system of inflicting physical punishment in Brazil. Contrary to what went on in the rest of the country—up in Pernambuco the abuse of political prisoners died down temporarily around August—the mistreatment of prisoners in Guanabara began anew that November. This second upsurge was in response to a fictitious plot to blow up a train carrying Carlos Lacerda back to Rio de Janeiro.[84]

The torturing and some of the killing in Lacerda's state took place in several locations. In the jails of the air force, at the billets of the Army Police, in Niterói and São Gonçalo, in the offices of CENIMAR, and on the section of the top floor of the Central Police Station used by DOPS. There were at least two more reported suicides when suspects jumped to their deaths from this notorious edifice on the Rua da Relação.[85] Persons taken into custody by the air force were likely to be delivered to one of three aerodromes in Guanabara: Galeão, Afonsos, or Santa Cruz. Following their arrival, some were beaten or threatened with a bullet in the brain. Everyone was held incommunicado for weeks, and a few were even kept in lockups under a tank of water, the sides of which were dripping wet. At night the guards pounded on the walls so loudly and so often that sleep was nearly unachievable. Requests for drinking water were routinely ignored. There were no doubt other questionable practices employed by the air force, if not in Guanabara, then surely in São Paulo, and most assuredly in other parts of the country.[86]

Although they possessed the most ferocious of the Guanabara torturers, one Capt. Portela, the Army Police reacted with fists and electric shocks on a smaller scale in 1964 than any of the other repressive agencies in Guanabara or Rio de Janeiro. This was because CENIMAR and DOPS had been given the nod to carry the ball. Political prisoners, along with those suspected of having some grain of information, were funneled into Rio to these two organizations. Often shifting from one agency to the other, the torturers from each entity went to work on the captives.

The navy had several types of accommodations in the Rio de Janeiro vicinity to receive sympathizers of the former government. First, there were at least four ships: the naval transports *Barroso Pereira* and *Ari Parreiras,* the already-in-use *Raul Soares,* and the Coast Guard vessel *Princesa Leopoldina.* Both the *Custódio de Melo* and the *Raul Soares* went to Santos to pick up São Paulo's prisoners. The *Ari Parreiras* and the *Raul Soares* were used as containers for ordinary seamen, some of whom were banged about or placed in remote cells that were unusually cold. On the *Raul Soares,* new arrivals were moved to a cage near the boilers where temperatures reached 122°F (50°C). This was the cell referred to as "El Morocco." There was another called "Night and Day." It was noted for having cold water up to the knees at all times. Lastly, and for those putting up any kind of a problem, there was the "Casablanca." Full of prisoners or completely empty, all of the ship's feces was deposited in this cubicle. Higher-ranking former naval officers, as befitted their former status, did not have to go through this plebeian nonsense. They were housed aboard the *Princesa Leopoldina* in air-conditioned staterooms. Further amenities at their disposal included radios, televisions, a swimming pool, and complete meals. Censorship was imposed—kind of. They were allowed to read only two newspapers—the two biggest dailies in the city: *O Globo* and *Jornal do Brasil.*[87]

Across the water from downtown Rio de Janeiro there was CAM, the Naval Munitions Center, in Niterói. The man in charge of torture there was the commandant, Capt. Maurício Dantas Torres. Under his direction, and with bayonets pressed to their ribs, political prisoners were made to stand in front of one of the impassive inquiry commissions until they confessed. A tidy number of these admissions of guilt were made for crimes that never took place except in the minds of the commission's members.[88] Jayme Navas da Costa, as example, accompanied by machine-gun-wielding guards, was made to carry the human waste from an improvised latrine—by hand—to a hole he had dug at gunpoint. Then his head was shaved and under the threat of another beating he was forced to sign a fake confession. All those taken to the compound at CAM were kept from bathing or shaving. Prisoners slept on cold concrete floors. After a couple of months of this routine, and without explanation, Jayme was moved to a humid cell under a staircase which lacked running water or a toilet.[89] There was no medical attention.

The latrines did not have to be spur-of-the-moment arrangements to inflict the degree of drama suffered by Jayme Navas da Costa. At the Fernandes Viana detention complex on the Ilha das Flores (Island of

Flowers), the toilet for one group of political prisoners was another cubicle with a hole in the concrete floor called the *boca de boi* ("Mouth of the Bull"). A gutter, roughly 1' 8" (50.8 cm) deep, ran to the boca de boi. It was into this trough that excretion took place. Yet there was a second purpose. The trough was also used as the channel through which drinking water was delivered to the inmates by the guards.[90]

There was more than one commander of the appalling on Ilha das Flores. Captain José Clemente Monteiro Filho was in charge of such things until, perhaps, being replaced by Captain Vasconcellos. Or, instead of being transferred, it could well have been that Monteiro Filho was simply traveling to the main CENIMAR complex in Rio to assist in their torture sessions when needed. Individual tortures like Solimar certainly moved back and forth between the two facilities with ease. Perhaps Monteiro Filho did as well.

Assisting the captains in the discharge of their duties were several sailors such as Seaman Sergio and Petty Officer III Class Pinhol. A physician, José Lino Coutinho, also helped out. He was just two years out of medical school in 1970. Ilha das Flores had been used as a naval/governmental lockup for years prior to the golpe, but it had never before had a medical doctor who carried out torture. Located at the "White House," or House 29 on the island, the rooms used by Dr. Coutinho were said to be a "virtual laboratory of agony."[91]

In addition to Niterói's smaller branch of DOPS, and a sports complex pressed into use as a holding pen, there was the Neves Concentration Camp for the politically suspect in nearby São Gonçalo. It was outfitted with its very own torture chamber, called the *sala do estado* ("Government Room").[92] For real depravity, however, one could consider oneself blessed not to have been put through what went on across the bay at the Naval Ministry or over at the main DOPS jail in the center of the former Brazilian capital.

Part of the fifth floor of the Ministry of the Navy building on the Cais da Bandeira in the heart of Rio de Janeiro was occupied by CENIMAR. Following the golpe, as one detainee after another was brought in, each came face to face with the prominent sign on a wall in the manager's office that read: "We Are Not Joking!"[93] Across the hall in the director's office there was another notice that was apparently an attempt to build office morale. Contrasted with what was going on only a few rooms away, it went: "Join

Hands, and with Love, We Will Reconstruct Brazil." The existence of these signs was made known in the comments accompanying the floor plan of CENIMAR's headquarters and its annex over on Rua Primeiro de Março that first appeared in *Correio da Manhã.* Both locations were used to inflict pain. The initial reaction on the part of the minister of the navy was to sue "the paper for disclosing military secrets. He was forced to drop the project when it was pointed out to him that such a move would be a public confession of the truthfulness of the torture stories."[94]

Late at night, after the secretaries had gone home, the Portuguese and the Americans[95] helped CENIMAR and DOPS subelites dispense a different kind of passion. Prisoners were dragged up from the basement and tortured senseless by professionals from both the Brazilian political police and naval intelligence. Torturing at night stretched all the way back to at least the police of Artur Bernardes. During his administration many prisoners from the Central Police Station were taken during hours of darkness to the beaches of Leblon, then largely uninhabited, and battered around until the guards became exhausted.[96]

Once the military deposed Goulart, enforcers like João Macedo and the busy Clemente José Monteiro Filho carried out the dirty work. Benedito Darcy, Petestrello Feijó, João Boneschi, João Alfredo Boeck, Gil Pellegrini, Julio Bierrembach, Sérgio Alex Toledo, the indefatigable Francisco de Assis Lima "Chico Pinote," and Miguel de Ginestra were all likewise known to lend a hand—or mangle one on someone's body. Then there was the tireless Solimar.[97] Solimar's complete name was either Solimar Adilson Aragão or Solimar Moura Carneiro. But accomplice and victim alike knew him as "Dr. Cláudio" and by another more-to-the-point handle: "Dr. Bottle Opener."[98] This second name was given him because of "his skill in extracting the last bit of information from the most stubborn prisoner. Solimar was very small, but his energy was prodigious, . . . [so much so that he could have] used drugs."[99]

A few of the Bottle Opener's associates also used pseudonyms to protect their identities. The usual bunch of interrogators in 1964 included CENIMAR officials such as Capts. Alfredo and Adriano, as well as Fernando Paranhos and Lts. Xavier and Gama Lima.[100] Obviously, the roles of inquisitor and torturer were blurred in the heat of the moment. Not that all of the types of physical punishment these men could conjure up involved heat. Some did and some did not. There were the customary electric shocks that fried the body like a piece of bacon. But just as common were various threats—both to the prisoner and his family—beatings, stranglings, and the soap flakes in the eyes therapy. All of this usually transpired while the victim was handcuffed into a chair. At least one person was left in this position for twelve full days. Different individuals were jammed, still bound, into a cold 6' 7" × 9' 10" (2 m × 3 m) cell for extended periods, along with drunks and vagrants picked up off the streets. There is one report of eleven persons being shoehorned into this diminutive confine. Toilets and proper ventilation were dreamed-of luxuries.[101]

With Goulart's downfall, political prisoners and torturers began to move to and fro between the DOPS nerve center on the Rua da Relação and CENIMAR in an almost never-ending pageant. Besides the abrasive treatment, many of the prisoners at DOPS were constantly sick with colds. This was a product of being forced to drink water out of the same metal can. The cells used by Rio's idea police apparently came in various dimensions. They ranged in size from 5' 3" × 3' 11" (1.6 m × 1.2 m) to 5' 11" × 3' 11" (1.8 m × 1.2 m). All were holes, and all were without windows, light, or fresh air. Then there were the *maracanã,* the *aranha negra* ("Black Spider"), and the *buraco do ratão* ("Big Rat Hole").

Named after the world's largest soccer stadium, the maracanã was located on the third floor of their headquarters in the center of Rio de Janeiro. It was not built to house the two hundred thousand screaming sports fans of its famous namesake. A paltry fifteen was all that it could hold. But this was really no problem since sentries regularly compressed fifty prisoners into this nifty thimble. The DOPS version was not to be confused with a torture facility in the North Zone of the city also called maracanã. It was part of the police substation in Olaria referred to as the Invernada de Olaria ("Olaria Hibernation Corral").

Run at one time by Lincoln Monteiro, the Invernada de Olaria was located at Rua Paranapanema 76 in Olaria. Its formal jurisdiction stretched from Bonsucesso to Mangaratiba. In August 1966, there was a report that the four cells at the Invernada were actually all fumigated and had their toilets fixed. Local businessmen paid for these repairs, as well as for the painting of the Invernada's cells with what were termed "happy colors." What it was like before it became a place of such joy can only be imagined. A hint can be seen in the fact that the Invernada was long noted among the working-class residents of Rio's North Zone as a place where apprehended people went missing. Another reference mentions that the Invernada was famous not only for torturing but for the "'fabrication' of 'dangerous' bandits." Besides robbing prisoners, the police assigned to the Invernada were said to have made money by discreetly selling bullets, including dum-dum cartridges, to the public.[102]

The maracanã in downtown Rio received the largest number of post-golpe political criminals. DOPS's main location had another gory lockup on its third floor not far away. There, the aranha negra was constructed in the middle of the hallway. Its door was positioned so as to absorb heat from a metal skylight. At night the Black Spider was a living inferno. Worse still was the buraco do ratão. In the humble estimation of DOPS agents, there were hundreds of the furry little creatures in the buraco.[103]

Things went from bad to unbelievable at DOPS when Alberto Amazonas was made head jailer. He rapidly became known for being constantly drunk on duty. He and his assistant, João Macedo, occasionally raped female prisoners and took part in or supervised many of the torture sessions in a special room called the *seção trabalhista* ("Workers' Section," or, more accurately, the "PTB Section"). Amazonas increased the severity of what was dished out following the reported attempt on the life of train-riding Carlos Lacerda in November. For novelty's sake, Amazonas even had his guards spike the prisoners' coffee with laxatives. He then ordered that the communal toilets were to be used but twice a day at specified times.[104]

Giving drugs to those in custody was not the exclusive domain of DOPS operatives. Assorted prisoners in assorted lockups were pumped full of truth serum or given amphetamines in their food so that they would become nervously excited and unable to sleep. The concept was not just to torture but often to bring about some kind of drug-induced stupor and more cooperative subjects in the process. At least since the uprising of 1935, such methods had been popular with the Brazilian police and military. One of the revolutionaries from the November 1935 affair was an American, Victor Allen Barron. He was probably killed after being given too high a dose of insulin by Filinto Müller's police. They were trying to get Barron to cooperate through drug injections. He had a physical condition that made such shots lethal. One Brazilian internal medicine specialist commented that overdoses of insulin were a common method of police execution up through the 1960s when the authorities wanted to leave as little evidence as possible of foul play.[105]

Guanabara's secretary for public security, Gustavo Borges, repeatedly denied that anything illegal was being done to political prisoners. This included injections. But when an Angolan student, José Lima de Azevedo, was picked up and tortured, he succeeded in smuggling a letter out of prison attesting to his ill treatment. The information found its way into the hands of *Correio da Manhã* journalist Márcio Moreira Alves, who began publishing reports of torture in that paper on August 12, 1964. The first article accused Borges of having lied about the arrest, intermittent abuse, and continuing imprisonment of forty-five political prisoners. From then on, there was something about the persecution of detainees almost daily, well into November.[106]

Coming from the upper classes, Alves and the owner of the *Correio da Manhã,* Niomar Bittencourt, had been among those dancing in the streets after Goulart's fall. They were also among those who did an about-face, wholly or in part, when the generals issued the cold shower of things to come: AI-1. Federal congressman Nina Ribeiro, however, states that Bittencourt's sudden anti-government position was a result of the favors she expected but did not get once the military grabbed office. A UDN delegate, Ribeiro was linked to Carlos Lacerda and would ultimately become a member of ARENA, the administration's party. As Alves began filing his copy from Recife, Bittencourt was threatened back in Rio, but the stories continued. *Última Hora* published some material, *Jornal do Brasil* even less; *Correio da Manhã* was the only major daily to give wide coverage to the post-golpe torture.

When *Correio da Manhã* published in its September 13 issue a front-page account suggesting that torture had been the cause of the May 8 death of army sergeant Manuel Alves de Oliveira, Castelo Branco was forced to do something to save face. Sergeant Oliveira died from being given a too lethal shot of dope or from one too many electric shocks, or both.[107] Acting under pressure from hardline war minister Costa e Silva, Castelo Branco gave orders for his chief of the presidential military staff, General Ernesto Geisel, to take a personal look at military installations in São Paulo, Guanabara, Recife, Salvador, and on Fernando de Noronha.

Starting from Brasília, the inspection would have been a lot of work for anyone. Geisel flew first to Recife and then quickly to Fernando de Noronha. This part of his journey took less than twenty-four hours.[108] However, for Geisel it was enough time to pretend that he cared. When asked what he had turned up, he stated that no torture had taken place and that everything was fine.[109] Those in custody for political reasons, in his view, were content with their treatment. "They receive good food and are visited by their loved ones on days predetermined by the authorities." The general added that "While they are not ideal, prisoners do have the minimum conditions necessary for personal hygiene."[110]

Not even a day later, Geisel completed his inspection, Costa e Silva said that he was satisfied, and Castelo Branco declared the matter closed.[111] Quite the reverse had actually taken place. Political prisoners had been moved to quieter centers of detention, and torture died down for a while. Castelo Branco was evidently made aware of what really had transpired but in his complicity did nothing. No torturers were formally charged, there were no transfers, and there were no further inquires.[112]

Vive la France!

Down in Porto Alegre, individuals linked to Leonel Brizola felt the generals had gone too far. They wanted to wake up the country and the world to the evils they knew were transpiring. Apparently they felt international attention was necessary to underline their distress. The military's security service intercepted the plans of this group on or about October 6, 1964. Deemed material "from a highly competent source," it stated that an attempt would be made against the life of French president Charles de Gaulle during his visit to Brazil.[113]

Nothing happened one week later, however, when the French leader arrived for his three-day state visit. The Mutt and Jeff appearance of the two men standing side by side was striking. Castelo Branco was 5' 3" (1.6 m), with a nearly nonexistent neck, while de Gaulle reached 6' 5" (1.96 m) and sported his famous nose. About the only item remembered from the encounter was their barbed exchange over the issue of government-by-bayonet. This tête-à-tête began when de Gaulle asked Castelo Branco in an impolite tone, "I have always wanted to know what a South American dictator is and why history is so full of them?" The Brazilian's rapid-fire answer was perhaps not what his guest expected. "A South American dictator is a man," Castelo Branco answered, "not necessarily a military man like you and me, who finds it extremely agreeable to hold onto power and extremely disagreeable to let it go. I shall let go of power on March 15, 1967. And you, what plans do you have?"[114]

Higher Education

It is unknown if the French president knew about the torture that was taking place in Brazil or whether, if he did know, he assumed it was part and parcel of any dictatorship. Yet the regime of Castelo Branco should have been called to task for a number of policies beyond the treatment of political prisoners. Even before the military's first ruler unpacked his bags in the Alvorada, his colleagues had acted in full force against the country's universities. Brazil's centers of scholarship had become breeding grounds of leftist agitation, and the dictators were determined to purify them of this menace. In their attention to detail, they invaded and occupied the University of Brasília. In São Paulo the conquerors made arrests, fired suspect professors, and rewrote the curriculum. The University of São Paulo was also hit with soldiers, who trampled about there with such abandon that the Department of Philosophy was nearly destroyed. The University of Minas Gerais was simply relieved of its chancellor and put under direct military rule. In fact, IPMs were set up on all university campuses along with special summary committees of "safe" academicians and others to lead a series of cleansings of undesirables from the ranks of higher education.[115]

As for the UNE, it was declared illegal. Not only was the National Union of Students' headquarters gutted and its inhabitants ejected at gun point, but the structure remained closed until it was demolished in 1980. The space it occupied was turned into a dusty parking lot and remains to this day the only gap in the expensive Flamengo beachfront skyline.[116]

Labor

Unions and other associations were also subjected to a series of political purifications. Since many of the then-current labor laws were ones that had been borrowed from Fascist Italy during the Vargas years, the new rulers of Brazil needed only to apply selected provisions to once again weaken the position of the Brazilian worker. Goulart had not used these statutes because of his ideological orientation, but this was not the case with the incoming generals. They were probusiness, particularly international business, and decidedly anti-labor. When this new way of doing things was put into action, hundreds of leaders from urban unions and worker organizations were fired. Other groups had their elections tampered with or annulled altogether. In the rural sector, the Peasant Leagues were broken up, and many officials and members from their ranks were arrested as Communists or Communist supporters. Other rural groups were not forgotten either. By June 27, 1964, 90 percent of the rural unions established in 1963 and 1964 had been shut down.[117]

Not quite five months into their revolution, the generals addressed the second reason for Jango's downfall. To satisfy the American and international entrepreneurial communities, Goulart's Profits Remittance Law was almost entirely scrapped. Foreign firms could thenceforth take home all profits except those derived from activities in the luxury sector. To further convince the foreign investor, wages were put on the block—not the wages of the officer corps, but those of the middle- and lower-class worker. These latter Brazilians were going to the front in the battle against inflation. On July 14, 1964, it was the public employees' turn. A year later, on July 13, 1965, their brothers in the private sector were likewise facing an order that mathematically squeezed take-home pay a little tighter each month. Everything was combined with attractive tax breaks for the multinationals, plus other perks, such as making strikes virtually illegal. Ultimately, job security for most workers and the benefits of a mediocre social welfare system for others would be trashed to boot. The dictators believed that all of these measures were necessary medicine for economic growth.[118] Economic dependence would have been a better expression.

When the Danger Passed

Golbery do Couto e Silva got up off the floor of the apartment in which he was hiding in Marechal Hermes. Dusting himself off, he was given the ministerial post in his own intelligence creation, the SNI. With a stroke of the pen, Castelo Branco brought into being a monster that would become one of the most ubiquitous spy organizations in the world.[119] And who better to run it than Dr. Go, the Machiavellian from IPÊS who was one of the masterminds behind the fall of João Goulart?

Concentrating mainly in the area of domestic spying, the Serviço Nacional de Informações was created on June 13, 1964. Responsible only to the head of state, the new body was to gather and sift information related to all manner of things construed in any way as part of the Doctrine of National Security. One should read between the lines, however, in that the SNI's true goal was to prevent anyone from doing to the new government what it had just done to the country's last one. With a secret budget in U.S. dollars, which only the president knew about and could control, of up to $4 million per year, the SNI was no minor-league operation. It specialized in what was happening in the minds, words, and actions of all internal opponents, potential or actual. To this end, every national entity, state institution, university, or firm doing business with the government was to have at least one SNI contact on the staff. In many instances the agency placed its own operatives in the field. Otherwise it simply recruited persons from existing pools of employees. This final group of secret stool pigeons, or ASIs (Security and Information Advisors), had a familiar totalitarian ring to the way they went about their affairs. At the Biblioteca Nacional, for example, workers, along with those who used the facilities, never knew who the informer really was, or, for that matter, to whom they were really talking.[120]

Slowly there developed more storm clouds within the Castelo Branco moderate-line dictatorship. Just over five and a half weeks after the birth of the SNI, the nation's leader gave in to the wishes of his supporters in the federal legislature by agreeing to extend his mandate past the last day of his original term of office, January 31, 1966, to the March 15, 1967, date he would mention to de Gaulle.[121] In spite of this extended mandate, the representatives themselves became the focus of the first major vote of confidence of the Castelo Branco administration. Not the elected members of the Federal Congress and Senate but the governorships of eleven states. These regional leaders were to be chosen in contests scheduled for October 3, 1965. As the vote had not yet been removed from enfranchised citizens, the government was anxious to protect its image, insisting to hard-line confederates that handpicked UDN candidates could bring home rigged victories.

Once the campaign began in earnest, nationwide attention came to be centered on Guanabara and Minas Gerais as the true crucibles of the military's political clout. In these two states, opposition hopefuls were disqualified, one by one, until the government felt its men were up against sure losers. The only hitch in all of this was that the carioca and mineiro voters, along with those in Santa Catarina and Mato Grosso, required by law to cast their ballots or leave them blank, elected the wrong men to office. It was a clear manifestation of wide-ranging displeasure over the way things had been going since the golpe.

The hard-liners were livid at this defeat and ended up forcing Castelo Branco, behind the smokescreen of compromise, to side with them if he wanted to stay in office. One of the deals cut allowed the elections' winners to take office if the government could name the secretaries of public security in each state.[122]

> This was an astute move. The [generals] . . . were aware that the states' security or police forces would have been a significant political trump card in the hands of the opposition. Magalhães Pinto, as governor of Minas Gerais prior to the 1964 takeover, and Carlos Lacerda, as governor of Guanabara, had both used their police forces effectively to aid the military coup. The lesson was not lost on the military, which did not wish to see the same instrument turned against it. Therefore, the military police of the individual states were placed under the direct control of the army and commanded by a general. In this way both the state [Polícia Civil and Polícia Militar] . . . came to be controlled by the federal government in an increasingly centralized repressive apparatus.[123]

The judiciary and the legislative branches of government were also scheduled for drastic reductions in their exercise of power. Castelo Branco saw this coming and tried to get the lawmakers to vote in the desired changes. When they balked at their own demise, he issued the second of the Institutional Acts on October 27, 1965.[124]

More Diktat

AI-2 began with a number of rationalizations that had become standard fare. There were clichés about economic, political, and moral reforms to promote crass capitalism (i.e., progress), followed by observations that he country needed tranquility (i.e., order) to achieve these changes. Agitators and elements of the old system threatened these positivistic goals, the dictators claimed. For the generals, democracy was an institution of presupposed liberty, based on responsibility, which rejected the right to oppose the political choices made for the nation by them. Then again, the voters (i.e., agitators) had just selected four state governors from the opposition. Not only that, but the federal legislature (i.e., elements of the old system) had just refused to vote in amendments to turn their body into a rubber stamp. In the face of these two political outcomes, the military proceeded to oppose their own maxim on democracy by pronouncing the way things would be done in the future.

Getting to the heart of AI-2, the generals decreed in Article 2 that from then on, whenever the president wanted to amend the constitution, he need only a simple majority in Congress. Originally, a two-thirds vote had been required. Article 4 gave the chief executive sole responsibility in budgetary matters and in issues pertaining to the armed forces. In Article 5, debate on bills before either house was limited to forty-five days. At the end of that period, the legislation would pass to the other house. After a month and a half, if still not voted on, the proposal would become law. Bills from the president, however, were to be decided upon by joint sessions within thirty days or they would pass automatically.

Article 6 packed the Supreme Court from eleven to sixteen justices and allowed the president to appoint every federal judge. These national magistrates, in turn, were ordained to hear all political crimes except those that fell under the jurisdiction of the military or electoral courts. Breaches of national security were the kinds of catchall cases reserved for military tribunals. Article 8 stipulated that anyone from the ordinary man in the street all the way up to a state governor could be tried before the Supreme Military Court for this type of hard-to-define transgression. The generals removed the direct election of Brazil's presidents and vice presidents from the people in Article 9. The two chief executives were to be elected by a voice vote from an absolute majority of federal legislators. Article 13 gave the president the right to declare a state of siege without approval from the Chamber of Deputies or Senate.

All job tenure, security, and nontransfer guarantees were suspended with Article 14. This was specifically aimed at problem judges and military officers not yet touched by the cassações. In Article 15, the president's option of suspending the political rights of citizens for ten years, along with the removal of mandates from out-of-favor politicians, was extended. Federal and state representatives who were so disciplined were not to have their seats filled in special elections. The administration stipulated that a quorum would consist of whatever number of noncensured members was left. This clause was used as a threat, forcing opponents of any government measure to join the team and vote as the military dictated or risk being removed.

Censured individuals were dealt with in Article 16. Not only were they prohibited from anything political but also they could be told where to live and where they could go. Breakers of the law could be imprisoned for terms of three to twelve months. Those responsible for providing any type of media forum to reprimanded persons for dissemination of their views could be fined between 100,000 and 1,000,000 cruzeiros ($55 to $548).[125] A national stool-pigeon system was even established, whereby any Brazilian could turn in persons who showed they were at odds with the "Revolution."[126] In Article 18, all political parties were declared extinct. New parties were to be formed later under rigid guidelines. Article 19 removed the right of appeal from all citizens touched by AI-1 and AI-2. Finally, the last relevant article, number thirty-one, allowed the president to close the federal legislature, state assemblies, and local municipal councils at will.[127]

The new political entities mentioned in Article 18 were allowed to form after November 20, 1965. There would be two bodies: an effectively powerless opposition, the Movimento Democrático Brasileiro (Brazilian Democratic Movement), or MDB, and the government's own Aliança Renovadora Nacional (National Renovation Alliance), or ARENA. The former police chief of Rio de Janeiro, Filinto Müller, was soon put in charge of ARENA forces in the Senate. He would later become the national president of the party and—unbelievably—head of the Brazilian Human Rights Commission. Müller's selection for this last post is a good indication of the depths to which the dictators had sunk.[128]

There were two additional institutional acts during the Castelo Branco administration. AI-3, issued on February 5, 1966, stipulated that governors, like the president and vice president, would be elected by a majority show of hands in their respective state legislatures. The mayors of the state capitals were then to be appointed by the newly elected governors. The plan of the military was to put a stranglehold on the opposition MDB. There were more intimidations and cassações when this failed. Congress was even closed on October 20, 1966, for one month and then reassembled for two special sessions: one on December 12, 1966, and the other on January 24, 1967. The purpose of reconvening was to ramrod the authoritarian Constitution of 1967 down the throats of the lawmakers.[129]

Castelo Branco may have wanted to be remembered as a moderate, but he kept caving in to his hard-line colleagues. Before leaving office, he apparently did so again and signed two measures into law. The first laid the groundwork for the most extensive media gag since the Vargas dictatorship. The second was yet one more attempt to regulate just what it was that constituted an offense against national security.[130]

During his final months in power, Castelo Branco was unpopular. He had sold Brazil to the United States. Commencing with the fall of Goulart, the men in Washington, D.C., "furnished 67 percent of the $2.5 billion in foreign public funds made available to Brazil. Approximately $1 billion was supplied through the programs of USAID, $525 million in loans, $400 million in loans for specific projects, and $80 million in technical assistance. An additional $478 million was conceded through purchases and grants of foodstuffs, together with $136 million in loans from the Export-Import Bank. The Inter-American Development Bank and the World Bank authorized loans of $819 million during this period. The American government, furthermore, guaranteed roughly $200 million in new investments from its private sector."[131]

With all of the money came all of the experts. Besides the team from USAID—now even larger and stronger with support from more than twelve stateside universities—there were helpers from the U.S. Weather Bureau; Federal Aviation Agency; Department of Labor; Department of the Interior; Bureau of Land Management; Geological Survey; Bureau of Reclamation; Bureau of Commercial Fisheries; Bureau of Public Roads; Department of Health, Education, and Welfare; Department of Commerce; Inter-American Geodetic Survey; and Census Bureau.[132]

For the average Brazilian, in contrast, the North Americans failed to improve anything. Aside from the arbitrary measures of the government, a 20- to 25-percent increase in the cost of living was the most noticeable consequence. Ultimately, a number of protests took place by students, housewives, workers, and even the business community. The home of the American consul in Porto Alegre and the United States Information Service centers in Brasília and Belo Horizonte were all bombed. An attempt was made on the life of presidential candidate and war minister Costa e Silva at Guararapes Airport in Recife. Some one thousand arrests took place in Pernambuco immediately following the incident.

There were more bombings in Recife: one at the headquarters of the Union of Students of Pernambuco, the other at the USAID office. Explosions likewise went off at the home of Brazil's foreign minister and at the finance and war ministries.[133] The Brazilian Catholic Church even began to go against the dictatorship. All of these things were an indication of increasing discontent. Many Brazilians from the middle class on down were starting to understand, too late, that their nation and their wallets were being picked by foreign and domestic business interests; that their personal liberties were being slowly eroded to advance this effort; and that their army, navy, and air force were not about to go back to the barracks.

Following some internal bickering, those in favor of more force came out from the shadows and chose Brazil's next leader. The new head of state would be the old minister of war, General Arthur da Costa e Silva. Although both the moderates and the hard-liners had their roots in the tenente movement of the 1920s, the latter also believed much more in authoritarian and nationalistic approaches. This, in turn, led straight back to the days when many of these men, or their loved ones, were members or sympathizers of Plínio Salgado's stiff-armed fascist Green Shirts.[134]

Costa e Silva was seen at first as a kind of compromise between the moderates and the hard-liners. He came to office with pledges to "humanize the revolution," "govern for the people," "respect the legislature," and "re-establish accords with the working class."[135] But since the makeup of the new dictator's ministerial team was top-heavy with the military old school, Costa e Silva's true sympathies lay somewhere else—or at the very least were manipulated like those of his predecessor. The armed forces side of his cabinet was composed of four hard-line generals: Lima (Ministry of the Interior), Médici (SNI), Portela (Presidential Military Staff), and Souza e Mello (Ministry of the Air Force). There was also one hard-line admiral, Rademaker (Ministry of the Navy); one hard-line colonel, Cavalcanti (Ministry of Mines and Energy); one probable hard-line colonel in the reserve, Passarinho (Ministry of Labor); one colonel who was a protégé of Costa e Silva, Andreazza (Ministry of Transportation); one neutral general, Soares (Ministry of Trade and Industry); and but a single concession to the moderates, albeit an important one: General

Aurélio de Lyra Tavares, chosen to be the new minister of the army.[136] Two key civilians to obtain cabinet posts, what's more, only made the situation more precarious. First there was the incoming minister of justice, a former head of the University of São Paulo law school, Luís Antônio da Gama e Silva, who represented the extreme hard line.[137] Second, and complementing Gama e Silva, was the incoming minister of finance, Antônio Delfim Neto.

One of Castelo Branco's main objectives had been to get a grip on the inflation produced in the process of destabilizing the Goulart regime. There were three main avenues by which his finance and planning ministers attempted to do this: by tightening credit, by reducing the deficit, and by controlling wages in a manner that allowed for annual increases, but at levels that fell below the rate of inflation. This last item was the notorious *arrocho salarial* (salary squeeze). The difference between the two administrations in this area was that Delfim Neto, 1) increased credit to control inflation while 2) retaining the arrocho salarial as a continuous feature. As originally laid out, the slow strangulation of the Brazilian worker in this game of wage-increases-versus-inflation musical chairs was to end on July 13, 1968.[138] In one form or another, however, the arrocho salarial would last into the next century.

Chapter 4

The Battle Joined

The sporadic protests that marked the end of Castelo Branco's government began again, and in earnest, soon into Costa e Silva's term of office. There were five main centers of opposition: the Frente Ampla or Broad Front, labor, the Brazilian Catholic Church, performing artists, and the country's secondary school and university students. The activities of all of these people were at times intermeshed if not interrelated. Actions in one sector or several sectors of the opposition provoked reactions by the government, which in turn usually resulted in countermeasures in the same or entirely different areas. As a consequence of this interplay, what few moderate views the new administration held were pushed to the background. Brazil's second military leader thus had his excuse. To meet the challenge, he adopted an even more rigid stance than had Castelo Branco, as demanded by his own hard-line colleagues. The country would become polarized. Before Costa e Silva left power in 1969, it would be the generals versus the revolutionaries.

The Frente Ampla

The Frente Ampla was a Carlos Lacerda concoction designed to propel him into office in 1972 as the next president of Brazil. Formed officially on

October 28, 1966, the Broad Front was a reaction to Castelo Branco's extended term of office, mainly by Lacerda and the governor of Minas Gerais, Magalhães Pinto. One of the more humorous aspects of Lacerda's efforts in opposing Castelo Branco's added stay at the helm underlined once again the governor-publisher's obsession to become president. It occurred when a small, satirical publication, *Pif Paf,* printed two montage photographs of Lacerda and Castelo Branco as long-haired maidens fighting it out to become "Miss Alvorada." Lacerda was called "Miss Carlota Corwina," alluding to his nickname, "The Crow." Castelo Branco appeared as "Miss Castelinho," or Miss Little Castle, in a direct reference to his small size.[1] The dictator shut down the paper.

Former presidents Juscelino Kubitschek and João Goulart were visited by Lacerda while they were in exile and agreed to the alliance. The two ex-presidents' followers were also urged to join the Front. Leonel Brizola wanted to arrange a secret meeting with Lacerda, but this was turned down. Leonel sought a get-together without journalists in rural Uruguay before the then ex-governor could see Goulart in Montevideo. When Lacerda insisted on everything being done out in the open and in the Uruguayan capital, Brizola backed off, broke with Jango, and began a campaign assailing his brother-in-law for supporting the Frente Ampla. Lacerda, however, was not completely transparent. He is said to have secretly sent money to support ex-admiral Cândido Aragão, then exiled in Montevideo. When asked why he decided to aid the Frente Ampla, Goulart replied that at that moment it was the only alternative. Jânio Quadros and Miguel Arraes, both also in exile, were similarly approached but rejected lending their voices to the movement.[2] Even with Lacerda in the saddle, it was clearly the stated objectives of the Front that attracted Juscelino and Jango. These included a general amnesty, a new democratic constitution, the right for workers to strike, a true range of political parties, plus the direct elections of presidents, vice presidents, governors, and the mayors of state capitals.[3]

With such a platform, the Frente began to grow in size and influence. Headway was made in several quarters, from the general populace to opposition politicians. Two rallies were held in the hopes of rekindling the pre-golpe mass meetings. The largest crowd, in Paraná, reached a size of more than fifteen thousand persons. Lacerda likewise hit the university lecture circuit, blasting away at the military regime. He was undoubtedly throwing down the gauntlet, testing Costa e Silva's promise to humanize the revolution.

Such was a genuine threat to the blooming national security state—a state that spoke of democracy while being dead set against it. The Broad Front could have blossomed into a legitimate opposition party. The dictatorship, however, was determined to continue with its unopposed recasting of Brazil, and not long after a student protest that left one youngster dead, a nervous government decreed the Frente Ampla illegal on April 5, 1968.[4]

More Problems

Labor was another area making the dictators jumpy. As soon as Castelo Branco signed the arrocho salarial into law, the military lost the workers, not that they had been very fond of each other anyway since March 31, 1964. One of the original stumbling blocks between the two sides had been the 1943 Labor Code.[5] The corporatist approach of the Italian Fascists, contained in this document, was used by Vargas, ignored by Goulart, and reanimated by the soldier-autocrats to keep organized labor ineffective. Under Costa e Silva, a multitude of new sham unions and labor associations were cobbled together all over the country. Each new countrywide federation—some had as few as one hundred members—got one vote in national affairs right alongside the single vote cast by Brazil's older and immensely larger unions. The government also bought votes through obligatory union taxes, which were deducted from an employee's wages whether or not the individual was a member. These funds were then redistributed to worker syndicates to help pay for various social programs. Most of the established unions, large and small, were co-opted in this arrangement lest they lose the monies allocated to them. More and more, the military rulers came to use labor organizations—ideally a sentinel of employee interests—as mere social-welfare-dispensing utensils.

Even so, it was really with the arrocho salarial that things began to sour quickly. In 1965 there were scattered strikes, one of which was by machinists in Rio de Janeiro. Two years later, in 1967, other workers tried to win back real control of their union from pro-government incumbents in Contagem, Minas Gerais. The armed forces rewarded those involved in the attempted change by stepping in and barring the leading candidate—because he was from the opposition. One state over, however, events moved in a different direction.[6]

SO GOES SÃO PAULO

In the paulista suburb of Osasco, the dictators let one proletarian committee from an automobile-parts manufacturer become legal 1965. From that starting point, other factory workers in São Paulo began organizing themselves. In 1967 José Ibrahim even won the presidency of the Osasco machinists' union. Ibrahim had at one time been a follower of Lionel Brizola. The year after his election, he became a member of the Vanguarda Popular Revolutionária.[7] Many of Ibrahim's fellow workers formed a coalition with local students to support MDB candidates in Osasco municipal elections. When the MDB won, student and labor representatives were given positions in the new administration.

In 1968 events began first up in Pernambuco in January, when militants from the PCB and PCR (Partido Comunista Revolucionário—Revolutionary Communist Party) promoted a work stoppage by sugarcane cutters. Other leftists helped pull off the next strike, a big one, down in Minas Gerais. That April, between twelve and fifteen hundred employees at the Belgo Mineira Steel Works seized a number of hostages from the management and took control of their part of the factory. Fifteen to sixteen thousand laborers from other industries in the area soon joined the largest stoppage in the city of Contagem. Their combined efforts brought the region to a virtual standstill. They demanded an across-the-board pay hike of 25 percent in addition to the government's year-end adjustment of 17 percent. After a period of negotiations, the demonstrators agreed to end the affair and go back to work for a flat 10 percent.[8]

These events were followed by a rally in the center of São Paulo at the Praça da Sé on May 1. Turning out were eight hundred activists, along with twenty thousand workers from all over the heavily working-class suburbs south of the city center, the ABC paulista (Santo André, São Bernado do Campo, and São Caetano do Sul). The throng quickly lost its patience once officials tried to placate it with meaningless speeches. When Governor Roberto Costa de Abreu Sodré got to his feet for just that purpose, he was pelted with stones, corncobs, eggs, potatoes, pieces of metal, and hunks of wood. Sodré was slightly injured in the deluge. The power to the microphone was cut, and the governor was chased from the rostrum. Things turned uglier as the crowd partially burned the speaker's platform and nearly succeeded in sacking the offices of New York–based Citibank. Dodging all the projectiles, São Paulo DOPS agents likewise ran for cover with Sodré.

Soon they were back with a contingent of machine-gun-brandishing naval police to protect this single American business. Apparently without firm orders to open fire, the police merely stood around looking ferocious, and the crowd finally dispersed by itself.[9]

The hard-line rulers countered with their own moves just over six weeks later by declaring a 10-percent raise for all workers, wherever the increase was not more than one-third of a regional Minimum Salary. That was the good news. The bad news was that the arrocho salarial was officially made permanent,[10] and this was just the appetizer. The generals had decided to lie in wait for the next bit of blue-collar unrest. An example must be made.

The opportunity came in São Paulo that July, when José Ibrahim reluctantly agreed to rank-and-file pleas at COBRASMA, an Osasco railroad parts company. COBRASMA workers hoped to replicate the protest just resolved in Contagem. With Ibrahim's approval, a strike was called for 8:00 A.M. on Tuesday May 16, 1968. Factory buildings were occupied, and fifteen engineers plus thirty supervisors were taken prisoner. Workers at several nearby firms then walked out in sympathy actions. The call was for a 35 percent raise, two-year collective contracts, and wage adjustments every third month. This last demand would have essentially put a damper on the arrocho salarial, and Costa e Silva, together with his advisors, was not prepared to go along. Two days into the strike, a force of thirty mounted police, aided by soldiers in full battle dress and two armored vehicles, clanked into COBRASMA to begin taking control. It took them five days to secure the factories and union facilities. The strike itself went on for another two weeks. By that time there had been hundreds of firings, arrests, and new cases of torture. All the strike leaders, including Ibrahim, lost their jobs and were hauled before military courts. The police occupation lasted for months. Many of those deprived of livelihoods were not thought sufficiently subversive to be detained. Nonetheless, they had to move their families to distant cities because, guilty or not, they were blacklisted in the entire state.[11]

The Church

That two Catholic priests had been among those apprehended following the Osasco strike was no accident. Beginning with the Second Vatican

Council (1962–65), the Church started a painful rethinking of a number of its philosophical positions. As in so many important movements, some of the ultimate ramifications of this conference may not have been among the actual intentions of its participants. Such was the case with the burning question of social justice. Before the conclusion of Vatican II, its originator, Pope John XXIII, died, and the new spiritual leader, Pope Paul VI, began his papacy by laying great emphasis on this same social theme. Commencing with his first encyclical, *Ecclesiam* (August 6, 1964), and focusing his remarks later in *Populorum Progresso* (March 26, 1967), Paul VI's thinking was felt by the more conservative elements in the Church to be so radical that he was suspected of having come under the influence of Marxism. To be more exact, his holiness was only verbalizing the humanitarian intent inherited from the work begun by John XXIII.[12]

In Brazil, the early central personality who preached the new teaching was Dom Hélder Câmara. The progressive side to Câmara's social activism stretched back to the early 1950s, when the National Conference of Brazilian Bishops (Conferência Nacional dos Bispos do Brasil—CNBB) was founded largely because of his efforts. Just after the golpe, Dom Hélder was made archbishop of Olinda and Recife, and it was not long before he was at odds with Brazil's new secular rulers. Among other things, almost as soon as he took up residence in Pernambuco, he was charged with protecting three subversive priests. There were, of course, other reactionary clergymen besides the archbishop of Rio de Janeiro, Dom Jaime de Barros Câmara, who looked with alarm on attempts to liberalize the Church or protect its wayward priests. Some, like Dom Adherbal Franco Moraes, who became an undercover DOPS agent, even collaborated with the dictators.[13]

On March 31, 1966, the second anniversary of the coup, Hélder Câmara further irritated the military and his conservative colleagues by refusing to preside over a victory mass. Four months later, the archbishop became involved in another controversy. This time events grew out of two meetings held by a trio of Catholic action groups looking into the situation of workers in the northeast. Both laity and clergy attended the gatherings, and local bishops soon added their approval and their own comments to the conference's combined teachings.[14] In clearly understandable terms, the priests affirmed that mother Church had her arms open for everyone. Her job was to unite the people of God:

> By preference, the maternal concern of the Church must return to those who suffer, to those who don't earn [enough] bread for themselves and their families, . . . to those who appear condemned to the stagnation of inhumane living conditions.
>
> Together, we cry out to the authorities, and to businessmen, to use your energies and resources to create new sources of social progress. We deplore and condemn all injustices committed against workers. We recognize and proclaim that pleading for a higher standard of living for laborers is true evangelism, [which ultimately will] prepare the country for Christ and his doctrine.[15]

Since the vast majority of workers, particularly rural workingmen and -women, were among those most exploited in Brazil, the statement, signed first by Câmara and then by fourteen bishops, presented an important challenge to the authority of obstinate worldly leaders.

In post-golpe Brazil, the Church was divided into traditionalists, moderates, and progressives. The traditionalists supported that age-old system of domination, fatalism, and conspiracy with powerful civilians that had been the hallmark of their success ever since the Church arrived in Portuguese America at the start of the sixteenth century. The moderates adopted a wait-and-see attitude, content to ignore the teachings of *Populorum Progresso* until they needed them, such as when the actions of the government were shown to be empty promises. Progressives felt that such positions betrayed the real intent of Christ. This final group wanted change and generally felt empowered by the pronouncements of John XXIII and Paul VI to effect that change.[16]

As for Father Câmara, he was targeted by General Itiberê Gouveia do Amaral, the head of the 4th Army, as the dangerous leftist-leaning agitator who was behind the bishops' declaration of support. The general then prohibited the publication of the document. His act rallied a number of astonished moderates in different parts of the country to Dom Hélder's side. The issue was no longer a northeastern affair.[17]

As the conflict intensified, Archbishop Câmara became a persona non grata with the dictators. The Mar del Plata and Medellín Conferences (1966 and 1968) reaffirmed the position of the progressives and even baptized their views as "Liberationist Theology."[18] In knee-jerk fashion, for the rest of 1967 and on into the following year, priests and their lay assistants began to be arrested—some were even tortured. Dom Hélder's house came under automatic weapons fire in October 1968 and was "plastered with extremist slogans."[19] The following May, in a direct warning to the archbishop, one of his subordinates, Padre Antônio Henrique Pereira Neto, was kidnapped by Pernambucan Polícia Civil, tortured, and executed. Four agents of the local Polícia Civil, an ex-agent, and the then head of the Department of Investigations of the secretary for public security were pointed out as being responsible for the torture and death of Father Henrique. But twenty years later, the statute of limitations expired without anyone ever having been convicted of the crime. In spite of this, the priest's mother refused to accept the lack of justice. She became a lawyer and wrote letters demanding action to three military dictators (Costa e Silva, Médici, and Geisel), among others. Yet for all her efforts Dona Isaíras Pereira and several members of her family received only anonymous threats and warnings to shut up. There was an attempt made to kidnap another one of her children, and a different son was falsely imprisoned as part of this muzzling effort. This treatment of the clergy was justifiable to those in power.[20] As one observer put it, "Ever since the military coup all those engaged in organizing against the prevailing social order—in the fields, the mills, or the schools—have been prosecuted. Repression is the only democratic institution left in Brazil. It strikes everyone, making no distinction between motivations: for the police it doesn't matter if someone is promoting social awareness among peasants or *favelados* (slum dwellers) because of Marxist, Christian, or simply humanitarian belief. All are included within the vague and all-embracing definition of subversion and are equally punished."[21]

These episodes only increased the Brazilian Church's opposition to the dictatorship. There were renewed calls for agrarian reform, respect for human rights, and social justice. The crushing misery of the lower classes and the National Security Doctrine—which had become the National *Insecurity* Doctrine for the large majority of Brazilians—were common themes from pulpits across the country.[22] These sermons were "focused directly on the regime's economic and social strategy; and it was becoming increasingly difficult to dismiss all criticism as a reflection of subversive Marxism disloyal to the central and traditional teaching of the Church. Rather the contrary, as apologists and supporters of the regime now found themselves faced with the need, both at home and abroad, to explain how strategies which imposed these heavy burdens on the poor and weaker members of society could be squared with Christian teaching."[23]

The Arts

Various entertainers, too, were hounded as the military tightened the noose of censorship. Creative citizens had been under pressure ever since 1964. But four years on, plays such as *O rei da vela* and movies like *Terra em transe* were not tolerated or the public waiting in line to see them, along with the actors, writers, and producers, were threatened. Ultimately some performers were dishonored by the system. Roberto Carlos let Sérgio Fleury provide his security. Wilson Simonal was accused of becoming a snitch. Tom Jobin supported the dictators. Others simply packed their bags and got out. Among those leaving were Gilberto Gil and Caetano Veloso, who went to London in 1969. Elis Regina flew to Holland in 1971. Also departing were Geraldo Vandré and Chico Buarque. Army agents reported back to 1st Army headquarters in August 1967 that a group of Communist sympathizers had been put together to conduct psychological actions against the public through their protest music. The main individuals in this group were Elis Regina, Gilberto Gil, Nara Leão, Chico Buarque, Edu Lobo, and Geraldo Vandré. Regina had problems with her later career because she sang at a military function before leaving the country. Vandré was said to be an actual Communist, and his father, João Fonseca, an important Communist in Paraíba.[24]

CHICO BUARQUE

One of Brazil's most gifted singer/composers, Francisco "Chico" Buarque de Holanda, opened his first play, *Roda viva* (Life's Merry-Go-Round), in 1968 to shocked yet packed houses in Rio de Janeiro. Moving on to São Paulo, the production again wowed audiences with its corrosiveness, such as when a woman playing the mother of Jesus simulated sexual intercourse with her son. In another scene one of the actors urinated in an army helmet. Buarque used devices of this kind to capture the attention of his audiences at their most sensitive level of understanding. The actual plot dealt with a singer, Benedito Silva, trapped in the rat race of life, who sells his career to his guardian angel to win the admiration of young fans. His new manager (actually the devil) guarantees their veneration in return for 20 percent of the profits. Silva gains the aficionados all right, but ends up committing suicide when he runs out of new music to offer his public. The same scenario then starts all over with his widow.

While *Roda viva* was a sellout, there were protests from some of those present over the subversive nature of the dialogue, in addition to several of the more shocking scenes. Brazil's military was determined to create a group of unquestioning followers of their own artistic ideas. Freedom of expression in their theater was unwelcome, especially when it demeaned the armed forces. A conflict of ideas was about to happen.

On the night of July 17, thirty members of a right-wing paramilitary group, the CCC (Comando de Caça aos Comunistas—Communist-Chasing Commandos), directed by João Marcos Monteiro Flaquer and led by air force sergeant Roberto "Padre" Bento, invaded a rehearsal at São Paulo's Ruth Escobar Theater and began beating everyone up. It mattered little that the cast had asked for police protection two weeks earlier. That request was conveniently forgotten. So too were any charges that could have been brought against two of the attackers, who were caught red-handed by DOPS agents. Flávio Ettore, one of those captured, was on active duty in the Brazilian army. Roberto Bento later worked for the army's DOI-Codi executioners in São Paulo as an interrogator and jailer. The CCC felt that they had made such an impression at the Ruth Escobar that they later traveled to Rio and attacked the Mesbla Theater when *Cordélia Brasil* was playing. The Communist-Chasing Commandos were linked to the air force. They had civilian as well as military members.

A similar setup, MAC (Movimento Anticomunista—Anti-Communist Movement), had connections with the army and the CIA. Both of these far-right groups would customarily leave their initials, in large letters, painted on a wall following an incident. On other occasions, they would leave complete expressions like, "Have you killed a Commie Today?" "How many corpses to build a Cuba?" and "Prestes . . . should be strung up!" Additional right-fringe organizations vying for the limelight included the Anti-Communist Front, the Anti-Communist Vanguard, the Anti-Communist Group, the Brazilian Anti-Communist Action, and the New Homeland Phalanx. Many of these groups took turns assuming responsibility for the sending of warnings and threats, for assassinations, and for the bombings of newsstands suspected of selling subversive publications.[25]

Roda viva appeared next in Porto Alegre, but the reception there was about the same. First two kidnappings, then another thirty CCC adherents armed with pistols and steel-cored rubber hoses, headed by army Lt. Col. Ilus, met up with some of the performers and stage personnel outside their hotel. The results were predictable. Several entertainers wound up in the hospital with busted up faces or bullet wounds. The rest of the company left town by bus for São Paulo. Lt. Colonel Ilus joined a motorized infantry regiment in Porto Alegre in 1974. It was reported that captured revolutionaries were kept in barbarous conditions in the confines of his unit. The CCC hounded Chico Buarque for years.[26] In late 1979, they sent him a message that read in part, "the Communist Chasing Command wishes you, wretched Communist activist who dirties our country—a terrible Christmas and the realization that our final confrontation will take place in 1979."[27] The CCC customarily signed their communications with the slogan, "Save Brazil."[28]

THE HYMN

For many years people thought that Geraldo Vandré did not get off so lightly. They said he was arrested and tortured so badly that he developed severe mental problems—even that he was castrated—for writing the song "Para não dizer que não falei das flores" (Don't Say Later That I Didn't Speak of Flowers).[29] If he was not physically castrated, Geraldo was certainly mentally emasculated. Years later, long after the generals had left power, he would not touch the topic of what had happened. He refused or threatened to terminate interviews that in any way looked like they would probe into the horrendous suffering the dictators had caused him. In his own words, this 1968 melody was a composition about "the love of peace [combined with] the ever present need that man has for a better life."[30]

Vandré's hit was given a couple of shortened titles on the street: "Caminhando" (Marching) and "Sexta coluna" (Sixth Column).[31] A CENIMAR agent who witnessed the song's first performance by Vandré at Maracãnzinho in Rio, on September 29, 1968, said that it was a skillful synthesis, in the best aesthetic form, of the basic postulates of Marxism. But the thirty thousand civilians gathered there did not think so. They applauded for a full ten minutes. The following weekend, DOPS agents Claide Rodrigues dos Santos, Gil Batista Lemos, Teobaldo Lisboa, Hugo Correa de Matos, and Francisco d'Avila Filho arrested seven leftist students at an encore performance for passing out subversive leaflets praising Vandré and his song and condemning the dictators. "Para não dizer que não falei das flores" became a near alternative national anthem in the late '60s and '70s at antigovernment demonstrations. Interestingly, the tune's popularity never really died out. It is still played in clubs and over the radio once in a while to spellbound audiences. These days it can now and again be heard when workers, who are still paid less than they are worth, go out on strike.[32]

Higher Education

Several sectors of Brazil's student population were uncomfortable with the dictatorship right from the overthrow. Since the country's students had largely been behind the deposed president—some had tried to push Goulart farther to the left than he had wanted to go—they became "prime target[s] for post-coup repression."[33] Consequently, the UNE and the university system were quickly brought under control. The government then promulgated a measure in November 1964 that created puppetlike student organizations.[34] This only added fuel to the already smoldering fire. Students and their leftist allies reacted by making their objections known in underground publications and fliers, as well as through recurrent acts of graffiti and vandalism. The events in the central market in Porto Alegre in October 1964 were a good illustration.

In a report sent to Brasília, the SNI stated that a group of individuals, all of whom were captured, showered the market with pamphlets. One headline read, "Neither Gorillas, nor the Crow, All Power to the People!" Others proclaimed, "War on Unemployment!" and "Better Salaries for Workers!" Simple anti-dictatorship slogans were scrawled on some banknotes. On other banknotes was a larger composition beginning with the question, "Brazilians, did you know that our armed forces have the highest number of officers of the rank of general in the entire world? Well, be informed. We in Brazil have 4,000 marshals, generals, and admirals. Together, the country pays them Cr$4,000,000,000 [US$2,400,000] per month." It was a dubious assertion. What came next, however, made more sense to the man in the street: "These officers are the best smugglers of luxury cars, TVs, and refrigerators in the country!"[35]

Throughout Castelo Branco's reign there was unrest in the scholastic community. Many intellectuals were not necessarily on the left, but those of them who came from the middle class definitely felt more and more that the revolution had betrayed their interests. The government's economic policies were provoking thousands of bankruptcies everywhere one looked. The plain fact was that six months into the golpe Brazilians were digging deeper into their pockets for basic necessities, as the following prices indicate.[36]

	April 1, 1964	September 1, 1964	Percent Change
Sugar (kilo)	Cr$125	270	+116
Bread (loaf)	70	170	+143
Onions (kilo)	60	300	+400
Gasoline (liter)	47	84	+79

The most conspicuous villain was the arrocho salarial. It had done in the lower classes and was now taking a bite out of the middle class—nearly devouring it. So it was that the sons and daughters of this essential stratum slowly added their voices, in ever-larger numbers, to those of progressive students once the military's economic intentions became clear.

The first boos at the Federal University of Rio de Janeiro were heard in 1965. In a plebiscite there, students voted to keep their center of higher learning out of government hands. Additionally, they protested against AI-2.[37] Students returning for the new school year at the University of Brasília followed this up with anti–Castelo Branco demonstrations on the ninth of March. A number of arrests were made. Four days later several intellectuals launched a message to the nation, calling for the return of democratic liberties.

In March 1966 the police savagely attacked a street protest being held by first-year university students in Belo Horizonte. The next month the UNE met secretly and decided to hold demonstrations against the dictatorship in Brazil's main cities. Polícia Militar strong arms of the law then invaded the faculty of medicine at the Federal University of Rio de Janeiro. The scholars were made to run a "Polish Corridor" in order to leave the campus. This was a gauntlet formed by police leading to a paddy wagon.

Apprehended persons were made to scamper to the vehicle while sub-elites beat them viciously with billy clubs. The Polish Corridor was also routinely applied on arrival at the police station in reverse order: from the paddy wagon into the building. There were hundreds detained.[38]

That September the military was at it again in Rio de Janeiro. This time, they took 126 students into custody for taking to the streets with cries of "Down with the Dictatorship!" Soon new graffiti appeared, reading, "Down with the Gorillas!" "Viva the PC!" and "Remove the Man with No Neck!" In Belo Horizonte, at the faculty of law, police with batons at the ready likewise surrounded some 300 future lawyers. Farther south, in Porto Alegre, the clubs were pulled out again against impudent students protesting the latest round of arrests in Rio.[39]

After Costa e Silva took office in mid-March 1967, the student front was quiet for most of the rest of the year, almost as if the students wanted to see whether he would make good on his campaign promises. All of this changed in 1968 as the military's pledges were shown to lack substance. Over the following months, the nation's leader even came to be referred to as "Bosta e Silva" (Shit and Silva), but of course not to his face. Costa e Silva's alias was not limited to left-of-center students. He was similarly known by the extreme hard line within the military.[40] The American chargé d'affaires in Brasília, Philip Raine, reported back to the State Department that Costa e Silva was a "good natured dolt portrayed in jokes about him heard everywhere in Brazil."[41]

Part of the reason for the pointed nickname grew out of an altercation with university students over agreements stretching back to the previous decade. Beginning in the 1950s, various educational accords were discussed or signed with the United States. In 1965 a mixed commission of officials from the Ministry of Education and Culture (MEC) and USAID was formed to study improvements in Brazil's elitist learning system. When the MEC-USAID got around to proposals for higher education, which came out in May 9, 1967, they were far from what was needed. Critics argued that the plan attempted to implant a first-world American model in third-world Brazil (some derided this as creeping imperialism), that it emphasized the gradual privatization of all institutions (hence, the middle class would have to pay more to see its children educated), that the government wanted to subordinate higher education to the interests of industry, and that there was to be more significance placed on the hard sciences at the expense of the humanities. What the young people were calling for was totally different: more democratic universities with more students being given the chance to study, special primer courses before taking college-entrance examinations, better and cheaper food at student cafés, a student medical network, plus more student cooperatives and bookstores.[42]

THE CALABOUÇO

During the second Vargas administration, a student restaurant had been established as part of the UNE's setup in Rio. It was later transferred to the Ponta do Calabouço, close to Santo Dumont Airport, where it became known simply as the Calabouço, owing to the jail for slaves that once stood on the property. The youngsters who took their meals there were usually from local high schools. On the weekends, when university restaurants were closed, poorer college students got in line as well.

The year 1968 was tumultuous for several reasons. The Vietnam War was without question the most horrific catalyst. But so too were the widespread use of birth-control pills and the melancholic effects of *Humanae Vita.* Even civil-rights issues in the United States and the Soviet-led Warsaw Pact invasion of Czechoslovakia played a part. Students around the globe began protesting these and related topics beginning on January 11 in Franco's Spain. Other young people in an almost endless panorama of African, American, Asian, European, and Pacific nations soon followed. In Mexico, France, and the United States protests resulted in repressive acts of violence by local authorities. The most important difference between what unfolded in quite a few of these nations and what transpired in Brazil was that the glaring fact that the latter was run by a four-year-old military dictatorship hiding behind the cloak of an opaque democracy.[43]

Students who frequented the Calabouço and those from the nearby Federal University's Department of Philosophy had a long history of being involved in efforts to promote social change. They were among the carioca voices prodding Goulart to the left, and following his fall their meeting place had been occupied by troops from the air force base across the street. Some undergraduates joined an activist group started by Elinor Brito called Frente Unida dos Estudantes do Calabouço (FUEC—the United Front of Calabouço Students) that met in the facility. Closed for a few months by government order, the Calabouço eventually reopened, and agents from DOPS began installing themselves inside to keep a watchful eye on the comings and goings. Earlier the Calabouço had a small medical center that provided free services to students. There were a number of subsidized enterprises such as a shoe repair, laundry, and barbershop.[44] While the Calabouço was shut down, students had several get-togethers to discuss what to do. A CENIMAR spy attended one of the gatherings at the Ministry of Education. The individual sent the following report back to his/her superiors: "A representative of the student restaurant Calabouço also spoke, condemning the reopening for, in their opinion, ignoring the proposals of the students. A column of the building was covered with a characterization of a colossus with the inscription 'MEC-USAID is a dwarf being humbled by a giant.' Everyone there shouted in unison, 'Down with MEC-USAID!' "[45]

Once the Calabouço started up again, the clinic was gone and the food in the restaurant not only got worse but also was more expensive. It seemed that an organized effort was being made to make the students go elsewhere. With political police putting an evil eye on freedom of expression, those in government began to discuss demolishing the Calabouço as part of the attempt to clean up the area around the Museum of Modern Art, or MAM. A meeting of the International Monetary Fund was scheduled to take place in the museum in September 1967, and one just could not have a bunch of noisy students in a nearby building that is covered with embarrassing placards.

Potentially rambunctious undergraduates were not the only people the government wanted out of the area around MAM because of the IMF meeting. Likewise vanishing from the streets were some three thousand sundry eyesores: bums, pickpockets, perpetrators of assaults and robberies, burglars, prostitutes, and homosexuals. A number of preventive arrests, including that of Elinor Brito, were made. She was charged with antigovernment activities. The Calabouço was bulldozed on May 15, 1967, amid promises that another student center would be built. And it was, in part, because a new but incomplete edifice began limited service at the end of September—after the IMF meeting. Elinor Brito was later released.[46]

ÉDSON LUÍS

To keep the government on track, and despite a military injunction, student activists planned a series of protests to demand that work on the medical section, as well as on the new Calabouço's other amenities, be completed. In the middle of one of these demonstrations, on March 28, 1968, the police decided to storm the restaurant. It was a straightforward enough task. However, as with so many other seemingly small events in history, this single act unleashed an avalanche of repercussions. Maybe it was an accident, maybe it was not—but it was there for all to see. One of the attacking members of Guanabara's Polícia Militar, Aluísio Rapôso, shot and killed Édson Luís de Lima Souto, a poor high school student who had not taken part in any demonstration. He was just eating lunch.

Stunned, Édson's acquaintances and classmates carried his body to the MDB-controlled state legislature, where revered lawyer Heráclito Sobral Pinto, among others, tried to convince the throng to turn the corpse over to the authorities for an autopsy. On hearing this, some in the crowd protested that Luís's body would just disappear, as had so many others since the golpe. The students listened but ultimately refused, and a postmortem was performed on the spot. The only way Édson Luís's corpse would leave the building—without further bloodshed—was on its last journey, straight to the cemetery.[47]

As his funeral cortege passed out of the legislature the next day, March 29, 1968, over twenty thousand persons, including eighteen attentive DOPS agents, met in nearby Cinelândia under banners and shouts of "And If He Had Been Your Son?" "Power for the Old, Coffins for the Young," "They Murdered a Student," and "Does a Bullet Kill Hunger?" Shortly, some ten thousand or so of the protesters began to move in the direction of the São João Batista cemetery along with those carrying Édson's body. As the crowd passed what was left of the building in Flamengo that had housed the now-outlawed UNE, an American flag was burned. In a show of sympathy, a number of residents along the route hung black banners from their apartment windows. Others tossed flower petals or small bits of paper. The tropical sky darkened, threatening rain as if on cue, and some members of the procession began to light candles. As they reached the final resting place, there were shouts such as "Get Rid of the Assassins!" "Brazil, Your Children Are Dying for You!" and the ubiquitous "Down with the Fascist Dictatorship!" Three more editions of the Stars and Stripes were put to the torch. There had been nothing like it since the suicide of Getúlio Vargas.[48]

Rapôso denied that he or any of the twenty-five men under his command had fired a single shot. Disregarding this, reporters—through the testimony of a witness, a diagram, the autopsy report, and a close look at the scene of the crime—concluded that the police had indeed opened fire. CENIMAR contended that Elinor Brito was responsible for the death of Édson because as president of FUEC she had urged armed resistance by students against the police. Officials there implied that she should be arrested and stand trial. In the raid itself, the authorities confiscated numerous objects as evidence. Along with leftist literature were items that ranged from the quixotic—pamphlets urging that a university education should be for everyone—to the patriotic—approximately one hundred paper Brazilian flags—to the idiotic—a blank roll of Telex paper.[49]

Two days after the funeral, on March 31, Nilton do Nascimento Silva informed his superiors at DOPS that he had almost been lynched while trying to eat at the Calabouço. A student and not-so-secret DOPS plant, he had been confronted by those tired of seeing his face at the restaurant nearly every day since 1963, who were particularly incensed following the killing of Édson Luís. Nilton was bound, and a quick trial was in the process of being arranged. There were background chants of "Hang!" "Hang!" The words "Police" and "Down with the Dictatorship" were written on his face. He was shoved around and separated from both his student identification and his 6.35mm Baretta. Taking Nilton's service revolver was to be expected. His Calabouço card was probably confiscated because of the motto all such IDs carried on their backsides, a motto which was now an insult both to the memory of Édson Luís and to those opposed to the military's despotism: "Fight for a Better Brazil!" Only after a great effort did Nilton manage to get away before anything more serious happened.[50]

STUDENTS IN THE STREETS

Although students at most carioca universities and some at other locations in the state went on a limited strike, the youthful indignation was not restricted to Rio de Janeiro. Demonstrators took to the streets in many major cities. Protests in Belo Horizonte and Brasília each drew ten thousand participants; of these, the Federal District's dissenters proved to be the most violent. More than one MDB legislator took part in that march; the list even included the vice president of the Chamber of Deputies. Nonetheless, the police waded into the crowd and mercilessly attacked everyone. Six federal lawmakers were billy-clubbed, a student was shot in the thorax, twenty people were injured, and another seventy arrested. At this, the protesters not yet chased away began rioting. For the rest of the night crowds roamed the capital's boulevards, eventually burning part of the reviewing stand set up for the military to give itself an anniversary-of-the-golpe pat on the back.[51]

From March 29, the day of Édson Luís's burial, until the sacking of the U.S. Information Service offices in Fortaleza nearly two weeks later, Brazil would be ablaze with student demonstrations[52] and the police repression that came with them. There was at least one more student killed by the police. The victim was sixteen-year-old Ivo Vieira in Goiânia. He died when the Polícia Federal felt it their duty to enter the metropolitan cathedral in Goiânia and shoot up the consecrated structure while chasing another group of students. In the northeast, students in São Luís perhaps verbalized their outrage in the most direct manner of all. Several walls in the city were painted with slogans that read, "Brazil is the New Vietnam!"[53]

On the same day that Martin Luther King Jr. was gunned down in Memphis, another kind of tragedy unfolded in Rio de Janeiro. April 4, 1968, is remembered not only as the day on which one of America's finest was silenced, but in Brazil as the day the police went to work with horses, clubs and swords on twenty-five hundred persons attending a forbidden requiem mass for Édson Luís held in Rio's Candelária Church, where there was enough space for a mere six hundred worshipers to attend. From time to time the overflow crowd in the square outside looked up nervously to watch planes from the air force circling overhead. A lot of people were soon chased away by tear-gas-throwing-DOPS agents[54] lobbing canister after canister from their patrol cars. Mounted troops then galloped in and waited for the religious service to end. Some two thousand Polícia Militar and a few hundred naval riflemen supported the cavalry.

At the end of the service, those paying their respects, led by two padres, attempted to leave the house of God, but this proved to be no easy matter. The mourners were indiscriminately clubbed, bloodied by horses' hooves, and arrested in one of the dictatorship's gloomier public-relations episodes. A total of 680 persons had been jailed by the end of the day.[55] Smaller scenes took place after masses in Recife, Belo Horizonte, Porto Alegre, João Pessoa, Goiânia, and São Luís. The observance in Recife was led by Dom Hélder Câmara and held in secret—probably for good reason.[56]

Most of Brazil's students remained quiet for the rest of April and May. Aside from altercations, like those between police and student-machinist

José Campos Barreto, known as "Zequinha," who also took part in the Osasco, Contagem, and May Day in São Paulo affairs,[57] there was but one student/police altercation that turned violent. At the Federal University of Paraná on May 12, six students were injured in clashes with the authorities.

June would bring more heated clashes, many of which arose from student occupations of university buildings. One such event occurred on June 20, when the office of the president of the Federal University of Rio de Janeiro was taken over. The undergraduates wanted to discuss what they did not like about Brasília's educational policies, and they wanted those in charge to listen. They also demanded that the authorities release already imprisoned students. After nearly eight hours of talks, and with police and more tear-gas-bearing DOPS units in position, and Governor Negrão de Lima promising over and over that he would withdraw his forces, the undergraduates made a break for it. Some one hundred got away, but five times that many were apprehended, submitted to the customary Polish Corridor, and taken to the practice field of the Botafogo Soccer Club to be insulted and roughed up all over again. There was a report of policemen being high on what were probably amphetamines. Other students, juveniles, and anyone else who looked guilty were stopped at police roadblocks all over Praia Vermelha, Urca, and Botafogo. Even local buses were halted and their youth removed.

The number of prisoners at the sports complex swelled to approximately seven hundred by nightfall. Five hundred or so were made to stand facing a wall with their hands on their heads. The remaining two hundred, mainly university coeds, were forced to lie spread-eagled on the ground. The sentinels of the revolution then circulated among them, swearing at them and urinating on their bodies.[58]

This was the first time that the Polish Corridor was used at Rio's Federal University. At least until the latter part of the 1970s, the police sporadically raided carioca institutions of higher learning, rounding up professors and students pointed out to them by spies as being involved with outlawed movements or even for questioning governmental positions. At one of these forays, on June 20, 1968, again at the Federal University of Rio de Janeiro, the police clubbed everyone running the Polish Corridor. Out of sadism, female students were made special targets. When possible they were separated from other detainees before leaving the buildings and individually herded into adjoining rooms. Some were then raped or had billy clubs twisted into their vaginas. The really fortunate ones got away after being only groped and insulted. It seems highly unlikely that similar scenes of criminal behavior did not take place in other Brazilian states during the same period. A cousin of Anonymous-1 was one of the coeds violated in Rio de Janeiro. In her family's opinion, her later suicide was a result of the horrible ordeal she suffered.[59]

BLOODY FRIDAY AND THE MARCH OF THE 100,000

With vivid displays and descriptions punctuating the morning newspapers, the generals faced one of their most serious threats the following morning, Friday, June 21, 1968. If ever there was a point in the long years of military rule that resembled a popular uprising, "Bloody Friday," as it was dubbed, was it. For at least ten hours, in direct response to what had taken place that Thursday, cariocas of all ages—not just students—fought the Polícia Militar, the Polícia Federal, and those omnipresent agents from DOPS. The center of Rio de Janeiro has never seen anything like it before or since. The downtown area, for one short day, became a virtual battlefield.

There were two phases to Bloody Friday. The first, starting at 8 A.M., was largely student inspired. Stirred up by such charismatic young people as Vladimir Palmeira, Franklin Martins, and Elinor Brito, after some preliminary speeches at the Ministry of Education, the students headed to the U.S. consulate on Avenida Presidente Wilson. Not many rocks were thrown at the edifice before DOPS and the tear gas arrived, and, like the previous day, an unknown number of the men in uniform were reported to have been on stimulants. In their haste, agents may have handed a few of the tear-gas canisters to students. The number of tins of the choking gas falling into protesters' hands, however, was too small to make much of a difference. The demonstrators were driven off but regrouped and struck at the authorities elsewhere in the adjoining streets.

The second eruption, beginning around lunchtime (normally 1 P.M.), brought locals and some city workers into the action, and in some cases into the crossfire. Ordinary people who witnessed the earlier fracas from the windows of offices and scattered apartment complexes began to help the students after the pause for the noonday meal. At an agency of the Banco do Brasil located at Rua Araújo Porto Alegre 64, some employees began clapping in sympathy with the demonstrators. *Jornal do Brasil* photographers took their snapshots, and the ones who later could be identified by DOPS operatives were fired.

As the government's first offensive line charged, hidden inside patrol wagons or high up on the backs of horses, they ran into barricades and skyrockets and handfuls of marbles, the latter to trip up the horses. Wires were even stretched across the streets to knock the legs out from under the animals. Several floors above, sympathetic onlookers tossed a medley of objects out of open windows. Nearly anything that was not of significant personal value was aimed at the helmeted heads or exposed bodies of the police below. Besides the assorted bottles, ashtrays, and flowerpots, toilet seats, chairs, bricks, blocks of ice, and at least one typewriter all took the quick way down.

Infuriated, the constables began firing rounds up at the buildings. On Avenida Rio Branco, about two thousand persons erected more barricades. Rocks from the city's famous mosaic sidewalks, full Pepsi bottles, and pieces of wood were their only ammunition. Cries of "Liberty!" "More Money for Education!" and "End the Repression!" were their only words.

The forces of imposed law and order nonetheless slowly won control. Anyone caught out in the open was fair target for subelite truncheons. Businesses lining the thoroughfares were entered and their patrons and employees waylaid. Workers at a Caixa Econômica Federal that was under construction were arrested, accused of throwing stones. The combined downtown office of the newspapers *O Dia* and *A Notícia* was busted into, and numerous persons on several different floors were taken into custody. As the police left the building they let off a tear-gas canister just to say good-bye. The nation's leading library, Biblioteca Nacional, was desecrated and also doused with the eye-burning fumes. The director of the repository of written learning rushed into the street to protest, only to meet with abuse from the political police. Helicopters floated over it all, scouting the crowds. The crew on one of these machines had the job—no doubt left out of the tales such men tell their grandchildren—of dropping on the protesters a chemical that opened up ugly wounds on exposed skin within a few moments.

By 8 P.M. that evening the war had ended. The hospitals reported that at least twenty-eight protesters were dead (three according to the official version) and hundreds more injured. Estimates put the number of arrests at one thousand; most of those detained were nonstudents. As for the other side, a falling brick killed one member of the Polícia Militar, Nelson Barros; another thirty-five got banged up; and ten patrol wagons were incinerated.[60] The next Wednesday, June 26, the March of the 100,000 took place in the former national capital.

Disgusted by what they had seen and read, a group of students, artists, journalists, and intellectuals put the protest together. Due to a growing awareness of the increasingly middle-class character of many of these events, few if any persons of noticeable African heritage or blue-collar workers participated. Perhaps even more interesting was the fact that the police let the whole thing come off without gassing or clubbing anyone. Costa e Silva wanted people to think he was a reasonable man. He, or those close to him, was behind the orders to lay off. A presidential interview was even arranged with some of the demonstration's leaders. When the face-to-face encounter took place, however, Costa e Silva abruptly ended the meeting over what he felt was disrespect. This was probably his reaction to a pointed question from one of the students, twenty-three-year-old Marcos Medeiros: "Listen here, Professor. I want to know the following: are you, Sir, going to or not going to release our [student] colleagues?"[61] The nation's leading military man failed to respond directly, but his progovernment allies were not of a like mind. They held a counter-rally in Rio two days later, on July 4, to try to reaffirm support for the repression. Anything short of another one hundred thousand would be seen as a failure—which it was—only half as many, some fifty thousand demonstrators, showed up.

Student clashes with the police over the government's educational policies, worker clashes with the police over the administration's wage policies, and kidnappings by the police and by right-wing elements for no reason aside from promoting fear became part of daily life for the rest of 1968. Bombings were carried out more and more in the second half of the year. The government attributed all of the violence to groups on the Left. But Col. Helvécio Silveira Leite of the SNI admitted, nearly twenty years later, that many of the explosions were really the work of the army.[62]

On June 24, DOPS in São Paulo telephoned DOPS in Rio to say that homemade explosives had already detonated at the French consulate, the offices of the secretary of education, Citibank, the newspaper *O Estado de São Paulo,* and the army's pharmacy and that an official car from the state of Guanabara had been torched. In Rio the first explosion was directed against the champions of free speech over at the Brazilian Press Association on July 22. Further actions, like the police invasion of the University of Brasília on August 29, provided another quarrel that led on December 13 to a hard-line revolution within the revolution. Originally, sparks flew in the capital when the Brasília chief of police orchestrated a provocation. Under his command a hundred DOPS agents, protected by two hundred Polícia Militar, entered the university's grounds to search for young people wanted for questioning. About five hundred students resisted. There was a twenty-minute conflict, followed by a capitulation and massive beatings. Just as thoroughly roughed up as the protesting students were several legislators who had the bad luck to be on the campus either by coincidence, or because they sided with the students, or because they were attempting to rescue their sons and daughters.[63]

The Lysistrata Speech

By September 3, Márcio Moreira Alves, now a federal deputy, could wait no longer. Fed up with bloodletting in the modernistic city, he rose from his seat in the House to speak out once more. Together with some forty members of the opposition, Moreira Alves had been lawfully harassing the administration's record on human rights. His comments had already covered police brutality, the torture of political prisoners, and the invasion of the University of Brasília. Elected as the MDP representative from the state of Guanabara, Moreira Alves favored a kind of oratory that was not what the military elite wanted to hear. Their mistake was in gagging the deputy too slowly. Simply putting a bullet through his brain on some darkened street would have better served their purposes. By failing to do so, the generals left themselves open for one of the most bittersweet sucker punches of their years in power.

In his remarks, called the "Lysistrata Speech" after the ancient Greek satirical comedy written by Aristophanes, Moreira Alves did not mention the real inspiration for his comments. Too few of the generals had ever experienced the wonders of an education in the classics. No need to go over their heads. Instead he chose something he knew they'd comprehend with ease. The Emboabas conflict in early eighteenth-century Minas Gerais was spooned up as the source of his discourse. In Alves's view, individuals from all walks of life, and in particular Brazilian mothers, were tired of the abusive violence by persons whose job it was to protect them. He therefore called on the public to boycott the annual holiday on which the armed forces paraded around with puffed up chests—National Independence Day, September 7. Once the horn blowing was over, civilians were told to keep up the pressure by giving soldiers the silent treatment. Hitting soldiers where it hurt most, in their libidos, he further urged "those young ladies who dance with cadets or who have a relationship with young officers to give the military the cold shoulder. Today what Brazil needs is for the women of 1968 to repeat what paulista women in the Emboabas War did. Refuse to open your doors to those who belittle the nation."[64]

No bad language was used. The word *sex* was never mentioned, but the meaning was clear enough. If they were with men in the armed forces, Brazilian women across the country were to put on a chastity belt until the violence ended. Moreira Alves later said that his remarks were not serious. Maybe, but the hard line thought otherwise. If the call to ignore the most military of Brazilian holidays did not galvanize the military against the opposition, the possibility of having sex withheld did. Copies of Alves's speech were reprinted by the hundreds and posted in even the most remote of bases. The military ministers then initiated a movement to lift his parliamentary immunity so that he could be tried for "offending the honor of the armed forces." Once they ended Moreira Alves's freedom of expression, they felt they could move on to deal with anyone else in the legislature who made trouble. Censorship would wind up being all the more complete.[65]

New Atrocities

Aside from the kidnappings, right-wing political murders, strikes, and student demonstrations, the month of October produced three fresh incidents on consecutive days. The last of these events, occurring on the third, was the bullying of the actors in the Porto Alegre version of *Roda viva.* Two days earlier, MDB deputy, Maurílio Ferreira Lima denounced PARASAR. The air force's Parachute, Safety, and Rescue Unit (Páraquedistas de Salvamento Aéro Resgate, or PARASAR), had been selected to spearhead the military's efforts at using terrorism against political opponents, especially the Communists. In that vein, select PARASAR officers met in a closed meeting on April 4 to plan the abduction of student and opposition political leaders. Among the targets were Carlos Lacerda, ex-presidents Jânio Quadros and Juscelino Kubitschek, Archbishop Dom Hélder Câmara, and General Olympio Mourão Filho, who had grown irritatingly discontent with the dictatorship. In all, forty individuals were to be grabbed and flown, or even freighted, some twenty-five miles off shore, and tossed in the ocean.

The PARASAR meeting brought forth other projects too. There were to be assassinations at Rio's branch of Sears, Citibank, and at the American Consulate. The Rio de Janeiro gas meter job was another PARASAR innovation. According to the plan put forth by air force General João Paulo Burnier, the huge gas repository, near the main bus terminal in Rio, was to be blown up during the evening rush hour. At the same moment a dam providing electricity to the city was to be dynamited. The combined death toll might well have been more than a hundred thousand people, and it all was to be blamed on the Communists. But thanks to the persuasive efforts of a single man at the April 4 discussions, Capt. Sérgio Carvalho "O Sérgio Macaco" ("Sérgio Monkey"), these tragedies never took place.

On the same day as the PARASAR meeting, other members of the unit were at the banned requiem mass for Édson Luís. Their assignment was to spot anyone throwing things from the windows of the nearby high-rises at the police. They then had the authority to enter the structure, find the guilty party, and kill them on the spot. It is not known if PARASAR ever carried out any executions at that time. Capt. Carvalho was later booted out of the air force over a squabble with Burnier. Gen. Burnier had been the leader of the short-lived Aragarças Revolt in 1959. He would go on to contribute his talents to CISA (Centro de Informações e Segurança da Aeronáutica —Air Force Intelligence and Security Center). In fact, CISA was the air force's intelligence and torture unit where Burnier personally asphyxiated the Brazilian-American, Stuart Edgar Angel, to death in 1971. The general secured Angel by the hair, holding his head in position, after the tied victim had a Jeep's exhaust pipe forced into his mouth.[66]

The day following the PARASAR unmasking, on October 2, as troops in Mexico City were getting ready to shoot to pieces hundreds of persons in the Plaza de las Tres Culturas, students from two rival *paulistano* universities went for each other's throats. The squabble involved the Philosophy Department at the University of São Paulo, who largely represented the interests of the idealistic Left, and nearby Mackenzie University, a bastion of the Right. Both schools occupy part of the same street, Rua Maria Antônia, in the Consolação section of downtown São Paulo. DOPS and the CCC had taken flying runs by the University of São Paulo at various times, opening up with machine guns on the front of the main building as they sped past.[67] Mackenzie students added rocks and bottles to the authorities' bullets.

Tensions continued to run high between the two ivory towers and fighting began in earnest at 10:30 P.M., when the Mackenzie side again started throwing stones and even some rotten eggs at high school and USP students on Rua Maria Antônia. The people at Mackenzie were incensed over efforts by their USP counterparts to solicit money on their common street for the upcoming congress of the illegal National Union of Students. The first skirmish lasted but a few hours before the police showed up. The next day, however, they were at it again with gusto. Mackenzie's students—the first in the country to support the golpe—were out in force, lobbing stones, tear gas, skyrockets, and projectiles from slingshots, along with acid, lime, ammonia, and who knows what else in plastic sack bombs. Over five hundred Molotov cocktails took to the air with a University of São Paulo destination. Pistols, rifles, and even a machine gun rounded out the arsenal of the conservative university's budding intellectuals. Slightly outmanned, and definitely outgunned, the USP philosophy majors hurled screams of "Fascists!" together with rocks, small missiles, and flaming cocktails back across the street.

At the end of the second day, the authorities managed to gain the upper hand, aided by the CCC, DOPS, FAC (Frente Anti Comunista—Anti-Communist Front), the young minds from Mackenzie, plus an elite group from the paulistano Força Pública named ROTA (Rondas Ostensivas Tobias de Aguiar—the Tobias de Aguiar Proactive Patrol). ROTA would go on to become one of the most active death squads operating in the metropolitan São Paulo region. Antônio Erasmo Dias, the Secretary for Public Security in São Paulo, personally led the combined operation. Miraculously, there had been but a single fatality, second-year USP student José Guimarães. Three persons received bullet wounds. Many others were injured. Five official cars were destroyed by fire, and no less than forty-one persons, including ten women and six journalists, were arrested.[68]

Murundu-Ibiúna

Not only were University of São Paulo undergraduates on a campaign to further the forbidden National Union of Students, they were against the military dictatorship, for socialism and the sexual revolution. Morality was a big issue among those in control of Brazilian universities well into the sixties. In 1968, not only were males expected to be properly attired (i.e., coat and tie), they were separated from female students in all living, study, and leisure-time activities at some schools. At least one center of higher learning kept students segregated by sex even in the lecture halls. Virginity for female students, as one might expect, was also one of the most touted items. The police unvaryingly tried to convince parents that daughters who became interested in antigovernment politics would be taking birth control pills within a few days. By and large, Mackenzie and USP students were split on these and other issues. Then suddenly, the progressive students lost much of their leadership.[69]

The unexpected blow came at Murundu, a small farm near the village of Ibiúna, itself not far from the western city limits of São Paulo, on October 12. The event was the thirtieth national congress of the outlawed UNE. Its clandestine directors decided on the Murundu site over two other possible locations because of its relative remoteness. It was felt that the isolation would produce a freer interchange of ideas by the participants. We will never know if this would have worked since the authorities were soon on to what was about to happen. They came by this information through the badgering of student prisoners and due to a few well-placed dedoduros. Another tip found its way to the police because there was a problem in providing the large number of people in attendance with food. Guesses, made from photographs, as to the number of students at Murundu range from 750 to 1,600. When the provisions ran out, selected delegates trekked down rain-muddied lanes to Ibiúna, then a community of a few thousand. With their hefty purchases of foodstuffs the strangers caused more than one eyebrow to rise and more than one tongue to wag.

Early on, the government's security forces had generally been able to infiltrate the student movement. This had been done primarily through telephone taps. Later, there were student moles like Saulo Garroux, who is said to have kept DOPS abreast of Communists he knew among the students in São Paulo and other places. There were also plants among the guerrilla warfare instructors in Cuba. These individuals, via the CIA and/or Brazilian army intelligence, informed local authorities which Brazilian students were taking courses in Cuba. On their return home, the suspect intellectuals were seized and tortured for information.[70]

Notwithstanding the spies, it was perhaps the disheveled appearance of the young people entering Ibiúna that led the authorities to nearly misread what was taking place. When a sizeable Força Pública contingent, supported by a delegation from DOPS, moved in on the farm not long after 7 A.M., they expected to do battle with an encampment of leftist guerrillas.[71] They found only 102 passive students and five reporters, all too indecisive to really react or try to flee en mass. The rest had left early or gotten away.[72] UNE's leadership had been made aware of the impending raid but felt it was hours off. Both sides were thus stunned by what unfolded. The Brazilian student movement as represented by the UNE, and unarmed protests in general, suffered a crushing defeat at Ibiúna. All of the important student leaders in Brazil were captured in this single swoop, marched back to a paved highway, and trucked off to São Paulo in assorted vehicles. Some, like José Dirceu, stayed in custody under the watchful eyes of DOPS at its headquarters near Largo General Osório. Many of the rest were merely booked and photographed before being let go. Their police records would come back to haunt them once things really got hot in Brazil on December 13.[73]

The Man Who Would Not Shut Up

The move to muzzle Márcio Moreira Alves proceeded through the bureaucratic jungle of Brasília at a cumbersome pace. By early December the petition to lift his right to say anything he wanted on the floor of the Chamber of Deputies had been considered by his peers on the judiciary committee but gone unanswered. In such cases, the rules called for measures to be brought before a joint session of the legislature for a vote. Though as the day of reckoning neared, it seemed apparent that the dictators were relying too much on the assumption that ARENA members would cast their ballots for the government's proposal. For their part, representatives on both sides of the aisle feared, rightly, that once Alves was stopped, no one in either party would be safe. The administration should have used more arm-twisting, along with a careful and descriptive explanation of what it might or could do to any legislator, beyond having his mandate canceled, should the vote go against it. When the yeas and nays were finally tallied, much to the displeasure of the generals, a sufficient number of ARENA politicians had voted with the MDB to soundly defeat the motion 216 to 141. There were 24 abstentions plus 12 blank ballots.[74]

Ato Institucional No. 5

The men in gold braid were caught off balance. Their reaction was to immediately implement the extreme hard-line approach they had kept under wraps since July.[75] On the day after the ill-fated vote, Institutional Act No. 5, or AI-5, was rolled out in order to heed "the demands for a political and judicial system which safeguards authentic democratic order premised on liberty and respect for human dignity." It was the darkest day of the dictatorship: December 13, 1968.[76]

Article 1 decreed that the Constitution of 1967 would be retained except as modified by AI-5. Article 2 stated that the president alone had the right to recess and convene the National Congress, legislative assemblies, and all municipal councils. Members of these bodies would receive only their base pay during periods of recess. Article 3 announced that the president had the power to intervene in any state or municipality at will and to nominate all of the governors and mayors of such entities. Article 4 gave the president the authority to suspend the political rights of any citizen for up to ten years. He could also cancel the term of office of elected federal, state, and municipal officials. Individuals losing their mandates were not to be replaced. The aim again was to remove uncooperative MDB politicians, and even some ARENA renegades, thereby stacking the deck in favor of the government party's faithful. A majority of each federal, state, or local legislature would be made up of approved representatives. Articles 5 and 6 allowed the administration to prevent any obstinate member of the judiciary and any public functionary from holding a nontransferable lifetime position. Persons who had their political rights lifted could not participate in any kind of political activities. When necessary, the government could spy on anyone, prohibit individuals from frequenting specific places, and force a person to reside in a location chosen by the authorities. Other restrictions could be implemented at the government's discretion. Last, the president could fire, forcibly retire, or otherwise remove any employee of the public sector, armed forces, or Polícia Militar.

Article 7 provided the president with the sole authority to declare a state of siege and to decide how long it would be in effect. Article 8 authorized the confiscation of personal property by the state of anyone shown to have enriched themselves illicitly. In cases where an individual later proved his or her innocence, their property was to be returned. Article 9 gave the president the power to declare additional acts and decrees in defense of the government. He could also, according to this same article, limit the right of peaceful assembly, in addition to censoring all mail and public diversions. Article 10 suspended *habeas corpus* in political, national security, and economic cases. All appeals to judicial bodies over the application and effect of AI-5 were forbidden in Article 11. Unlike AI-1 and AI-2, Institutional Act 5 had no time limit. With his counterfeit show of legitimacy spelled out, Costa e Silva next issued Complementary Act No. 38, which shut down the federal legislature.[77]

The intent of AI-5 soon became clear. Opponents of Costa e Silva, including legislators opposed to the hard-line approach to Marcio Moreira Alves, were shortly being picked up or pestered by the police or other entities of the security apparatus. The list included ex-president Juscelino Kubitschek, lawyer Heráclito Sobral Pinto, and bothersome journalists such as Hélio Fernandes and Carlos Lacerda. Sobral Pinto had at first been in favor of the golpe. But he was long noted for his Christian humanism and his view that all deserve legal representation regardless of the political agenda of any government or individual. He was soon at odds with the dictators. Lacerda was arrested when it was pointed out to Costa e Silva that the former governor's name had not been included on the list of those with suspended political rights. Costa e Silva remarked that Lacerda should not be excluded since he had authored the Frente Ampla and promoted disunity among supporters of the military. Lacerda was taken to the country's best urban lockup at the time, the jail on Rua Frei Caneca at the Marshal Caetano de Farias Polícia Militar station, where he promptly went on a hunger strike.[78]

Meanwhile, a letter from Cardinal Dom Jaime Câmara, Lacerda's physician, and another from his daughter, Maria Cristina, arrived at Costa e Silva's office. The latter communiqué, on April 20, had one passage that was especially revealing about the relationship between Lacerda and the country's military dictator. It read, "During my father's long life, have you forgotten that the best thing that happened to you was the attainment of the presidency of the Republic?" The implication of Lacerda's collusion in Costa e Silva's road to the Alvorada was clear enough. On April 21 he ordered the meddlesome newspaperman's release. That December, however, Lacerda's political rights were revoked for ten years.[79]

Arthur da Costa e Silva rolled up his sleeves in the new year. Further complementary decrees, institutional acts, and other instructions were churned out of the nation's capital at an almost regular pace. The year 1969 also brought a fresh round of expulsions within the military and police forces, the national legislature, state assemblies, city councils, and in a number of mayoral posts. Gone too were three Supreme Court judges, as well as the president of that noble chamber, Gonçalves de Oliveira, who quit in protest. On February 1, 1969, Costa e Silva then reduced the Supreme Court from sixteen to eleven judges and all crimes of national security, or those considered to be against the military, were transferred to the jurisdiction of the Supreme Military Tribunal.[80]

Censorship of the press and all other media was likewise vigorously tightened up. The military would ultimately get even with several newspapers that had caused it trouble. *Correio da Manhã* was first in line. It was slowly strangled to death through a loss of advertising, much of it foreign, and because of other financial problems. As soon as AI-5 was dictated, an officer from the army, navy, or air force took up residence in the offices of every major newspaper, magazine, and radio and TV station in the country. Their job was to review, edit, and censure all items for public consumption. It took editorials and news stories a week to pass through this screening. There were opposition newspapers that sprang up, but, as one might expect, they had an even rougher time of it. Some, like *Pasquim,* had their editors thrown in jail and a number of newsstands selling their tabloids bombed. After March 1, 1969, the men in uniform moved out of most press rooms. They were replaced by orders that arrived over the phone, by telegraph, in letters, or on mere scraps of paper.[81]

On the second of June, the Polícia Militar and the fire departments in all states, territories, and in the Federal District were placed under the command of the minister of the army. No criticism of the government, the armed forces, or any of the institutional acts was tolerated. Some seventy educators at a number of Brazilian institutes of higher learning, most notably the University of São Paulo, were forced into retirement. Students engaged in antigovernment political activities were expelled. Obligatory courses in patriotism were established.[82] In 1971 Márcio Moreira Alves commented on these compulsory classes:

> Another policy of the military regime that strengthens the Fascist analogy is the "Civic-Education Program." A law passed in 1969 makes civic education a required subject for all students at all levels from kindergarten to postgraduate studies. The official texts, printed and distributed by the Ministry of Education, are a mixture of praise for the regime, slander of the previous liberal-democratic system, and appeals to primitive symbols of patriotism, such as the national anthem and flag. Every mention of the military stresses its right to guide the country, its selflessness and heroism. Such political control of teaching, along with the permanent purges of "subversive" books, is intended to produce docile generations for the future.[83]

Armed Resistance

With the official closing of society to any true bipartisan discourse, a number of Brazilians took up arms as the only viable alternative. Not that violence by those at odds with the dictators was anything new. Brazil's leftists had touched off their own explosions following the golpe, selectively and on a limited scale. Besides the attempt on the life of then war minister Costa e Silva at Recife Airport, the prime targets of many of these blasts were U.S. cultural institutions and diplomatic missions, along with their American employees. Leftists even tried, unsuccessfully, to detonate a bomb at the house of U.S. Air Force colonel Jerry Jay Hunt in Rio's South Zone suburb of Leblon. The device was thrown from a passing car in the early morning hours of September 25, 1967. It landed at a point where the sidewalk met a wall, next to the road, and did not cause major damage.[84]

Concurrently, as the sixties wore on, the *foco* (lit., focus) theory of Régis Debray, from the Cuban Revolution, came more and more to be a central issue in Brazilian Communist debate. The idea held that a small team of dedicated rural guerrillas could bring off a national uprising by lighting the first fires of rebellion among penniless peasants if supported by urban revolutionaries. This was tempered with a call to conclude the endless discussions, cries to pick up weapons, and the urging to get down to the business of a proletarian uprising.

Earlier in the 1960s, the Cubans had been against funding Francisco Julião's Peasant Leagues, perhaps because they felt that Julião lacked the correct revolutionary zeal. Ché Guevara was one of those in opposition.[85] This attitude of the Cuban government changed later in the decade, especially after Julião and his wife traveled to China, where Mao agreed to partially finance the leagues. Money then arrived via Cuba from Moscow. MRT (Movimento Revolucionario Tiradentes—Tiradentes Revolutionary Movement) radicals, affiliated with the Peasant Leagues, were soon being taught guerrilla tactics in the island nation. As their courses finished, members slipped into Brazil and started training camps of their own in Bahia, Goiás, Maranhão, Mato Grosso, and Rio Grande do Sul. These efforts were largely unsuccessful because of bad planning, squandered money, and detection by the authorities.[86]

Of those who went to China for training, most notable was the Maoist-leaning Ala Vermelha (Red Column) of the Communist Party of Brazil. The only thing was the first member of the group to return home was a future dedo-duro, Tarzan de Castro. Tarzan was picked up in São Paulo but was transferred to the Fortaleza de São João in Rio de Janeiro. He decided somewhere during the five-hour car ride to Rio to switch sides. He was then allowed to escape to spy on fellow comrades. Eventually Tarzan was sent to Uruguay to report back about the movements and plans of Brazilian refugees. What he discovered, however, may well have been limited because rumors began to circulate that he was a CIA plant.

Groups on the Brazilian left other than the MRT also spent time in Cuba, learning how to bring down the dictators using the rural foco base. The CIA suspected that by as early as the end of August 1967 more than 300 Brazilians had received guerrilla training on the island. By 1972, Brazilian army intelligence was aware of 30 individuals who had been sent to Havana by Leonel Brizola, along with 94 from the ALN (Ação Libertadora Nacional—National Liberation Action), plus others from MOLIPO (Movimento de Libertação Nacional—National Liberation Movement) and the VPR. Toward the end of that November, at least 219 Brazilians had been dispatched to Cuba for training. DOPS and the military intelligence services were kept informed, sometimes in great detail, largely through the work of Brazilian double agents who infiltrated the assorted bands of leftists. One was Boanerges de Souza Messa. Another was Cabo Anselmo. As a result of their penetration many of the Cuban-taught Brazilians were detained either after they returned to Brazil or even as they attempted to reenter the country. Anselmo was different. Once back on his native soil, he "made contact with Sergio [Sérgio] Fleury and subsequently furnished information that led to (by his estimate) 100–200 arrests. He was directly responsible for the liquidation of the entire VPR unit in Recife. Anselmo had the personality for his role, repeatedly talking his way out of confrontations with suspicious comrades. He later claimed to have known 'six or eight' other infiltrators."[87]

In April 1973, together with the ALN and VPR, the MR-8 (Movimento Revolucionário 8 de Outubro—8th of October Revolutionary Movement),[88] PCBR (Partido Comunista Brasileiro Revolucionário—Brazilian Revolutionary Communist Party), and VAR-Palmares (Vanguarda Armada Revolutionária-Palmares[89]—Palmares Armed Revolutionary Vanguard) held a tribunal in which Cabo Anselmo and Sérgio Fleury were condemned to death *in absentia*. An infiltrator reporting back to Brasília stated that the plan to execute Fleury had been to the point of being ready to carry out when VAR-Palmares decided that the moment was not right. The leader of the plot was Onofre Pinto. Still, a bungled attempt was made to kidnap Fleury. Along with seven others, Onofre would later be captured and tortured to death by Fleury and his men. DOPS agents in São Paulo eventually wanted to do in Anselmo too, but Fleury kept it from happening.[90]

THE URBAN GUERRILLA

Carlos Marighella was another kind of Marxist. He stood by while the foco theory was put to the test in Bolivia by Ché Guevara and in Brazil's Caparaó Mountains by the guerrillas linked to Leonel Brizola. Brizola attempted to establish Cuban-style focos in Rio Grande do Sul. According to CIA data, Brizola was also thought to be concentrating his efforts in the states of Mato Grosso and Goiás. These focos, at his insistence, were to be composed entirely of Brazilians. No Cubans would be sent to Brazil. For some unspecified time, however, Cuban money apparently did fund the Caparaó venture.[91]

In each case the armed forces moved in and easily killed the insurgents. Marighella was one of those whose experience of Brazilian realities told him that foco tactics had a better chance of success in the anonymity of larger cities by showing people that resistance was possible. The establishment of, and cooperation with, focos in the countryside would come later. Yet whether rural first or urban first, the whole thing was moot since both approaches were unacceptable to the Luís Carlos Prestes–run PCB. The official position of the party was to avoid armed quarrels at all cost and to promote instead the so-called peaceful road to socialism. But the foco strategy, wherever it was to be employed, was too appealing to be brushed aside by the old master. Voices would not be quieted, and the subsequent polemics resulted in splinter groups breaking off to go it alone. Carlos Marighella's ALN was one of the more important new revolutionary forces emerging in this process. Like its leader, the ALN was decidedly a proponent of an immediate armed struggle in Brazil's concrete jungles.

Marighella was the charismatic son of an Italian immigrant who, in spite of his Socialist views, had avoided being deported back to the old country. The huge number of European immigrants to Brazil at the end of the nineteenth and beginning of the twentieth centuries caused no end of problems for the ruling classes. Newcomers had to put up with low pay, long hours, unsafe working conditions, and savage treatment at the hands of their employers. Some of those who refused to go along with this system became radicalized, particularly in the largest urban areas. The government countered with the creation of the country's first political police, and through mass deportations to both internal and external destinations.

Carlos Marighella joined the party at age eighteen and endured his first political arrest three years later, in 1932. In 1936, following the failed Communist Revolution of November 1935, he was jailed again and severely tortured for twenty-three days. Using aliases such as Armando Silveira Lopes, Orlando José dos Reis, and "Orlando" for protection, he was nonetheless found out and picked up once more by the police of Getúlio Vargas in 1939. This time a blowtorch was turned loose on the soles of his feet, needles rammed under his finger nails, and a few teeth torn from his gums. He ended up spending most of the next six years in captivity in two island prisons, Fernando de Noronha and Ilha Grande.[92]

Before being shipped off, Marighella had developed a reputation for telling the police nothing despite the methods used to try to break him.

With the PCB code name of "Fraga," he was an important thinker and rose to a position of prominence on the party's ruling executive committee. Marighella was released and served on the Constitutional Assembly as the deputy from Bahia when the PCB was momentarily decriminalized at the end of the Estado Novo in 1945. His last arrest came nearly six weeks after the golpe on May 12, 1964. On that occasion, it took eight DOPS agents, a bullet in the lower abdomen, and a rap on the head to bring him in after being surrounded inside the Eskye Cinema in Rio's Tijuca suburb.

What a contrast it must have been for Marighella, laughing along with the rest of the audience at the Bob Hope comedy *Call Me Bwana,* to suddenly see the house lights come on and the police rushing to grab him, shooting as they came. The chief of public security, Gustavo Borges, became angry at *Correio da Manhã* for the coverage it gave to Marighella's mauling. Borges wrote a letter to the paper in which he claimed that Marighella had violently resisted arrest, that he had attempted to use a hidden gun, that the apprehension was nevertheless made by a single DOPS operative, and that members of the audience irritated with Marighella's attitude had actually administered the beating. *Correio da Manhã* ridiculed the statement by Borges and even produced photographs of the arrest.[93]

MORE REVOLUTIONARIES

Marighella's ALN was only part of the picture. The radical left in post-golpe Brazil had its origins in the Socialist and Anarchist movements at the turn of the century, and especially in the PCB.[94] Then called the PC do B, or Partido Comunista do Brazil, the PCB was founded in 1922. There was a rupture in 1929 when the Trotskyite element left. From that point, numerous divisions occurred. By 1968, over two dozen different groups had been created. Some had come and gone for one reason or another. Others had merged and broken away again. Money and guns for those involved in the present armed struggle were obtained by any means possible. Well-organized bank robberies, a specialty of the ALN, became common. On one occasion a train was stopped and relieved of the wages it was carrying for railway workers just outside of São Paulo.[95]

São Paulo was, in fact, the center for much of the urban guerrilla activity in the late 1960s. A secretary and mistress of the recently deceased paulista governor, Ademar de Barros, even got into the act—albeit involuntarily—

of financing the rebels. Apparently, Ademar had entrusted several safes to the woman, Ana Gimol Capriglione. One was filled with kickbacks from the tacitly legal numbers racket so enjoyed by the Brazilian working class, *jogo do bicho* (lit., "game of the animals"; a numbers racket). The governor's bribes were daringly "liberated" by VAR-Palmares. The take was between US$2,400,000 and $2,450,000. Capriglione had four other safes belonging to Ademar hidden in various parts of Rio de Janeiro. All were loaded with dirty money. Capriglione and a future governor of Guanabara/Rio de Janeiro, Chagas Freitas, intended to split the one that VAR-Palmares took. Later, when key members of VAR-Palmares fell into police hands in São Paulo, $400,000 of the money disappeared into the wallet of high-profile policeman Sérgio Fleury.[96]

Weapons were somewhat easier. Besides small arms, which were not difficult to obtain, the rebels wanted the latest equipment, and sometimes they got it. In one original and highly irritating raid on a 2nd Army hospital in São Paulo in the winter of 1968, POLOP (Organização Revolucionária Marxista–Política Operária, or the Revolutionary Marxist Political Worker's Organization) came by a few dozen of the most modern rifles in the Brazilian army. Some six months later, in January 1969, army captain Carlos Lamarca, along with a corporal and a VW van filled with arms, crossed over to the guerrillas' cause. The van contained sixty-four FAL rifles, ten machine guns, and cases of ammunition. Among other actions, Lamarca, along with thirteen men, would lead the subsequent sack of Ademar's concealed strongbox.[97]

Other spectacular examples of leftist activity in the first years of the armed conflict included the assassination of U.S. army captain and CIA agent Charles Chandler in his car on October 12, 1968, in São Paulo. The revolutionaries had accused Chandler of having personally tortured prisoners in Vietnam. Perhaps mistakenly, he was likewise said to have been a U.S. operative in Bolivia at the time of Ché Guevara's execution. Chandler surfaced in São Paulo in a Portuguese language course following his tour of duty in Bolivia. During this period he reportedly defended torture in a speech to university students in Campinas. An unconfirmed report states that Chandler carried out the same functions in São Paulo that Dan Mitrione did in Minas Gerais. On January 20, 1969, DOPS shot and killed Marco Antonio Brás de Carvalho, alias "Marquinho." Marquinho was said to have been one of Chandler's assassins.[98]

The slaying of Chandler was followed on September 4 by the abduction of American ambassador C. Burke Elbrick. The Elbrick action, carried out by a combined unit from the ALN and MR-8, produced an enormous government crisis and the grudging release into foreign exile of fifteen political prisoners. Among those freed were Gregório Bezerra, José Ibrahim, and José Dirceu.[99] A note left in the American ambassador's limousine by the kidnappers read in part, "This is not an isolated act. It is another one of the innumerable revolutionary acts already carried out: bank holdups, where funds for the revolution are collected, returning what the bankers take from the people and their employees; raids on barracks and police stations, where arms and ammunitions are obtained for the struggle to topple the dictatorship; invasions of jails when revolutionaries are freed to return them to the people's struggle; the explosion of buildings that signify oppression, the execution of hangmen and torturers."[100]

In addition to demanding the release of the fifteen prisoners, the guerillas insisted that the entire message be read over the air and published in the country's principal newspapers. The message ended with a notice "to those who torture, beat, and kill our comrades. We shall not allow these atrocities to continue. This is a last warning. Anyone who persists should beware. Now it is an eye for an eye and a tooth for a tooth."[101]

The armed forces had smarted over giving in to the ALN and MR-8 for decades. Col. Dickson Grael was eventually accused by a man who was Brazil's 1969 military attaché to the United States and supposedly one of his friends, General Artur Santos Moura, of being behind the plan to publicly execute all of the fifteen prisoners, one each hour, until Elbrick was let go. Grael's involvement in such a scheme was probably untrue. The men in Brasília wanted to get even with Grael for blowing the lid off the Riocentro bombing of 1981. Grael died in 1988, and the accusations against him surfaced the year following his death.[102] By the time the American ambassador was released on September 8, 1969, he had become sympathetic to some of the positions of his captors. Elbrick was immediately transferred back to the States and dismissed. At one point in the mid-1970s he wanted to get together and reminisce with one of the revolutionaries, Fernando Gabeira, who had held him prisoner. The State Department, however, advised the former ambassador against such a meeting, and it never came off.[103]

The desire to secure the release of imprisoned comrades led leftist activists to carry out more abductions in 1970, notably those of the consul of Japan in São Paulo and the German and Swiss ambassadors. The order of kidnapping was determined by the investments of each country in Brazil. Several of the political prisoners who were exchanged for the German ambassador, Ehrenfried von Holleben, had been tortured not long before their release, some by mock executions. A group led by "Cirilo," which was the alias then being used by Carlos Lamarca, carried out the kidnapping of the Swiss ambassador. The price for the diplomat's release was seventy political detainees. They were flown to exile in Salvador Allende's Chile. The German ambassador's kidnapping was blamed on Lamarca by the press. It was undertaken by a combined VPR-ALN unit and resulted in forty revolutionaries being jetted off to Algeria. A probable attempted kidnapping of the U.S. consul in Porto Alegre came to naught in early April 1970.[104]

The Reaction

To deal with what were immediately dubbed terrorists, the dictators relied on large-scale "urban pacification programs"—a tranquil-sounding name for massive police and army dragnets. These sweeps resulted in hundreds and sometimes thousands of suspects being ensnarled in surprise roadblocks or neighborhood searches. Besides the occasional criminal, anyone whose papers were not in order was liable to be arrested, roughed up, and taken to headquarters for a thorough interrogation.[105]

On August 29, 1969, Costa e Silva suffered a debilitating stroke that set off a grab for his office by members of the military hierarchy. The civilian vice-president was ruled out. Not only was he not from the armed forces, he had opposed the enactment of AI-5. In his place, the three military ministers, Augusto Hamann Rademaker Grünewald from the navy, Aurélio de Lyra Tavares from the army, and Márcio de Souza e Mello from the air force, took over the functions of the impaired head of state. Even as the armed forces haggled among themselves over which general would eventually succeed Costa e Silva, and partly in reaction to the Elbrick affair, the new triumvirate tightened the reins of government.

> On 5 September [1969] it issued Institutional Acts Nos. 13 and 14, which aimed at strengthening the legal framework of the repressive apparatus. Institutional Act No. 13 established that all political prisoners exchanged for kidnapped dignitaries were to be banished from Brazilian territory and in fact gave the executive the power to banish from Brazil for life all those considered to be "inconvenient, harmful, or dangerous to national security." Institutional Act No. 14 amended the Constitution of 1967 to make death penalties, life imprisonment, and banishment applicable in cases of "adverse psychological, revolutionary, or subversive warfare" as well as in external war. The definition of these kinds of warfare was left deliberately vague, as the "enemy within" was potentially any citizen.[106]

Three further items provided the final legal touches. Late in September, a so-called National Security Law (Lei de Segurança Nacional) was decreed. Modeled after the Cold War thinking of the Doctrine of National Security, the new statute aimed at gagging all those residing on Brazilian soil who might be opposed to the regime. Specifically throttled in were union organizers, strike promoters, editors, and media owners. So too were those who had ideas about disrupting legislative sessions, attempting to organize or reorganize outlawed political parties, promoting violent or nonviolent resistance, defaming public institutions (like the military) or constituted officials (like the military leaders), or even defending anyone accused of committing one of these new crimes against the Brazilian state.

The first of the other two matters of note allowed the government, through the constitution change, to oblige each and every citizen to inform on his or her neighbors. Last, just in case they had forgotten something, the autocrats gave themselves the power on November 11, 1971, to enact secret laws. The exact scope of such measures was not commented upon in the official publications of the administration. Used until 1973, these ordinances came into play to arrest persons on unknown charges.[107]

In early October 1969 the heads of Brazil's armed forces met to put an end to all of the jockeying by the presidential hopefuls. General Emílio Garrastazu Médici, a former chief of SNI and at the time the commander of the 3rd Army, stationed in Rio Grande do Sul, was talked into the position. He accepted, he said, for reasons of patriotism. Often called "Milito" (a variation of "Little Emílio"), Médici, like each of his predecessors, promised to restore the country's democratic institutions. What Milito did do was run the most lethal apparatus ever assembled in Brazilian history. Opponents of his regime were hunted down, tortured, and killed, along with their wives, husbands, children, parents, brothers, sisters, friends, and sometimes even those who simply happened to be in a suspected terrorist's personal address book. At one point, Médici's ex-Integralist minister of justice, Alfredo Buzaid, formally denied to the press that the torturing of political prisoners was taking place in Brazil. He then invited foreign correspondents to come to the country and verify the government's statement. The following week, however, Buzaid said that he had never made the invitation.[108]

MARIGHELLA

One of the first big victories in the new administration's fight came on November 4. In a São Paulo police ambush led by Sérgio Fleury, who liked to be called "The Pope" by his men,[109] Carlos Marighella was reportedly shot dead in the backseat of a blue Volkswagen bug. There are several versions of how the shooting took place. One author states that Fleury snuck up to the VW and briefly tried to get Marighella to surrender. When the legendary revolutionary made a sudden move with his hand toward a small black briefcase, the Pope opened fire. Fleury's men, fearing that their boss was involved in a shoot-out with Marighella's bodyguards, began discharging their weapons in all directions. An out-of-control crossfire among Fleury's team was the end product, leaving one policeman wounded and two dead: policewoman Stella Borges Morato, who was rushing the Volkswagen, as well as Friederich Adolf Rohmann, an immigrant dentist from Germany driving by in his car.

However, some of the policemen who supposedly took part gave a slightly different version. They claim that Fleury, who had been on lookout, faking that he was necking in a car with Morato, left the vehicle and began to walk in the direction of Marighella's automobile. He told Morato to wait behind, but then she decided to follow her chief after some seconds. Hearing her footsteps, Fleury, startled into thinking it was one of Marighella's men, turned and fired, killing Morato instantly.[110]

A number of ALN militants and sympathetic Dominican priests had been taken into custody and tortured shortly before Marighella's death in an attempt to discover his whereabouts. Leading the gruesome duties of inflicting pain for information was policeman Raul "Pudim" Ferreira. Still, the major reason for the successful operation, more likely than not, was the infiltration of CIA or police spies into the guerrilla organization Marighella had put together. An attempt was later made by the ALN and VPR to kidnap the Pope and avenge Marighella's death, but this second try ended only in more shooting, blood, and dead leftists.[111]

LAMARCA

Less than a year later, in October 1970, Marighella's replacement, Joaquim Câmara Ferreira, was also eliminated. The demise of "The Old Man" or "Toledo," as Ferreira was called, like the death of his predecessor, ended up being shrouded by the government. Its story was that he had suffered a heart attack and died on October 23, 1970, while resisting arrest by Fleury and his associates. But, a non-government account holds that Ferreira was taken to a fazenda and executed by Fleury himself.[112] This essentially finished the ALN. So too would be the fate of the advocates of the rural foco. The following September, in a massive police and army sweep, Carlos Lamarca, or "João," if one were to use his VPR code name, and another comrade, José Campos Barreto, or "Zequinha," were killed outside Pintadas, Bahia.

Popularized accountings hold that the two were ambushed while seeking shelter from 104°F (40°C) tropical heat in the shade of a brauna tree. But documents at DOPS in Rio de Janeiro suggest otherwise. That material contends that the pair ran for their lives after being discovered. Lamarca did not make it farther than a few yards before he was shot in the back. Zequinha was evidently the healthier of the two. He got nearly a third of a mile away (five hundred meters) before turning to pick up a rock to throw at his pursuers. As he did so he screamed "Down with the dictatorship!" The spy police documents claim that he was cut down in a hail of bullets.

The shooting of these two defenseless men was an attempt to settle old scores. There is no disagreement about the fact that the pair were starving, sick, and in rags. They could not have put up much of a fight even if they had wanted to. During the three days leading up to their deaths, Zequinha had carried an ill Lamarca around the Bahian *caatinga,* or scrub-savanna badlands, looking for a physician. It is reported that Fleury could have gotten there first, but he knew the execution of this particular deserter was to be carried out by the military themselves. The lucky man to kill Lamarca was Nilton Cerqueira. Dalmar Caribé shot Zequinha. Both were members of the Equipe do Cão, or "The Team of the Dog," led by Cerqueira, the chief of DOI-Codi in Bahia. Lamarca had undergone some plastic surgery, but the results did not change his appearance much.

One of those in the race to unearth Lamarca's trail, Fleury had led his own group of paulistano police around in the caatinga for three months, standing aside only at the last moment. People suspected of knowing something appear to have been tortured. Some peasants were slaughtered outright. The father of Zequinha, José Barreto, had his farm in Cabeça D'Anta, Bahia, taken over by Fleury after his men had machine-gunned two other sons (one miraculously survived). When Sérgio and his men finally left, they stole everything that was not nailed down, including the poor man's meager savings.[113]

Lamarca's body was shot an additional forty-eight times. It was taken to the morgue in Salvador, where the teeth were pulled out and made into a choker. Once this grotesque piece of jewelry was completed, the military in attendance took turns placing it around their necks one at a time to be photographed. They then called Fleury to the little ceremony. By way of thanks, the defenders of Brazil let the Pope wear the necklace and have his picture taken too. The number of prints was kept small, and their circulation was limited.[114]

ARAGUAIA

The violent deaths of Lamarca and Zequinha were perhaps surpassed by a single dramatic event in provincial Brazil. As 1972 unfolded, the largest armed conflict in rural Brazilian history secretly began in a remote section of Pará called Araguaia. A near blackout of the affair by military censors kept news of the ensuing three-year war from reaching the public.[115]

It all started in the late 1960s when a handful of Brazilian Maoists moved into this nearly 12,500-square-mile region. They won the confidence of the locals by helping them with agricultural projects and medical necessities, and by constructing a small school. At their peak, no more than sixty-odd[116] guerrillas were involved. Many were from São Paulo. It is unclear just how the armed forces determined that there was a threat in Araguaia. Once they did, however, between ten and twenty-six thousand[117] soldiers, aviators, and elements of the Polícia Militar, in three different waves lasting into early 1975, were thrown against the insurgents. Nearly all of the Communists were wiped out. Noncombatants, too, figured in the fatalities as Médici's forces showed little pity to those living within the field of battle. Anyone was a potential enemy; and anyone could have vital information. More than a thousand local people, including women and children, small businessmen, members of the clergy, and even some fazendeiros, were rounded up during the operation. They were subjected to all the resources at Brasília's disposal to insure victory.

The military would sweep into an area suspected of guerrilla activity and start herding up every peasant it could find. Commanders reasoned that these persons knew the surrounding forests better than anyone. In order to secure the release of a wife or a child and to avoid torture, they usually cooperated. The carrot was an empty promise of free land should they act as trackers for the army patrols and civilian sharpshooters sent in to pick off the rebels. The only way returning squads could prove they had ambushed members of the opposition was to bring back their severed heads and right hands. The authorities then paid a reward according to the importance of the dispatched leftist.

Despite this take-no-prisoners policy, a few Communists were captured and sent to Brasília, where they were killed. Others were tortured to death by specialists—like Messias Martins Reis and Benedito Rodrigues Silva—sent in from other states or by army major Sebastião Rodrigues de Moura, "Sebastião Curió." Curió also used the alias of Dr. Patricio dos Santos. He would continue his career in the army as a torturer in Rio de Janeiro, enter the SNI, and become involved in the corruption schemes of President Fernando Collor de Mello. In 1980 he succeeded in organizing the destitute open-pit miners of Serra Pelada in Pará and had the town of Curionópolis named after him, even serving as its mayor.[118]

Before victims were put out of their misery, electric shock and the pau-de-arara came to be used extensively in Araguaia as intelligence-gathering tools. Likewise put to good use were two simpler but no less effective methods of torture. With the *forno* ("Oven"), prisoners were laid on their backs and pinned to the ground under a body-length sheet of zinc. The heat under this blanket of metal was so intense by midday that everyone subjected to it cracked. There was also the *forquilha* ("Wishbone"), where subjects were tied by their legs, upside down, to the limb of a tree.

Soldiers said that the increased blood to victims' brains really helped them reflect better on just what they were going to say when cut down. Those who died while undergoing interrogation had their corpses dumped in the forest or stuffed into tires and burned.

Even some important locals were taken prisoner when it was believed they were aiding the rebels. A particular fazendeiro, for example, was flown over the city of Marabá bound, blindfolded, and suspended in the air from a helicopter. It was both a warning to the landowner and an attempt to terrorize the people back on firm ground into lending a hand. The fazendeiro became mentally unbalanced as a result of the ordeal.[119]

OBAN

In the rest of the country the repressive apparatus—which had been created on the anvil of national security, itself a reaction to the Socialist experiment in Cuba—coupled to the reaction Castro generated in the United States, was refined and took on a new focus of urgency. Brazil's military government felt that only a concentrated effort could keep it from loosing its grip. Western Civilization depended on them. Thus, in São Paulo on July 1, 1969, the intelligence service from the army, or CIEx, the air force's CISA, the navy's CENIMAR, along with DOPS,[120] the Polícia Federal, the Polícia Civil, the Força Pública, and the Guarda Civil were all placed under one paramilitary umbrella called OBAN (Operação Bandeirantes—Operation Bandeirantes). The organization was the brainchild of army colonel Erar Vasconcelos. So impressed were his colleagues that Vasconcelos was later made a general.

OBAN was an undertaking that specialized in three areas: search and arrest, interrogation, and the sifting and analysis of information. The operation was not linked openly to the powerful 2nd Army in São Paulo. So the 2nd Army's commander, General Canavarro Pereira, being the discreet officer that he was, ran the affair out of a structure known as "Grandma's House" at Rua Tutóia 921 in the Paraíso suburb. This building was neatly hidden behind São Paulo's 36th District police station. Prisoners within its walls were subjected to abuse in several forms—including the spiritual. Army chaplain Roberto Pontushloa Filho distributed Bibles while admonishing those held captive that they should drop their leftist ways and return to the true path of righteousness. Sometimes assisted by an evangelical pastor, Pontushloa was remembered by those he attempted to soothe and convert because he always wore a .45 caliber pistol in a holster around his waist and a camouflage uniform. It was said that he never counseled the torturers dishing out the punishment.[121]

The free hand provided plain-clothed OBAN agents in the legal area, together with round-the-clock maliciousness, produced striking results. Grandma's House had an up-to-date array of nonstop torture devices and the men to run them all imported from DOPS. One of the specialties was the already mentioned *cadeira de dragão* ("Dragon's Chair"). Two members of the thought police, Fábio Lessa Sampaio and Ivahyr Freitas Garcia, had designed the apparatus. The pau-de-arara was, of course, one of the more ubiquitous features of the information gathering sessions at Grandma's House. The police often sniggered when referring to it as the *paulígrafo* ("Polygraph"). A staunch supporter of utilizing this crude lie detector was the chief of one of the interrogation teams, Capt. Orestes Faria, also known as "Dr. Átila." After each victim was bound into the pau-de-arara and hoisted into place, Faria would have newspapers spread about on the floor. This was done to collect the defecation that resulted from the repeated shocks to captives' genitals. When a couple was tortured together in this way, Átila would be sure to turn the man's face to a position in which the man could see him or his staff insert their fingers and other objects into the anus of the woman, dangling helplessly like skewered meat. When victims passed out and the authorities were not yet finished, they were occasionally taken to the office of a Dr. Isaac, south of the city, in Santo Amaro. He administered just enough medication to get the individual ready for another round of electricity, iron bars, and probing fingers. One final report speaks of a man known only as Dr. Eiraldo. He "stood out from the rest. An army captain, Eiraldo would come up to . . . [a victim] at daybreak, greeting him with, 'I'm here to wish you Good Morning! I woke up today with a desire to torture you!' During his sessions, he always used a peaked hat from the Nazi army and liked to give the Nazi salute, affirming repeatedly that 'Hitler is our spiritual father.'"[122]

OBAN's funding came from multinationals such as Ford, General Motors, Grupo Ultra, and the like. Much of the money was dug up through the activities of Henning Albert Boilesen, a Danish-born naturalized Brazilian and one of the directors of Grupo Ultra. Boilesen was an enthusiastic reactionary who prodded other businessmen into contributing support and cash. He provided uniforms and trucks from his own company to OBAN—as well as a reward to the police who participated in the assassination of Carlos Marighella. Some said he was a CIA agent. His interest in the way OBAN did things went right into their interrogation rooms, where he took part in torturing detainees, at times with an apparatus called the *pianola Boilesen* ("Boilesen Piano"). The pianola Boilesen was a sophisticated piece of equipment that had been specially designed by the CIA to be used in Vietnam. Boilesen introduced it to Brazil and donated it to the Brazilian army. It consisted of a machine that could run on 110 or 220 volts of domestic current. It had a keyboard, and through a system of transformers it could deliver different intensities of electricity to anything it was hooked up to. Identified by the antigovernment forces, Boilesen paid the price for his zealotry. He was cut down by gunfire outside his home on April 15, 1971.[123]

DOI-Codi

But this was still in the future. By early 1970 the dictators had decided that other, slightly more refined, OBAN units would be started in the rest of the country. One of the other changes concentrated everything into the watchful hands of the army. The revamped setup was renamed DOI (Destacamento de Operações de Informações—Operation and Information Detachment). It had the same three functions as OBAN, and there was more than one DOI, each busy working out of Codi (Centros de Operações da Defensa Interna, or Centers for Internal Defense Operations) facilities, jurisdictionally established all over Brazil. These latter entities were carved out of the already existing military districts.[124]

Anyone judged to be politically dangerous whom these new units grabbed was killed. To leave as little trace as possible and to limit the number of witnesses to a trusted handful, the CIEx ran a group of human slaughterhouses in the late 1960s and 70s. These structures were located first in Rio de Janeiro in São Conrado and later up in the mountains at Rua Arthur Barbosa 668 in Petrópolis. In São Paulo, a house at Avenida Teresa Cristina 58 in Ipiranga, nearly adjacent to the impressive Independence Monument, was used for this purpose. When army intelligence decided it needed more space in São Paulo, a nightclub in Itapevi named Querosene ("Kerosene") was rented for two years. In 1975, for reasons of security, the former nightspot was substituted with a fazenda some 18 1/2 miles (30 km) outside the city. It was well that the army took such precautions because of what went on in these places. If you were taken to one of them, you were not meant to come out still breathing. You were not even to come out in one piece. Victims were either tortured to death or given an injection used to kill full-grown horses.[125] Bodies were cut into chunks—sometimes numbering as many as fourteen—placed in individual plastic bags and buried in diverse places.

The men carrying out the erasures were experts. Heading the team in São Paulo was DOPS detective Alcides Cintra Bueno Filho, known as Porquinho ("Little Pig"). He is described as a slob of a man who stuffed food in his pockets to snack on while dandruff fell untreated from his balding, oversized head. Alcides's eyebrows were joined in the middle, and he possessed a peculiar voice, one that went from a lower to a higher pitch when he got excited. With his bad taste in clothes, habit of grinding his teeth, and the rest of his attributes, the behind-the-back comments at headquarters about him never seemed to end. Yet there is no denying that Porquinho did not know how to ingratiate himself with the powerful. He provided security for his idol, Guanabara governor Carlos Lacerda, whenever the latter was in town. Once approved by the 2nd Army, Alcides's day job at DOPS became one of analyzing how to dispose of the corpses of those who had been tortured to death. Each case was different, yet similar. The work required a man with his talents, as the dictators knew they would not be in power forever.

First, the fingertips were sliced off to hinder the process of identification. Many times the small bits of skin, nail, and bone were thrown into heavily trafficked streets so as to be ground into the pavement. Next, the corpse was cut up. Sometimes heads were switched in the morgue. Last, the body was disposed of. If the victim was to be buried, the body was usually taken to a cemetery in the Perus section of São Paulo and left in a pauper's grave. If it was to be deposited in water—the Rio Novo and the Jurumirim Dam were often used—the lower abdomen and stomach had holes stabbed into them so that the gasses would escape. That way the remains would not bobble to the surface. Before being removed, the carcass was hog-tied to minimize the space needed for transportation. Otherwise, bodies and parts of bodies were placed in sacks along with blocks of concrete to be certain everything stayed put on the bottom. Sometimes already dead leftists were shot several times, placed in the trunks of cars, and taken elsewhere. A fake gunfight was then arranged so that the security forces could get their man in the act of committing a crime or resisting arrest. It has been claimed, although never proven, that Carlos Marighella suffered this last fate.[126]

The DOI-Codi network brought forth another refinement in 1972: specially trained hit teams. These groups of triggermen were schooled in ways to simulate suicides, pedestrian accidents, and automobile mishaps. In São Paulo they were led by a lieutenant in the Polícia Militar[127] and called GTA, a twist on the Tactically Armed Groups that made up the ALN's live-action units. The Polícia Militar took an active role in furnishing men for these kinds of activities. This is evident from the fact that it ran a counterinsurgency school—the so-called *escola de torturadores* (School of Torturers)—on the Guarani fazenda, some 168 miles (270 km) from Belo Horizonte. Students were taught to think like terrorists. The use of sabotage and explosives was part of the curriculum. A former alumnus of the school declared that they were ready to blow up electrical transmission towers, to bring about power outages, and to do whatever was necessary to turn the population against the urban guerrillas. In Rio, their base was established at CISA, where they went by the code name of *grupo coruja* ("Group of the Owl"). So that people on the outside would not catch on, secret words made up part of the workaday argot of these men and women. *Plantar* (to plant), for example, meant to bury someone; *levar para as duzentas* (to take to the two hundreds) signified throwing a victim from a boat or plane into the ocean; and *códio 12* (Code 12) indicated a fatal automobile accident or some other kind of death in transit.[128]

In 1973 the security apparatus started Operation Radar. This was a project designed specifically to go after the leadership of the PCB. One of the ways this was done was through dedo-duro Severino Teodoro de Mello. Arrested initially in 1974, Teodoro was taken to the nightclub in Itapevi but then miraculously transferred to another lockup, where he was turned into a stool pigeon. He signed a contract to this end and apparently received a monthly wage. The information that this one man provided allowed the authorities to seize those responsible for the newspaper *Voz Operária* and most of the PCB's central committee—except for Prestes, who had made it out of the country to Moscow. The apprehended disappeared forever into the government's death houses.[129]

What really went on while the generals were in charge can never be totally and accurately described. But the crackdown was doubtlessly so complete that when Orlando Geisel (brother of Ernesto) was minister of the army from 1969 to 1974, he apparently ordered the execution on their return to Brazil of all leftists who left the country. His principal targets were those who went to Chile during the Allende government.[130]

It would be safe to say that the repressive apparatus—instructed, funded, and equipped in part by foreign specialists—produced a deluge of domestic terror the likes of which set a record in the long course of Brazilian history. No previous regime had so completely suppressed—or, if this was not possible—eliminated political opponents. Every means at the government's disposal was considered. There were many, many types of torture in this quest, everything from gouging out eyes to cockroaches being placed in anuses. The sheer magnitude of this undertaking—at least 326 types of torture can be identified—caught the attention of a shocked, civilized world.[131]

Into the future, the Brazilian armed forces, its leaders no longer sophomoric lieutenants from the 1920s but obdurate generals still intoxicated from the refrains of *tenentismo,* will be remembered for two things. First, it will be recalled how they ran the country to the very edge of bankruptcy with a policy of economic growth through massive foreign borrowing.[132] Second, few will be able to forget what they did to all those who opposed them during the two-plus decades of military rule. From the mid-1960s to the mid-1980s their fervor would act as a catalyst for the activities of death squads against uncharged common criminals. In the meantime, revolutionaries, political adversaries, idealists, urban and rural workers, students, priests, and the guiltless were all gagged, forced into exile, or tortured and murdered in one of hundreds of ways. The following case is a sorrowful illustration.

PAIVA

Rubens Paiva had led the parliamentary commission put in motion by Goulart to look into the activities of the Instituto Brasileiro de Ação Democrática, the conspiring generals, and the mostly American sources of funding. As the commission uncovered one piece of the puzzle after the other, the military plotters added Paiva to the list of persons who would have their political rights removed once they took power. He was number ninety-two on the first list of cassações, which was published on April 10, 1964. Rubens was hounded, yet he never left the country for foreign exile. Seven years after the golpe he was arrested at his home in Rio de Janeiro by air force agents and taken to the 3rd Air Zone base next to Rio's Santo Dumont Airport. There he was bound, tortured, and handed over to the DOI unit working out of the headquarters of the 1st Battalion of the Polícia do Exército. What transpired next is only partially known. That which is documented is that torturers such as Majs. Francisco Moacyr Mayer Fontinelli, Paulo Armando Albuquerque Maranhão, Demburgo, Capt. Leão, the busy Sgt. Juvenal Antunes Pereira, and DOPS detective Luiz Timotheo de Lima were active at the facility. One of two physicians was usually in attendance—Ricardo Agnese Fayad or Amílcar Lobo.[133]

In the early morning hours of April 11, 1971, Amílcar Lobo was on night duty and received an urgent call ordering him to come and look at a prisoner at the Army Police compound. Lobo's role, like Fayad's, was to help the authorities produce more agony through his academic knowledge of the human body. In this capacity, he occasionally worked the CIEx death house in Petrópolis. As Lobo arrived at the military complex on Rua Barão de Mesquita in Tijuca,[134] he was ushered to

> an open cell at the end of a corridor. There, a nude man was lying on a bunk with his eyes closed, very beat up. He had black-and-blue marks on his face, chest, abdomen, and thighs. I turned him on his side and found contusions on his back and rump. He then rolled back to his original position, opened his eyes, looked into mine, and said in a low voice, "Rubens Paiva."
>
> At that moment, the major [from DOI] smiled and in a joking tone indicated that the prisoner had complained a lot about stomach pains. I could verify the existence of two recent injuries, one on an eyebrow, the other at the edge of his mouth. I began to feel his abdomen and discovered it was a hard as a board. I immediately suspected hemorrhaging in the area due to the liver or spleen. The prisoner opened his eyes again and repeated with a voice full of emotion, "Rubens Paiva!"[135]

Later in the day, Paiva was probably taken to the house in Petrópolis where he died and his body was cut into quarters. The pieces were buried at assorted points near the end of Recreio dos Bandeirantes Beach.[136] Lobo also substantiated that other political prisoners were likewise dismembered in order to hinder identification and buried in remote places. The official DOI version of what became of Paiva was that he was abducted from them several days after he had been taken into custody while being moved from one lockup to another. Those who knew Paiva immediately rejected the story. He was 5' 11" (180 cm) tall and weighed 220 lb. (100 k), and the authorities claimed that he had managed to escape from the backseat of a VW Bug into a waiting car. How did he overpower three armed escorts in the vehicle while handcuffed?[137]

GEISEL

By 1973–74 it was evident to a number of generals that their plan of growth via foreign loans had not paid off as predicted. "The national security state [thus] became concerned with the establishment of different mechanisms to develop social and political support."[138] In that spirit, on March 13, 1974, the next national dictator, General Ernesto Geisel, took office. He admitted to the head of his security detail that "to kill is barbarity, but it has to be." He urged that leftists be disposed of without a trace.[139] The torture and murder of radicals accordingly continued even as Geisel announced in August the slow implementation of a strategy he called decompression or distension. The new policy aimed at a gradual easing of the police-state atmosphere in certain sectors of society. Censorship was to be partially lifted and AI-5 revoked (although it would be replaced with other laws that did many of the same things). Even the democratic process was to be opened a nudge. The incoming government felt that ARENA could win the national legislative elections in 1974, just as it had done in 1966 and 1970. They were only half right since the MDB won the Senate and increased its overall strength in the Chamber of Deputies, a victory that extended to many of the state assemblies.[140]

Still, the hard-liners were not about to go quietly. In the period following Geisel's assumption of office, they were responsible for a number of events that galvanized first liberal sectors of the Brazilian Church and then the public at large. Two involved the death of someone from the middle class. Since the days when Brazil was a colony, it has always been more problematic for the authorities when victims of elite violence came from the middle classes or above, or when they were influential members of the working class. On March 17, 1973, a well-connected University of São Paulo student, Alexandre Vannucchi Leme, was tortured to death by the paulista police. The authorities said he was a terrorist, but in fact he was just an ALN sympathizer. Leme's murder was followed in 1975 and early 1976 with the torture deaths in São Paulo of a prominent upper-middle-class TV Cultura news director, Vladimir Herzog, and a machinist, Manoel Fiel Filho, by DOI-Codi operatives. Herzog's death got more press than did that of Fiel Filho because of who he was. Vladimir was a former editor of the international section of the magazine *Visão* and had voluntarily presented himself for interrogation at the 2nd Army's DOI-Codi compound at Grandma's House in São Paulo's Paraíso district.

Paraíso means *paradise* in Portuguese. It was a contradiction that no doubt crossed the minds of many persons as they entered the complex and heard the gates clank shut behind them. Herzog's case was no different. The authorities mistakenly thought Vladimir was connected to the PCB. Major André Leite Pereira Filho interrogated him about this and that and about his politics. Soon two intimidators became part of the questioning: Waldomiro Bueno Filho from the 2nd Section of the Department of Criminal Investigations and DOPS/DOI-Codi functionary Pedro Antônio Mira Grancieri, also known as "Capitão Ramiro." Experts in torture, the two men and their own assistants quickly went to work. After Herzog's initial denials, salt may have been forced into his mouth in an attempt to get him to confess. Usually this would have been followed by a gas mask that delivered ammonia to the lungs. The joint effect was similar to drowning. He ended up being smacked around and tied into the Dragon's Chair. What Waldomiro and Grancieri did not understand was that Herzog had a weak heart.[141]

Herzog's death, the official explanation was suicide,[142] provoked an instantaneous reaction from the paulista intellectual elite. This last fact—his social class—made his death more important than the loss of just another revolutionary or worker. Colleagues, students, and lawyers went on strike or demanded an inquiry. The situation was explosively reminiscent of the first hours following the deaths of Getúlio Vargas and Édson Luís.

THE CRY FOR REASON

The archbishop of São Paulo, Dom Paulo Evaristo Arns, felt betrayed. Slowly he had become involved with the opposition movement. Shortly after the arrest of Herzog, he visited the governor and then the head of the 2nd Army, General Ednardo d'Ávila Melo. Both men emphatically assured him that he need not worry. Nothing out of the ordinary was going to occur. "Then, a few days later, Herzog turned up dead: people were just presented with the corpse. Cardinal Arns . . . [mentioned] how shaken this had left him. He questioned whether he had done enough, and he had this sense of at least having to do something more now. He couldn't allow the incident to go unsung. So he presided at [an ecumenical Mass for Herzog. Then as] ... thousands of people show[ed] up, with the police cameras all clicking away ... [the cardinal made] it the turning point for the society."[143]

Some eight thousand persons packed their way into the cathedral at the Praça de Sé. Another thirty thousand filled the square outside, despite a police blockade of the downtown area. The throng would have been even larger had it not been for the barricades. Those who got through heard Cardinal Arns, two rabbis, and a Presbyterian minister deliver a thunderous eulogy. The main message, in the words of the archbishop, was a simple one—so simple that even the dictators could understand: "ENOUGH!"[144]

In Brasília, these occurrences, and the 1974 election returns, served to exacerbate the tension in the military hierarchy. On the one side were the hard-liners, particularly ultraconservatives within the intelligence community who did not favor a reduction in autocratic rule. Opposed to them were the moderates, including Ernesto Geisel. If Geisel's scheme to decompress the situation was to work, he would have to show in some way that he too had had enough. He did not have to wait long. Geisel warned General d'Ávila Melo to restrain the DOI-Codi torturers under his command. But d'Ávila Melo, not a fan of decompression, felt that he was strong enough to stare down Geisel's ultimatum. So he ignored the advice, and it was not long before the nation's military ruler and d'Ávila Melo were at an impasse.[145]

The incident that precipitated the showdown was yet another torture-murder. The victim was Manoel Fiel Filho. An activist in a São Paulo metalworker's union, Fiel was picked up in early January 1976 on charges of being a Communist and delivered to one of DOI-Codi's dungeons.[146] Another prisoner, who observed what transpired shortly thereafter, testified that Fiel's inquisitors were responsible for his death. Fiel had been taken to a torture chamber and placed on a pau-de-arara. Even with the radio turned up, the machinist could be overheard pleading with his captors, "For the love of God, don't hurt me so much that you kill me!"[147] Sgt. Luiz Shinji Akaboshi then roared, "Where are Flores, Afonso, and Fiore?" "You know!" "Why don't you tell us, you Communist coward and tramp?"[148]

While hanging suspended, Fiel was beaten, kicked, clubbed, and then revived with a bucket of water. Although he knew little and could not help, his abusers would not relent. Fiel was dragged to the Dragon's Chair and "given terrible shocks to his fingers and head. He bit his tongue. The pain was unbearable. They took him out of the chair and asked again, 'Where are Flores, Afonso, and Fiore?' "[149]

Fiel collapsed, only to be elbowed in the spleen and kicked. There was no sign of life. They had finished him. The radio was turned off. After a few minutes the sergeant went to the office of his superior and reported in the best police parlance a euphemism for someone's having been executed, "Chief, the omelet is ready."[150]

The official account labeled it all another suicide. In November of the year Fiel "took his own life," twenty-eight political prisoners wrote a twenty-nine-page letter to the Brazilian Lawyers Association complaining of torture and faked suicides at the hands of the authorities. The message mentioned three further murders, in addition to those of Herzog and Fiel Filho, which were similarly covered up. The names listed were those of Severino Viana Collon, João Lucas Alves, and Manoel Raimundo Soares.[151]

But before the political prisoners had even composed their letter of protest, Gen. Geisel focused his resolve on the covert actions of 1975 and 1976. The death of Fiel Filho had been a proverbial last straw. Geisel's military hard-line opponents had pushed him too much. The challenge to presidential authority had become too blatant. He consequently fired (transferred to the reserves) General d'Ávila Melo on January 20, 1976. Sacked as well would be another inflexible general, Confucio Danton de Paula Avelino, the head of army intelligence and one of the main barriers to Geisel's decompression policy.[152]

The hardliners were shocked at Geisel's move, but they were not done. That July, a German missionary, Father Rodolfo Lunkenbein, working with Native Brazilians in the state of Amazonas was murdered by fazendeiros. In September, the Bishop of Nova Iguaçu, Dom Adriano Hipolito, was kidnapped, beaten, painted red, and dumped nude on the street. Afterwards, a car bomb exploded in front of the offices of the CNBB. And in October, again in the state of Amazonas, the police shot and killed Father João Burnier. This priest's crime had been that he had protested the torturing of local women.[153]

As these adversities were grabbing the headlines, a more cautious Dom Eugenio Sales, the Archbishop of Rio de Janeiro, was hiding political refugees from leftist movements in neighboring countries in the very heart of Rio. Between 1976 and 1982, his diocese used eighty apartments in the city, plus the Convent of the Carmelitas, to help some five thousand exiles escape South America and the terrors of Operation Condor. They arrived in droves or one at a time. Many only had his address, Glória 466, scribbled on a scrap of paper. It became their passport to his help and a plane ride out of Brazil to safety.[154]

MORE LABOR WOES AND PESKY GUESTS

A further thorn in Geisel's side and that of his successor were the strikes. Workers had grumbled but had been kept quiet until a small manifestation of displeasure on May 1, 1977, in Osasco. Two years later, it was a different story. There were hundreds of strikes all over the country which produced several dead workers and countless injured ones. In 1980 the industrial actions continued and came to be centered in the ABC paulista. Things really got rolling on March 16, when roughly sixty thousand workers, meeting at the Vila Euclides Stadium in São Bernardo do Campo, decided to walk out if their demands for better salaries were not met by April 1. With no real progress in discussions, when the deadline arrived the strike was called. The effect was a massive industrial slowdown. On the ninth, however, the strike was called off. This prompted the military leaders to move unflinchingly. On the seventeenth, the minister of labor, Murillo Macedo, fired forty-two union leaders, including thirty-three-year-old union president Luiz Inácio Lula da Silva. The very next day, four thousand protesters went to battle with some three thousand police assisted by twenty transporters filled with troops from the army. On the nineteenth, when Lula and several associates in the union leadership were taken into custody for breaking the law on national security, an estimated forty thousand machinists reacted with an immediate demonstration of solidarity.

Government dictates against the right of assembly, against striking, and against shows of musical support by such out-of-favor artists as Chico Buarque were passed. Some of those who tried to attend Buarque's performance at Vila Euclides Stadium anyway were stopped and roughed up. The situation was quickly getting out of hand. On the twenty-first, ten thousand or so protesters marched to the Praça da Sé. On May 1, with Lula still in prison, eight thousand subelites tried to contain roughly one hundred thousand strikers and their families, friends, and sympathizers, all of whom were protesting an administration that was clearly anti-labor. The country seethed for weeks in the wake of the injuries and the bombs set off by the police themselves. Lula was finally released on May 20, 1980, following an eleven-day hunger strike.[155]

In late March 1978, American president Jimmy Carter traveled to Brazil on a largely American initiative. The main topic on his agenda was the sale of nuclear technology to Brazil by the Germans. Of secondary importance was the issue of the torture and murder of opponents to the military regime. Geisel defended his interests on the first item in the name of progress. He denied that the second matter was something with which the American should be concerned. Carter then visited with Cardinal Arns at the home of activist minister Jamie Wright. There were four other individauls in attendance: the president of the Brazilian bar association, Raimundo Faoro; the publisher of *O Estado de São Paulo,* Julio Mesquita Neto; an influential São Paulo businessman, José Mindin; plus the head of the National Economic Development Bank and the only government official present, Marcos Vianna. Though he did not resolve either subject, by meeting with Arns, Wright, and the others the American president sent a clear message to the dictators, at least on the question of human rights. The whole problem of civil liberties had become a touchy subject between the two countries. In June 1977, the year before President Carter's visit, the generals abrogated a U.S. military assistance package since such help came with a new requirement for a human rights report to the American Congress. In part, this new condition was a result of the Senator Frank Church hearings in 1975, which gave Brazil a less than favorable human rights evaluation. In addition, and also in June of 1977, the American president's wife, Rosalynn Carter, traveled to Recife and met with missionaries who said they had been "treated like animals while in jail."[156]

Those in the Kitchen

But what of this "frying of omelets?" How high up did the knowledge, practice, and approval—however unstated—of murder and mayhem go in the Brazilian security apparatus? Was everything merely the work of a few isolated officers and a select group of men under their commands? One way to come to grips with these questions, one way we can get a glimpse at the enormous range of men in uniform who had to have been involved is to return to the words of army physician Amílcar Lobo. Entering his unit's intelligence section to talk with Col. José Luís Coelho Neto about the physical state of one of the prisoners sometime in winter 1971, Dr. Lobo recounted that the door to Coelho Neto's office was closed when he arrived. Major Rubens Paim Sampaio, Col. Freddie Perdigão Pereira, and an older man dressed in a suit were in the office talking. They did so for some minutes, whereupon Lobo partially entered and indicated that he did not have much time. At that, Sampaio came to the door and opened it. Lobo could hear the stranger continuing to speak aggressively and could see him gesturing a lot to Col. Pedigão.[157]

The civilian went on,

> "Last month, I witnessed the interrogation of a detainee that produced very good results. The scoundrel was hanging in a *pau-de-arara* when [his torturers] decided to shove a Billy club, like this one"—here he picked up a wooden club he found on a table with his left hand—"into the guy's ass. And that's just what they did. The prisoner cried out, trembled, but still refused to speak. So they rammed the truncheon in and out while beating the fellow on the upper part of his body. [After this] it didn't take long for the man to open his mouth and yap for more than an hour. You know, Coelho Neto, everything depends on how you do it. Nobody resists. Nobody is made of iron."
>
> At that point, Colonel Coelho Neto looked at me, made a little sign with his hand, and added, "General, excuse me for interrupting, but Lobo, who is a physician over with the Army Police, is in a hurry and has to discuss an important matter with me. Give me a minute, Sir, please?"
>
> "Oh, I was already leaving anyway." He extended his hand to the colonel, who shook it and saluted while smiling. Then the two men walked to the door. Sampaio and Freddie straightened up discreetly. I said, "Good

day," and the man left. Colonel Coelho Neto looked uneasy [but] smiled and indicated that I should enter his office. On leaving, I asked him who was the individual he was speaking with when I arrived. He answered, "Oh that was General Figueiredo."[158]

General João Baptista de Oliveira Figueiredo became the military's final post-golpe head of state on March 15, 1979. He had been the national chief of SNI before traveling the short distance to the Alvorada. With his connections to the intelligence community, Figueiredo should have been able to halt the excesses of the hard-liners quickly—he did not. Up through 1980, that faction of the Brazilian armed forces continued to scheme, to kidnap, and to bomb.

Besides detonations at the labor disputes in São Paulo, once Figueiredo took office the following explosions or attempted bombings took place: October 4, 1979: a fire bomb went off in the car of journalist Hélio Fernandes in Rio de Janeiro; January 18, 1980: a device was deactivated in Leonel Brizola's room at the Hotel Everest in Rio de Janeiro; January 27, 1980: a charge went off at a Rio samba school, where the Partido Movimento Democrático Brasileiro, or PMDB, was having a rally; May 22, 1980: a time bomb was found still ticking at the National Confederation of Agriculture in Brasília, where Gregório Bezerra was scheduled to speak; May 30, 1980: two bombs exploded at the building occupied by the weekly Rio newspaper *Hora do Povo;* June 27, 1980: another device was set off at the union headquarters of the Journalists of Minas Gerais; August 29, 1980: a blast at the offices of the Brazilian Lawyers' Organization killed a secretary. Another, in the town council chamber in Rio de Janeiro, ripped off an arm and blinded a servant. The final event was the explosion at the Riocentro convention center on April 30, 1981.[159]

A musical extravaganza was scheduled to take place inside the Riocentro complex, and several of the performers were considered security risks by the military. The hard-liners were likewise troubled by the fact that the PCB had organized the event. Anyone who attended was thus viewed with suspicion. No less than two, and possibly as many as four, devices were to be planted in the stands—each designed to maim and kill. So much the better if those who were there just for the music had their wits scared out of them. The public would be told that all of the damage was the work of the VPR.

When the evening of the thirtieth arrived, and the rhythms started to make their way into the night air, army sergeant Guilherme Pereira do Rosário sat on the passenger side of a parked Puma sports car just outside the festival. He was getting ready to go into action. However, there was some kind of mix-up. The bomb he was assembling went off in his lap, killing him instantly. The driver of the vehicle, Capt. Wilson Machado, was seriously injured but managed to live. Two army tough guys had been caught in the act.[160]

The Riocentro affair pressed the embarrassed hard-liners into a corner. It allowed Figueiredo to continue Geisel's rapprochement policies, now renamed *abertura* (opening). What this meant in practical terms was that the political atmosphere began to thaw at a rate slow enough for the most important officers to accept, or at a speed hardly perceptible to outsiders. One of the decrees along the way, in 1979, even instituted a kind of amnesty for the antidictatorship forces, provided they go along with a blanket pardon for anyone involved with the application of the military's security measures.[161] Figueiredo was covered by the edict.

In the late 1980s, Luís Carlos Prestes, back from exile, used to walk along the sidewalk on the beach side of Avenida Vieira Souto in Ipanema for exercise. Occasionally he would pass a retired João Figueiredo and his bodyguards coming toward him from the opposite direction. The reaction was always the same. The two men never said a word.[162]

Plate 1. President João Goulart being photographed by his wife, Maria Tereza, in 1963.
Bloch e Nova Editora Manchete

Plate 2. Leonel Brizola in 1963. Arquivo Nacional/*Correio da Manhã*

Plate 3. Luís Carlos Prestes (seated at right). Arquivo Nacional/*Correio da Manhã*

Plate 4. Colonel Vernon Walters in 1964. Arquivo Nacional/*Correio da Manhã*

Plate 5. U.S. Ambassador to Brazil Lincoln Gordon. Johns Hopkins University

Plate 6. Cabo Anselmo (in front) at the CGT machinist union hall in 1964. Walter Firmo/ Agência JB

Plate 7. The Golpe of 1964 in progress. Troops on their way. Bloch e Nova Editora Manchete

Plate 8. Celebrating in Copacabana over the fall of Goulart on April 1, 1964, as the presidential aircraft passes overhead. Bloch e Nova Editora Manchete

Plate 9 The burning of books at the National Union of Students building in Flamengo shortly after the *golpe*. Paulo Muniz/*Life*

"Wherever they burn books they will also, in the end, burn human beings." Heinrich Heine

Plate 10. General Castelo Branco (sitting), the first military dictator following the Golpe of 1964. Going clockwise, he was succeeded by General Costa e Silva, General Médici, General Geisel, and General Figueiredo. A Cavalry officer, Figueiredo was drawn as a bow-legged hint of the "Amigo da Onça" ("False Friend"), a cartoon character made famous by Péricles de Andrade Maranhão. Cássio Loredano/*Jornal do Brazil*

Plate 11. "General" Golbery.
Ique/*Jornal do Brasil*

Plate 12. Gustavo Borges holding an example of Miguel Arraes's offensive communist garments destined for rural workers in Pernambuco. *O Dia*

Plate 13. Cecil Borer in 1964. *O Cruzeiro*

Plate 14. An injured Carlos Marighella being questioned by police in May 1964. Arquivo Nacional/*Correio da Manhã*

Plate 15. A pause in the torturing of Gregório in Recife in April 1964. Anonymous

A tortura por dentro

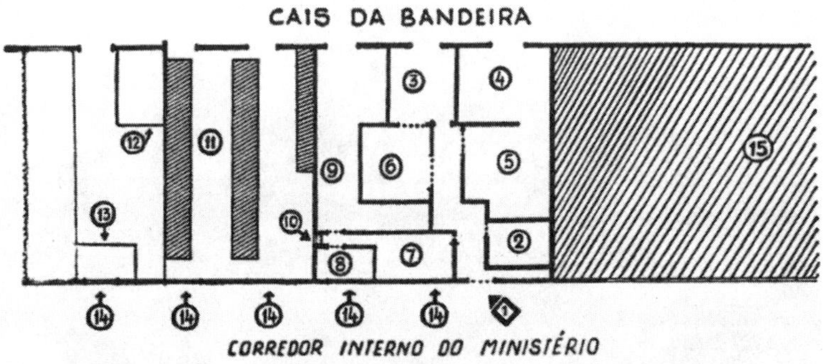

CENIMAR·DEPENDÊNCIAS PRINCIPAIS

Torture from The Inside

Wharf of The Flag

1 Entrance
2 Waiting Room—Some suspects handcuffed here for more than 48 hours
3 Director's Office—On one wall was the sign "Join Hands, *and* with Love, We Will Reconstruct Brazil."
4 Office of the Associate Director
5 Office of the Manager—Displayed on one wall was the notice 'We Are Not Joking!'
6 Interrogation Room
7 Clerk's Office
8 Cloakroom
9 Photographic Lab
10 Closet with a false back leading to secret area
11 Confidential card files and telex
12 Torture chamber
13 Torture chamber
14 Permanently closed windows
15 General offices of the Navy, occupying the rest of the floor

Internal Corridor of the Ministry

CENIMAR • PRINCIPAL OFFICES

Plate 16. Floor plan of the main CENIMAR torture facility in Rio de Janeiro in the 1960s with translation. Arquivo Nacional/*Correio da Manhã*

Plate 17. Geraldo Vandré. Arquivo Nacional/*Correio da Manhã*

Plate 18. An unsigned depiction of Carlos "The Crow" Lacerda perched at one of the rivers where indigents were murdered. The sign on the approaching truck, packed with such people, reads, "TRASH." The placard in the water, loaded with human remains, says, "Work of Governor Carlos Lacerda." *Última Hora*

Plate 19. Charge of the Light Brigade into the crowd outside Candelária Church at the forbidden requiem mass for Édson Luís. Evandro Teixeira/Agência JB

Plate 20. Milton Le Cocq carrying the hat of Mineirinho (behind Le Cocq, shirt open), 1960. Between the two men, in the background, is a young Sivuca. Arquivo Nacional/*Última Hora*

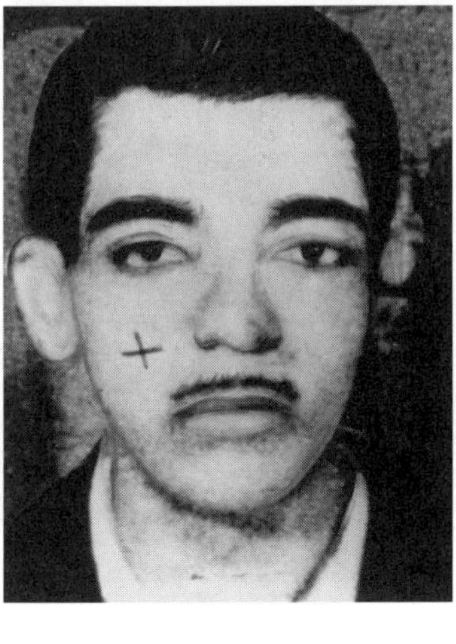

Plate 21. "Horse Face." The "X" on his cheek was added at a police station following the murder of Le Cocq to indicate that Horse Face was a target for death. *O Cruzeiro*

Plate 22. Smiling for the camera aboard a Varig flight to Rio, Mariel Moryscotte under arrest in 1973. Vitor Santos/Agência JB

Plate 23. A death-squad warning decal on a car in Rio de Janeiro. Crister Kågéll

Plate 24. Astorige Corrêa, "O Correinha," with his trusty Winchester in 1967. *Fatos e Fotos*

Plate 25. Sérgio Fleury on February 24, 1978. Agência O Globo

Plate 26. The Polícia Civil in Rocinha, Rio de Janeiro's and South America's largest shantytown, on January 29, 2004. Michel Filho/Agência O Globo

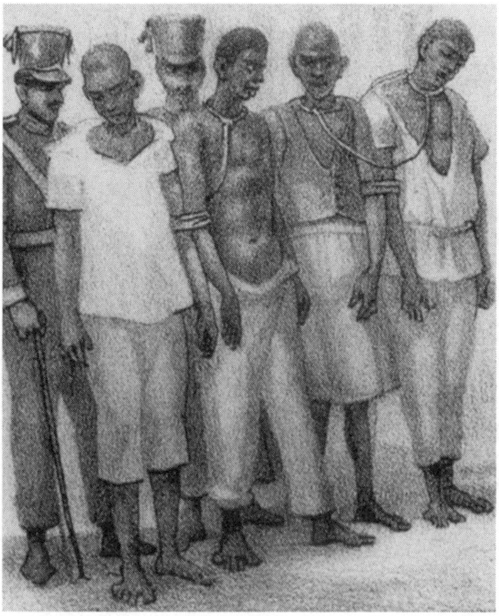

Plate 27. Police with their captives in Rio de Janeiro in the 1820s. Debret/Acervo da Fundação Biblioteca Nacional–Brasil

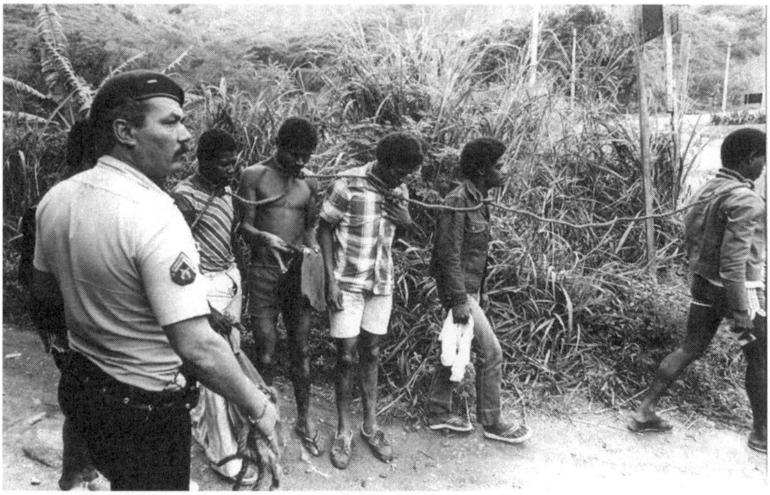

Plate 28. Polícia Militar in action in rural Rio de Janeiro in 1982. Luiz Morier/ Agência JB

Slaves of the New Age

Terror to the Year 2000 *and Beyond*

Chapter 5

The Real Rural Bandits

IT IS OFTEN forgotten or ignored that in Brazil the treatment of common criminals, plus all the other so-called dregs of society, never really changed. Brazil's military dictators, via their executors of policy, were by no means concerned about who would be denounced, arrested, or ground up—if suspected of nonpolitical transgressions. In this they were no different from the rulers of the country who came before them or from those who came after them. Castelo Branco, Costa e Silva, Médici, Geisel, and Figueiredo simply underwrote time-honored practices for dealing with individuals labeled by the upper classes as *marginais* (marginals; that is, criminals). What caused so much outrage was that during their tenure in Brasília they applied many of these same procedures to the now excused, often middle-class, agitators of social order.

In the rural areas of Brazil, the dual system of justice based on social class was put into practice against the peasants who flocked to a lay religious leader in Canudos (1893–97), just as it was against the displaced poor and their "monks" in the Contestado affair (1912–16). And, it was used all through the period of the cangaço right up until 1940. Regional or national elites—or both—invariably hounded the religious revitalizations, interrupted now and again or paralleled by violent peasant protests and strikes. Opposition began at the level of general disapproval but could quickly move up the scale to open hostility, particularly when profits—real or anticipated—were involved. There was little room for discussion and still less for tolerance.[1]

The notable exception, of course, is Juàzeiro do Norte in Ceará. Padre Cícero Romano Batista turned that village into a messianic center which came to be the largest such community Brazil has ever known. In 1909 Juàzeiro's population was about fifteen thousand. Although defrocked for a time, Padre Cícero paternalistically provided for many of his people's wants and needs and grew to be one of the most influential backlanders of his day. There were a number of reasons for his success. Perhaps the primary explanation was his concession to the local men of influence not to step on their economic toes. He accomplished this by allowing his followers to work outside Juàzeiro do Norte on the fazendas or other establishments of these men. He also permitted a number of sects to establish themselves within Juàzeiro or even in satellite communes around it. Cícero did not want to appear to be monopolizing power—he was well aware of the way the elites had eradicated Antônio Conselheiro and those at Canudos. Last, he kept the forceful at bay through a strict policy of political neutrality until he found it beneficial to do otherwise. These were important concessions that helped to pacify regional elites.[2]

A Sweeping Chronicle

The occurrence of Brazilian resurgence movements has a clear connection all the way back to 1578 and the death of Portuguese King Sebastião I at the hands of the Moors in the Battle of Alcazarquivir. The demise of Sebastião was a catastrophe for Portugal. It marked the end of her expansionist period, and, two years later, the loss of independence to Spain for six decades. Yet many whispers had it that Sebastião had, in fact, not died in the fighting. It was said that he would return one day to free Portugal from the yoke of the Spaniards. Some took these rumors to an extreme, believing that the next appearance of the slain king would personify the Second Coming of Christ. Those who felt otherwise looked on such views as ignorant heresy.

Once firmly implanted on the Brazilian mainland, Portuguese Catholicism continued to reflect this interpretative duality. Each position took different roots in the emerging nation. The traditionalists ingested the conventional dogma and pomp of official Church teachings, and, in turn passed on a religious orientation that was tailor-made for the conservative palates of the nobility and those identified with them. In opposition, there emerged a religious conviction emphasizing release for the masses. This second form of the faith was more universalistic, immediate, and since there was usually a lack of priests in the interior, it was often administered by the laity. Even though Sebastianism was expunged from the formal Church, it never fully left the religious realities of rural, folk-Catholics. What this meant was that the great bulk of Brazil's peasants were inclined to rally behind substitute religious personalities when these individuals preached that the long dreamed of millennium was near at hand.

Messianic/millenarian components could be found in Brazilian provincial Catholicism for another reason. They served as the only avenue by which the rural poor could flee from otherwise chronic boss control and domination.[3] This was particularly the case when the lower classes fell into the category of being called *povo miserável* (sorry masses) during times of unusual hardship. Brazil's entire social history, inundated with practices of worker exploitation, is top-heavy with instances of utopian-religious escapism right up to the present crop of evangelic soul savers.[4]

Rural potentates, be they the coronéis of yesterday or the mechanized fazendeiros and multinational organizations of today, have perpetually condemned and battered what in their view was and is a disgusting peasantry. Not only did they abuse them, they also disposed of them in the ebb and flow of production. This rejection of a people as people by the elite can be traced to the days when an influx of poor European immigrants came to Brazil to do the work once done by slaves. Coupled to this was that fact that until 1850 land could be obtained through occupation. After that date, it had to be purchased.

By the end of the nineteenth century, the swarm of rural laborers of all ethnicities, races, and hybrids understood that little had changed since the declared end of slavery twelve years before on May 13, 1888. Perhaps the main lesson passed from father to son was that there would be no open talk of justice and land redistribution if one wanted to remain alive. Peasants could be seen but not heard. They were to ask for as little as possible. They represented the weak part, the poor part, in this relationship based on one side's control of and willingness to use violence on the other—just as they had in times gone past. Elites wanted to believe and continued to believe that the lower classes were childlike, unsophisticated, and inept if left on their own. It was something in their genes, they sometimes argued—both theirs and in those of the powerless. Hence the latter had to be made to be orderly at any cost if progress was to be assured.

This was how it was before the combined effects of mass media, technology, and the populism of the second half of the twentieth century kindled the possibilities for change. Dovetailing into this scenario was the fact that while Brazil's population as a whole was increasing, its rural population was decreasing. Rural people were leaving the countryside, either by choice or because they were forced out of agriculture, and moving to the metropolitan areas in the hopes of a better life. Their dreams were often so strong that it mattered little if they had to start out in the teeming favelas, in a park, or even under a bridge in urban Brazil. Countless thousands were willing to take the chance. By the mid-1960s the transition was complete; as of that time the majority of Brazilians lived in urban environments. This evolution can be seen in figure 5.1.[5]

FIGURE 5.1
Rural and Urban Population from 1930 to 1990 in Percent

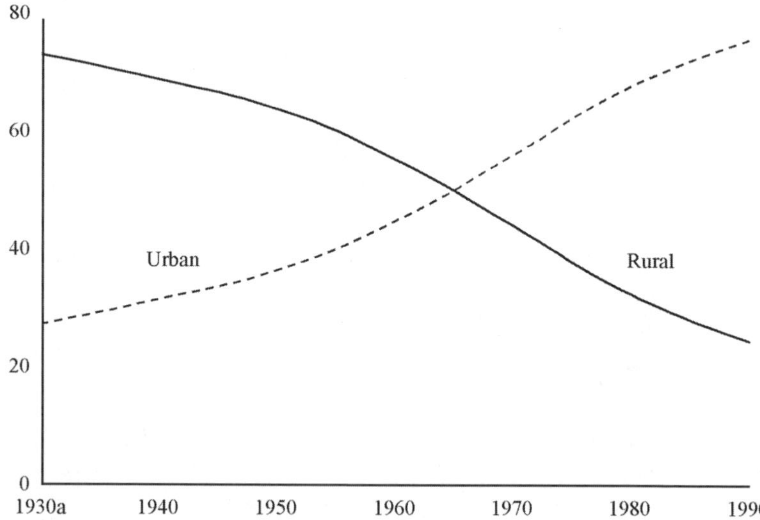

	1930[a]	*1940*	*1950*	*1960*	*1970*	*1980*	*1990*
Rural Population	73.0%	68.8	63.8	55.3	44.1	32.4	24.5
Urban Population	27.0	31.2	36.2	44.7	55.9	67.6	75.5

a = estimate

One legacy from the João Goulart years is that from his time forward a number of rural workers took another path. Because of an increasing awareness of their plight, some provincials—only a handful at first—decided that the time was ripe to claim or to occupy land. This had actually been the common denominator all along, and when it took hold, no longer did rural workers seek out the *beato,*[6] the reincarnation, or the Savior in the same way. They did not give up their religion; they merely adjusted its fatalism to allow in fresh ideas from the outside. A number of radical priests, who embraced principles from the Theology of Liberation, encouraged a good number of these peasants. As a result, a significant slice of rural labor began shifting its consciousness to the here and now, to the profane aspirations that in Brazil had lain behind many messianic and millenarian movements in the first place. Unobtainable, indeed unthinkable, earlier, the uniting bond between innumerable Brazilians since the first half of the 1960s has been the land and the burning desire that just maybe they can own it, or possess it, or simply live in peace on a piece of it.

End-of-the-Century Statistics

As of 1996 there were 916.7 million acres (371 million hectares) of land that could be used for agricultural purposes in Brazil. Of this territory, 62 percent, or 568.3 million acres (230 million hectares), was used for crop production or for grazing livestock. That left 348.4 million acres (141 million hectares) that were only pushing up weeds. Intensifying the issue, 1 percent of Brazil's elite controlled 44 percent of the country's agriculturally viable real estate, including undeveloped land. That this latter portion is significant was shown by the fact that properties *over* one thousand hectares (2,471 acres) in size produced 11 percent of the country's basic foodstuff. Those concerns *below* ten hectares (24.7 acres) turned out 16 percent of Brazil's comestibles.[7]

Also in 1996 it was estimated that five million Brazilian families (or, conservatively, twenty million people if one included a wife and two children) would have liked to own a small parcel of this unused agricultural area. In response to the outcry that ensued and with only one omission, national and state administrations occasionally promised to give away land, but only when it was politically expedient to do so.[8] Yet even as these tired assurances were given and given and given again, the povão still wanted land! They have always wanted land. Since colonial times, the circle of wait and frustration has produced only conflict after bloody conflict.

The Coming of the UDR

A return to civilian rule in 1985 and the presidency of José Sarney did not significantly alter anything in rural Brazil. The military governments and erstwhile political parties that had been formed to represent the interests of the landed elite remained in continuous opposition to any significant alterations of the agrarian setting. In pre-golpe Brazil, these parties had included the União Democrática Nacional, Partido Social Democrático, Partido Republicano, and the Integralist Partido de Representação Popular. This of course ignores groups that were not specifically political parties but only associations. Before the tumultuous events of 1964, one of the most important of these creations was the Sociedade Rural Brasileira (SRB—Brazilian Rural Society). Formed in 1919 to represent the interest of the fazendeiros, the SRB always managed to drag its feet on questions of land reform. It became one of the main rural movements behind the downfall of President João Goulart, even going so far as to arm many of its members and allow its offices in São Paulo to be used as organizational headquarters for the Marcha da Família com Deus pela Liberdade.[9]

From the country's earliest days, rural potentates had used *jagunço* and capanga enforcers to protect themselves.[10] Although the terms came to be used almost interchangeably with a host of others, a jagunço normally did the killing for his rural bosses when called upon to do so. Otherwise he supervised laborers on a rural estate. A capanga was different. He was an armed bodyguard, usually hired privately. The capanga carried out all kinds of horrific acts for his employer and/or landlord. Murder and mayhem were standard assignments.

The União Democrática Ruralista (Rural Democratic Union, or UDR), was and is no different from the SRB. They are simply another page in the book of terror. Formally started in Goiás in 1984 in response to José Sarney's meager land redistribution plans, the UDR is an outgrowth of the TFP (Sociedade Brasileira de Defesa da Tradição, Família e Propriedade—Society for the Defense of Tradition, Family, and Property). UDR supporters represent a conglomeration of rural elites opposed to land reform, the progressive Church, and Communism. They are in favor of hands-off capitalism and the unregulated arming of all landowners.[11] By 1990 the UDR had mushroomed. "There were 230,000 members with two hundred chapters in nineteen states."[12] At that time, the leader of the UDR was an orthopedist turned farmer turned cattle breeder named Ronaldo Caiado. Charismatic, Caiado holds decidedly old-school opinions. Alex Shoumatoff, who heard Caiado give a speech to other ranchers, paraphrased him as follows: "You are the master[s] of your property, and nobody can tell you what to do. You got yours by your own sweat, and if others don't have as much as you do, it's because they don't deserve it. So why should you share it with lazy, incompetent inferiors? Why should we, who know what to do with the land, hand it over to people who have never farmed or ranched? We are the ones who feed the country, who provide the grain and beef. We are the heroes. The riches of Brazil have always come from people like us, from private initiative."[13]

Caiado's strength grew to such a degree that the UDR effectively killed President José Sarney's land-reform package. Caiado ran for president in 1988, along with a host of other candidates in a two-tiered election. While Ronaldo did not gain enough votes to advance to the runoff phase, his clout was nonetheless sufficient to give the victory to conservative Fernando Collor de Mello over progressive Luis Ignácio Lula da Silva.

Collor, who came to national prominence promising to clean out graft and rein in corrupt power brokers, aptly called *marajás* (maharajas), only feigned land reform once taking office. He was later impeached on graft and corruption charges, thus becoming the first Brazilian president to be thrown out of office. Collor de Mello's family had a history of duplicity. His uncle Lindolfo Collor was a minister in the initial national government of Getúlio Vargas. Lindolfo was supposed to have been a man so blinded by ambition and the pursuit of wealth that he once cheated his own father-in-law out of a large sum of money. He had likewise defrauded the governor of Minas Gerais—and a presidential hopeful—Antônio Carlos in connection with the installation of a bogus telegraph station during the days leading up to the election of 1930. Fernando Collor de Mello's father, Alagoas state senator Arnon de Mello, shot and killed a fellow legislator in the Senate but was let off because he was actually aiming at another person.[14]

Caiado evidently thought he was being witty when he claimed that the UDR was not against agrarian reform per se. "On the contrary, we always were against entities such as the CPT [Comissão Pastoral da Terra—the Pastoral Land Commission], the progressive Church, and leftist political parties that used [agrarian] reform to promote themselves."[15] Such discourse was simply pretense. So too was the UDR's pronouncement that it "repudiates all kinds of violence," and that it "never supports armed conflicts."[16] Peasants knew that these were embellished lies. To this day, a common chant in the interior, whenever the landless rural poor suspect the UDR of complicity in some killing, goes:

> Punição!
> Punição!
> UDR na prisão![17]
>
> ———
>
> Punishment!
> Punishment!
> Put the UDR in prison!

Every affiliate of the UDR was rumored "to have an executive committee that overlaps with the death squad in the State Department of Public Safety."[18] Thus the UDR regularly employed hit men to knock off troublesome individuals in the interior of the country. And the fix was evidently in so well that a *mandante* (the hirer of an assassin) did not have to worry about going to jail. Looking at the twelve-year period 1987 to 1999, a CPT investigation determined that in eighty-six cases that were brought before the courts where mandantes were suspected of having ordered the murder of 1,167 rural workers, just seven mandantes were deemed culpable and only five received prison terms.[19] Another CPT study showed that a mere thirty-three of the actual killers had been found guilty by the end of 1993.[20]

Subelites

Many of the people retained as assassins in the CPT inquiries came from Goiânia—a short one hundred or so miles from the federal capital in Brasília. Their services could be arranged by word of mouth, through some of the city's lawyers and real estate agents, or through the torpedoes themselves. A firm specializing in rural security called A Solução, or The Solution, was at one time the best known of these dubious concerns.[21] A veritable Brazilian version of Murder Incorporated, A Solução was founded by no less than Col. Irineu da Silva Mattos, former head of the Department of Public Safety in Goiás.[22] How common were the services provided by such groups? By the year 2000 the trend in using hired killers in rural settings was actually on the rise, as can be seen in the scattergram presented in figure 5.2.[23]

The prices for an execution varied with the importance of the target. By 1994, it had become much more expensive (an average of forty times more expensive) to have a judge, sheriff, mayor, or bishop killed than to have someone involved in organizing agricultural laborers killed. Sixty to 70 percent of the following rates had to be paid in advance before a contract was finalized. All figures are rounded and given in U.S. dollars at the black market rate—a better indication of the real worth of the cruzado, Brazil's currency at the time. Observe that the price list does not mention what it cost to do away with a humble agricultural worker. This was evidently so

FIGURE 5.2
Rural Assassinations by Hired Killer from 1964 to 1999 in Percent

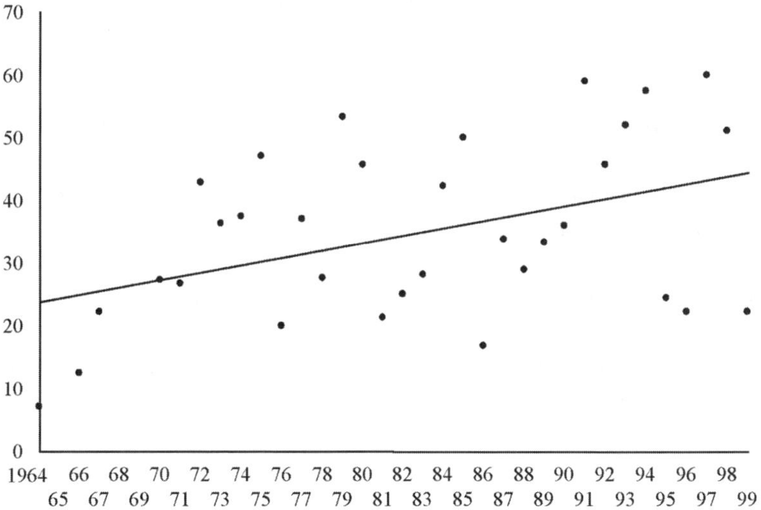

easy that a fazendeiro's own jagunços could carry out the task with very little rigmarole.

Rural union official	$329 to 987
Rural city councilman, lawyer, or agent	987
Priest in the agrarian reform movement	2,632 to 3,290
Rural judge, sheriff, mayor, or bishop	19,737 [24]

The city of Imperatriz, in Maranhão, was also a noted place to hire gunmen. One of the first victims, in 1951, was the mayor, Urbano Rocha. Davi Alves da Silva, whose brother Daniel was a federal congressman, made a fortune commanding groups of hired killers in the area in the 1980s. Anyone who needed a killer had only to go to the dilapidated and nameless bar at one end of the municipal market. They could as well approach the men standing outside the hunting shop owned by Joaquim José Branco.[25] One of the most disgraceful cases involved a CPT priest and activist for the PT (Partido dos Trabalhadores—Workers' Party). It occurred on May 10, 1986, when Geraldo Rodrigues da Costa shot Padre Josimo Moraes Tavares twice in front of a church in Imperatriz. Two landowner brothers, Osmar Teodoro da Silva, also know as "Paulão," and Nazareth Teodoro da Silva, who went by the nickname "Deca," hired Costa to rub out the cleric. Father Josimo died in the hospital when physicians discovered they had no anesthetic for an operation. The murderer was soon arrested, but it took authorities fifteen years to apprehend the Silva brothers, which happened only because of a series of stories in *Jornal do Brasil.* Deca was let go after a night in jail for lack of a formal arrest warrant. The only thing rural workers got out of the deal was the blood-soaked shirt of Padre Josimo, which they used at subsequent rallies as a flag nailed to a wooden cross.[26]

Pará, one state away, also had firms specializing in eradication. There was even a pecking order among private assassins; the most powerful thugs used small planes, stayed in the best hotels, and drove stolen cars. Ambush was the method preferred by these men. One Sebastião da Terezona was even said to have shot rural workers simply because they stood in line to collect their pay. Most professional triggermen in Pará, especially those in the southern part of the state, had a policy of never burying their prey. They cut out the entrails and hung the bodies in trees by the necks so that the meat would dry. More recently, they chopped off ears, gouged out eyes, tore off limbs, and burned the cadavers. The remains were then left for Urubu vultures and dogs.[27]

Perhaps not as harsh, but similarly effective, the police themselves, especially the Polícia Militar, came more to the forefront as the killers of agricultural workers. Over the years, these representatives of law and order threatened, attempted, or carried out the homicides of rural laborers and their families. Enforcers of laws created by the elite largely for the elite, they often committed these offenses together with members of the elite (judges, rural entrepreneurs, landowners, and so on) and the henchmen of the elite (capangas, jagunços, etc.).[28] In the three figures (5.3a–c), the participation of several types of police are noted in respect to rural assassination, attempted murder, and the threat of murder against rural workers during various years. The lack of data for the years 1985–89 and again from 1996 to 1999 was due to the source consulted.[29] Nonetheless, the point seems clear enough. In the legends, PC+PF means the Polícia Civil and Polícia Federal, PC+PM stands for Polícia Civil and Polícia Militar, Fed Hwy Police equals Federal Highway Police, and Nat Park Police designates the National Park Police. The final presentation in this series, figure 5.3d, combines the three forgoing figures, when they are comparable, in order to better appreciate the origin and entirety of these particular forms of rural violence. Figure 5.3d, like its three-dimensional acronym of cinemagraphic usage, is a vivid revelation of the suspect party. The Polícia Militar was the main instigator of homicides, attempts at homicide, and threats of homicide.[30] Clearly those entrusted with the responsibility and privilege of protecting the public were protecting the interests of someone else.

Coming to an understanding of the totality of this slaughter—not just of those murders reputedly committed by law enforcement—has been another question. Various watchdog organizations competed with each other for several years in this undertaking. Different figures were the unfortunate result. From 1985 on, however, CPT generally had the field to itself. Its data, and that of the Movimento dos Trabalhadores Rurais Sem-Terra (Movement of Landless Rural Workers) (MST), *Ciência Hoje* (CH), and Amnesty International (AI), are presented in graph form in figure 5.4. Observe that figure 5.4 excludes attacks by Native Brazilians, cases without dates, kidnappings, suicides, accidents at work, the disappeared, other causes, and victims of the Araguaia conflict (1972–75). MST lists sixty dead in the region of Pará during the Araguaia affair. It fails to mention that these were rebels and not rural workers.[31]

FIGURE 5.3a
Murder by the Police in Rural Areas from 1985 to 1999

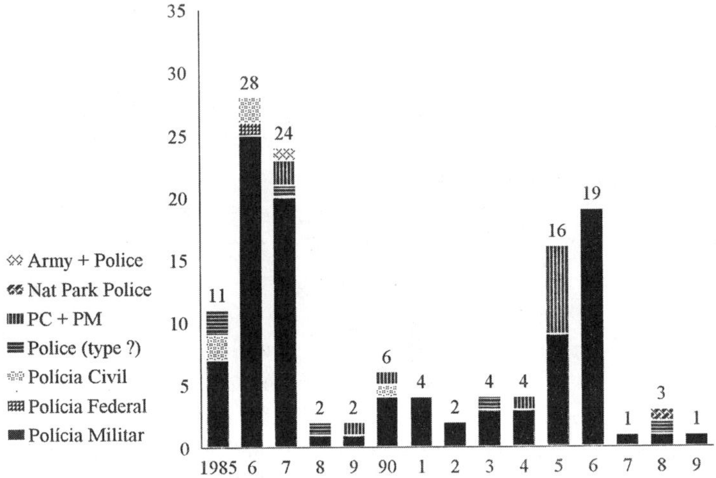

In the legends for figures 5.3a to 5.3d, PC+PF means the Polícia Civil and Polícia Federal, PC+PM stands for Polícia Civil and Polícia Militar, Fed Hwy Police equals Federal Highway Police, and Nat Park Police designates the National Park Police.

FIGURE 5.3b
Attempted Murder by the Police in Rural Areas from 1990 to 1995

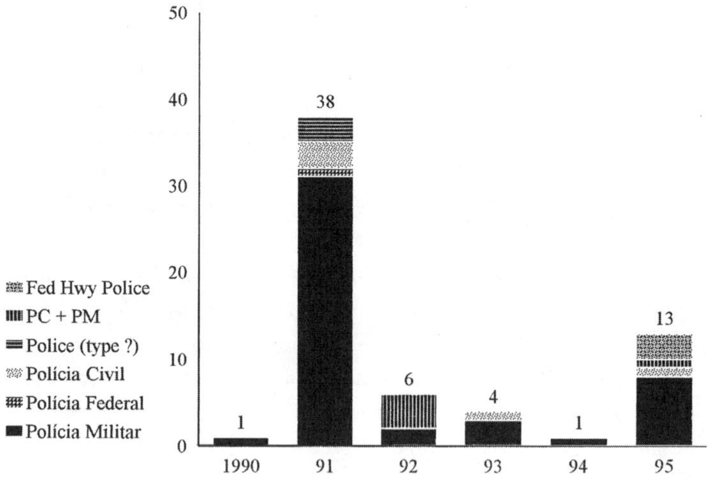

FIGURE 5.3c
Murder Threats by the Police in Rural Areas from 1990 to 1995

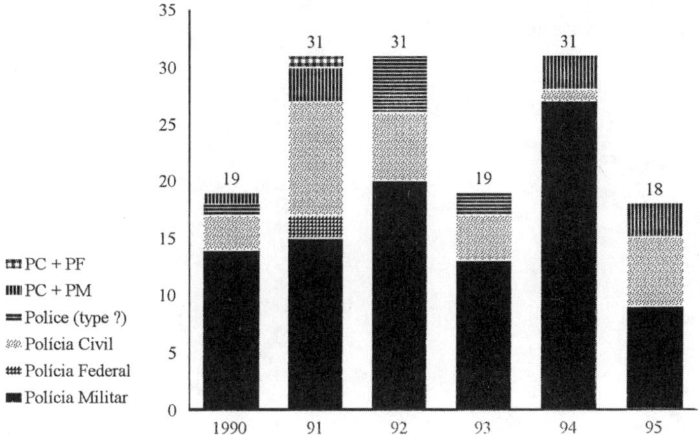

FIGURE 5.3d
Murder, Attempted Murder, Threats of Murder by the Police in Rural Areas from 1990 to 1995

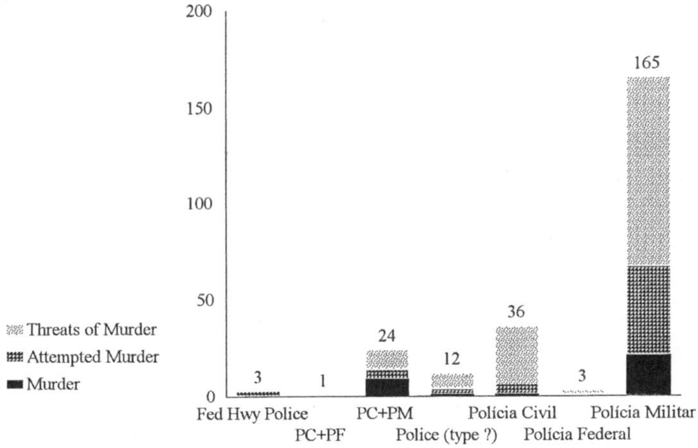

FIGURE 5.4
Rural Murders according to the Movimento dos Trabalhadores Rurais Sem-Terra, Ciência Hoje, Comissão Pastoral da Terra, and Amnesty International in Rural Areas from 1964 to 1999

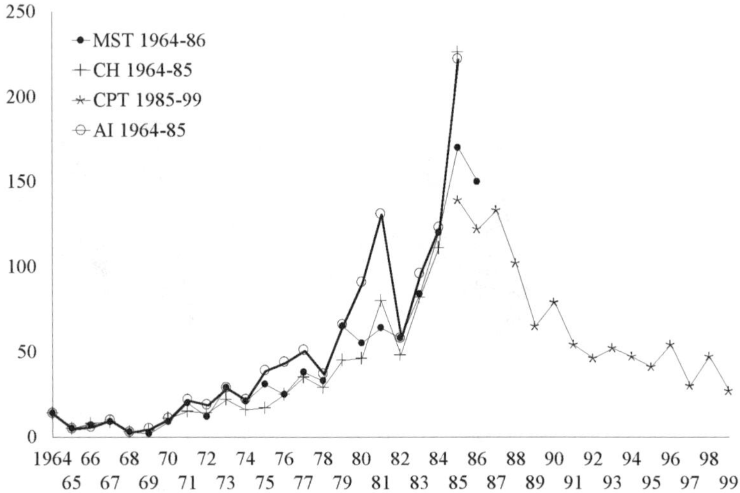

The slow decline in the number of rural assassinations after 1985 is credibly due to the work of the CPT at exposing the problem both to Brazilians and to a wider international audience. Its ability to do this work came in part in 1985 with the demise of the military dictatorship and the rebirth of civilian rule. The incoming democratic administration was not as tolerant to such things as had been the generals before them. One additional event in 1988, however, also served to keep the numbers dropping. It was the cold-blooded murder of a national treasure.

Francisco Alves Mendes Filho

Know by everyone as "Chico" Mendes,[32] Francisco was a lowly rubber tapper from Xapurí, in the state of Acre, who became a world-famous ecologist. Darci Alves Pereira ambushed Mendes as he stepped from the backdoor of his house on the evening of December 22, 1988. Chico had been *anunciado* (warned) several times that he was on a hit list because he had blocked the way of landowners. He knew he was marked for elimination, and he wanted those who had threatened him prosecuted or made to back off. He tried the usual legal channels. He even sent several telexes to the governor, Flaviano Melo; to Polícia Federal chief Romeu Tuma; to the Minister of Justice, Paulo Bossard; and to President José Sarney. No one from the government ever answered his pleas.[33] The authorities in Xapurí assigned a couple of Polícia Militar to guard Mendes, but the bodyguards' submachine guns were curiously replaced with defective pistols just before he was killed. One of Chico's daughters was asked who she thought really killed her father. Without hesitation, she replied, "It was the UDR."[34]

Darci Alves Pereira carried out the murder at the wish of his father, Darli Alves da Silva. Darli and a brother, Alvarino, are said to have had some thirty rural workers killed between 1973 and 1988: two in Minas Gerais, three in Paraná, and the rest in Acre. They fled to Acre, where warrants for their arrests were sent to the state superintendent of the Polícia Federal, Mauro Sposito. Being one of Darli's friends, the superintendent did nothing.[35] In Acre, Darli was a member of a group of ranchers who had wanted Mendes out of the way. Both Darci and Darli were charged with the murder. At their trial, nearly two years later, Márcio Thomaz Bastos, a courageous lawyer who had defended numerous political prisoners during the just-ended period of military rule, assisted the prosecution. The defense of the father-and-son duo was headed by João Lucena Leal, one of the Polícia Federal torturers in Fortaleza during the dictatorship before becoming a criminal defense lawyer. In his former profession, Leal had maimed and crippled prisoners as late as 1973.[36] Despite apprehension in some quarters, the two defendants were found guilty, and each was sentenced to nineteen years' confinement. Key testimony was provided by fifteen-year-old Genésio Ferreira da Silva, a relative by marriage of the defendants, who lived at Darli's fazenda. He swore before the court that Darli had instigated the crime. In addition, the boy stated that several male members of the Alves family had killed fourteen other persons in or near the area.[37]

In February 1992 Darli's conviction was overturned and the case was sent to a higher court. He was kept in jail, however, on another murder charge, this time from the state of Paraná. There was talk of deporting Darli to Paraná to stand trial. Then, on February 14, 1993, apparently with the acquiescence of the new governor of Acre, Romildo Magalhães, Darli and Darci escaped from prison by walking through the front gate. The breakout was timed to take place during the national confusion produced by Carnival. Another son, Darlizinho, sold twenty head of cattle to finance the escape, which included the rental of an airplane.

It is said that Darli and Darci went first to Bolivia, then to Paraguay, and then back to Brazil to their property near Xapurí, called Fazenda Paraná. There followed a Keystone Cops–style chase in several rural areas—at one point it included even the Bolivian National Guard—that frustratingly produced only dead ends and rumors on the whereabouts of the two fugitives. Though the Brazilian courts upheld Darli's earlier guilty verdict *in absentia,* it was not until just after dawn on June 30, 1996, that he was finally taken into custody again. Darli was seized on a fazenda in Medicilândia, Pará, which he had acquired using a false name. Five months later, on November 26, Darci was captured. Darli had his sentence increased by twelve years for the Paraná killing, but the entire verdict was eventually vacated, and he was transferred to a semi-open institution where he was locked up only at night. During the day the mandante behind the murder of Chico Mendes worked as a public functionary in the city of Agrovila de São Sebastião and received a salary of approximately $150 per month.[38]

The Continuing Drama

Since none of the sources whose figures for rural murders are depicted in figure 5.4 gives the entire picture from 1964 to 1998, figure 5.5[39] combines the research by MST with that begun in 1985 by CPT.[40] The years 1985 and 1986 were subtracted from the CPT data to make it fit with the more moderate MST material. Remember, figure 5.5 is only an estimate of the total package. Although tentative, it does offer the dimension of being able to suggest where these killings are taking place by state and geographical region.

The nine most precarious states were Pará in the north, with 577 assassinations, followed by Maranhão, Bahia, and Pernambuco in the northeast; Mato Grosso and Goiás in the center; and Minas Gerais in the southeast. Then came Paraná in the south and Rondônia back in the north. It is significant to note that the north had more killings, 765, than did the northeast, 662. But the difference is really moot since these regions are separated only by a line drawn on a map. It is more germane to observe that three of

FIGURE 5.5
Rural Murders from 1964 to 1999 by State and Section

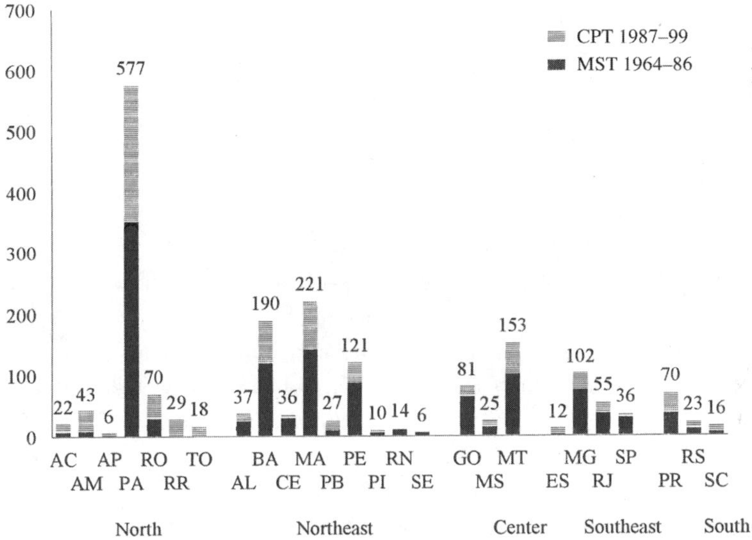

Abbreviations: AC = Acre; AL = Alagoas; AM = Amazonas; BA = Bahia; CE = Ceará; ES = Espírito Santo; GO = Goiás; MA = Maranhão; MG = Minas Gerais; MS = Mato Grosso do Sul; MT = Mato Grosso; PA = Pará; PB = Paraíba; PE = Pernambuco; PI = Piauí ; PR = Paraná; RJ = Rio de Janeiro; RN = Rio Grande do Norte; RO = Rondônia; RR = Roraima; RS = Rio Grande do Sul; SC = Santa Catarina; SE = Sergipe; SP = São Paulo; TO = Tocantins

the four most unsafe states—Pará, Maranhão, and Mato Grosso—are neighbors. If one throws in Bahia, Minas Gerais, and Goiás, the latter with all those murder services, then one sees an arc of rural assassination, at times over a thousand miles wide, curving from Bahia on the Atlantic, through the center of Brazil, up and out the mouth of the Amazon River to the north.

There is more to this tragic story; not every assassination was successful, and botched jobs were likewise part of the picture. Supplementary crimes were committed as well, some of which went unreported. The CPT material was the lone statistical source for these additional offenses—so far as they were known. Moreover, it cannot be stressed enough that nearly all of these misdeeds were perpetrated against rural workers and or individuals concerned with their welfare. This added data is summarized below for the years 1987 to 1998.[41]

Assaults	14,939
Attempted Murder	724
Destruction of Homes	13,165[a]
Illegal Confinement	5,794[b]
Injuries	4,286
Kidnapping	235[c]
Murder Threats	1,826
Torture	616

a = 1988–98; b = until 1999; c = until 1992

It should be pointed out here that assaults and injuries have been in decline for some years. Most of the other categories remain roughly stable. Conversely, the responding authorities and other subelites, augmented their destruction of the places of residence of anyone caught trying to occupy land. Commencing In 1988 with 132 homes demolished, the figures jumped to 2,782 in 1998. Although these structures were typically temporary and ramshackle, they were, nonetheless, a home to someone that was ripped apart or burned to the ground without respect to the contents, be they material or human.

Several of these injustices could be anticipated under the circumstances of intending to permanently occupy someone else's property. What was unexpected was the number, some 5,794, or nearly 445 a year, who were illegally kept from leaving rural settings. The intriguing question here is thus: Why was this figure so high? The most plausible answer is that the number reflected a large part of an incessant phenomenon.

Debt Peonage

Slavery in Brazil was supposed to have ended with the Lei Áurea in 1888, but the decree was really effective only in the urban areas. The enslavement of Asian, black, indigenous,[42] and white Brazilians, along with their various mixtures, continued, albeit at a more discreet pace, in the interior of the country after 1888. The need for servile labor was and is just too great to be totally offset by a law enacted in far-off Rio de Janeiro.

From the moment Princess Isabel affixed her signature to the emancipation document, whispered comments to the effect that the practice of enslaving people or maintaining them in conditions of virtual servitude stubbornly lingered on.[43] The practice certainly continued until the 1930s and was apparently winked at, even from the office of Gétulio Vargas. It seems that Vargas was, at a minimum, indirectly involved in the enslavement process through one of his top lieutenants. More likely than not, Getúlio knew about such goings on if only in one case. Granting this assumption, he simply ignored what he was told, was aware of, or heard others discussing.

In the old Federal District, Police Chief Filinto Müller was the key link. His post required a presidential appointment. Filinto used this position fully, becoming a close Vargas confidant with direct access to the leader of the country. In the 1930s, and no doubt into the 1940s, Júlio, one of Müller's, brothers ran a fazenda with the incredible name "Abolição" (or "Abolition") in the family's Nazified native state of Mato Grosso "where prisoners worked. All laborers who put up a fuss about their wages were arrested and sent there. They were forced to work for free, receiving only a small piece of meat, from 4 A.M. until sunset under the system of the billy club."[44]

Besides Júlio, Filinto had another brother, Fenelon. Both men became state *interventors* during these years—jobs as governors that also needed presidential sanction.[45] Others in the Müller clan were just as questionable. One of the cousins "had a Rosary made from the ears of prisoners."[46]

Vargas's early social welfare legislation never really touched the rural worker. What there was of it was never designed for this purpose. Perhaps he was afraid of the displeasure such policies would cause among the fazendeiros. Perhaps he just felt that rural labor did not matter. In April 1942 American diplomats reported,

> There is a large and complicated body of legislation which presumably regularizes labor relations and confers certain social benefits on the employees of industrial and commercial enterprises. However, these laws are not uniformly enforced throughout the country and enforcement tends to be increasingly lax as one gets farther away from the Eastern seaboard. The government establishes minimum wage rates, presumably based on the cost of living, which vary from place to place and according to occupation. The . . . daily wages in the interior of Brazil [are] . . . two milreis [or 9.7 cents] per day for unskilled field labor.[47]

Later that year, the American government remarked on what this meant for Brazil's rural citizens during the first Vargas administrations. "*Seringueiros* or rubber gatherers of the Amazon valley are kept in virtual slavery through debts for necessary supplies which cannot be paid off from their low wages and accumulate year after year. In some parts of Matto Grosso working conditions are equally bad."[48]

The events of the third and fourth decades of the twentieth century were not unique to some unenlightened period in Brazilian history. One hundred years after slavery was abolished, when its practice should have been nothing but a bad memory, cases of enslavement—called "modern debt peonage" today—could still be observed. Slavery's continuing existence in Brazil was the result of several policies designed to preserve and perpetuate large pools of unemployed and underemployed individuals throughout the country.

THE MINIMUM SALARY

When he was making a play for working-class support in 1943, one of the measures Vargas initiated was a program that his administration hoped would ease the dilemma of these out-of-work or partly working persons. The already mentioned Minimum Salary was not a radical measure because Getúlo was afraid of losing favor among the landowning elite.[49] The Minimum Salary is an artificial wage representing the least amount of money an employer must pay an employee each month. Before double-digit inflation was brought under control in 1994, the government used to adjust the Minimum Salary upward every thirty days, although several months sometimes passed before an increase was announced.

Understanding what a Minimum Salary is is one thing. Understanding what a Minimum Salary buys is quite another. In 1988, three-quarters of the way through the time frame of this study—and still during the period of high inflation—anyone who earned one Minimum Salary brought home barely enough money to buy a *cafezinho* (a demitasse-sized cup of coffee) for himself, a hypothetical wife, and two hypothetical children after each of the day's three meals. Note that this says nothing about the meal itself, or about rent, electricity, gas, transportation, clothes, schooling costs, entertainment, medical expenses, and so on. Official data for 1988[50] showed that just over 29 percent of the economically active population[51] earned up to one Minimum Salary. Over half, or 53 percent, were paid between one and two Minimum Salaries.[52] What this meant in the hard light of day was that the majority of Brazilians competed for jobs on whose salaries it was impossible to exist. Employers knew (and still know) that they could offer rock-bottom wages because, through their government, they kept so many persons fighting over the scraps. Employees were generally afraid to make waves for fear of being fired, and unions, with the exception of the João Goulart administration, were historically weak.

THE HOOK

In rural areas, this discussion merges into all too common narratives. It often begins when an unemployed person is already moving about the country looking for work. Somewhere, he meets up with a *gato* (lit., cat; slang for recruiter) who offers him a job. In much of the northern part of Brazil, the high season for recruiting rural workers is the month of May, after the seasonal rains have subsided. It is then that the landowners need more hands to work the fields. It is also then that gatos began prowling small communities with large numbers of economically inactive people. The gato typically attempts to gain the confidence of a laborer with generous doses of one of Brazil's national drinks, *cachaça,* or sugarcane brandy. The recruiter might even pay the peasant's hotel and other bills. The hook is then set with an offer of a seasonal or temporary job at an appealing salary on a fazenda in another state. For those who accept the deal, transportation is always provided free of charge—apparently.

Arriving in the Promised Land, the duped field hand quickly discovers that his employer has little intention of living up to any agreement consummated by a gato. What is more, the hoodwinked worker is told that he will have to pay for his trip, that his living conditions are nearly subhuman, and that food and other necessities are available only in company stores at inflated prices and will have to be purchased on credit; the charges will be deducted from the worker's wages. He will be then legally kept from leaving as his bills grow faster than they can be paid off. In some places there are variations on this enslavement dynamic. Yet in all instances, jagunços are nearby, ready to intimidate and, if need be, kill agitators, complainers, and anyone caught trying to escape. These bullies rely on several levels of inducements and arrangements to maintain order beyond the pervasive threat of the club. Such things as revolvers, machine guns, walkie-talkies, helicopters, planes, and larger-than-usual police bribes are all commonplace. This payola to the authorities produces situations in which the police are reluctant to help escaped rural workers. Sometimes the police work with the landowner and his jagunços to keep things quiet and out of the press. It is often standard operating procedure for officers of the law to arrive at some estate or business too late to investigate allegations of contemporary servitude.[53]

CASES

There are occasions when the mountains of muscle and corruption fail to keep the national news media oblivious to what is happening. Surely local journalists are bought off or even run newspapers that favor fazendeiros either in their vicinity or in general. For this reason the reports that make it into the larger tabloids and CPT reports are no doubt only the tip of the iceberg. Cognizant of this probability—and of this drawback—every major daily newspaper in the cities of Rio de Janeiro and São Paulo was scrutinized to try to uncover cases of slavery in the ten-year period leading up to the centennial anniversary of the Lei Áurea.[54]

From 1978 to 1987, Brazil was composed of twenty-three states and three territories. During this short interval, the papers examined ran stories making a minimum of 253 charges of slavery in twenty of these national entities.[55] In one news report, where 177 cases were listed in a single article,[56] it proved impossible to sift out complaints occurring between May 1985 and November 1986, as exact dates were not provided. In a different description of the same report, 167 rural concerns were accused of running business that practiced modern-day servitude. Subtracting the 177 incomplete accountings from the rest of the cases, but remembering that 1985 and 1986 are underrepresented, the yearly analysis for the remaining 76 instances was as follows:

1978	*1979*	*1980*	*1981*	*1982*	*1983*	*1984*	**1985**	**1986**	*1987*
0	14	3	8	1	6	7	**10**	**17**	10

A state-by-state breakdown (excluding Tocantins, which was formed in 1990 by dividing Goiás) could be made for all 253 charges. São Paulo, the most significant manufacturing and commercial center as well as the most populous state, led the list with 60 allegations during this period, followed by Pará with 49; Bahia with 34; Rondônia with 29; Pernambuco with 25; Mato Grosso with 13; Minas Gerais with 9; Paraná with 8; Mato Grosso do Sul with 6; Acre, Goiás, and Rio de Janeiro with 3 each; Amazonas, Ceará, and Rio Grande do Sul with 2; and Alagoas, Amapá, Maranhão, Santa Catarina, and Sergipe with one apiece. Keep in mind that these are numbers of cases, not numbers of victims.

One hundred and ninety-five instances (77.4 percent) took place in rural environments. Two charges (.8 percent) were made in the urban sprawl that comprises the city of São Paulo, the biggest in South America. Fifty-five accusations (21.8 percent) could not be classified as either urban or rural because the news articles failed to provide enough information.

The sex of the victims also was not reported on a consistent basis. What can be determined in respect to gender is that some businesses enslaved mainly adult males, while others—as in the case of one candy factory in metropolitan São Paulo—were women-only establishments. A few enterprises used minors or even children exclusively.[57] The youngest coerced

wage earners were four-year-olds with noticeable mental problems who worked at charcoal production in rural São Paulo.

It appears that Paulo Maluf, the controversial former governor of São Paulo, was tied to a different slavery accusation involving youth of the same age, through his investments and position. Maluf had been the military's civilian candidate for president during the election of 1985, once they decided to hand back the government—Maluf lost. He tried again in 1989 but never made it past the first round of Brazil's two-tiered election process. Saying that Maluf has had a checkered career would not be far off the mark. His manipulative dealings and Swiss bank accounts became notorious in Brazil. In 1971 he was the dictatorship's appointed mayor of São Paulo. It is said that in the same year he gave the go-ahead to the construction of the clandestine cemetery already mentioned in the paulistano suburb of Perus. It was there that numerous executed political radicals along with some death-squad victims were buried. The men in uniform liked Maluf so much that they made him governor of São Paulo in 1978. Once declared elected, he stated that one of the priorities of his administration would be to transfer capital to the rural areas of São Paulo in order to harmoniously develop and defend the small and middle-size businessman. It was during his term as governor (1978–82) that stories began linking his name to charges of slavery in the state's interior.[58]

While the race of these victims was also never indicated, photographs accompanying several articles and the stories themselves indicate that all shades of Brazilians were exploited during the years studied. Information about the number of people held in conditions analogous to slavery was either left out, unknown, or only guessed at in several of the narratives, and thus an accurate head count was not possible. However, then secretary of labor Plínio Sarti said he received an average of three accusations per month, mainly against enterprises in the states of Pará, Maranhão, and Rondônia. In Maranhão the regional secretary of labor delegate, Paulo Marinho, estimated in 1985 that thirty-five to forty firms maintained about a thousand persons as slaves.[59]

The largest group of what could be called present-day bondspeople was estimated at thirty-five thousand persons state-wide in São Paulo.[60] The smallest numbers were occurrences in which a single individual was enslaved. This was observed in only two cases, one in Bahia and the other in São Paulo. The latter case involved a man who spent twenty years as a slave on a fazenda. The man's daughter discovered him when he was fifty-six. She had lost contact with her father. The victim was held on a property near Penápolis owned by Devanir Marques Correia. He had been starved many times over the course of his captivity. Never allowed to speak with other people, he had been forced to wear clothes made out of empty sacks of manure.[61]

Various other reports suggested that peasants were being sold to landowners. A 1984 exposé reported that 150 men had been rescued about 209 miles (337 km) from Fortaleza in Ceará. They were being shipped by truck to Goiás, three states away. Had they arrived, each of them would have been sold to local fazendeiros for Cr$400,000, or about $375 and change. The article pointed out a disturbing reminder that this was not the only shipment. It was one that was detected.[62]

An unknowable number of these victims were hired on as rural laborers only to be whooshed into the manufacturing sector. Consider the plight of six hundred northeastern workers who were contracted in 1982 by an industrial entity in Itapevi, a city some eighteen miles (thirty kilometers) from the center of São Paulo. After a tiring journey through several states, they were confined to the construction site where they were to work. Each man was provided with skimpy sleeping facilities, nearly nonexistent wages, and food that was either almost raw or putrid. Much of the latter was full of cockroaches and other insects. The pistol-packing guards pounced instantly on anyone who opened his mouth in protest. Thrashings and death threats accompanied the enforcers and helped to keep the recruits docile.[63]

Then there was Antônio Oliveira e Silva. Around October 1984 he was attracted by an offer of employment on a cocao plantation in the interior of Rondônia. Silva signed up and with eleven other farm hands squeezed into a Jeep. They were taken to an isolated fazenda in the forests of Ariquemes, 119 miles (192 km) from the state capital of Porto Velho. There they were forced to work as indentured servants. After four months they discovered that they were not going to be paid, but by then no one was allowed to quit or stop working. Silva and fifty others escaped in October 1985. They were starving and in rags when found. An additional two hundred workers, guarded by armed jagunços, were left at the fazenda. Silva stated that the houses for the workers were holes in the ground covered with canvas.[64]

Another group, this one made up of eighteen men from the state of Alagoas, also decided to try to flee from their inferno, a Martinópolis sugar plantation. Originally part of a force of twelve hundred freighted-in workers, eighteen managed to get around the enterprise's security system and make their way to the state capital in June 1987, thanks to a free lift from a bus driver. They had been promised employment as cane cutters or in other more skilled positions. Each was to have been compensated between Cr$8,000 to Cr$30,000 (then about $345 to $1,295) per month. Once at the plantation, where they were watched over by the usual subelites, they were informed that their wages would be only Cr$3,500. From this reduced figure, Cr$2,600 was to be taken out for food. So these workers received Cr$900 every four weeks, or just under $39 at the official rate of exchange. But as the real value of the cruzeiro was always its black market exchange rate, this figure had a purchasing value of about $19.50, or roughly 50 percent less than the government-imposed bank rate from 1978 to 1987. The menu, by the way, never varied. The only meal of substance each day consisted of rice and one fried egg.[65]

THOSE RESPONSIBLE

Of course the accounts presented here do not tell the full story since they relied on news reports from two major cities to measure illegal activity in other states. Still, there is enough material to suggest that something grim was taking place in the rural areas of Brazil. Who was responsible for all of this? What kind of person, what kinds of businesses, would commit such acts against living, breathing, humans—against fellow Brazilians? We can begin to arrive at an answer when we observe the names of the accused employers in these 253 occurrences. There were numerous important elites and corporate bodies named in this section of the inquiry. Sometimes, as in the case of Paulo Maluf, they were very close to personal knowledge of such policies. The Maluf family has always controlled Eucatex (see below) since its founding in 1951.[66] But the practice of contemporary enslavement appears to be so prevalent in Brazil that proclaiming one's innocence due to oblique financial or administrative connection falls on deaf ears.

The list of accused parties included the investment firm Sul America; Daniel Ludwig, the American billionaire and father of the Jari project; and business elites like Jeremias Lunardelli, Maria Pia Matarazzo, and Alysson Paulinelli. Matarazzo was a member of one of the richest families in Brazil. Paulinelli had been minister of agriculture in the military government of Ernesto Geisel. The list also included Nassib Mofarrej, then head of the Sheraton Hotel in São Paulo; Bradesco, the largest private bank in Brazil; Volkswagen, the German auto manufacturer; Votorantim, the principal industrial conglomerate in the country; Supergasbrás, number one in the natural gas field; Cacique, Brazil's coffee giant; Papelok, the nation's most significant paper and cardboard concern; Camargo Corrêa, an organization that was first in the construction field, third in metals, thirteenth in cement, and twenty-seventh in electric products; Encol, the nation's second-largest real-estate outfit and construction business; Suzano de Papel e Celulose, Brazil's second-biggest maker of paper and cardboard products; Paranapanema, second in minerals; Eucatex, the fourth-largest wood products firm; Ripasa Celulose, Brazil's fifth-biggest in paper and cardboard; Piraquê, the eleventh-biggest enterprise in the Brazilian food industry; Banco Mercantil, seventeenth in banking; Atlântica Boa Vista, thirtieth in real estate; Vale do Rio Grande, thirty-seventh in agriculture; and Gameleira, sixty-third in the distillation business.

Even so, as organizations, Palhinha and Coopersucar perhaps best exemplified the breadth of the forced labor situation in the country. This is because in Brazil's corporate world of 1987, they were at the opposite extreme in terms of size. Out of 118 competitors, with 31 employees, Palhinha occupied position number 108, the eleventh-smallest firm in Brazil's beverage trade. Coopersucar employed 3,178 individuals. One wonders how many of them were functioning as de facto slaves, and how many other persons in this field at other establishments were likewise modern-day bondservants. Coopersucar was twelfth in importance in its business specialty: alcohol production. One final detail: the president of Coopersucar, Roque Quagliato, was the national director of the UDR.[67]

What about the Situation after 1988?

Did the continued presence of a civilian, democratically elected government coincide with noticeable reductions in both the number of rural assassinations and the number of Brazilians held in debt peonage in the final years of the twentieth century? While the total number of rural murders is down, the number of assassinations by hired killers is up. And the number of rural murders, including those by hired killers, has remained high in Bahia and Maranhão and at a disturbing level in Amazonas, Minas Gerais, Mato Grosso, Pernambuco, Paraná, Rondônia, Roraima, and Tocantins. In the state of Pará, however, the slaughter of rural laborers has reached near-epidemic proportions. The event that occurred at Eldorado dos Carajás in Pará in 1996, and the subsequent day in court in 1999, serve to illustrate what has changed with the change of governments.

It was just another massacre, like others now remote in the thick morass of such events in Brazil. On the morning of April 17, the governor of Pará, Almir Gabriel, ordered the police to clear a road, PA-150, Pará's main north-south thoroughfare, of approximately fifteen hundred MST supporters. Formed in 1985 with the goal of giving the rural poor a real voice in the nation, by 1996 MST had grown into an organization that used land occupation as its principal weapon. The group that marched down PA-150 had just left the fazenda Macaxeira, a parcel of territory briefly taken over in protest of Brasília's sloth-like speed at land redistribution to the poor. The authorities had kept abreast of the Macaxeira events, probably by army intelligence.

At 3 P.M. some 268 Polícia Militar took up the last of their positions on both sides of road as the landless demonstrators walked in their direction. A different kind of Polish Corridor was in the making. Many of the police removed their Velcro-affixed nametags so as to avoid identification. They carried handguns, rifles, shotguns, and four machine guns. A wise man would have known that this was not the usual kind of response. In the state's largest city, Belém, the police had been called out to watch over other types of protest—without the weaponry. A study later showed that the citizens of Belém, more so than any other of ten state capitals surveyed, wanted the police to shoot to kill in confrontations with the MST.[68] Sentiments in rural areas of Pará doubtlessly ran higher.

Filmed by a journalist, a little after 4:30 P.M. the police began discharging their weapons. Many of the protesters tried to surrender or flee in panic. The authorities, however, were out for blood. They chased people into the surrounding woods and structures, shooting as they went. A total of nineteen MST adherents were killed and another sixty-nine wounded or injured. Six bodies had bullet holes; four of these victims had been shot in the forehead at close range. Ten people were beaten before they died. But "some corpses had more than 50 stab wounds."[69] As for those who surrendered or were taken prisoner, about fifty, they were placed on the road and then kicked, slapped around, and pelted with choice four-letter words.

Away in the capital at a safe distance, President Fernando Henrique Cardoso (1995–2003) started out by referring to the event as a battle between the forces of the archaic and the modern. Those he lumped into the "outdated" corner were the MST and its supporters. Weighing in against this group were the forces of the government, of modern Brazil, of which he was the leader. When his statement was met with astonishment and after growing public repulsion over the affair, Cardoso backtracked, calling the slaughter unacceptable, unjustifiable, and shameful. The governor of Pará then confiscated the Macaxeira fazenda, the starting point of it all, supposedly for distribution to those without property. Three years and four months later, the three police charged with giving the order to fire upon the protesters were acquitted in Belém. The widows of the nineteen slain protesters witnessed this pretense of justice. As the downcast wives and mothers left the tribunal, members of the Polícia Militar waiting outside subjected them to more threats, more insults, and more foul language.[70]

The MST, however, did not quit. Following a series of fazenda occupations, the slayer of Brazil's hyperinflation—but nothing else—President Cardoso, tried his best to control the landless agricultural worker.[71] According to his own figures, Cardoso's administration had done more to assist rural families than had any other Brazilian government. Cardoso claimed to have helped some four hundred thousand families. Was this merely an empty boast by a president often belittled for being out of the country too often to help anyone? Maybe, in light of the fact that Cardoso's economic policies forced the same number of rural families to migrate to the cities to look for work during just the period 1995 to 1998.[72] Most of these new city residents only added to the already-swollen favelas choking Brazil's larger urban areas. By the year 2000, for example, Rio de Janeiro would have 752 of these shantytowns.[73]

Fernando Henrique's own fazenda, Córrego da Ponte in Buritis, Minas Gerais, would be invaded more than once. Done to call attention to a president with empty promises, the most conspicuous of these occupations occurred in early April 2002. On that occasion, some 250 MST members took over the president's rural home. They ate his imported and domestic food, and drank ninety bottles of imported wines, whiskeys, and cognacs. His cachaça and six cases of his beer were also passed around and guzzled. Two turkeys plus fifty chickens were butchered and eaten. The trespassers messed with Cardoso's private papers, lounged around watching his cable TV, used his private phone, and slept in his bed. They broke dishes and left tractor lights on just to run down the batteries. They even smoked cigars given to Fernando Henrique by Fidel Castro. After twenty-two hours, the gatecrashers were overrun and arrested by a military unit sent in to regain control.[74]

New tactics by the MST moved it further to the political left and to the occupation, not just of fazendas, but also of numerous government buildings in fourteen state capitals. In response, President Cardoso initiated a series of proposals that appeared to do something, but really did little for anyone except those who needed little anyway. The first of his measures made it more difficult to apply for or receive the deed to land that the applicant had already occupied or previously occupied. Second, the president created guidelines whereby the federal government passed responsibility to the states. Each region was given special funds and empowered to commandeer lands within its borders for dispersal to duly registered individuals. More attention was paid to CONTAG, one of five unions vying to represent rural labor.[75] All of this, the president claimed, was necessary to keep the MST from ever again occupying any public buildings (or lands) in their quest for justice for Brazil's rural poor. The nation's leader indicated that the Polícia Federal, and the army if necessary, would be used to guarantee the freedom of access to public structures. Transgressors would be punished under the National Security Law, the very same statute that had been created and used by Brazil's military dictators. He backed everything up by saying that it was being done to protect democracy.[76]

One of those who thought Fernando Henrique Cardoso had gone too far, indeed, that he was "recreating DOPS in the rural arena,"[77] was Catholic bishop Dom Thomás Balduíno, president of the CPT. In Dom Thomás's words,

> The democracy the government says exists is only rhetoric; in practice, it's dictatorial [and] authoritarian. The grave steps taken to control the MST are measures that will cause a complete paralysis of the process and even a regression of agrarian reform. Because the MST took action . . . the answer

> of the government was repression. . . . The authorities close their eyes to rural violence and prefer to criticize violence in a movement. But, if we add things up, the number of rural atrocities is massive; yet to occupy buildings is viewed as the ultimate act of violence.[78]

As for Brazilians held in conditions of slavery in the country where bondage was the most prolific in human history,[79] the institution seems to be alive and well in remote parts of Brazil. One report indicated that during the first four months of 2000, 279 persons were removed from situations of servitude by functionaries from the Ministry of Labor in the states of Pará and Mato Grosso.[80] The UDR too was still around, still employing hit men to guard fazendas from occupation attempts by the displaced rural poor and, needless to add, to prevent escape attempts by the contracted rural poor.[81]

If these journalistic descriptions are to be believed—there were many, many instances that never made it into print—then there is support for the premise that the ages-old institution of human servitude continues to exist in the Federal Republic of Brazil. Moreover, it appears to be a sad fact that the promise of the Golden Law, which was supposed to have ended the enslavement of *all* Brazilians just over a century ago, has only been partially met. King Profit called all the shots, at least during the ten-year period immediately prior to the centennial celebration of Brazil's abolition. Crass capitalism seems to have been the real culprit. This headlong chase after profits kept the situation stagnant and made for a mere cosmetic interpretation of the 1888 decree.

In sum, both the 1978–1987 survey of articles and the CPT figures clearly show that most of the accusations of illegal servitude took place and will probably continue to take place in rural parts of Brazil. Extrapolating the latter investigation back onto the former, it appears that most of the victims came from and will continue to come from the countryside as well. The one variable that these citizens have in common is not a racial one but an economic one.

The real rural bandits in Brazil have always had things both ways. It took until the end of 2002 for a fazendeiro to be convicted in a civil action and made to pay a fine for keeping slaves.[82] The men who run Brazil's interior (some might venture to include the country's underpaid urban labor force too) have determined that if and when you work, you will work as a slave, or as close to it as possible. Maximum profit is the name of their game. Workers and their families are not looked on as humans with human needs in this contest. They are viewed as disposable tools. If they put up any kind of a fuss, or if they try to get a morsel of land to live on, they risk being killed. Indeed, a germane application of James Joyce's contrite comment on history might be that it is a nightmare from which Brazil's rural poor have never been allowed to awake.[83]

Chapter 6

Urbancide

THE NATION'S TWO largest cities led the way in dealing with the metropolitan part of the question. This is not to say that the methods or the disposition to use them were anything novel in Brazilian history, or even anything specific to Rio de Janeiro or São Paulo. Since colonial times, elite security was maintained through the selective use of overt violence both in the cities and countryside. The military governments merely took the gloves off these tired and tested ways of maintaining a mollified social order. Indeed, the povão understood that even their children were not immune. The sanctity of childhood was for those who could afford it. For the urban poor, accusations against their offspring resulted in many a bullet or in being packed off to an overcrowded youth detention facility to be abused, tortured, and perhaps murdered by the guards or mauled by those brought in to quell outbursts. Individuals a little older and fortunate enough to be left alive might end up in an overcrowded adult detention facility to be abused, tortured, and perhaps murdered by the guards or slaughtered by those brought in to quell outbursts. When they came to the attention of the enforcers, urban working-class adolescents and adults were both situationally considered human rubbish—rubbish that should rightly be discarded.

One of the first reports to make the press about ill treatment in juvenile lockups was back in 1951. It concerned the SAM (Serviço de Assistência aos Menores, or the Social Service for Minors) facility on Rua Clarimundo de Melo in that slice of Rio de Janeiro called Quintino Bocaiúva. The principal abusers were guards Lido Fernandes, Jorge Pinheiro, Irineu Werneck, Paulo Ferreira, Pedro Mostardeiro, and Inspector Rangel. Someone called "Tatú" was said to be the most perverse.[1]

Children and adolescents coming out of these institutions were often beyond help. The story of one such young man, Fernando Ramos da Silva, underscores the immensity of the problem. Known as "Pixote," he was an abandoned child whose story was made into an internationally acclaimed movie in which he played the leading role (*Pixote: a lei do mais fraco,* 1980). Following the production and several short stints on TV soap operas, Pixote returned to a life of poverty. At nineteen, married with two children, and living in a favela, he was assassinated by the police in 1987. Ten years after his murder, the guilty parties still had not been punished. His two executioners were finally brought to trial but had their sentences reduced by the Tribunal de Justiça Militar, on September 16, 1995. Pixote lived his short life in São Paulo, the richest of Brazil's states. One report, looking at the years 2000 to the end of July 2003, revealed that an average of nearly thirty-one adolescent murders a month were taking place among those young people who had served time in São Paulo state youth reformatories.[2]

As for incarcerated adults, beginning in colonial Brazil mature prisoners were subjected to horrific treatment. Like slavery, The Portuguese carried this bias toward those in custody with them from the mother country. In those earlier years, the elite had their own ways of dealing with miscreants. But slowly established penal institutions emerged, and by the start of the nineteenth century Rio's wrongdoers were sent to living infernos like the Aljube if they transgressed a civilian or military statute. Slaves were sent to the Calabouço. Masters could likewise forward their bondservants to the Calabouço just to be whipped or to be chastised in some other way. Other slaves may well have administered these thrashings and additional ghoulish eventualities.[3]

Efforts at maintaining order among persons in bondage were later transferred to any Brazilian in detention. It is only to remember the atrocities committed in such institutions during the times of Artur Bernardes, Getúlio Vargas, and the post-1964 military dictators to see that the events in the then latest link of the chain, the massacre in 1992 of 111 inmates by the authorities at Carandiru Prison in São Paulo, was nothing unusual.[4] The individual ultimately held responsible for giving the order to open fire at Carandiru, Polícia Militar colonel Ubiratan Guimarães, was sentenced to 632 years' imprisonment for the deaths of 102 inmates and the attempted murder of 5 others. Eight years later it was nonetheless arranged for Ubiratan to take part in a parade commemorating the 1932 Constitutionalist Revolution. The largely white audience applauded the colonel, who is white, as he passed the reviewing stands in the Jeep of his girl friend.[5]

The First Death Squads in the Americas

The morality was thus in place in 1957 when federal police chief and army general Amauri Kruel approved a proposal made by Cecil de Macedo Borer.[6] Borer had been an interrogator at the Polícia Central in Rio de Janeiro during the late 1930s and the 1940s. An imposing figure even in old age, back then he had been physically fit and one of the select few chosen to work for the Tomato Heads, the Polícia Especial of Euzébio de Queiroz Filho. Later he was assigned to the Quadro Movel (Mobile Squad), the semi-secret unit whose members were mainly nominated by and directly responsible to the chief of police, Filinto Müller.[7] In 1957 he was moved upstairs to head the uniformed Polícia Civil transit section, which patrolled the capital's streets on motorcycles.[8] Borer's suggestion to Kruel that year resulted in the creation of the Grupo de Diligências Especiais (Special Diligence Group), or GDE. Amauri Kruel had another reason, a morbid one, for adopting Borer's plan. Kruel's brother Riograndino Kruel had been one of Borer's contemporaries in torture/questioning at the Polícia Central in the 1930s and '40s.[9]

Eurípedes Malta de Sá, a thirty-three-year police veteran and former Integralist, headed the GDE.[10] The rest of the crew was made up of Itagiba José de Oliveira, João de Deus Dorneles, and Salvador Correia de Oliveira. The novel unit had the green light to eliminate each and every delinquent circulating in the city. There were to be no questions, no paperwork, and no prisoners taken alive. When it was decided to go after a specific suspect, the individual's death had already been agreed upon. If his whereabouts were known, Eurípedes, who was an imposing six feet five inches tall, would pick up a large shopping bag that he kept in the station house. Inside he carried a machine gun. Eurípedes would then call his men together, and they would drive away to murder the wrongdoer.

Bodies were often unceremoniously dumped in an outlying working-class district north of the city called the Baixada Fluminense. Reporters were now and then let in on what was about to happen, and sometimes they even followed Eurípedes and his men. The next day, Rio's newspapers would announce that another bandit was out of circulation.

All this changed on February 25, 1958, when a member of the GDE team, João Dorneles, killed Edgar Faria de Oliveira in a shoot-out with suspects in a hillside shantytown. The dead man, an innocent bystander who had been on his way home at the time, was a driver for Radio Tupi. His unexpected death was a mistake that invaded middle-class reality. At that juncture, justice in Brazil was not just for the upper echelon but also for selected members of this buffer class. A trial might not have been on the agenda had the victim been less noticeable. In this case, it was the interests of the victim's employer that were served, not Edgar Faria de Oliveira's. The hearing that ensued on December 13, 1959, against four defendants, including Dorneles, resulted in verdicts of manslaughter. The prosecution appealed but lost eighteen months later.

After the reading of the verdict, the Grupo de Diligências Especiais was never heard of again. Amado Ribeiro, a young journalist at *Última Hora,* had already started to refer to the GDE as the Esquadrão da Morte, or Squadron of Death.[11] Ribeiro was not the first to coin a phrase for this kind of activity in Rio de Janeiro. As early as the 1880s there had been a person or group of people referred to as "Mão Negra," or "Black Hand," who went around killing marginals and no doubt other undesirable elements. In fact, arbitrary behavior by the police goes back even farther, to individuals such as Miguel Nunes Vidigal in 1809. Vidigal had been second in the chain of comand of the Guarda Real de Polícia (Royal Police Guards).[12] It could be argued that the carioca and *fluminense* (a person or thing from the State of Rio de Janeiro) police have been de facto death squads since the time of this early-nineteenth-century official. In the late 1950s, however, Amado Ribeiro's terminology stuck. It did not take long for the rest of the city's newspapers to pick up the expression. Eurípedes Malta soon retired from the police force and opened a restaurant near the beach in Rio's Barra da Tijuca suburb. The place would serve as a watering hole for many members of the Esquadrão over the coming decades.[13]

On December 5, 1960, when Carlos Lacerda took office as the first governor of the freshly created state of Guanabara, he was already a walking, talking controversy, and his administration would be remembered for a number of noteworthy accomplishments as well as for a number of inglorious fiascoes. One of the more interesting of the second category involved a reorganization of the state's Polícia Militar. A product of this process was the creation of a new group by Guanabara's secretary of security, Gustavo Borges, to combat crime.

"O Gringo"

The command of the new squad was given to detective Milton Le Cocq de Oliveira. Le Cocq was a peculiar blend of the odd and the efficient. Known as "O Gringo" ("The Gringo"), he began his career as a member of the Polícia Militar. Later he transferred to the motorcycle detachment of the Polícia Especial. The Tomato Heads, while under Euzébio de Queiroz Filho, were actually an extension of the palace guards protecting the interests of Getúlio Vargas. Their style of policing served as a role model for the various groups of Polícia de Choque (Shock Police) of our own era.[14]

Le Cocq chose a number of persons he knew from the Polícia Especial to be part of his new team. Among them were José Guilherme Godinho Ferreira ("Sivuca")[15] and Hélio Guaíba Nunes. The rest of the group was made up of Euclides Nascimento, Jamie de Lima, Hermenegildo de Souza Cavalcanti Filho "Jacaré" (or "Alligator"), Lincoln Monteiro, Ivo Americano Alves de Brito, José Nunes Curvello "Arrepiado" ("Goosebumps"), and Espencer Manga "Chocolate." Sometimes Aníbal Beckman dos Santos "Cartola" ("Top Hat") was asked to participate.[16]

Le Cocq instructed his men never to accept money to kill anyone. Nor were they to shoot unarmed or surrendering citizens.[17] He was noted for insisting that all suspects be allowed at least one opportunity to give themselves up. Stoic, Le Cocq was tall, had blue eyes, and sported a neatly trimmed mustache. Having never been to France to learn how to use one, or perhaps it was only one more manifestation in his strong personality, he was almost never without his most noticeable trademark: an unusually worn navy-blue beret.[18] Notwithstanding this quirk, there is no ignoring the respect he earned from his peers. O Gringo personally knew the ins and outs of many of Rio's South Zone favelas. He put this knowledge to use by consistently taking the point position on sweeps into these shantytowns. It was an almost foolhardy macho gift, this penchant he had for leading his men into the thick of battle.[19]

At the start, Le Cocq's renovated death squad had a number of stunning successes. Soon they notched their pistols with a large number of executions. Today the majority of their victims are recalled only by their once-dreaded nicknames. In alphabetical order, killed or in prison were "Buck Jones," "Cara de Tigre" ("Tiger Face"), "Careca" ("Head"), Casemiro, "Coroa" ("Crown"), "Dentinho" ("Little Tooth"), "Eru," "Exu," "Fidel Castro," "Formiguinha" ("Little Ant"), Geneci, "Luís Ruim" ("Bad Luis"), "Manuel Olhão," "Mexicano" ("Mexican"), "Micuçu," "Mineirinho" (here "Thin Mineiro"), "Mino," "Murilhão," "Os Irmãos Buda" ("The Buda Brothers"), Pedro Meganha, "Praga de Mãe" ("Mother's Curse"), and "Vicentino." Following the death of Mineirinho in late 1961, many of the casualties of summary justice began to be dumped into the Guandu River.[20] It was quick, it was easy, and the soaking disfigured the evidence.

O DIA

It is at this point that an analysis of a Rio blood-and-guts newspaper proves useful. Since neither the national government nor the state ministries of justice report crime statistics to the public on an annual basis, one must wait for their arbitrary reports[21] or face the laborious task of assessing the volume of a particular crime through some other means. Not that death squad homicide would ever be reported in this way anyway. As a consequence, to try to assess their number, as well as gather some of the details of the general universe of victims, a case-by-case methodology using newspapers was adopted. In this respect, the carioca daily *O Dia,* which specialized in crime for many years, was selected and read from June 5, 1951, the date of the very first issue. *O Dia* was not published on Mondays until June 11, 1979. Each day's issue was examined until December 31, 1998. Beginning in 1999, *O Dia* went through an editorial change resulting in a much-reduced coverage of crime.[22] For that reason, it was decided to conclude the Rio de Janeiro portion of the research at the end of that year, after forty-seven and a half years of *O Dia*'s had been examined. The total number of cases uncovered was 14,770.

Without doubt, *O Dia* registered a large number of extermination group killings in the state during this period. Reporters from carnage specialty tabloids like *O Dia* perform daily checks of police stations for *boletins de ocorrência,* or notices of an incident. The *boletins* were and still are required police paperwork. When a *boletim* was issued concerning a murder, the journalist assigned to cover that station invariably followed it up by including a story about the occurrence in the next day's edition. Instances that failed to make the *boletins* included those where victims were killed and buried secretly, or those who had their bodies disposed of in such a manner, or at such a distance, that their deaths went unnoticed by the long nose of the press. For example, in the state of Bahia, a policeman named França regularly took common criminals out to sea off the city of Salvador and dumped them in the Atlantic Ocean.[23] In spite of this and other seeming methodological drawbacks, carioca criminologist Marcio Luiz Donnici insists that using the boletins is the best way to measure the number of extermination-group victims. In his opinion, one simply cannot trust statistics made available to the public by the police.[24]

The cases that were chosen for study were homicides that fit one or more of the extermination group *modus operandi*. The criteria for inclusion were worked out in discussions with two Brazilians who were hired to read the newspapers. The individuals were selected because they are university graduates who grew up in and still reside in a poorer section of Rio's North Zone. As such, they witnessed a different, often brutal, facet of police behavior; one that is not usually seen by foreign tourists in the plush South Zone beach and body beautiful communities.

The examination of *O Dia* began in late 1981. Soon the researchers agreed on a list of *keys* (police parlance for elements of the modus operandi) used to determine whether a killing would be included or discarded. As the years passed and the procedures of the various extermination groups changed, the list of keys grew to twenty-four. Each investigator was supervised by the author and randomly checked for accuracy. Many apparent homicides were rejected. In order to be included, victims had to have several of the keys listed below:

1. Marks of torture, often a result of being beaten.
2. Pronounced neck abrasions from rope strangulation (but not from being hung).
3. Abrasions on wrists from handcuffs.
4. Abrasions on ankles from shackles or ropes.
5. More than one caliber of bullet used.[25]
6. When bullets were found, they came from the same kinds of revolvers used by the police.
7. One shot, the coup de grace, often discharged into the victim's head.

8. No stabbings.
9. Body discarded in remote or out-of-the-way place.
10. Body found with other victims.
11. Body found in a place where bodies had been found in the past.
12. Body discarded in working-class neighborhood.
13. Victim killed elsewhere since little blood was found next to the body.
14. Body with few clothes (usually just trunks or underwear on males).
15. Body discarded at night.
16. Neighbors in the area never reported hearing gunfire.
17. A death-squad symbol and or a warning by one was left on or near the corpse.
18. A death squad "public-relations" spokesperson[26] announced the disposal site of some bodies to the press.
19. Neighbors mentioned seeing a black VW bus or other kind of transporter, with several men inside, in the vicinity the night before a corpse(s) was/were discovered.
20. Tire marks found near the body.
21. Many corpses lacked identification documents.
22. Many corpses not claimed by relatives.[27]
23. Victim of a subelite who shot first and asked questions later.
24. Victim of a process known as *queimando o arquivo* ("burning the archive") wherein potential witnesses are executed.

When it was available, the following data was collected for each victim:

1. Date of newspaper article
2. Sequential order on date
3. Weekday
4. Page(s) in newspaper
5. Sex
6. Race[28]
7. Age
8. Profession
9. Type of profession
10. Social class[29]
11. Crime(s) of which accused
12. Suburb of residence
13. Suburb where the body was found[30]
14. Zone of residence
15. Zone where the body was found[31]
16. Group responsible for the killing
17. Whether or not a gunfight had occurred
18. Whether a suspected queima o arquivo had taken place

Undeniably Le Cocq and his colleagues went to work on what they and their superiors defined as criminal activity. When looking at the *O Dia* material from 1958 to 1968, the importance of the years 1960 and 1961 becomes apparent. What took place later, on August 27, 1964, also contributed to the legacy.

Suspected Death-Squad Murders Reported in *O Dia* for the State of Rio de Janeiro (including Guanabara) for 1958–68

1958	*1959*	*1960*	*1961*	*1962*	*1963*	*1964*	*1965*	*1966*	*1967*	*1968*
2	7	21	14	13	24	24	33	34	28	35

Removals

In the meantime, the Lacerda administration hit upon another idea to placate the wishes of the affluent huddled in Rio's South Zone. Using American financing—through the Alliance for Progress—the residents of various favelas were forced to relocate to commuter cities in the distant environs. Their former homes were demolished. It was argued at the time that these removals were in the best interests of the favelados since they would gain new, safe, and hygienic housing in the process. But Cidade de Deus, Vila Aliança, Vila Esperança, and Vila Kennedy, as the new communities were called, all quickly deteriorated into new shantytowns. In part this was provoked by the fact that the new settlements were some one and a half to two hours from the city center, which is where many residents worked. Exacerbating the distance issue were the additional bus and train charges former South Zone slum dwellers were obliged to pay to get to work. These fares were based on distance, and they drastically reduced the already-at-the-starvation-level wages of lower-class workers forced to live in and on the social periphery.

The slums selected by the Lacerda administration for destruction in 1963 and 1964 were all located in the South Zone. All were festering sores that needed to be removed lest the smugness of the better off and the postcard landscapes of the world-famous city be smudged for tourism. Under the direction of Sandra Cavalcanti, secretary of social services in the Lacerda government, the entire project suffered a black eye as resistance put up by favelados stiffened. In December 1963, women and children blocked the entrance to the Pasmado shantytown when the authorities came to eject them. A week later, the governor's representatives were back in force. Once they gained control, everything that was not removed was burned that night—including the slum. The fire caused a scandal, especially when it was announced that the blaze was started by unknown causes.[32]

MATA-MENDIGO

If the Pasmado fire gave Lacerda and his advisors a shiner, what they were accused of doing with mendigos in the South Zone was an albatross that never left the governor's neck. It even dangled for years from the neck of one of his trusted subordinates. The calamity began in August 1962, when two correspondents from the newspaper *Última Hora* began investigating the strange deaths of several mendigos who had turned up drowned in two outlying rivers. During the course of their investigations, the reporters uncovered a policy on the part of a police agency, the Department of Mendicancy (Delegacia de Mendicancia), to treat detained beggars as human litter.

To line their own pockets, it was also standard policy to rob beggars once taking them into custody. Any impoverished person putting up any kind of problem was seized and thrown into a death cell to be tortured senseless or killed. They were later driven to specific bridges over the Guandu and Guarda Rivers and tossed over the railing. Some had to be whacked over the head first. Many of the victims were found with their hands and feet bound and with stones tied around their necks so that they would drown faster. There was even said to have been a secret cemetery where the police entombed more than one hundred individuals.

Some of the other cages for mendigos at the Repression of Begging Service complex had been given the names of police *célèbres* that were painted outside each cell. There was the Aristides Ventura, named after a man who had been the first commander of the Pelotão de Exterminio, or Extermination Platoon. Another was the Cecil Borer. Already by that time, members of Rio's multitude without power suspected that Borer was more than just another DOPS official. The so-called drownings were given extensive coverage by the press, especially *Última Hora,* which ran daily articles complete with all the gruesome details from January 23, 1963, until the end of March.

The accumulating evidence endedup implicating Governor Lacerda as being partially responsible. He is said to have given the approval to the formation by Borer of a death squad to be a Nazi-like final solution to the problem of beggars in the city. Front-page editorial cartoons of the bespectacled governor in *Última Hora* lampooned the affair for some time.[33] Lacerda had been dubbed The Crow up until that point because of his hovering over the unanswered murder of Nestor Moreira in 1954.

There ultimately were demands for the governor to fire Borer. When he refused, a move was started for Lacerda's impeachment. Nothing ever happened, of course, to Lacerda or Borer. But seven policemen, including the chief of the Department of Mendicancy, were eventually tried (sacrificed?). Six were found guilty and sentenced to prison. One died in jail while awaiting trial. Lacerda, however, pardoned and reinstated a number of these convicted police when it was decided to beef up the force with specialists shortly after the 1964 golpe. The entire affair did not further the plans for higher office of "Mata-mendigo" (or "Kill-a-Beggar"), as Lacerda was called by some of the media while the story was hot. There were never proved rumors through the years that Sandra Cavalcanti, once again, may well have been the person really accountable. These suspicions were used against her when she ran her own losing campaign for the governorship of Rio de Janeiro in 1982.[34]

A different and less promoted theory holds that Newton "Nini" Cruz, then the prosecutor for the Public Security Office, and not Sandra Cavalcanti, had given the go-ahead to "clean" the streets. This was done in preparation for Rio's four hundredth birthday in 1965 and the planned visit to the city by Queen Elizabeth II. Additionally, there were many mendigos who were taken to remote roads and left to die in the winter cold. This fact was not reported in the press. An army officer, Newton Cruz became a general and a chief of SNI (1978–83) . He was accused of being involved in two sorry events: 1) in 1981, Cruz is said to have known in advance that a bombing would take place at Riocentro, 2) in 1982 he was the progenitor of the kidnapping and murder of the former editor of the magazine *O Cruzeiro,* Alexander von Baumgarten, Baumgarten's wife, and boatman Manoel Augusto Valente Pires. For his part in the Riocentro cover-up, Cruz was only charged with lying under oath and disobeying an order. He was not sentenced in the 1999–2000 reopening of the Riocentro case because of the statute of limitations. His role in the Baumgarten affair was thrown out of court for lack of evidence. General Cruz tried to get elected governor of Rio de Janeiro in 1994, but lost.[35]

Horse Face

The most significant milestone in the history of the Esquadrão da Morte was the murder of Milton Le Cocq on August 27, 1964. O Gringo and Aníbal Beckman had been looking for Manuel Moreira, a.k.a. "Cara de Cavalho" ("Horse Face").[36] Twenty-year-old Moreira was an obscure bandit who had mistakenly been released from detention while being held on murder, weapons, and vagabond charges. Free, he had made his way as a small-time assault and robbery specialist who also extorted prostitutes and other hold-up artists. Eventually he tried to squeeze money out of "Nado," a jogo do bicho *banqueiro* (numbers-racket banker; area don).

Horse Face had made a fatal blunder. Jogo do bicho had long depended on the police for its existence. At first banqueiros bribed the police to leave them alone. Gradually the relationship matured to the point where they were buying protection from the men in uniform. Nado was soon complaining to his contacts in the police department, and it was not long before Le Cocq, along with three other detectives in a VW bug, were out on Horse Face's trail.

They ran into Horse Face not far from Maracanã Stadium, but his girlfriend, Niza, alerted him and he fled in a waiting taxi. The VW followed, and the procession came to a halt when the police succeeded in nudging the taxi to the corner of Ruas Teodoro da Silva and Emílio Sampaio in nearby Vila Isabel. Everyone in the car except Le Cocq wanted to pull their guns on Horse Face. Sitting in the front passenger seat, Le Cocq said no, stuck his head out the window, and shouted at the taxi that they were the police. Horse Face did not wait. He began to shoot, killing Le Cocq and seriously wounding the driver. Unable to move the bodies of their companions out of the way, the two detectives in the back seat could only watch helplessly as Manuel Moreira escaped on foot into the early evening.

One of Le Cocq's group, Sivuca, stated in a long interview that Le Cocq had actually gotten out of the car before being shot. There has been speculation that a rookie policeman, Hélio Vígio, who was one of the police in the backseat of the two-door VW, shot Le Cocq. This theory has never been thoroughly investigated. It holds that Cara de Cavalho's subsequent execution was a spectacle put on to cover up an accident or differences among the police.[37]

Whatever the reality, the death of O Gringo exploded like a bomb in the corridors of the carioca police. A massive manhunt for Horse Face was begun immediately. A Cr$500,000 reward (nearly $360) was offered for the capture and conviction of the assassin.[38] One of Brazil's most renowned journalists at the time, David Nasser, made a dramatic plea on TV in which he implored Governor Lacerda, Gustavo Borges, and the police commissioner to go after criminals in their very homes. He urged the killing of ten bandits for every policeman who fell in the line of duty. Nasser's television remarks were reprinted in *O Cruzeiro,* yet he was not the originator of the proposal. It appears to have been made first by Amauri Kruel while the general was head of the Departamento Federal de Segurança Pública (Federal Department of Public Security) from 1957 to 1959. At Le Cocq's funeral, a note calling for this same ten-to-one ratio was pinned to the murdered detective's coffin for all to see. It was signed "João Ninguem," or John Nobody.[39] The superintendent of the Polícia Civil, Sales Guerra, even went so far as to decree the arrest of all twenty-year-old Mulattoes who had short hair, who resembled Horse Face, and who looked suspicious. He emphasized that, if necessary, his men were to shoot to kill.[40]

The authorities stumbled over one another deciding what to do next. There were heated arguments that turned ugly. One inexperienced detective, Jorge Galante from the Invernada, shot and killed Perpétuo de Freitas, Le Cocq's only serious rival on the force, because Perpétuo wanted to capture Horse Face alive.[41] Le Cocq's group was determined that Horse Face be gunned down on sight. They had already agreed that no other alternative would be acceptable. As the chase to find Horse Face unfolded, no small number of favelas were stormed and checked. When it was rumored that Le Cocq's murderer was in Tijuca, upwards of three hundred police pounced on the suburb and busted into some thirty homes. Even Governor Lacerda got into the act, going with a posse to the house of a physician on Rua Lôbo in Anchieta when the bandit was said to be there.[42]

One witness later remarked that there was a lot of torturing done to get information. Incensed subelites summarily executed some persons at the sides of deserted roads. Others were killed because they resembled Horse

Face. But Horse Face managed to stay a step ahead of the police. Avoiding the closing dragnet, he took Niza to a hotel in Duque de Caxias. Leaving her there, he went to São João de Meriti to meet two accomplices, brother and sister Milton Alves Luíz and Vanilda Alves Luíz. As they discussed where he could hide, Vanilda suggested their parent's country place. It was small and modest. It was perfect.

The only hitch in the plan was Milton, also known as "Zé Carioca." After Horse Face and Vanilda left, he stayed behind and happened to fall into police hands. The police went right to work on Milton. He was thrown on the floor of a police car. With an officer's boot mashing down on his neck, a gun was fired next to his head every few miles to browbeat him. The intimidation worked. Zé Carioca took the group to his and Vanilda's parents' house in remote Saco Fora, located in the municipality of Cabo Frio, which was several miles up the coast from the former capital. Milton and Vanilda's father, Pedro Alves Luíz, their mother, and the fugitives from Rio were inside. Thirty-six days into the operation, at 3 A.M. on October 3, 1964, the authorities finally had their man surrounded.

There are two versions of what happened next. The first account, by eyewitness reporter Amado Ribeiro in *Fatos e Fotos* on October 17, holds that following an initial barrage of gun fire, an order was barked out for everyone in the house to leave with their hands in the air. The older couple, Niza, and Vanilda quickly scampered outside. Horse Face frantically screamed and swore at the waiting police that he was ready to die, but that he would "take another cop to hell with me!"[43] He tried to escape through a window, but a burst of machine-gun fire forced him back. He countered by shooting his Colt 45 wildly before being struck in the head with a bullet.

Sivuca's description of the trip to Cabo Frio and the killing of Horse Face are substantially different. He was one of the police who went to Cabo Frio, and thus his recollection must be told. In Sivuca's account, the police got the names of the two siblings wrong, using Wilma for Niza and Oswaldo for her brother Milton. Pretending to be part of a medical team, Sivuca entered the Jacarezinho favela, where Oswaldo resided, and after a dramatic all-day search managed to find him. They told Oswaldo that a car had hit his sister and that she was dying. Because she wanted to repent her sins, she had sent them to find Oswaldo so that he could tell them where their parents lived. Trailed by a car full of police, Sivuca drove Oswaldo to Cabo Frio with the unsuspecting Oswaldo volunteering information all the way. Sivuca guaranteed that Oswaldo was not tortured. After killing Horse Face, Sivuca states that there were three people left alone inside the cottage: the two parents plus Wilma.

Sivuca's version was published thirteen years after Horse Face's murder. His report not only suffers from the time factor but has the following additional flaws: Why did Wilma (Niza) not know where her parents lived? Can we really believe that the police did not torture Oswaldo? And what about the third female in the Cabo Frio Home? Keep in mind that the *Fatos e Fotos* version was made by an eyewitness was corroborated and added to by Percival de Souza and was upheld by the next day's edition of *Correio da Manhã*. Percival de Souza later changed his story to one in which Horse Face's girlfriend was tortured on the pau-de-arara but confessed where her man was only after having been shown a photograph of a beautiful female competitor—complete with a romantic inscription to Horse Face. He maintained that the police forged the dedication.[44]

The final description contends that once arriving at Cabo Frio, ten men simply kicked in the door and began shooting, yelling as they fired away that they were the police. Horse Face sprang out of bed but was shot before he could reach his pistol on a table.[45]

All accounts, however, agree about the ensuing series of events. The police assembled around the murderer of Milton Le Cocq. Then, one by one, they fired round after round into the already lifeless body. So much flesh was shot out of the corpse that some of it was permanently stuck to one wall and the floor. The number of bullet holes reported to have been made in Horse Face's body ranges from more than 50 to 155. Someone even brought one of Le Cocq's revolvers, just so he could fire it into Manuel Moreira for O Gringo.[46]

The sheriff of Cabo Frio, Jorge Bretz, received an anonymous phone call at 6 A.M. the same morning. The voice said that he should go to the home of Pedro Alves Luíz "because there's a present there."[47] Bretz went to the small house and, after recognizing what was left of the body, got in touch with the secretary of security for the state of Rio de Janeiro. The sheriff remarked that he did not know who the murderers of Horse Face were, but that he did not think they were from the state police. He went on to point out that the night of the crime, three cars filled with men passed through the center of his city in the direction of the Luíz place.[48] The Esquadrão da Morte had come of age.

Weeks earlier, at Milton Le Cocq's funeral, federal congressman Fioravante Fraga was among those who gave a speech. He spoke to the dead martyr, saying, "Le Cocq, you died; but you will always be remembered. You are the leader, you are the bright star that all police have to follow."[49]

Truly he was. Almost before Le Cocq was in the ground, the Esquadrão was out killing in his name. In Guanabara, the assassination of unwanted elements continued even though the hunt for Horse Face was over. Besides fugitives from justice, many arrested and even already sentenced prisoners were taken from their cells and executed. Their bullet-ridden corpses began to be noticed on the sides of roads or bobbing down outlying rivers. It was not long before a man who called himself "Rosa Vermelha" ("Red Rose") became a part of the Esquadrão's early culture. His role was to telephone newspapers and announce where fresh *presuntos* (hams), or victim's bodies, had been rudely dumped. The choice of the word *ham* as slang for *cadaver* comes from the fact that Brazilians invariably eat ham cold, and thus the association with the meat of a cold corpse.[50]

The Shield of Le Cocq

Meanwhile, former brothers-in-arms of the dead policeman organized to carry out the ten-for-one mandate. On August 27, 1965, the first anniversary of his murder, they began calling themselves the Scuderie Detetive Le Cocq (the Shield of Detective Le Cocq). Euclides Nascimento was made the first president, and journalist David Nasser served in this same post in an honorary capacity. Founding members were Euclides Nascimento, Hélio Guaíba Nunes, Sivuca, Luiz Mariano dos Santos, Ivo Americano Alves de Brito, Adaylton Chaves, Manoel Bittencourt da Cruz, Euvaldo Raimundo Nascimento, João dos Santos Cardoso, Luiz Gonzaga de Aguiar Marques, Antonio Lopes dos Santos, Affonso Solano Guimarães de Oliveira, and Joel Ferreira Crespo. Euclides Nascimento, Hélio Guaíba, Sivuca, and Ivo Americano had been members of Le Cocq's original team. One source places the entire above list, plus Le Cocq himself, among those detectives who were members of the Esquadrão. Likewise included are the names of Police Commisioner Morvan Lopes, plus Guanabara police officers Hélio Vígio, Arlindo Domingos da Cruz, Silvio Carneiro "Silvinho" ("Little Silvio"), João da Silva Coelho "Coelhão" ("Big Rabbit"), Justino da Silva, and Mariel Moryscotte.

The Scuderie has always wanted the public to believe that its formation was solely to raise funds so that it could provide Le Cocq's widow with financial assistance. In later years, members said it was a charity organization whose twofold purpose was to promote the camaraderie of the public and the police and to assist the widows of slain police colleagues. They even claimed to have contributed money to help orphans and to pay for rabies vaccinations.[51]

Some say Mariel Araujo Moryscotte de Mattos, known to friend and foe alike simply as "Mariel," designed the Scuderie's first logo. Others mention one of Mariel's snitches, Waldemiro Teixeira Gomes, also called "O Cromado" ("The Chromed One"), as the artist. The emblem had a skull and crossbones inside a circle, which had a border with the group's name. Beneath the universal warning symbol, at the bottom of the circle, were eventually inscribed in large block letters "E.M." The members of the Scuderie insist that the acronym stands for Esquadrão Montada (Mounted Squadron). But ask anyone on the street what the two letters really mean, and you will invariably be told, Esquadrão da Morte.[52] In the first years of the Death Squad, the Scuderie was nothing more than the public-relations wing of the parent organization.

The "Mounted Squadron" claims to have offices in six Brazilian states plus the Federal District. Foreign representatives are said to be in Argentina, England, Germany, Italy, Switzerland, and the United States. This includes links to Scotland Yard, the Carabinieri, and the FBI.[53] While the actual number is subject to conjecture[54] and names of most Scuderie members are kept secret, the identities of some associates are used to try to add legitimacy as well as create a bandwagon effect to gain new adherents. Besides indigenous elites—members of the military establishment, judges, lawyers, engineers, and physicians—one can find at least one exgovernor, Esperidião Amin; soccer great Pelé; musician Sérgio Mendes; and old blue eyes himself, Frank Sinatra.[55]

Although Sinatra never attended meetings, other members and their families certainly did at the Scuderie's address: Rua Paula Ramos 402 in the Rio Comprido suburb of Rio de Janeiro.[56] This was no underground affair. The Scuderie Detetive Le Cocq had four phone numbers listed in the 1997 Rio telephone directory: 273–0543, 273–1449, 273–1596, and 273–7446.[57] On December 13, 1982, it became a registered public agency, a police benevolent society in the state of Rio de Janeiro. With this legal loophole, the public relations section of the Esquadrão da Morte could avoid paying national federal income taxes. It was also eligible for direct or indirect state subsidies.[58] Whether or not the Scuderie ever availed itself of these options is unknown.

The Scuderie was not to be taken lightly. Members displayed their affiliation openly until well into the 1990s. Each was given a hand-size decal to be affixed to the rear window of his automobile. And it was not to put in just any old part of the rear window, either. The decal was always in the center, toward the right-hand edge.[59] The logo served as a warning on two levels. First, "Don't mess with this car or you'll be killed!" and second, "Don't do anything suspicious or you'll be killed!" As to the first piece of advice, in 1986 Scuderie president Sivuca was proud of the fact that in twenty years not a single member's car had been stolen. The implication of the second suggestion needed little clarification. The numbers of Scuderie decals on automobile rear windows began to drop by the middle of the 1990s. This was because at that time there was a series of shootings of occupants of cars with the decals. The purpose was not merely to kill someone viewed as an enemy but also to procure weapons thought to be in the vehicles.[60]

As well as the E.M. logo, the Scuderie put out a newsletter aptly titled *O Gringo*.[61] There are busts of Le Cocq that one can purchase. There are also key chains, pens, pins, T-shirts, and baseball hats. All bear the group's emblem. The Scuderie even has an anthem, "Hino da Scuderie Detetive Le Cocq" ("Hymn of the Shield of Detective Le Cocq"), which is available as a phonograph record. The lyrics are:

Nossa luta não é por gloria
Nossa meta é servir todo irmão
Na coragem, no amor, na justiça
Está o segredo da nossa união

Só queremos unir esforços
Para plantar nessa nossa canção
Na amizade, na paz, no exemplo
Está o segredo da nossa união

Juntos vamos seguir
Seu legado vamos todos cumprir
Nossas mãos vão se unir

Para formar a corrente

E cada elo há de ser um irmão
Consciente do nosso dever
Seja no dar ou pedir
O ideal é um exemplo a seguir[62]

Our fight is not for glory
Our purpose is to serve all brothers
In courage, in love, in justice
It is the secret of our unity

We want only to unite forces
To give seed to our song
In friendship, in peace, in our example
It is the secret of our unity

Together we are going to follow
His legacy we are going to complete
We will join hands
To form a chain

And each link shall be a brother
Conscious of our duty
Even when we give or ask
His ideal is the example to follow

The Men of Gold

The Esquadrão da Morte was not the only extermination group in Rio de Janeiro following the murder of Le Cocq. In November 1969, during the darkest days of the military dictatorship, the secretary of public security for the state of Guanabara, Gen. Luiz França de Oliveira, created Os Homens de Ouro (The Men of Gold).[63] At first the group consisted of seven policemen, then nine, eleven, and finally twelve officers of the law.[64] The golden men were: Aníbal Beckman, Nelson Duarte, Nils Kaufman,

Humberto de Matos, Elinto Pires, Jaime de Lima, Lincoln Monteiro, Vigmar Riberio Gonçalves, Hélio Guaíba Nunes, Mariel, Sivuca, and the then head of the Scuderie Le Cocq, Euclides Nascimento.[65]

All but Nelson Duarte, Nils Kaufman, Mariel, and Elinto Pires had been in on the chase out to Cabo Frio to take care of Horse Face.[66] Headed by detectives Odilon Castelões Moreira César and Godofredo César Mattos, the golden ones were formed—or so the public was informed—to combat a wave of assault and robbery cases against night taxis, truck drivers, supermarkets, and banks. Disguised as anything from garbage men to priests, Os Homens de Ouro enjoyed a limited number of successes in eliminating the menace to professional drivers. But they failed to counteract the robberies of supermarkets and banks. This was because the latter were being hit more and more often by well-armed leftist revolutionaries. Following the golpe, bank robbery became more common, particularly near the end of the 1960s and into the 1970s.[67] The authorities would need more than just twelve men to put an end to such endeavors.

Turning once again to the *O Dia* material, it at first seems amazing that the various manifestations of the Men of Gold were credited with only four murders from the time the group was founded until it was disbanded in late 1971. Two took place right away, in November 1969. Both victims were lower-class males (one was black; the other's race is unknown) accused of assault and robbery plus homicide. The following month two more corpses were attributed to the Doze Homens de Ouro (Twelve Golden Men). No class or racial data was reported. The victims, however, were said to have been guilty of trafficking in narcotics. This would indicate that the Men of Gold were involved in suppressing crimes other than those of their original directive. As for the low number of golden killings reported in *O Dia,* either this group committed more crimes than were credited to them or the volume of homicides laid at the feet of the Men of Gold was blown totally out of proportion[68] or some of both.[69] There is no denying that along with all of the publicity surrounding The Men of Gold, most if not all of its members became involved in an illegal way with the very crimes they were supposed to be fighting.[70] For some it was narcotics. For others it was extortion or becoming—as in Sivuca's case—too mixed up with jogo do bicho bankers.

Sivuca has been accused of killing some two hundred suspects. Nonetheless, in November 1991 he was elected to the post of state legislator for Rio de Janeiro. His campaign posters bore the slogan "Rio with Security." Three years later, state prosecutor Antônio Carlos Biscaia seized the records of *bicheiro* (a jogo do bicho don) Castor de Andrade. The records indicated that Sivuca, who was still serving as a state assemblyman, had accepted a bribe or bribes from Andrade. Sivuca was not alone. Likewise said to have received enticements from Andrade were important civilians and individuals in all levels of Rio's state and city governments and in sections of the Polícia Civil and Polícia Federal. Fellow death-squad advocate, founder of the Cavalos Corredores (Race Horses) extermination group, and state assemblyman Emir Larangeira was also said to be on Castor's list. The most notorious hit by the Cavalos occurred in 1993 in a Rio favela located in Vigário Geral. To take revenge on the killing of four policemen, the Cavalos Corredores, together with other police forces, entered the shantytown and gunned down twenty-one residents.[71]

RINGO

It was Mariel Moryscotte, however, and not Sivuca who provoked the biggest storm, taking a number of his golden colleagues with him as he was raked over the coals. Mariel began life modestly in 1940. He was born in the center of Niterói, but the family moved to Salvador while he was still an infant. In 1943 his mother became a widow, remarried, and moved the new family back to Rio. By the end of the 1950s Mariel had finished elementary school and was working as a weaver. He is said to have regularly brought his earnings home to his mother in Bangu. He also worked as a swimming instructor on the side. This was how he got the chance to work as a lifeguard on the beaches of Copacabana. To complement things he rapidly found a part-time job as a wrestler on TV. His life outside the ring also took him into new territory. He began to be known as somewhat of a tourist gigolo at the Copacabana Palace Hotel. He had sex with at least one married couple staying at the hotel and with countless women.

It is true that while on duty at the beach he rescued former presidential candidate Gen. Henrique Teixeira Lott from the surf. But he incurred the wrath of his superiors for things like renting out the fire department's motorboats to sightseers. For that Mariel was transferred to Sepetiba. Although he did not look like he was of African descent, Mariel claimed that his transfer was because his complexion was darker than his superiors wanted.[72]

Then again, the future Man of Gold was not about to stay put. He applied to the Polícia de Vigilâcia (Vigilance Police, a former unit of the Polícia Civil), was accepted, and began to patrol areas of Rio's North Zone.

Now closer to the bright lights again Mariel's spirit was still in Copacabana, and he often returned to his beachfront haunts to meet friends in restaurants and bars along Rua Prado Júnior. He also hung around the local police stations and volunteered to go on raids. Soon Mariel was visiting Copacabana's second-rate nightspots and moonlighting as a bouncer and bodyguard for some of these establishments. There were fights and more questionable behavior. Once he left a police paddy wagon while on patrol to beat up an innocent pedestrian just because he felt like it. Another time Mariel and some of his buddies from Prado Júnior got into a fight at the La Licorne Club when two customers refused to pay their inflated bar tab. Not long afterward one of the patrons, a jockey, had both of his legs amputated as the result of a questionable automobile accident. His companion died in the crash. Mariel was fingered as being behind the tragedy. Nothing was done.

Perhaps his superiors turned their heads because Mariel had arrested the escaped criminal Nélson Bassani in 1967. Mariel had decided to let Bassani—who was serving 117 years in prison—go in return for a bribe and information. It was this knowledge—all of it about Copacabana's underworld—that made Mariel indispensable and nearly untouchable. He became an informant to the 1st Army's DOI-Codi. A promotion came the following year, and another at the start of 1969. In November 1969, to the surprise and even annoyance of many of his police colleagues, Mariel Moryscotte was made one of the last Twelve Golden Men.[73] In his own words, "It was the biggest piece of luck that happened in my life."[74]

If the Golden Men had been created to pacify the press and the public, then the group was put on the block for the same reason. It had become too controversial and too illegal. The idea of police death squads, however, did not die a slow death. Only administrative changes were really made. It is unknown how many Golden Men were concurrently members of the Esquadrão. Most probably were, though there was an important difference. The names of those associated with the larger and more infamous group were secret so that those in positions of command in the state governments did not have to worry about the public outcry. The Esquadrão would never be given over.

Just as it is difficult to tell how many members of the Golden Men were members of the Esquadrão da Morte, so too is it nearly impossible to know who was a trigger man for the Death Squad. One might actually say "Death Squads," because at first glance there would appear to have been more than one gang of killers in action. As the 1960s became the 1970s, *O Dia* reported no fewer than five different groups that had at one time or another carried out extralegal executions of supposed fluminense and carioca criminals. A list[75] of these vigilante groups, together with an interpretation of their names from the Portuguese, is presented below:

Name	*Translation*
1. Esquadrão da Morte	The Squadron of Death
2. Doze Homens de Ouro	Twelve Golden Men
3. Gangue da Baleia	Gang of the Whale
4. Gangue da Caveira	Gang of the Skull
5. Onze de Ouro	Eleven [Men] of Gold

Both the Gangue da Caveira and the Gangue da Baleia were probably the Esquadrão da Morte. Since many members of the two Golden Men groups were also members of the Esquadrão da Morte, it is evident that until the end of the 1970s the Esquadrão was *the* major hit squad in the area that was connected to, but not officially sanctioned by, the police.

It is important to point out that as the seventies wore on there developed more than one Esquadrão. In other words, several police precincts had individuals who became part of the phenomenon. No formal memberships were required. It all worked very unceremoniously; sometimes members knew the identities of other members, other times they did not. This lends support to the observation by a former Polícia Civil colleague that among the police each knows who kills and who does not.[76] Few of these people come to light because there is a fear of reprisal coupled to the tendency to close ranks.

Mariel's exploits, however, were known by too many to be kept secret for long. He was fired from the police department on October 20, 1971. That December he was charged with the murder of five persons while leading a section of the Esquadrão and with the forgery of signatures on traveler's checks. The checks were lifted off unsuspecting foreign tourists by prostitutes in a ring of thugs put together and run by Mariel. The other members of Mariel's bloc of the Esquadrão included detectives César dos Santos and Luís Carlos dos Santos, "O Tigrão" ("The Tiger"). Waldomiro Teixeira was one of the group's principal informants. His day job was that of chauffeur to the singer Aguinaldo Timóteo.[77]

Before the trial, "Ringo," as Mariel sometimes called himself, skipped town. He came to the surface in Salvador, living the life of a carefree celebrity. He was seen in the company of Pelé, Carlos Alberto, and Clodoaldo, all of the Santos Soccer Club. Mariel used his police ID to enter private resorts. He even had the cheek to speak briefly with the Bahian secretary for public security, although it is said that possibly he was not recognized due to the thick beard he had cultivated.

Mariel remained a fugitive. He was spotted back down the coast in Rio de Janeiro at least once. He journeyed to Asuncion more often. Paraguay held his business interests with "Fininho-I." The two men had formed the largest auto theft and drug distribution organization in the South-Central part of Brazil. Mariel got 70 percent of the profit on whatever Brazilian cars the pair could smuggle into dictator Alfredo Stroessner's Paraguay.[78]

The former Man of Gold taunted the authorities. He telephoned TV stations and said he would appear on particular shows.[79] He traveled freely among the restaurants in Rio's South Zone. At Alvaro's in Leblon he was recognized. Someone whispered in his ear that a patron had called the police. Unbothered, Mariel continued to sip his whisky. Ten minutes later he asked for his bill and said, "Look, I already waited ten minutes and the police didn't come. I'm leaving 'cause I can't wait any longer."[80] Ringo was ultimately arrested at about noon on March 9, 1973. He had been on his way south from Salvador to Rio de Janeiro, traveling leisurely in a car. Flown to Rio in handcuffs, Mariel was tried the following month.[81] One of the witnesses for the prosecution was one of Brazil's most intelligent criminals ever, Lúcio Flávio Villar Lírio.

NOCA

Lúcio Flávio was said to have had the highest IQ of any bandit to pass through the hands of the carioca police. He could quote from Sartre and Dostoyevsky just as easily as he could paint or sculpt. On the other side of his personality lived one of Rio's most feared lawbreakers. During a life of crime spanning more than a decade, he was charged with some five hundred offenses and accumulated sentences in excess of one hundred years. He took part in eighteen jail breaks. The authorities said that he even tried to blame some of his lawlessness on the Esquadrão da Morte. Or at least the police displayed Esquadrão paraphernalia confiscated from him to reporters after one of his arrests. Whether it was really Lúcio Flávio's is anyone's guess.[82]

There is little doubt, however, that Lúcio Flávio was bluffing about having the goods on Mariel Moryscotte. They had long had various dealings. At one point Mariel tried to get "Noca,"[83] as Lúcio Flávio's intimates called him, to buy some of his hot cars. Lúcio Flávio refused with a quip that became celebrated. "It used to be that a cop was a cop and a thief was a thief. When police begin to mix with thieves . . . they make mess of everything."[84] Later he would come to the point. "I know that I'm a bandit; Mariel doesn't know what he is."[85] These pieces of wit were not entirely accurate. Brazil is replete with phraseology indicating that the relationship is not as ambivalent as Lúcio Flávio's observations would indicate. To give but one example, consider the expression "A única diferença entre um polícia e um bandido é a farda." This translates as "The only difference between a policeman and a bandit is the uniform."[86]

Noca testified that Mariel had tried to sell his group a protection package. In return, they were to rob for him.[87] Another witness stated that he had seen Mariel and four others leave a car in Praça Mauá. The individual, Francisco Rosas da Silva, a.k.a. "Horrible," trailed the vehicle from the northern suburb of Penha, where the Esquadrão had recently been active, after hearing a number of shots. A final voice, Lúcio Flávio's brother-in-law, "Fernando C.O.," informed the court that he, Lúcio Flávio, and Flávio's brother Nijini were on Mariel's list of individuals to be eliminated. Whether Mariel was behind it or not—film maker Hector Babenco thinks that he was—all of the members of Lúcio Flávio's gang who were taken into custody with him were murdered in prison. This included Lúcio Flávio, who was stabbed to death in his sleep. His assassin, cellmate Mário Pedro da Silva, "O Marujo" ("the Sailor"), was likewise killed, as was the killer of O Marujo. This appears to have been a process of queimando o arquivo.[88]

The testimonies of Lúcio Flávio, Fernando C.O., and Francisco Rosas da Silva were certainly not the only ones the court considered, but they were definitely some of the most interesting. On June 19, 1973, judge

Deocleciano de Oliveira found Mariel guilty of the traveler's check scam and sentenced him to sixteen years imprisonment plus one additional year in an agricultural colony. The extra year was given because the judge felt that Moryscotte was a danger to society. Of the twenty-seven members of Mariel's gang, only two got off. Three other policemen were sent to prison for lesser terms. Later, in 1975, Mariel was given twenty-one years and two months for his part in one of the Esquadrão killings. The victim had been Oldair de Andrade Lima, "O Jonas."[89]

Taken to the island prison on Ilha Grande, Mariel escaped in February 1976. There are several variations of how he did it. One of the most often cited is that Sivuca helped him.[90] Mariel, for his part, liked people to believe he swam the 2.3 miles to the mainland—without anyone's help.[91]

Recaptured in the interior of São Paulo that April, Mariel spent the next four years in Rio's old Casa de Correção, renamed the Lemos Brito Penitentiary. Somewhere someone got to the appropriate person, because Mariel was given three cells for his private use. Interested in painting, Moryscotte had one cubicle turned into an atelier. He passed his time with his art, writing about prison conditions, studying journalism, or watching his own color TV. Mariel also gave the occasional interview, during which he usually complained about a number of things. His favorite pet peeves were three films that he vigorously tried to block: *Lúcio Flávio: o passageiro da agonia* by Hector Babenco, *Eu matei Lúcio Flávio* by Antônio Calmon, and *República dos assassinos* by Miguel Faria Jr. Each movie dealt with the Esquadrão, and each had a character very much like Mariel Moryscotte. Mariel's lawyers argued that all of these cinemagraphic creations were prejudicial to the legal processes involving their client.[92]

The sentences against Mariel began to be overturned or thrown out of court on appeal. He won his lawsuits against the films and was awarded a sizable compensation in the process. He got married. And, on April 29, 1980, the long-awaited day arrived. He was among a group of twelve prisoners who were allowed to work for judge Francisco Horta. This meant that Mariel could go home on weekends. He had been given an open parole after serving not quite seven years of his sentence.[93]

It did not take long for the former Golden Man to return to his old stomping grounds in Copacabana. At this time too, Mariel tried to muscle in on the jogo do bicho territory of the banqueiros who controlled a number of locations where bets could be made in Niterói. On October 8, 1981, at about 5:30 P.M., Mariel was parking his car on Rua Alcântara Machado in the center of Rio. A meeting of banqueiros was taking place nearby at the headquarters of "Raul Capitão," or "Raul Captain" (the nickname of Raul Correa de Mello). He had invited Mariel to the gathering. But before Mariel could turn off his motor, a person who has been described as a well-built black male approached the car and professionally fired six bullets from an Ingram M-10 into Mariel before fleeing. Moryscotte died soon thereafter. No one was ever charged with the crime.[94]

At Mariel's funeral another graveside demonstration took place similar to the one that had accompanied the burial of Milton Le Cocq. There were three main differences between the two events, however. First, so many banqueiros and suspect police attended Mariel's entombment that one reporter commented, "I've never seen this many bandits assembled at any one time."[95] Then there was the routine of firing handguns into the air. When Le Cocq died, no one had fired their revolver in such a dangerous way. At Mariel's funeral some two hundred shots were aimed skyward amid whoops and shouts of "We're going to get the guy who did this." One bullet went astray and skinned a bystander's head. Finally, some mourners tried to get the ball rolling to form a "Scuderie Mariel Moryscotte." But there were no takers. The empty plan and its namesake were sealed in concrete in crypt no. 30751 of the Caju Cemetery.[96]

The White Hand

If Mariel's life was an enigma, so too was Rio's next major death squad. "Mão Branca," or the "White Hand," burst upon the scene in February 1980, when a man with a Portuguese accent began calling Rio newspapers to announce the next list of persons to be executed by Mão Branca. This much of the story is agreed upon. In dispute are the numbers of killings. One source claimed that approximately 160 persons were murdered in a three-month stretch.[97] The *O Dia* data, however, confirms only 91 Mão Branca slayings. Then there were the discussions of who Mão Branca was and whether there was more than one assassin. Again, the list of victims from *O Dia* would suggest that a group was behind these summary killings. If one looks at the three consecutive days with the most Mão Branca murders, Saturday to Monday, March 16–18, 1980, six persons were killed on Saturday, eight on Sunday, and six again on Monday. While it is possible that one individual carried out twenty assassinations in three days in different parts of greater Rio, it would seem to be a tall order. The last, and perhaps the most fascinating, question was, Did Mão Branca really exist?[98]

The answer actually begins with corrupt elements of the Polícia Civil and the Polícia Militar. For a period of time immediately prior to the appearance of Mão Branca, some Polícia Militar had attempted to usurp members of the Polícia Civil who were providing protection to jogo do bicho banqueiros. Their plan was to furnish this service themselves. It was not merely for gambling since the banqueiros also controlled the distribution of drugs in Rio. This provoked a reaction by some banqueiros, who began having individual Polícia Militar members assassinated as the two police organizations bickered among themselves. The chiefs of jogo reasoned that the Polícia Militar was rocking the boat.

While the police concentrated on themselves, crime in the former capital began to increase as local lawbreakers saw these events as a rare opportunity. This rise in illegal activity eventually caused the carioca populace and press to complain to the secretary for public security.[99] At the apex of the affair, *Última Hora* reporter Jorge Elias[100] telephoned Marcio Luiz Donnici at his law offices in Rio and asked if he would suggest a name for a new death squad. Marcio refused, but nonetheless noticed a few days later that the journalist had written a story in his newspaper, exposing for the first time the existence of Mão Branca.[101] The entire Mão Branca story was a farce. It was designed to sell newspapers.[102] Who then was responsible for the summary executions? The reply has to be the Esquadrão da Morte, since each crime was carried out in a style identical to the modus operandi used by the Esquadrão up to that point in time.

Rumblings in South America's Largest City

Contemporary vigilante death squads that have links to the police were born in the Americas, in Rio de Janeiro. Like a growing cancer, the idea caught on, particularly when the middle class became fearful and urged more police management of the povão. During the unbridled days of the military dictatorship, ten years after the formation of the GDE, a sister organization came to the public's attention in São Paulo. It too began with the homicide of a detective, this time David Romero Parré, on November 18, 1968. An accused thief and marijuana distributor named Carlos Eduardo da Silva, or "Saponga," shot Parré in the head and chest while he was looking for a suspect in São Paulo's Buraco Quente ("Hot Hole") favela. The policeman died in the ambulance, which was whisking him to the renowned Hospital das Clínicas. Saponga got away without a trace.

In the wake of the murder, the police began a massive sweep in Buraco Quente. More than a hundred people were arrested, but nothing was discovered. Favela residents knew the procedure. They had to go along with being roughed up by the authorities and maintain their silence or face being killed by Saponga and his associates.

Following the detective's burial, after the customary swearing and threats by those present, and after the shots into the air with their revolvers, a group of Parré's colleagues met that evening. One of the promises tossed around was that there would be ten criminals killed for every dead policeman. In so doing, those present acknowledged their connection with the Rio police. During the heated discussions one of the policemen picked up a telephone and called a newspaper.[103] "David will be revenged. We've already found photos of Saponga and ten others. These guys will be the first: 'Lourival,' 'Chininha,' 'Nego Sete,' 'Adalberto,' [and] 'Ademar,'" he told the reporter on the other end of the line.[104]

Three nights later, on November 22, Francisco Pereira Filho, or "O Neizão," who, it was claimed, was the first São Paulo death-squad victim,[105] was discovered shot to pieces not far from a dam south of the city. This murder was followed the next afternoon by the execution of Antônio de Souza Campos, known as Nego Sete, and another telephone call to the press. The caller said he was "White Lily," the public-relations officer of the São Paulo Esquadrão da Morte. He informed the reporters where they could find the second presunto.[106]

Notícias Populares

As in Rio, it was decided to look for these São Paulo victims in a local blood-and-guts newspaper. This is because in São Paulo, as in Rio and the rest of the country, official statistics are either not forthcoming or not reliable in respect to extralegal assassinations by police-connected extermination groups. One could sift through all deaths registered at coroners' offices, trying to filter out death-squad slayings.[107] Using this methodology, the researcher would have to determine vigilante cases primarily from the official data on the corpse. Missing or misfiled records would only add to the burden. The comments by witnesses, family members, and reporters would be absent. The *modus operandi* worked out in connection with the Rio de Janeiro cases would not be listed. Queimando o arquivo cases could not be included. Accordingly, the coroner's office option was considered but rejected.

São Paulo's major newspaper specializing in violence, *Notícias Populares,* was chosen as the best, easiest to use, and most consistent source of material. *Notícias Populares* began circulation on October 15, 1963. Unlike *O Dia,* it was published daily right from the start. Each edition from the first until that of December 31, 1999, was examined—totaling thirty-six years, two and a half months' worth of issues. This represented a shorter period of consultation than in Rio, although one that produced more cases: 17,905 instances of probable death resulting from extermination-group activity. This larger number was expected given the bigger state population of São Paulo over Rio de Janeiro. *Notícias Populares* correspondents relied on police boletins de ocorrência just as their counterparts at *O Dia* did. The same keys utilized in Rio de Janeiro again became useful in determining which events would be included in the São Paulo part of the study. All occurrences from the state of São Paulo were measured for the same variables as those in Rio de Janeiro.[108] Added together, the grand total of killings for both states was 32,675.

THE LITTLE LEATHER STRAP

Back on the streets, poorer paulistas must have wondered if they would wake up and find their loved ones' blood-spattered bodies on the pages of *Notícias Populares.* Police violence in the period following Parré's death took on a new magnitude in São Paulo. Saponga remained at large for nearly two months following the murder. He was finally located at a farm near the Cantareira Mountains in Tremembé, about two hours by car from the heart of São Paulo, in early 1969. The first man to shoot him was detective Astorige Corrêa de Paula e Silva, known as "O Correinha" ("The

Little Leather Strap"). Correinha would go on to lead one wing of the São Paulo death squad spawned by the murder of Parré. A host of police followed Correinha by sadistically firing round after round into Saponga's already-lifeless corpse. It is said that dozens of red roses had to be placed in the bandit's coffin to cover all the bullet holes in his cadaver.[109]

It was at about this time that the first break occurred in identifying a member of the emerging extermination group. In their zeal, members of the squad came across and gunned down a new victim named Bacuda. But Bacuda did not die right away. He lived long enough to finger one of his assailants, a man who had his arm in a cast. On the other arm he sometimes wore a watch he had taken off the still-warm wrist of Saponga. A friend of Bacuda stated positively that the man was detective Sérgio Fernando Paranhos Fleury.

THE POPE

Being the son of an undertaker was a fitting beginning for Sérgio Fleury. He was born in 1933, and like Mariel, in Niterói. His family also moved, but not up to Bahia. They traveled the shorter distance to the Vila Mariana suburb of São Paulo. When Sérgio was still a youth the senior Fleury passed away after being contaminated while performing an autopsy. Since the father had been a city employee, and as a way of compensation, the paulistano government paid for young Sérgio's high school education. When he graduated at seventeen, Fleury joined DOPS. Sérgio made a good cop and advanced rapidly. He became a clerk in the office of the secretary of public security. Next followed a stint in homicide, then seasoning in the 6th Police Division. During these years he took a law degree and worked as a special agent of RUDI (Ronda Unificada do Departamento de Investigações—Department of Investigations Unified Patrol). RUDI was a part of DEIC (Departamento Estadual de Investigações Criminais—State Department of Criminal Investigations), which was located at the Palácio da Polícia Civil (Headquarters of the Polícia Civil). In 1960, ten years after becoming a member of the force, Sérgio was advanced over more senior officers to the position of special deputy in charge of radio-equipped patrol cars.[110]

Handcuffed suspects brought in by Fleury and his team to DEIC discovered why that promotion had been made. They were forced to stay in a waiting room where a sign in plain view gave a military-era preview of what was to come: "Contra a Pátria, não há direitos" (Against the country, you have no rights).[111] Then, ushered into the bowels of the building, where upwards of eight hundred prisoners were squeezed into cells, the accused was subjected to the culture of the stick. This meant special treatment to bring about a confession or draw out information. For that purpose, the subject might find his inquisitors wrapping his wrists with cloth before a session in which his body would be twisted into abnormal positions or hung from the rafters. The rags minimized the marks. Sometimes his shoes were removed and he was placed in a chamber with a wet floor, which was repeatedly jolted with electric current. There was also a special room fitted with nozzles that shot powerful streams of water and sand at prisoners, forcing them back against the opposite wall. Some could not resist this unique torture and died. They were hauled out, stood up by two police, had a lit cigarette stuck between their lips to feign life, and dragged away. Still others were rolled up in rugs and removed. The bodies were discarded in various parts of the city and wound up in the reports of unwary local police as unsolved crimes.

With the advent of anti-dictatorship armed movements in the 1960s, DOPS director Benedito Nunes Dias adopted a policy of treating urban guerrillas in the same manner as common criminals. This produced a traffic jam of those waiting to be tortured. It also produced the most callous of mutilators, ones like Hélio Nico of the robbery division, who regularly played poker with his police colleagues while all about him were individuals groaning and crying out, dangling from their respective pau-de-araras. As in those days thirty years before when Filinto Müller was chief of police in Rio de Janeiro, and his people used a continuously revved up motorcycle engine to muffle the shrieks of those being tortured, DOPS in São Paulo used a police band to blare out off-key music in front of the building whenever called upon for the same function. Owing to a lack of skewers for the pau-de-araras, at one point even a small flagpole was used. The national symbol of Brazil apparently was still attached. Members of the FBI, who came to the city to watch DOPS at work, were said to have become uneasy when witnessing such routines.[112]

Attending to the medical requests of the torturees was one Dr. Pereira, or, more familiarly, "Pereirinha" ("Little Pereira"), who was actually only a male nurse. He walked about the cells each afternoon and evening dressed in white with a stethoscope hanging from his neck. Chain-smoking, he would check pulses, dab a bit of mercurochrome here or there, give a prisoner a pain killer, and guarantee, "You're going to be OK, my son." Pereira then told those in charge of the lash which tortures to administer and which to curtail.[113]

Besides the eight hundred prisoners at the Palácio da Polícia Civil, there were another eight hundred over at Tiradentes Prison, plus two hundred more at the Hipódromo penal complex. In the best Kafkaesque manner, few prisoners knew why they had been locked up. Some inmates languished for months or even got lost in this morass. New arrivals were called *mofo* (mold or mildew). Since many apprehensions occurred on Friday, a kind of extortion took place in which freshly brought in individuals paid a so-called contribution so that they would not have to spend the weekend in jail. Others, owing to their better attire, their connections with the world of crime, or their ability to generate additional arrests, were auctioned off between the police who were there. The winners of these bidding wars had the right to torture their living acquisitions until relatives paid a desired amount or the information for more important apprehensions was obtained.[114]

Fleury too was known to help himself. At one point in his career, he led periodic charges into an area of São Paulo known as the "Boca do Lixo" (Mouth of Trash). This was the territory of nightclub floozies and cheap hotels. Sérgio arbitrarily invaded the prostitutes' nearby apartments, stealing some things, throwing other items out the windows, and burning the rest. One of the things he quickly put in his pockets were the drugs. Fleury used to inject himself in the legs and feet with narcotics.[115] He was also a heavy drinker. Both vices were perfect for a man who referred to the Boca do Lixo as the "Boca do Luxo" ("Mouth of Luxury").

Fleury was a regular patron at many of the area's restaurants. One evening, he and his men were having a friendly drink at Moisés Bar in the Boca when one of the police noticed that blood was dripping from the underside of Fininho's yellow Simca, a stylish car of the times. The vehicle's trunk contained the body of a new presunto. Undisturbed, Fininho pointed to his key chain. On it was a freshly detached human ear, strung together with the keys. The globules of blood were falling to the street from its former owner. Unperturbed, they laughed and continued drinking.[116]

None of this kept Sérgio, who sometimes used the alias of "Dr. Vidigal Barreto," or simply "Vidiga," from becoming one of the most important agents in the Social Section of DOPS, which he joined in August 1969. In 1977 he would be made director of DEIC.[117] His posts came with a lot of paperwork, yet he never got too far from the action. Many times political detainees were ushered before him in scenes that were set up in advance. In a drama that was repeated several times, Fleury wore a steel helmet from the Nazi-era German army. As the prisoner was let in, he was startled to see Fleury being saluted with a "Heil!" by one of his assistants and responding in kind. Pushed face to face with this myth of a man and his cold, blue-eyed stare, many a prisoner started talking.[118] But Fleury was not just an ornament in this theater of the macabre. He took a personal role in the murders of many suspects, occasionally informing his victims, who were separated from the rest and always kept in the nude, "My name is Lucifer!"[119] "Fleury went every afternoon to cell 5 [at DEIC], where the Esquadrão da Morte had under guard those prisoners who would be shot on some road and then left at a curve in the highway. He always said to one of us, 'You'll be a legal presunto.' Sometimes he'd choose a prisoner and tell him that he was going to be set free. The poor fellow would be taken from his cell to a place where he could shave, have a manicure, and get his hair cut. After he got cleaned up, the illusion would be shattered and he would wind up being a presunto."[120]

Fresh mofo had all their money and personal items removed, theoretically to be stored in the Secção de Valores (Valuables Section). Only thing was, warden Olintho Denardi; the chief of the Secção de Valores, Orlando Trevisan; and two jailers, Leonildo Tangerino and Geraldo de Cavalli Almeida used the Secção as their personal treasure chest.

Tiradentes also contained political prisoners, although the number of ordinary inmates was larger. The health of all captives was allowed to lapse, venereal disease went largely untreated, and teenage males, some as young as sixteen, were regularly mixed in with older prisoners. When Hélio Tavares, a member of the Esquadrão da Morte, was put in charge of the facility, he had every inmate's head shaved. Tavares even took part in an evidently common ordeal. At the entrance to the "Correctional Wing" there was a pool of water not quite forty inches square (1 m^2). Prisoners were made to place their heads in the water. Whenever they raised their heads to breathe, the guards smacked them with their fists and pieces of wood. The torture ended only when the jailers got tired of the game or when the victim passed out. Other prisoners were burned with cigarettes and cigarette lighters. Or they were forced to take their clothes off and walk in a circle all night while chanting "Our Father Who Art in Heaven" without stopping.

Tiradentes likewise possessed a cell in its own "Special Wing" where future presuntos were kept. The window in this cell was covered with a piece of wood so that no one could see in or out. A list, or *grade,* was kept on each inmate. The grade contained an incarcerated person's name and the date of his capture. Those who had been in one place too long without anything having been done to move them on in the legal maze were taken to the cell in the Special Wing to await further action. A priest who saw the cell when it was in operation said that it was full of prisoners. A friend of Fleury's since childhood, the clergyman, Marcello Duarte de Oliveira, or Padre Agostinho, was threatened with imprisonment and/or assassination.[121]

Like Fleury and O Correinha, most members of the early paulistano Esquadrão da Morte were police. There was José Campos Corrêa Filho, João Carlos Tralli, Ademar Augusto de Oliveira and his brother Antonio Augusto de Oliveira. Not to be left out were João Balduino, João Bruno, Ernesto Milton Dias, Angelino Moliterno, Amador Navarro Parra, Eduardo Xavier, Nathaniel Gonçalves de Oliveira, José Gustavo de Oliveira, Cleómenes Antunes, Walter Brasileiro Polim, Abílio Armando Alcarpe, José Rosa, and former DEIC director Hélio Tavares. Also included were Antonio Lazardo Constanzia, Samuel Pereira Borba, Paulo Bordini, Josacyr Cuoco, Raul Ferreira, Salvio Fernandes do Monte, and Silas Silva Nicoleti. Alberto Barbour was the group's public relations specialist. Then there were those who were known only as "Luis," "Severino," "Indio," "Carlos" (a.k.a. "Little Carlos Iron Bullets"), "Dirceu" (alias "Jesus Christ"), and "Japa." Japa was the group's sole Brazilian of Japanese extraction.[122]

By 1973, when some of these men were under investigation for homicide, José Campos Corrêa Filho, or "Campão," was said to have been involved in nine murders. He was even accused of being the most evil of the group. Another narcotics user, João Carlos Tralli, who was known by the nickname "Trailer," was thought to have killed seventeen. But there were many more police officers involved with both the carrying out of summary justice and the use and trafficking of narcotics. In fact, when the district attorney for São Paulo looked into the activities of approximately two hundred Esquadrão suspects, only one was found *not* to be a member of the Polícia Militar or Polícia Civil.[123]

So it was with Ademar Augusto de Oliveira, also called Fininho-I.[124] His street name means "[Marijuana] Joint-1," and there was ample reason for such a title. Fininho-I used, smuggled, and sold drugs himself. He was said to be Fleury's right-hand man and Mariel's partner in their drug and auto theft ring. Fininho-I regularly tortured prisoners at DOPS. In addition, it was reported that he killed or helped to kill twenty people while a member of the Esquadrão da Morte. One of them was a barber at DEIC whom Fininho-I stabbed in the buttocks. A vein was cut and the man bled to death. Fininho-I was eventually imprisoned but escaped and fled to Paraguay.[125]

Topping the list of all-time kills were Fleury with twenty-two and Correinha with thirty-nine. A more recent accounting, however, attributes ninety-seven executions to O Correinha while acknowledging that he admits to only around twenty.[126]

Hélio Bicudo

Everything started to come undone because of one man. With the 1968 execution of David Parré, the military government became nervous about the country's international image. When another person wanted by the paulistano police, Adjuvan Nunes, "O Guri" ("The Little Boy"), shot his way out of a police encirclement, killing policeman Agostinho Gonçalves de Carvalho, in July 1970, events crystallized. Guri's name was placed on the Esquadrão's list of bandits to be executed on sight. Esquadrão members did not have to wait long, as Adjuvan was quickly found in a desolate area east of the city, between Vila Carrão and Itaquera, and murdered. The right side of his face was shot fourteen times. A 12-guage shotgun, fired at point-blank range, opened up a hole clean through his body where his heart had been. Nine other suspects were killed in the days that followed.

Public prosecutor Hélio Pereira Bicudo was one of those who initially thought that the Esquadrão was a manifestation of the Polícia Civil's not wanting to be incorporated into the Força Pública. The extralegal activities were seen as an effort to stop this amalgamation by showing a new vigor at rooting out and eliminating marginais. With the death of Guri and the slaughter that followed, Bicudo began looking at matters differently. He had tried to get the authorities to do something back on March 3, 1969, when AI-5 repression was in full force. Some seventeen months later, with no letup in AI-5, he found himself again requesting the state attorney general's office to take action. Asking the dictators was dangerous; getting them to act was nearly impossible. Officials in Brasília did not really want anything done to the members of the Esquadrão; they just wanted them to go away. Their solution was another pretense at justice.

Following bureaucratic discussions and maneuverings, the job of investigating the activities of the Esquadrão was offered to Bicudo himself. If he refused, he would have to shut up. If he accepted, so many roadblocks would be placed in his path that he would fail. The result would be the same in either case. It was felt that Bicudo was just a second-rate prosecutor anyway. Clearly, though, the military's *apparatchiks* did not know whom they were up against. For although small in stature and unpretentious, Hélio Bicudo was one of the most courageous Brazilians of this or any century.

There followed more posturing, until finally the autocrat himself, Emílio Médici, issued a notice on August 7, 1970, to all state governors. The circular seemed to place limits on the acts of barbarity that could be committed by the police. It called for the governors to arrange an investigation, independent of their state's judiciary, into police vigilantism. In São Paulo, the inquiry was assigned to the department of public security. Headed by army colonel Danilo Darcy de Sá da Cunha e Mello, it found nothing, did nothing, and suggested nothing. Governor Abreu Sodré also denied the existence of the Esquadrão on a popular evening television program, *Pinga Fogo,* on December 8.

Knowing that the state police were involved, Bicudo met with the minister of justice, Alfredo Buzaid, at the latter's Rio de Janeiro office to ask that another weapon in the government's arsenal, the Polícia Federal, help to scrutinize the dealings of the Esquadrão.[127] It was a bad idea. The Polícia Federal, at least in Rio de Janeiro, was accused of having had two rooms at one facility where officers regularly employed the pau-de-arara until 1985. They tried to cover their tracks when a local judge caught on to what they were doing. The metal bar and tires were not a pau-de-arara, a Polícia Federal representative told the magistrate, but part of the equipment used for karate practice. What about all of the blood on the ground? "Why, it got there from a police barbeque," was the answer.[128]

Buzaid promised full support for Bicudo's efforts but never provided any actual assistance. Unperturbed, Bicudo pressed on. With the help of municipal judge Nélson Fonseca and two prosecuting attorneys, José Sílvo Fonseca Tavares and Dirceu de Melo, Bicudo began looking into the activities of the Esquadrão. He and his team consulted with prisoners at Tiradentes prison and they listened to witnesses. They interviewed Padre Geraldo Manseroll, who had taken the pictures of the arm-in-a-cast Fleury. Fininho-I later made an attempt on Manseroll's life. The policeman pushed the priest from the scaffolding surrounding his church while he was making repairs. Fininho-I had hidden in the belfry. Manseroll spent time in the hospital, recuperated, and wisely left the country.

Waiting for him to return home, a swarm of police ambushed Nego Sete one afternoon in a part of the city not far from São Paulo's international airport. As soon as their mark got off a bus, a cop yelled out for him to halt. Sete took off running, arrived at his small house, and was shot dead as he opened the door by the police waiting inside. Fleury and his men made a neighbor wash up the blood. They then loaded the body into a vehicle and dumped it on the old road to Rio in the community of Mogi das Cruzes. Not only had Padre Geraldo photograph several of the police and witness much of the actual killing, he also took down the license numbers of the vehicles used by the Esquadrão.

From the moment Nego Sete was drilled full of holes until the promulgation of the so-called Lei Fleury on November 22, 1973, a spectacle that needs no adjectives took place in Brazil. In 1970 and 1971 Bicudo brought charges against thirty-six police.[129] There were seventy-three accusations of murder, three of attempted murder, and two for falsification of documents. The total number of homicide victims was fifteen. The results of three of the cases have been lost from the public record. In seventy-five indictments an eventual verdict was reached, but just four guilty findings—three for murder and one for attempted murder—were returned. Moreover, two of the three men convicted of homicide were allowed to go free pending appeal.[130]

Sérgio Fleury was the most important member of the force to be charged. Bicudo thought that the trail led all the way up to the São Paulo secretary for public security, Hely Lopes Meirelles, and even to the governor himself, Roberto Costa de Abreu Sodré. But clearly the men on top were not about to let a detective they considered a national hero for his work at putting down the red plague, and certainly not the leader of the police, much less the state governor, fall victim to this upstart public prosecutor. The threats to Bicudo's life, the countless intimidating telephone calls—received mainly by his wife and children—did not seem to be working. The only way out was a feeble one. On August 2, 1971, Bicudo was fired.

Some six weeks passed, and tax inspectors searched the former public prosecutor's office. Someone claimed that Hélio had not paid his taxes—charges that were totally unfounded. Later, when visiting his sister in Rio de Janeiro, Bicudo and his wife took a taxi from Leblon to Méier. At some point in this otherwise routine trip, the taxi driver began to act nervous. He mentioned to Bicudo that they were being followed. Reaching the home of his sister, Hélio invited the driver in to wait and see what a telephone call to another relative, this one at a carioca police station, might produce. Hélio had taken down the number of the car tailing them. After a short pause, the taxi driver abruptly left the house, hopped into a taxi driven by another individual, and sped away. Perhaps Bicudo failed to make the connection, but many police, owing to their low pay, held second jobs as taxi drivers. When the relative returned his call, the exprosecutor was informed that his pursuers were, in fact, members of the department—keeping a watchful on their famous visitor from São Paulo.

Bicudo's homegrown guardians placed him under an even more determined gaze when he returned to São Paulo. They learned of his comings and goings and broke into both his residence and his downtown office at night. Nothing was destroyed, but a person or persons unknown removed numerous documents. This invasion of privacy and theft took place when Hélio was preparing *Meu depoimento sobre o esquadrão da morte,* an exposé on his efforts to bring the members of the Esquadrão and several of those connected to them to justice.[131]

Fall of a Pope

The legal processes continued for another two years against Fleury and other members of the São Paulo death squad, until the government began to realize that its star policeman might actually go to jail after all. In record time, the generals then composed and passed a milestone of Brazilian jurisprudence. Gen. João Baptista Figueiredo took personal command of the effort. The Lei Fleury (Fleury Law) was the result. It was created to save Sérgio Fleury from a fate so many felt he deserved. The statute allowed magistrates to take into consideration the past good behavior of persons accused or convicted of a crime but appealing the charge or the verdict, and, if warranted, grant them conditional liberty during the legal process.[132]

Sérgio Fleury's legal proceedings outlived him. At around 1 A.M. on May 1, 1979, Fleury died mysteriously at the Ilha Bela Yacht Club in São Paulo. The official version of his death, approved in Brasília, stated that he had lost his balance while hopping from one tied-up boat to another, fell in the water, and drowned. This could have been provoked by the fact that he was stone drunk at the time. But there are those who feel that Fleury was knocked off by the mob, owing to his arrest and torture of Tomaso Buscetta in 1972. Though if not an accident, a more plausible scenario would be that the state he served came to consider him a liability. In this scenario, sometime during the unfolding *abertura* a decision was made that Fleury had outlived his usefulness. He knew too much, and what do you do with a torturer and head of an extermination group once redemocratization comes? Or, more accurately, those in power must have wondered, "What could he do to *us* once civilian rule returns?" Lending support to this thesis is the curious fact that an autopsy was forbidden on orders that originated in the office of Fleury's superior, Celso Telles, if not higher up in the government. Harry Shibata, the head mortician for the state of São Paulo, likewise discounted the drowning theory altogether.[133]

However much the ruling elite wanted the death squads to fade away in their transfer of power, it is best to remember that the dictators were concerned only about the blatant features of death-squad operations, such as point men who were high-profile police like Sérgio Fleury. They were unconcerned about homicides that largely went unnoticed, particularly those unseen by the international press. This apathy on the part of the dictators was nothing novel. Crimes that cry out for justice, including arbitrary killings of the povão, have always been committed in Brazil. Despised for becoming the beasts of burden that were once slaves,[134] the murder of the poor by enforcers preceded the volatility of the first subelites and the buzzwords invented by journalists. The impunity of crimes perpetrated in the name of authority outlived Vidigal, Müller, Fleury, and all the henchmen in Rio de Janeiro, São Paulo, and every other state across the nation. Long before the end of the twentieth century, rationalizing ethics were already a ghastly part of day-to-day life in Brazil. People were and are born, raised, and done away with. It has become so common that the bodies of the poor, dead or alive, are virtually ignored or are stepped over in trite abandon.

Examination of the Data

ALL CASES

The kinds of individuals whom death squads in Brazil typically went and continue to go after can now be determined. Who these people were/are has been the subject of all kinds of speculation. There have been reports that they are mainly blacks and mixed-race individuals, or unruly adolescents, or that they are just bandits clogging up the judicial process.[135] Yet, without a careful analysis of a large number of probable cases, such conclusions are based on little more than hearsay or invention. As the first extensive analysis of the victims of death-squad activities in Brazil, it is hoped to lay some misnomers to rest while giving motivation for additional research in other more fruitful areas.

We will hypothesize here, in light of the long historical importance of class rather than caste in Brazil, that the majority of victims will be poor. This is not to negate the importance of race. It is to state only that the poverty variable should manifest itself more strongly than color in the Brazilian cultural mosaic. Obviously, not the entire country could be evaluated in this effort. Brazil has a landmass larger than the contiguous forty-eight states of the USA. What follows, then, is the first exploratory accounting of several significant variables of extermination group victims, so far as those variables and victims could be determined from *O Dia* and *Notícias Populares* news articles based on the boletins de ocorrência, in the states of Rio de Janeiro and São Paulo, for a majority of the last fifty years of the twentieth century. Figure 6.1 presents a graphic rendition of the annual suspected occurrence of these assassinations in arguably Brazil's two most important states. There were thirty-two cases in Rio and thirteen in São Paulo where the gender of the victim could not be determined. The actual combined number of victims in the graph was as follows.

FIGURE 6.1

Suspected Death Squad Victims by Number and Year in the States of Rio de Janeiro and São Paulo

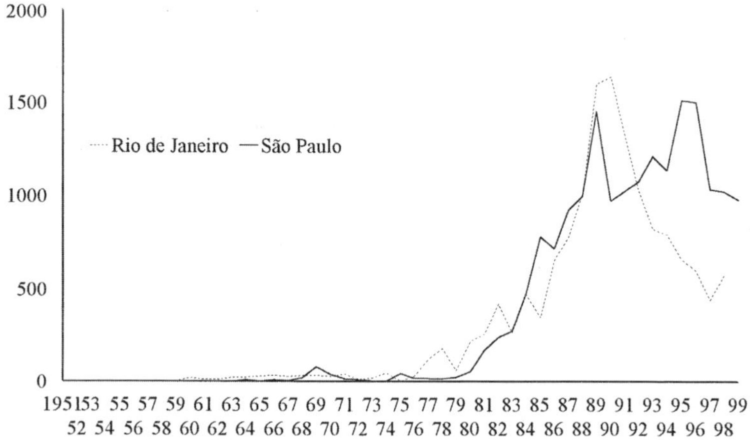

	Rio de Janeiro	*São Paulo*	*Total*
Females	783	632	*1415*
Males	13955	17260	*31215*
Total	*14738*	*17892*	**32630**

FEMALE CASES

One of the more intriguing features of the yearly report concerns the relatively small number of female fatalities. That is, 783 or 5.61 percent of the Rio cases, 632 or 3.66 percent of the São Paulo cases, and 1,415 or 4.33 percent of the aggregate instances were females. If we construct a null hypothesis theorizing that there is no significant difference in the numbers of each gender among death squad victims in these two states, then chi-square analysis[136] demonstrates that there were considerably fewer females in the sample than what we might have expected through random chance, $X^2 = 366.04$ with 1 df. Significance $10.83 = p < .001$ (one-tailed test). A visual construction of the feminine side to this ongoing carnage can be observed in figure 6.2.

When looking at the two prior diagrams, the increments in the Y-axis, or the left-hand column, should be taken into account so as not to equate

FIGURE 6.2
Suspected Female Death Squad Victims by Number and Year in the States of Rio de Janeiro and São Paulo

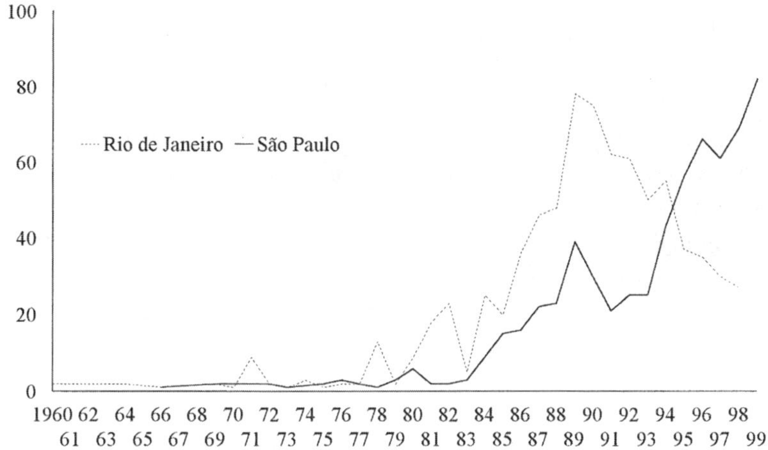

the number of female victims being anywhere near the totals for both sexes. And, while the actual numbers will be contrasted against other variables later, at this point it should be said that the greatest reason for female slayings involved members of this gender being in the physical vicinity of a male marked for execution. Many females were thus done away with in a process of queimando o arquivo. Usually lacking any charge of criminal activity in the news reports whatsoever, most females were killed by extermination groups so as to get rid of anyone who could testify against those groups.

AGE

When available, the ages within the sample were likewise of interest. The range of ages for female victims in Rio de Janeiro, with 626 cases reporting spanned three months to seventy years, with the mean ($\bar{x}$) being 25.3 years of age. In the same order for males in Rio, the figures were 11,382 cases: two to seventy-eight years, $\bar{x}$ = 25.0. For the state of São Paulo, the breakdown for females with an age given was 527 victims: three months to seventy-five years, $\bar{x}$ = 23.9. And finally, male victims in São Paulo had the following characteristics: 13,665 instances: one to sixty-eight years, $\bar{x} = 23.9$.

Setting aside the span of ages for the moment, we can readily observe that both genders in Rio de Janeiro were older than their counterparts in São Paulo—by over one year. When we couple in the race of the victims, the oldest group were black women in Rio de Janeiro at 26.4 years on average—one and a half years older than their sisters in São Paulo. The youngest group were mulatto males in São Paulo, at 24.0 years, excluding the low numbers of indigenous and Asian victims. But perhaps the most enticing item of all is that the average age in every category was in the twenties. This runs counter to the commonly heard view that the majority of victims are in their teens. Most of the fatalities uncovered in this analysis were nearing or had passed their twenty-fifth birthday. The death squads' prey are not juveniles but young adults.

	Rio de Janeiro		*São Paulo*		*Total*
	Female	Male	Female	Male	
Asian				$n = 17$ 23.0	*$n = 17$ 23.0*
Black	$n = 78$ $\bar{x} = 26.4$	$n = 1865$ 24.9	$n = 33$ 24.9	$n = 963$ 24.4	*$n = 2939$ 25.2*
Indigenous				$n = 1$ 20.0	*$n = 1$ 20.0*
Mulatto	$n = 128$ 25.3	$n = 1771$ 24.9	$n = 101$ 24.6	$n = 1719$ 24.0	*$n = 3719$ 24.7*
White	$n = 93$ 25.3	$n = 1305$ 26.2	$n = 80$ 23.8	$n = 1050$ 25.4	*$n = 2528$ 25.2*
Total	*$n = 299$ 25.6*	*$n = 4941$ 25.2*	*$n = 214$ 24.3*	*$n = 3750$ 24.5*	$n =$ **9204**

RACE

The total number of victims that could be assigned a race are set out in the following table. This data is listed cumulatively by gender and state for the entire investigated period. The single indigenous male was not included. Percentages are given for each cell, column, and row (the latter in parenthesis).

	Rio de Janeiro Victims		*São Paulo Victims*		*Total*
	Female	Male	Female	Male	
Asian	$n = 0$	$n = 0$	$n = 0$	$n = 19$	$n = 19$
	-	-	-	.5	.2
				(100.0)	
Black	$n = 93$	$n = 2149$	$n = 41$	$n = 1136$	$n = 3419$
	26.3%	38.7	17.4	26.6	32.9
	(2.7%)	(62.9)	(1.2)	(33.2)	
Mulatto	$n = 149$	$n = 1941$	$n = 108$	$n = 1922$	$n = 4120$
	42.1%	35.0	46.0	45.1	39.7
	(3.6%)	(47.1)	(2.6)	(46.7)	
White	$n = 112$	$n = 1436$	$n = 86$	$n = 1187$	$n = 2821$
	31.6%	26.3	36.6	27.8	27.2
	(4.0%)	(50.9)	(3.1)	(42.1)	
Total	$n = 354$	$n = 5526$	$n = 235$	$n = 4264$	$n =$ **10379**
	(3.4%)	*(53.2)*	*(2.3)*	*(41.1)*	

Knowing that 26.3 percent of the Rio females were black while just 2.7 percent of the black victims were females who came from Rio is valuable in its own right. It is much more revealing, however, to look at how the race of the fatalities changed over time in relation to the proportions of racial groups in the state populations. For our purposes, there were three national censuses that enumerated race by state: those conducted in 1950, 1960, and 1980. The 1970 census did not ask the race question. The 1990 census was never carried out. There are figures for 1991 and 2000 but, as of this writing, neither is yet available listing color by state of residence. From the three completed surveys, tables of racial percentages in the Rio and São Paulo state populations can, nonetheless, be projected for the missing periods.[137] Using those projections together with the occurrence of victims in the study, we can construct graphs depicting the over- and underrepresentation of all victim racial groups by percent relative to their frequency in the actual or estimated state populations. These two percentages were then subtracted from one another to determine if a particular cluster is represented in excess or not among respective death squad victims.

Observe that the best possible fit, one that shows no preferences on the part of the extermination groups, would be along the zero along the X-axis in figures 6.3a-b. As the number of female victims was small, those results

FIGURE 6.3a
Percentage of Over- or Underrepresentation of Suspected Female Victims by Race Compared to Their Proportion in the Censuses of the States of Rio de Janeiro and São Paulo

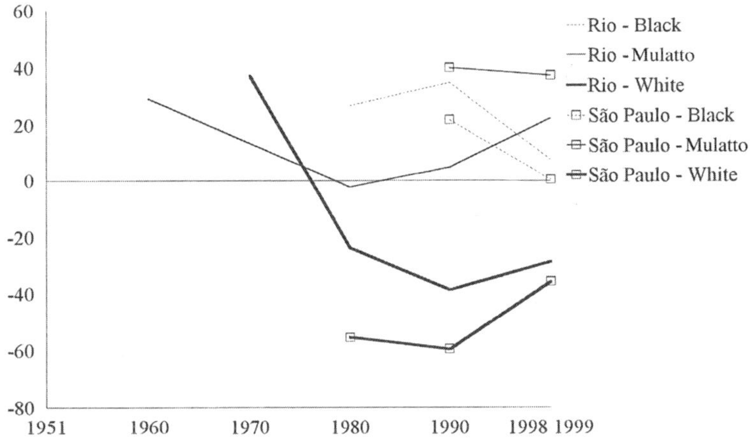

should be viewed only as indicative of emerging trends. These two graphs plainly demonstrate, however, that in comparison to the numbers in their respective states, over time extermination groups in both Rio de Janeiro and São Paulo kill more nonwhites and fewer whites than one would expect from their representation each state's racial composition. Only Asians were murdered in a manner that came close to zero, so we can assume they suffered no special malice or preferential treatment. In second place, mulatto males in Rio de Janeiro do not appear to have been targeted far out of proportion to their actual numbers in that state.

It is likewise essential to consider how a particular racial group fared over the course of the study compared to other groups, irrespective of its proportion in the population. From the four figures 6.4a–d, the visible inferences regarding when a particular cluster was most at risk can be distinguished. Starting in Rio de Janeiro, a majority of the female targets, since 1991, have been mulatto. Beginning in 1981, Rio males were usually nonwhite. By 1988, the largest number of males began to be black. In São Paulo, the occurrence

FIGURE 6.3b

Percentage of Over- or Underrepresentation of Suspected Male Victims by Race Compared to their Proportion in the Censuses of the States of Rio de Janeiro and São Paulo

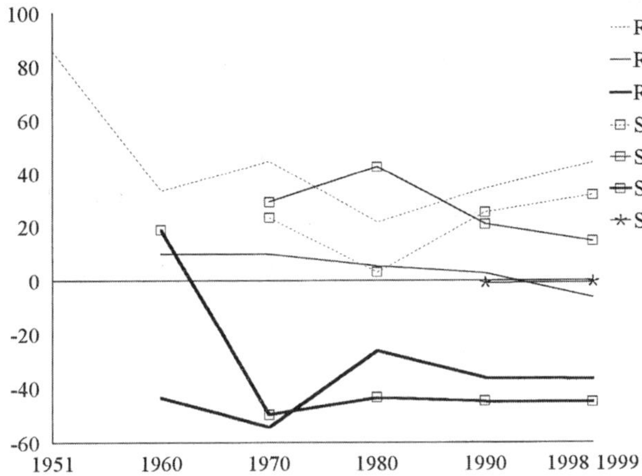

of mulatto females among the fatalities jumped in the last year of the study from eight to twenty-five. Only time will tell in which direction this last curve will go. It might prove best to recall, in this regard, that for the ten years 1990 to 1999, white women were killed less often than mulatto females in but a single year—1995. Mulatto males in São Paulo were perhaps the most dramatic of all the victims in respect to race. Since 1980, for the last twenty years of the research, they were the most common fatalities. Together with high numbers for mulatto females, this may be indicative of their rapid growth in the state. Many of these individuals were impoverished immigrants from other parts of the country, particularly rural sections of Brazil's northern states. Their reason for moving to São Paulo was invariably to find work. These desires ran headlong into any real opportunity to do so, plus one additional fact: São Paulo is a dividing line between the darker-skinned north and the lighter-skinned south of the country. The lack of opportunities to find adequate employment by the newcomers may well have been exacerbated by suspected subelite prejudices in this border state.

Figure 6.4a

Suspected Female Victims by Number, Race and Year in the State of Rio de Janeiro

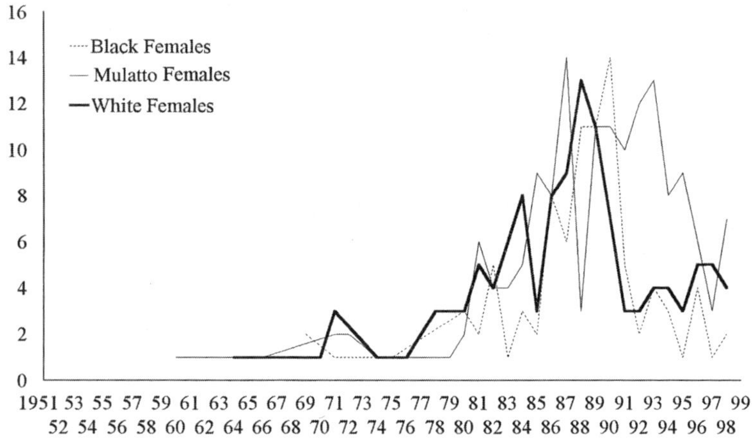

Figure 6.4b

Suspected Male Victims by Number, Race and Year in the State of Rio de Janeiro

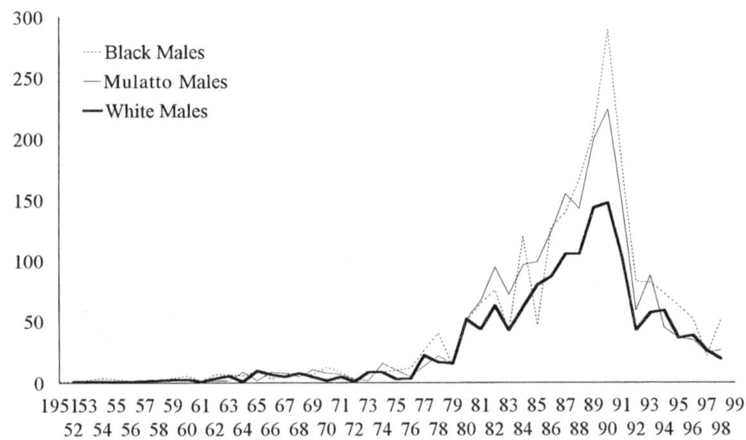

Figure 6.4c
Suspected Female Victims by Race and Year in the State of São Paulo

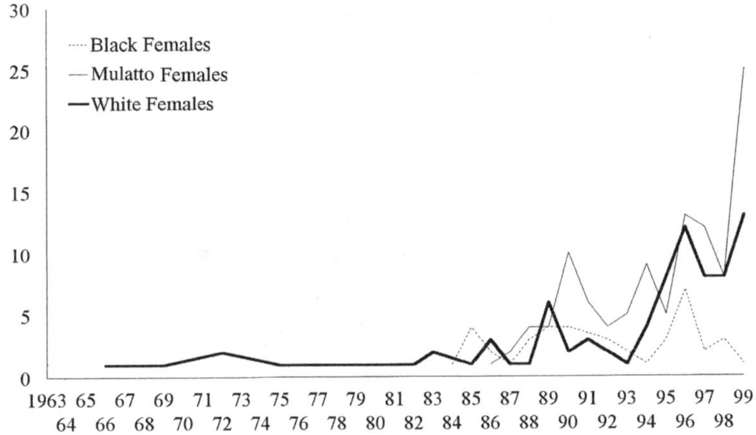

Figure 6.4d
Suspected Male Victims by Race and Year in the State of São Paulo

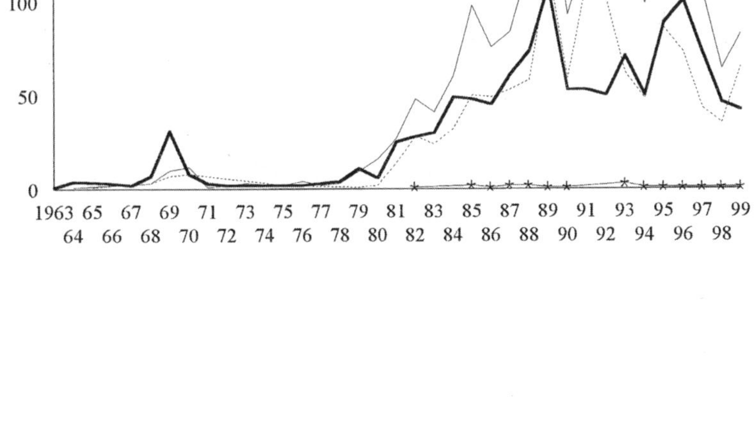

OCCUPATION

The victims in this research held a total of 355 different professions. Many poorer people held two and even three jobs. This fact was a product of Brazil's low salaries and suggestive of a gap between Brazil's rich and poor. Following the conclusion of this research, in 2002, it was reported that whereas the salary of the 20 percent poorest Americans would have to be multiplied by a factor of eight to reach the income level of the richest 20 percent of Americans, the take-home pay of the 20 percent poorest Brazilians would have to be multiplied by thirty-three. That's over four times the distance between the economic top and bottom in the USA and Brazil.[138]

Keeping the Brazilian side of this disparity in mind, it will now be convenient to summarize the number of victims into the ensuing general list of major occupational types. Just as with the other variables, not all news reports listed the victim's profession.

	Rio de Janeiro	*São Paulo*	*Total*
Blue collar	1282	2459	*3741*
Illegal activities	44	22	*66*
Religious orders	2	2	*4*
Retired	15		*15*
Students	97	173	*270*
Subelites	292	178	*470*
Unemployed	127	385	*512*
White collar	110	69	*179*
Total	*1969*	*3288*	**5257**

Besides the heavy bias toward blue-collar workers, 71.2 percent of the sample, one of the more curious revelations in the table is the impressive number of subelite fatalities—particularly in Rio de Janeiro. This was probably due to the fact that these individuals receive low salaries coupled to the opportunities they possess to commit crimes. It could likewise be true that some members or former members of the security apparatus were eliminated to settle old scores, or because they would not cooperate with some planned illegal activity. While it may appear that there were more killings in São Paulo among blue-collar workers, students, and the unemployed, such is actually not the case. This is because many more people live in the state of São Paulo than in Rio de Janeiro. From the following table, constructed using available census data,[139] it can be seen proportionate to their numbers in the population of each state, that these groups were not overly represented among the victims.

	1950	*1960*	*1970*	*1980*	*1991*[a]	*2000*
Rio de Janeiro	4,674,645	6,649,646	8,994,802	11,291,631	12,807,706	14,392,106
São Paulo	9,134,423	12,823,806	17,770,975	25,042,074	31,588,925	37,035,456
(difference)	(+95.4%)	(+92.9%)	(+97.6%)	(+121.8%)	(+146.6%)	(+156.3%)

a = 1990 unavailable

The percentages beneath the figures for São Paulo indicate how much larger the population was in that state over the number of inhabitants in the state of Rio de Janeiro. Looking at the year 1970, for example, for every resident of Rio de Janeiro, there were nearly two persons from São Paulo.

ALLEGED OFFENSES

Next, we shall look at the reported crime or crimes of the two groups of victims. We will omit those cases with no narrated crime(s) in the newspaper articles. Remembering that some persons were charged with several crimes at one time, there were a total of 4,901 individuals accused of an offense in the state of Rio de Janeiro, and 5,806 in the state of São Paulo. The totality of persons said to have committed some infraction was thus 10,707. Since 13,263 separate accusations were recorded in the newspapers, each victim was thus stated to have been responsible for an average of 1.24 breaches of Brazil's norms and morés. Be aware that all of these infractions were not necessarily codified statutes. Some offenses were not wrongdoings in the strict sense of the word, but were exactly that in the normative worldview of the subelite killer(s). Charges such as wrong race/ethnicity, transvetitism, and homosexual/lesbian were stated in *O Dia* and *Notícias Populares* as the reason for a particular execution; but of course they can hardly be seen as crimes per se on the international stage.

There were a total of ninety-six possible transgressions recorded. Of these, only those with combined aggregates of one hundred will be examined here. Minus five cases where gender was not reported, the charges with more that a hundred victims by number, sex, and state were:

	Rio de Janeiro		*São Paulo*		
	Female	Male	Female	Male	*Total*
Armed robbery		54		75	*129*
Assault and robbery	26	1510	34	2397	*3967*
Escape from detention	1	46	2	65	*114*
Ex-juvenile inmate		10	1	94	*105*
Ex-prisoner	1	104	1	196	*302*
Family member of a target[a]	96	179	67	190	*532*
Female with male[a]	409	-	245	-	*654*
Homicide		238	1	257	*496*
Homicide of police personnel	1	73		28	*102*
Narcotics violation	65	1953	99	979	*3096*
Rape		138		94	*232*
Resisting arrest	1	3		170	*174*
Robbery	6	100	9	478	*593*
Theft	6	102	5	417	*530*
Transvestitism		55		60	*115*
Vehicular theft	5	350	4	758	*1117*
Total	*617*	*4915*	*468*	*6258*	**12258**

a = elimination of witness category

Examining this data—in light of the ratios of persons living in each state—it can be argued that both states displayed significantly higher instances of some types of rule-breaking despite the actual numbers recorded for that particular kind of wrongdoing. In Rio de Janeiro, females were eliminated out of proportion to their numbers in the state population for being a: 1) family member of a target, and 2) female with male, while male victims were murdered in vivid numbers for: 1) homicide of police personnel, 2) narcotics violation, and 3) rape. In São Paulo, males were the only gender shown to have committed a significantly higher proportionate number of offenses over those committed by their opposites in Rio de Janeiro. Notwithstanding their larger state population, these charges included: 1) ex-juvenile inmate, 2) resisting arrest, 3) robbery, and 4) theft. There were, as well, several additional offenses where a less than dramatic but still significant over representation existed for Rio de Janeiro's male victims. Perhaps escape from detention, but certainly being the family member of a target, accused of homicide, or transvestitism fell into this category.

Looked at only by racial background and gender, when known, and no longer by state, the above charges totaling one hundred both in the columns and rows, exhibited the following characteristics:

Rio de Janeiro

	Black		*Mulatto*		*White*		
	Female	Male	Female	Male	Female	Male	*Total*
Armed robbery		2		6		3	*11*
Assault and robbery	6	242	3	237	3	136	*627*
Escape from detention		5		4		1	*10*
Ex-juvenile inmate							
Ex-prisoner		9		8		5	*22*
Family member of a target[a]	12	28	13	15	12	10	*90*
Female with male[a]	44	-	78	-	54	-	*176*
Homicide		48		30		23	*101*
Homicide of police personnel		7	1	7		4	*19*
Narcotics violation	3	215	21	196	3	110	*548*
Rape		34	1	22		11	*68*
Resisting arrest							
Robbery	2	12		10		7	*31*
Theft		17	2	14	1	6	*40*
Transvestitism		3		8		15	*26*
Vehicular theft		32	2	35	2	46	*117*
Total	*67*	*654*	*121*	*592*	*75*	*377*	**1886**

a = elimination of witness category

In Rio de Janeiro, black and mulatto males, usually in that order, made up the bulk of those reported to have committed every offense except being a transvestite. In São Paulo, the same can be said of mulatto males, who led in all but four categories: escape from detention, homicide of police personnel, resisting arrest, and transvestitism.

São Paulo

	Asian		*Black*		*Mulatto*		*White*	
	Male	Female	Male	Female	Male	Female	Male	*Total*
Armed robbery			4		10		6	*20*
Assault and robbery	2		170	9	265	2	175	*623*
Escape from detention			1		2		4	*7*
Ex-juvenile inmate			5		17		1	*23*
Ex-prisoner	1		17	1	32		8	*59*
Family member of a target[a]		1	11	12	24	8	9	*65*
Female with male[a]		16	-	40	-	31	-	*87*
Homicide			20		33		18	*71*
Homicide of police personnel					3		5	*8*
Narcotics violation	2	5	78	27	134	15	78	*339*
Rape			9		14		6	*29*
Resisting arrest			9		9		10	*28*
Robbery		2	40	1	56		331	*133*
Theft	1		33	1	55		25	*115*
Transvestitism			7		6		11	*24*
Vehicular theft	3		38		69	1	56	*167*
Total	*10*	*24*	*442*	*91*	*729*	*57*	*445*	**1798**

a = elimination of witness category

When these victims were considered by their social class, the strata in Rio de Janeiro and São Paulo from which those murdered without benefit of a judge, without benefit of a trial, and without the benefit of a judicial sentence becomes all too recognizable. Assault and robbery plus narcotics offenses, led the list of charges with a whopping 65.8 percent of the cases. Take note that in Rio, the largest category was not assault and robbery but narcotics violations by persons in the lower class. In the state of São Paulo, however, the most common charge was assault and robbery by members of this same under priviledged societal layer. Please continue to observe that these data cannot be directly compared owing to the difference in total state populations.

Rio de Janeiro	Upper	Middle	Lower	*Total*
Armed robbery		3	23	*26*
Assault and robbery	1	15	1001	*1017*
Escape from detention		2	36	*38*
Ex-juvenile inmate			9	*9*
Ex-prisoner		1	92	*93*
Family member of a target[a]		14	242	*256*
Female with male[a]		14	229	*243*
Homicide		5	173	*178*
Homicide of police personnel		3	61	*64*
Narcotics violation	4	31	1675	*1710*
Rape		1	100	*101*
Resisting arrest			3	*3*
Robbery		2	86	*88*
Theft		1	89	*90*
Transvestitism		1	33	*34*
Vehicular theft		17	175	*192*
Total	*5*	*110*	*4027*	**4142**
			97.2%	

São Paulo	Upper	Middle	Lower	*Total*
Armed robbery			35	*35*
Assault and robbery	2	6	1073	*1081*
Escape from detention			49	*49*
Ex-juvenile inmate			90	*90*
Ex-prisoner		1	164	*165*
Family member of a target[a]		2	251	*253*
Female with male[a]		1	182	*183*
Homicide	1	3	171	*175*
Homicide of police personnel			22	*22*
Narcotics violation	2	11	922	*935*
Rape		1	63	*64*
Resisting arrest			66	*66*
Robbery		3	360	*363*
Theft		3	335	*338*
Transvestitism	1	1	52	*54*
Vehicular theft		6	176	*182*
Total	*6*	*38*	*4011*	**4055**
			98.9%	

a = elimination of witness category

GEOGRAPHIC CONCERNS

Turning the analysis to those administrative sub-divisions of the state of Rio de Janeiro and to those accusations of criminal activity with at least one hundred charges in both columns and rows, it is evident that the majority of alleged offenses were confined to specific regions. The breakdown of these events is given first by regional residence of the victim and then by the region in which the individual's body was found (see map) when reported in the consulted news sources. This material is not presented in alphabetical order, but by the most number of accusations between regions and offenses.

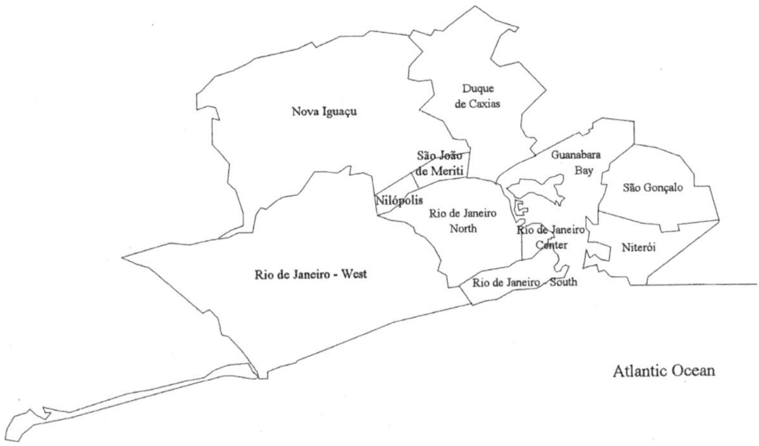

Rio de Janeiro—Ranked Residence of Victims by Offenses with More than 100 Events in Both Columns and Rows

	Narcotics violation	Assault and robbery	Family member of a target[a]	Female with male[a]	Homicide	*Total*
Rio de Janeiro – North Zone	625	134	56	40	28	*883*
Nova Iguaçu	154	178	49	45	29	*455*
Rio de Janeiro – West Zone	222	89	54	37	19	*421*
Duque de Caxias	118	82	30	22	11	*263*
São Gonçalo	52	53	17	13	7	*142*
Niterói	70	34		9	9	*122*
Rio de Janeiro – South Zone	82	22	4	7	5	*120*
Total	*1323*	*592*	*210*	*173*	*108*	**2406**

a = elimination of witness category

Rio de Janeiro—Ranked Location of Corpse by Offenses with More than 100 Events in Both Columns and Rows

	Narcotics violation	Assault and robbery	Female with male[a]	Vehicular theft	Family member of a target[a]	Homicide	Rape	*Total*
Rio de Janeiro–North Zone	802	437	99	173	62	55	32	*1660*
Nova Iguaçu	246	306	83	33	65	64	37	*834*
Rio de Janeiro–West Zone	282	212	67	49	54	33	16	*713*
Duque de Caxias	178	167	42	19	32	15	15	*468*
São Gonçalo	92	89	29	13	14	12	11	*260*
Rio de Janeiro–South Zone	110	62	1	13	3	9		*198*
Niterói	85	50	18	10	8	14	1	*186*
São João de Meriti	53	53	18	20	13	11	7	*175*
Rio de Janeiro–Center	81	40	3	14	1	3	2	*144*
Total	*1929*	*1416*	*360*	*344*	*252*	*216*	*121*	**4638**

a = elimination of witness category

We cannot construct a ranked presentation for the state of São Paulo in respect to residence of the victims because only Santo Amaro qualified with both rows and columns adding up to one hundred or more—and then only for 111 presumed narcotic violations. The reason for this centered around the fact that even though concentrated in Santo Amaro, victims' residences could be found all over the city of São Paulo and throughout the state. Such was not the case in Rio de Janeiro. In the latter capital and state of the same name, it would appear that victims originated by and large in a limited number of residential districts surrounding the metropolitan part of Rio de Janeiro. On the other hand, the discarded bodies of the São Paulo victims were discovered in a nearly closed circle of outlying suburbs around Sé, the center of the city. This description too, is arranged by districts and alleged crimes with the most number of allegations as to

São Paulo—Ranked Location of Corpse by Offenses with More than 100 Events in Both Columns and Rows

	Assault and robbery	Narcotics violation	Vehicular theft	Robbery	Theft	Female with male[a]	Family member of a target[a]	Homicide	Ex-prisoner	*Total*
Santo Amaro	310	165	86	68	60	40	28	29	30	*816*
Guarulhos	146	51	53	36	34	26	19	19	8	*392*
Osasco	144	32	20	19	25	8	13	9	16	*286*
Capela do Socorro	82	67	25	17	12	21	19	16	12	*271*
Guaianazes	65	47	17	25	19	10	3	7	7	*200*
São Bernardo do Campo	80	30	30	5	17	7	12	11	2	*194*
São Mateus	62	49	22	15	7	10	11	7	6	*189*
São Miguel Paulista	64	30	24	15	18	3	6	6	5	*171*
Diademia	57	25	24	17	16	6	10	12	2	*169*
Butantã	51	33	31	16	6	2	7	2	2	*150*
Brasilândia	55	27	18	6	16	5	5	7	4	*143*
Itaquera	64	13	17	10	6	2	3	4	5	*124*
Itaim Paulista	44	24	13	13	2	6	9	5	5	*121*
Jabaquara	54	20	14	7	9	8		4	4	*120*
Sapopemba	37	14	30	7	13	2	4	3	6	*116*
Tucuruvi	35	22	19	9	11	3	3	8	2	*112*
Santo André	49	26	13	7	3	4	4	2	1	*109*
Total	*1399*	*675*	*456*	*292*	*274*	*163*	*156*	*151*	*117*	**3683**

a = elimination of witness category

where the body of each victim was discovered. The *barrio* or suburb plan for the city of São Paulo from 1990 was used in locating subdivisions. Observe that Santo Amaro had more than twice as many bodies found within its boundaries as Guarulhos, the second-place district. In addition, numerous victims were uncovered in nearby Capela do Socorro, particularly in the areas bordering around Santo Amaro. Others came to light in Jabaquara and Diadema, again near the region of Santo Amaro. Each of these are working-class areas filled with an overabundance of slums, underemployment, and misery.

Looking now at the variables of gender, race, residence of the victims, and where their bodies were discovered in Rio de Janeiro, this discussion will examine only those vicinities with at least one hundred total reports. On page 291, in alphabetical order, the figures *not* in parenthesis represent those victims who actually resided in the area; the numbers in parenthesis are the numbers of suspected death-squad assassinations in the locale.

A simple rank ordering of the neighborhoods would begin with the North Zone of Rio de Janeiro followed by Nova Iguaçu, the Western Zone of Rio, Duque de Caxias, São João de Meriti, the Southern Zone of Rio, Niterói, the Central Zone of Rio, and São Gonçalo. But, if we lump Nova Iguaçu, Duque de Caxias, and São João de Meriti into the area normally called the Baixada Fluminense, it surpassed the North Zone as the region with both the largest number of victim residents and the most numbers of killings, when race and gender could be determined. The summated figures for residence were Baixada 463 versus 451 for the North Zone, and 1,974 vs. 1,885 for location of the corpse.

GROUPS RESPONSIBLE

Following twenty-two years of research on a near half-century of cases, eighty-four death squads were uncovered in the states of Rio de Janeiro and São Paulo. Keep in mind that several groups operated in conjunction with another collection of individuals. For ease of reference, the names of these purveyors of death are translated where appropriate, even if they have been translated earlier, and presented below starting on page 292.

	Black		*Mulatto*		*White*		
	Female	Male	Female	Male	Female	Male	*Total*
Duque de Caxias	1 (9)	41 (218)	12 (22)	53 (205)	6 (20)	22 (129)	*135 (603)*
Niterói	2 (5)	23 (79)	1 (4)	15 (68)	1 (4)	9 (40)	*51 (200)*
Nova Iguaçu	8 (17)	93 (415)	12 (30)	94 (400)	10 (23)	54 (252)	*271 (1137)*
Rio de Janeiro–Center	1 (4)	19 (54)	- (2)	15 (48)	- (1)	6 (31)	*41 (140)*
Rio de Janeiro–North Zone	8 (22)	178 (715)	22 (41)	157 (580)	6 (27)	80 (500)	*451 (1885)*
Rio de Janeiro–South Zone	- (1)	21 (59)	4 (4)	19 (53)	-	12 (40)	*56 (157)*
Rio de Janeiro–West Zone	9 (16)	89 (340)	7 (23)	63 (282)	4 (15)	30 (240)	*202 (916)*
São João de Meriti	5 (9)	20 (80)	6 (6)	19 (72)	1 (3)	6 (64)	*57 (234)*
São Gonçalo	-	- (76)	2 (5)	23 (121)	- (5)	14 (83)	*39 (290)*
Total	*34* (83)	*484 (2036)*	*66 (137)*	*458 (1829)*	*28 (98)*	*233 (1379)*	**1303 (5562)**

1. Alma ("Soul")
2. Amigos dos Amigos ("Friends of Friends")
3. Army
4. Bando/Gangue da Caveira ("Gang of the Skull") (probably the Esquadrão da Morte)
5. Bando Maldito ("Evil Gang")
6. Batalhão de Extermenío ("Extermination Battalion")
7. Bate-Bola ("Kick Ball")
8. Caçadores de Banditos ("Bandit Hunters")
9. Carrascos da Sivuca ("Sivuca's Hangmen")
10. Cavalos Corredores ("Race Horses")
11. Cocota ("Pussy" [pejorative])
12. Comando Policiamento Metropolitano ("Metropolitan Police Commandos")
13. DAS + DRE (probably DRE of the Polícia Civil)
14. DESIPE
15. Doze Homens de Ouro ("Twelve Golden Men")
16. Elo ("Link")
17. Esquadrão da Morte ("The Squadron of Death")
18. Flôr ("Flower")
19. Gangue da Baleia ("Gang of the Whale")
20. Gangue dos Paraibas ("Paraibans' Gang")
21. Group of guns for hire including at least one Polícia Militar
22. Grupo do Oito (police—unit unknown)
23. Guarda Civil (Civil Guards)
24. Guarda Ferroviário (Railroad Police)
25. Guarda Municipal (Municipal Police)
26. Guarda Rodoviário (Highway Police)
27. *justiciero(s)* (citizen vigilante[s])
28. Manto Azul ("Blue Cloak")
29. Mão Branca ("White Hand")
30. Mascara Negra ("Black Mask")
31. Narcotics Police (unit unknown)
32. O Moita ("Thicket")
33. Onze de Ouro ("Eleven [Men] of Gold")
34. Polícia Civil (Detective Bureau)
35. Polícia Civil: DAS

36. Polícia Civil: DEGRAN
37. Polícia Civil: DEIC
38. Polícia Civil: DEPATRI
39. Polícia Civil: DISE
40. Polícia Civil: DRE
41. Polícia Civil: DRE + Polícia Militar: P2 + Polícia Militar
42. Polícia Civil: DRF
43. Polícia Civil: GARRA
44. Polícia Civil: GARRA + Polícia Civil
45. Polícia Civil: GOE
46. Polícia Civil + Polícia Militar
47. Polícia Civil + POLÍNTER
48. Polícia (police: unit unknown)
49. Polícia Federal (Federal Police)
50. Polícia Federal + Polícia Militar: CIOE
51. Policiais da Secretaria de Segurança Pública (Secretary of Public Security Police)
52. Polícia Marítima (Maritime Police)
53. Polícia Militar: Apolo-44
54. Polícia Militar + Army
55. Polícia Militar: BOP
56. Polícia Militar: Cavalaria Eny Cony dos Santos (Eny Cony dos Santos Cavalry)
57. Polícia Militar + civilian(s)
58. Polícia Militar: COBRA
59. Polícia Militar: Comando Leopardo (Leopard Command)
60. Polícia Militar: Comando Tigre (Tiger Command)
61. Polícia Militar: DPO
62. Polícia Militar: DRE
63. Polícia Militar: DRRFCGF
64. Polícia Militar/Força Pública (uniformed Police)
65. Polícia Militar + GARRA
66. Polícia Militar: GATE
67. Polícia Militar: P2
68. Polícia Militar + private citizen(s) + private guard(s)
69. Polícia Militar: ROCAM
70. Polícia Militar: Ronda Setorial (Neighborhood Patrol)

71. Polícia Militar: ROTA
72. Polícia Militar: RP Mont
73. Polícia Militar: Tático Comando (Commando Group)
74. Polícia Militar: Tático Móvel (Mobile Group)
75. Polícia Militar: Tático Móvel + ROTA
76. Polícia Militar: Tático Sul (Southern Group)
77. Polícia Mineira (generic for "Death Squad")
78. POLÍNTER: DRE
79. Private guard(s)
80. Robbery Police (unit unknown)
81. Rosa Vermelha ("Red Rose")
82. Sigla-8 ("Monogram 8")
83. Sombra ("Shadow")
84. X-9 (police informant)

The acronyms stand for:

BOP = Batalhão de Operações Especiais (Special Operations Batalion)

CIOE = Compania Independente de Operações Especiais (Independent Special Operations Company)

COBRA = Comando de Busca Resgate e Assalto (Search and Rescue Attack Command)

DAS = Divisão Anti-Seqüestro (Anti-Kidnapping Division)

DEGRAN = Departamento das Delegacias Regionais de Polícia da Grande São Paulo (Department of Regional Police Stations of Larger São Paulo)

DEIC = Departamento de Investigações Criminais (Department of Investigations)

DEPATRI = Departamento de Investigações sobre Crimes Patrimoniais (Department of Property Crime Investigations)

DESIPE = Departamento de Supervisão Integrada de Penitenciarias (Department of Combined Penitentiary Control)

DISE = Divisão de Investigações sobre Entorpecentes (Investigation of Narcotics Division)

DPO = Destacamento de Polícia Ostensivo (Ostensive Police Detachment)

DRE = Divisão de Repressão a Entorpecentes (Repression of Narcotics Division)
DRF = Divisão de Roubos e Furtos (Robbery and Theft Division)
DRRFCGF = Delegacia de Repressão a Roubos e Furtos contra Estabelecimentos Financeiros (Financial Institution Robbery and Theft Division)
GARRA = Grupo Armado de Repressão a Roubos e Assaltos (Armed Repression of Assault and Robbery Group)
GATE = Grupo de Ações e Taticas Especiais (Action and Special Tactics Group)
GOE = Grupo de Operações Especiais (Special Operations Group)
P2 = Serviço Interna (Internal Police Security Service)
POLÍNTER = Serviço de Polícia Interestadual (Inter-State Police Service)
ROCAM = Rondas Ostensivas Com Apoio de Motocicletas (Motorcycle Supported Proactive Patrol)
ROTA = Rondas Ostensivas Tobias de Aguiar (Tobias de Aguiar Proactive Patrol)
RP Mont = Regimento de Polícia Montada (Regiment of Mounted Police)

The majority of killings by these entities were largely the activity of two factions—and *not* the Esquadrão da Morte. By the end of the project, the long-infamous death squad was operating without the tell-tale warning symbols left near its victims. To be sure, there had been a changing of the guard. Ostentatious displays of disdain and impunity became more and more infrequent as the research continued. In part, this came about because of the bad press such behavior produced abroad. The name of the Esquadrão was still invoked from time to time, but by the mid-1980s the more polite reference to subelite vigilantes became "grupos de exterminio," or extermination groups. It may, however, prove useful to those interested in the history of the Esquadrão da Morte to present the total number of summary executions attributable to them and their various alias groups in *O Dia* and *Notícias Populares*. Bando Maldito appeared in 1969 and operated only in São Paulo. Carrascos da Sivuca murdered one person in 1984.

	Rio de Janeiro	*São Paulo*	*Total*
Esquadrão da Morte	179	85	*264*
Bando Maldito		6	*6*
Carrascos da Sivuca	1		*1*
Doze Homens de Ouro	2		*2*
Gangue da Baleia	3		*3*
Gangue da Caveira	33	2	*35*
Onze de Ouro	2		*2*
Total	*220*	*93*	**313**

An elaboration of the major extermination groups in Brazil's two most important states in more recent years is a different story. Hélio Bicudo remarked that the death squads usually have a connection to the police.[140] Of the eighty-four execution groups uncovered in this project, seventy, or 83.3 percent, had a clear relationship with law enforcement. But this link was obviously higher as some groups (private guards, citizens, and even members of the armed forces) used a name to disguise their identity.

Even so, looking at vigilante-type killings by the open and sometimes combined police units with the greatest number of executions in the states of Rio de Janeiro and São Paulo, one cannot ignore the presence of the Polícia Militar/Força Pública or the Polícia Civil. The former group wins the prize hands down for the most death-squad type executions in both states, although the Polícia Civil in Rio de Janeiro seemed to be overly involved with the dealing out of lethal punishment.

	Rio de Janeiro	*São Paulo*	*Total*
Polícia Civil	220	86	*306*
Polícia Militar/Força Pública	1708	3535	*5243*
Total	*1928*	*3621*	**5549**

One should not forget that the state of São Paulo has had a much larger population than the state of Rio de Janeiro for many decades. In the next table, this fact would tend to mitigate the apparent excess of instances where the Força Pública opened fire on suspects in the state of São Paulo more so than in Rio de Janeiro. It would not explain, conversely, why the Rio de Janeiro Polícia Civil seemed to be much more trigger happy than their detective colleagues in São Paulo.

	Rio de Janeiro	*São Paulo*	*Total*
Polícia Civil	93	33	*126*
Polícia Militar/Força Pública	1001	2179	*3180*
Total	*1094*	*2212*	**3306**

The picture of police involvement takes on another dimension if we spread out the cases by their years of occurrence in the study. No instances of direct involvement by these four police agencies was recorded before 1960. But figure 6.5 demonstrates a dramatic increase after 1982 in the number of Brazilians murdered by the very police sworn to protect them. Why was this? What took place in that year involved the military government's relaxation of press censorship relating to police issues. The arbitrariness of subelites had to be covered up once journalists began reporting more aspects of suspected extermination group killings. What better way to do this than by stating that the victims shot at their police pursuers?[141] Both Rio and São Paulo recorded dramatic increases in cases where firearms suddenly appeared in the hands of the accused beginning in 1982.

If we plot the killings of all four police groups over the years of this study, it becomes apparent in figure 6.5 that the São Paulo Força Pública

FIGURE 6.5

Suspected Victims by Most Active Death Squads in the States of Rio de Janeiro and São Paulo

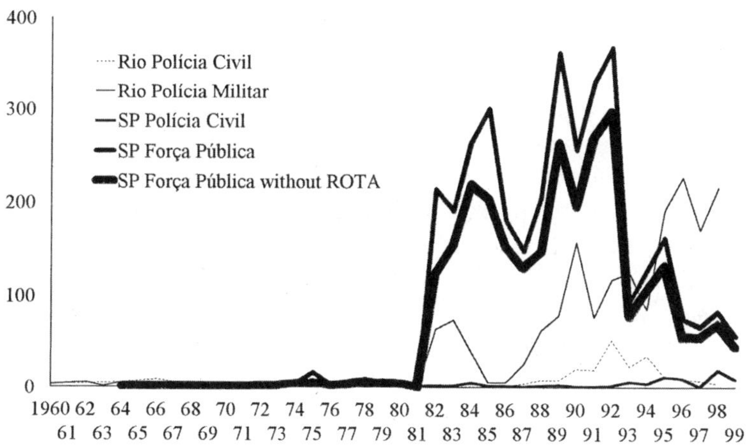

did not execute an inordinate number of citizens compared to the Polícia Militar in Rio de Janeiro except in the years 1984, 85, 86, and 1991. Yet the Polícia Militar material for Rio de Janeiro does display one dramatic event: since 1993, it has been increasing far beyond what one should expect from the state with a smaller population. The reason for this jump is not known. But, it does indicate that since 1993, Rio de Janeiro has been a state with proportionally many more death squad-type slayings by members of the uniformed police than in São Paulo. The activities of the Força Pública, on the other hand, took on a new dimension in 1969,[142] with the formation of the Rondas Ostensivas Tobias de Aguiar.

Known as ROTA by one and all, the Tobias de Aguiar Proactive Patrol is an arm of offensive paulistano police who literally shoot first and ask questions later. This research uncovered 802 ROTA killings within greater São Paulo between 1975 and 1999 (or 33.4 a year). The indefatigable Hélio Bicudo has a pertinent opinion here too. He called ROTA "a new version of the Esquadrão da Morte."[143] The comparison is not far from the truth. Watching their gray vehicles cruise the streets, many persons cannot help but feel nervous. They would have to be recent migrants to the city not to have heard the stories about them. Perhaps it is only to be expected that ROTA has as its operational territory the largest, richest, and one of the poorest metropolitan areas in South America. It could be argued that their primary unwritten role is to maintain an urban lid on things. When they stop at someone's door, it is not to take the suspect back to the police station. A vehicle from the morgue later arrives to do the necessary transportation. With neighbors and the curious gawking at the proceedings, the point has already been made, "this could be you!" Indeed, one creditable source stated that ROTA units regularly competed among themselves to kill the highest number of victims. Even ROTA's superiors get into the fray by arguing against those police opposed to extermination group tactics and operations.[144]

As for the race card, it showed that fluminense and carioca Polícia Militar, but not the Polícia Civil, went after nonwhite victims slightly more often. This was not the case in São Paulo. There, the Força Pública seemed to prefer individuals classified as mulatto. The indigenous victim was not included in this analysis.

	Asian	Black	Mulatto	White	*Total*
Rio de Janeiro					
Polícia Civil		26	28	14	*68*
Polícia Militar		191	178	103	*472*
Total		*217*	*206*	*117*	**540**
São Paulo					
Polícia Civil			2	13	*15*
Força Pública	5	229	350	246	*830*
Total	*5*	*229*	*352*	*259*	**845**

In respect to social class, the ensuing table sadly underlines what has been previously demonstrated. Police extermination teams were going after the poor.

	Upper	Middle	Lower	*Total*
Rio de Janeiro				
Polícia Civil	1	5	156	*162*
Polícia Militar	1	27	1348	*1376*
Total	*2*	*32*	*1504*	**1538**
			97.8%	
São Paulo				
Polícia Civil		3	56	*59*
Força Pública	5	27	1194	*1226*
Total	*5*	*30*	*1250*	**1285**
			97.3%	

EXECUTION DAY

The second-to-last item to be determined is the day of execution. Was there a specific day in the week when the extermination groups in the two states were more active? The answer is yes there was. In figure 6.6, it can be seen that the hit teams in both states had a slight preference for Sundays for dispatching their victims. Seemingly, this was because the intended target was often at home on this day of rest. Little did he or she know that they would be resting forever.

FIGURE 6.6
Death-Squad Killings by Day of the Week

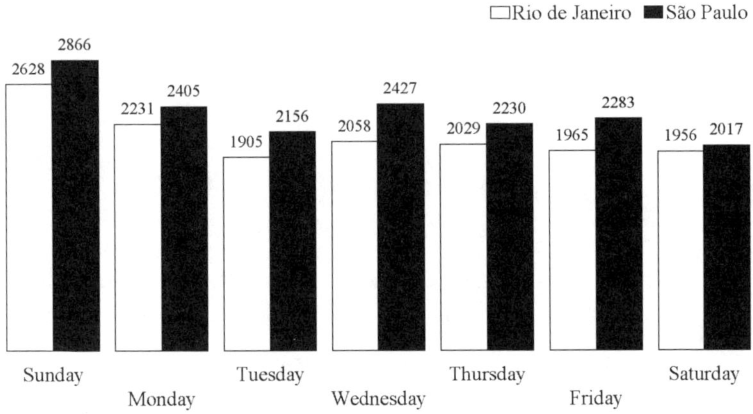

Finally, we come to the question commonly put in the form of a statement: Rio de Janeiro is the most violent place on earth. If it is, or if it is not, the veracity of such a position cannot be answered here. What can be shown, albeit inexactly by this research is only whether suspected death squads were more active in the state of Rio or in the state of São Paulo. Keep in mind that there were and are many other types of homicide and many other types of violent crimes committed by individuals and groups besides those realized through tacitly approved death squads. There may well be, in addition, more violent cities that lack dependable statistics. With these limitations considered, the ensuing percentages are estimated death-squad murders per hundred thousand members of the population in ten-year intervals in the two states in question. These statistics are computed with 1951 and 1998 as the starting and ending points for Rio and 1963 and 1999 for São Paulo.

The figures speak for themselves. If we ignore the interval for 1951–59, when the two states were not comparable, one's chances of becoming the victim of an extermination group—during the last thirty-six years of the twentieth century—were nearly three times as high in the state of Rio de Janeiro as they were in São Paulo.

	1951–59	*1960–69*	*1970–79*	*1980–89*	*1990–99*
Rio de Janeiro	.47	3.34	5.47	50.42	58.72
São Paulo	n.a.	.80	.92	21.74	33.77

This chapter lends support to that body of evidence pointing out the kind of urban individual usually falling prey to police bullets in extralegal circumstances. Victims are typically male, in their early twenties, and poor. They are nearly always working class and often nonwhite. Contemporary death squads in Brazil are usually some variation of the Polícia Militar who eliminate suspects for essentially property crimes. Yes, even assault and can have a monetary connection—if you are in dire need of money. If Rio de Janeiro and São Paulo are indicative of the rest of the nation, then the data presented here and in chapter 5 suggest that the victims of elite violence in Brazil are the same both in the countryside and in the larger communities. Their social class is by far the most uniting variable—as it is for so many things in this ongoing Brazilian dilemma.[145]

Epilogue

In 1991, no less a personage than Paulo Sérgio Pinheiro remarked that with the return of democracy the number of death-squad-type slayings would eventually subside.[1] The data just examined suggest that there was a degree of plausibility to his prediction. On December 3, 2000, however, Paulo Sérgio, who was secretary for human rights during the Cardoso presidency (1995–2003), admitted that "in democratic countries, where the population is not in insurrection, there are no other police that kill as much as the ones in Rio and São Paulo."[2] The point is that democracy returned to Brazil in 1985, and be it urban or rural, the figures are going up again. At the end of 2002 *Jornal do Brasil* recounted that the police in Rio had slain 834 individuals that year. On February 1, 2004, *O Globo* informed its readers that the Polícia Militar in São Paulo had killed 868 persons in 2003, which was an increase of 60 percent over 2002. Likewise, in April 2004 it was revealed that the number of rural workers murdered rose 69.8 percent in 2003 over the previous year, or from 43 to 73 killings. More Native Brazilians too were assassinated—23 in 2003 against just 7 in 2002.

As for slavery, accompanying commentary by Paulo Sérgio's successor, Nilmário Miranda, promised that sometime before 2006 forced labor would be eradicated. But not two months later it was stated that three inspectors and their driver from the ministry of labor in Brasília were machine-gunned to death in Minas Gerais while investigating possible cases of slavery. The primary suspects were assassins hired by fazendeiros.[3]

All of this love of democracy and wishful thinking by government ministers puts the objective before the means to achieve it. To return to Richard Quinney, he would point out that the only real solution is to first deal with the wounds that have been bleeding for centuries. Brazilians must look within themselves to do this.[4] Otherwise, they will have a democracy representing only the aspirations of the few.

Many of the same moral values that drove the dictators, indeed, that have almost always driven Brazil's wealthy, remain entrenched in Brazil's class-based cultural heritage. Instead of spending money on decent living conditions, adequately paid jobs, and university educations for the poor—allowing all to walk in dignity—these interests will see to it that the poor continue to be corralled and controlled by funds spent on new, more efficient weapons, shiny new police cars, and more police to ride roughshod over the poor. An episode in the Rocinha favela might serve to underline this. It begins with the realization that there are a very limited number of ways the working class can make enough money to afford the good-life items presented in the media as legitimate goals for all in the panorama of Brazilian capitalism. Thus, in a Mertonian-like way, poorer urban Brazilians frequently become *innovators* by grasping at such goals through involvement with illegal activities, even if only in a *de jure* sense.[5] For women, this repeatedly means prostitution. For men, it can mean becoming a holdup artist or selling narcotics.

In 2004, drug traffickers from the Vidigal favela tried to take over the narcotics operations in nearby Rocinha. Rocinha is the largest shantytown in the Americas. It stretches over a massive area on two sides of a huge hill in Rio's South Zone. Many of the residents of both Vidigal and Rocinha are the maids, day laborers, and others who work for rich South Zone employers. A turf war developed, producing intermittent bursts of automatic arms fire over several nights in April. Grenades, ammunition, rocket launchers, and even mines were captured by the authorities and put on display in pointed admittance of the firepower of the warring shantytown residents. These weapons were regularly supplied to favela gangs by black-market negotiations with the police and military—a common phenomenon for years in Brazil.

Several killings took place in or near Rocinha. A tunnel and a road had to be closed by the police. The press was ablaze with reports of a well-to-do couple trying to escape in their car from gang members wearing fake police clothing. The female driver of the car was shot dead. The story went on for days. Little coverage, however, was given to the povão who had been slain either by the gangs or the police called in to quell the situation. Instead, the editorial pages were replete with ways to restore the middle/upper-class sense of order while ignoring the knowledge that as soon as the authorities left, the situation would default to its former level. There were urgings to have the police install a more permanent and visible presence in Rocinha. The governor and others called for the army to be brought in to eradicate anyone connected with narcotics. There was even a serious suggestion to wall in the roughly fifty-six thousand inhabitants of Rocinha plus the inhabitants of Vidigal and two other nearby favelas. The proposed barrier was to be three meters high, or a little over 9'10".[6] With police guarding the entrances, this would have produced South America's first Warsaw Ghetto—lacking only an accompanying ruling to force favela residents to wear a some type of identifying symbol prominently displayed on their clothing.

In the centers of power in Rio de Janeiro, the cheapest alternative was the one finally adopted. Elite units from the police were repeatedly dispatched into the slums to overwhelm those opposed to lopsided ethics. After shooting one drug kingpin, they chased around in the hills for weeks, looking for his replacement. In the accompanying clamor, two items were ignored: whom were these gendarmes really protecting, and what were these gendarmes really protecting? Several of those taken in for questioning from the invading Vidigal favela were later murdered while in custody. There was talk that is was done in revenge.[7]

The Past Is Never Dead . . .

Certainly the ultimate question concerns the future of this country where violence by representatives of the elite has become virtually pornographic in size and scope. What will be the fate of a people so inundated for so long with the view that the poor are somehow intrinsically inferior to the rich? Can anyone succeed in giving the povão a lasting sense of worth? If the country's history gives us the answers, they certainly are bleak ones. Vargas started meekly on this crossing, and Jango inspired him and tried to augment their victories. Neither man succeeded. Anyone who takes up this mantle must know that the battle is against a millennium. The entrenched oligarchies are the real villains. For truly the privileged in Brazil have crafted an environment that echoes their own—one where conniving is king, where deceit is an art form, and where people have believed for too long that such things are normal. Brazil has been called the most unequal nation on the planet by the coordinator of the United Nations' activities there.[8] Approximately one third of the population lives in conditions described as miserable.[9] What that means in more accurate terms is that one third of all Brazilians live in slums like Rocinha, subject to ersatz justice and the threat of annihilation. Charles Darwin observed a similar situation while visiting Brazil in 1832.

> I may mention one very trifling anecdote, which at the time struck me more forcibly than any story of cruelty. I was crossing a ferry with a Negro, who was uncommonly stupid. In endeavouring to make him understand, I talked loud, and made signs, in doing which I passed my hand near his face. He, I suppose, thought I was in a passion, and was going to strike him; for instantly, with a frightened look and half-shut eyes, he dropped his hands. I shall never forget my feelings of surprise, disgust, and shame, at seeing a great powerful man afraid even to ward off a blow, directed, as he thought, at his face. This man had been trained to a degradation lower than the slavery of the most helpless animal.[10]

Notes

Introduction

1. R. S. Rose, *Beyond the Pale of Pity: Key Episodes of Elite Violence in Brazil to 1930* (Bethesda: Austin and Winfield, 1998), 7–19.

2. Ibid., 2–3.

3. This portion of the military is an addition to the original definition presented in ibid., 3.

4. Richard Quinney, *Class, State and Crime: On the Theory and Practice of Criminal Justice* (New York: David McKay, 1977), 116.

5. Lobo, Antonio de Sousa Silva Costa, *Historia da sociedade em Portugal no seculo xv* (Lisbon: Nacional, 1903), 235.

6. *Newsweek* (New York), December 8, 1997, 62.

7. Rose, 3.

8. Robert Conrad, *Children of God's Fire: A Documentary History of Black Slavery in Brazil* (Princeton: Princeton University Press, 1983), 129–32, 176–78.

9. Charles Boxer, *The Golden Age of Brazil, 1695–1750: Growing Pains of a Colonial Society* (Berkeley: University of California Press, 1962), 2.

10. Rose, 26–27.

11. Mary Karasch, "Slave Life in Rio de Janeiro, 1808–1850," Ph.D. diss., Department of History, University of Wisconsin, 1972, 154; and Thomas Ewbank, *Life in Brazil: Or a Visit to the Land of the Cocoa and the Palm* (New York: Harper, 1856), 438.

12. Boxer: 8; and *Race Relations in the Portuguese Colonial Empire, 1415–1825* (Oxford: Clarendon, 1963), 112.

13. Boxer, *The Golden Age of Brazil, loc. cit.;* Jorge Benci, *Economia Cristã dos senhores no governo de escravos: livro brasileiro de 1700,* 2nd ed., Serafim Leite (ed.) (Porto: Apostolado, 1954), 139; and Ewbank, 439.

14. *Revista Illustrada* (Rio de Janeiro), February 18, 1886, 5; Carl Schlichthorst, *O Rio de Janeiro como é, 1824–1826: huma vez e nunca mais* (Rio de Janeiro: Getulio Costa, 1943), 134; Luiz Edmundo, *O Rio de Janeiro no tempo dos vice-reis,* 4th ed. (Rio de Janeiro: Conquista, 1956), vol. I, 71; Karasch, 384–85; Ewbank, 281, 440–41; Daniel Kidder and James Fletcher, *Brazil and the Brazilians: Portrayed in Historical and Descriptive Sketches*

(Philadelphia: Childs and Peterson, 1857), 132; Robert Walsh, *Notices of Brazil in 1828 and 1829* (London: Westly and Davis, 1830), vol. II, 359; and *Jornal do Brasil* (Rio de Janeiro), May 30, 1988, sec. 1, 11.

15. The term originated in 1831 when the English were tricked into believing that a statute signed by the Marquês de Barbacena, a member of the Brazilian nobility, would free all slaves entering the country. The marquis' efforts created Brazil's first *africanos livres,* or freed Africans, for a while. It was not long, however, before these released people were re-absorbed back into the general slave population due to the need for captive workers.

16. R. S. Rose, "Slavery in Brazil: Does it Still Exist?" *Review of Latin American Studies,* vol. IV, no. 1, 1991, 97–98, 101–7; *Folha de São Paulo,* May 7, 2000, Mais!, 16–17; and *Jornal do Brasil,* May 13, 2000, Idéias especial, 4.

17. Marcos Arruda, *et al., The Multinational Corporations and Brazil: The Impact of Multinational Corporations in the Contemporary Brazilian Economy* (Toronto: Latin American Research Unit, 1975), 1; June Hahner, *Poverty and Politics: the Urban Poor in Brazil, 1870–1920* (Albuquerque: University of New Mexico Press, 1986), 45–46; and Thomas Skidmore, *Black into White: Race and Nationality in Brazilian Thought* (New York: Oxford University Press, 1974), 125.

18. Michael Hall and Paulo Sérgio Pinheiro, "The Control and Policing of the Working Class in Brazil," paper presented to the Conference on the History of Law, Labor and Crime, University of Warwick, September 15–18, 1983, 4; and Dalmo de Abreu Dallari, "The *Força Pública* of São Paulo in State and National Politics," *Perspectives on Armed Politics in Brazil,* Henry Keith and Robert Hayes (eds.) (Tempe: Arizona State University Press, 1976), 86.

19. Hall and Pinheiro, 5.

20. Paulo Sérgio Pinheiro, "The Legacy of Authoritarianism: Violence and the Limits of Democratic Transitions," paper presented to the 16th Conference of the Latin American Studies Association, Washington, DC, April 4–6, 1991, 4–6; and Richard Quinney, *Critique of Legal Order: Crime Control in Capitalist Society* (New York: Little, Brown, 1974), 24, 47–50, 139, 149–55.

21. Karl Marx and Frederick Engels, *Manifesto of the Communist Party: A Modern Edition* (London and New York: Verso, 1998), 35; Billy Jaynes Chandler, *The Bandit King: Lampião of Brazil* (College Station: Texas A&M University Press, 1978), 214; Linda Lewin, "The Oligarchical Limitations of Social Banditry in Brazil: the Case of the 'Good' Thief Antonio Silvino," *Past and Present,* no. 82, 1979, 116; and Eric Hobsbawm, *Bandits* (New York: Delacorte, 1969), 50–53.

22. Kevin Anderson and Richard Quinney (eds.), *Erich Fromm and Critical Criminology: Beyond the Punitive Society,* Heinz Osterle and Kevin Anderson

(trans.) (Urbana: University of Illinois Press, 2000), 96; Richard Quinney, *The Problem of Crime* (New York: New York University Press, 1970), 30–31; and Michel Foucault, *Discipline and Punish: The Birth of the Prison,* Alan Sheridan (trans.), 2nd ed. (New York: Vintage Books, 1997), 298.

23. Ruth Landes, *The City of Women* (New York: Macmillian, 1947), 6.

24. Maria Luiza Tucci Carneiro, *O anti-semitismo na era Vargas: fantasmas de uma geração, 1930–1945* (São Paulo: Brasiliense, 1988), 158–80, 184–88, 201–2, 208, 213, 266–71, 273, 277–78, 280–85, 288, 325, 331, 336–37, 348, 524, 543–49.

25. Craig Calhoun, "Why Historical Sociology?" *Handbook of Historical Sociology,* Geard Delanty and Engin Isin (eds.) (London: Sage, 2003), 384.

26. Richard Quinney, "The Existential Question, What is Real," *The Critical Criminologist,* vol. VI, no. 2, Summer-Fall, 1994, 3.

27. Nicolau Sevcenko, *Literatura como missão: tensões sociais e criação cultural na Primeira República* (São Paulo: Brasiliense, 1983), 33–34; and *Jornal do Commercio* (Rio de Janeiro), October 16, 1907, 4.

28. Eduardo Barbosa, "As 1200 mortes do Esquadrão da Morte," *Violência,* June 1–14, 1973, cited in Ettore Biocca, *Estratégia do terror: a face oculta e repressiva do Brasil,* Maria de Carvalho (trans.) (Lisbon: Iniciativas, [no date]), 213. Many individuals erroneously think death squads appeared first in Central America. The two countries usually mentioned are Guatemala and El Salvador, where they occurred in 1966 and in the 1970s respectively. *Harper's* (New York), June 1999, 52; and *New York Times,* October 22, 1987, A11.

Chapter 1. The Muscler of Governments

1. *Correio da Manhã* (Rio de Janeiro), August 25, 1954, sec. 1, 3.

2. John W. F. Dulles: *Carlos Lacerda, Brazilian Crusader, Volume I: The Years 1914–1960* (Austin: University of Texas Press, 1991), 168–69; *Brazilian Communism, 1935–1945: Repression during World Upheaval* (Austin: University of Texas Press, 1983), 7; Israel Beloch and Alzira Alves de Abreu (coords.), *Dicionário histórico-biográfico brasileiro, 1930–1983* (Rio de Janeiro: Forense-Universitária, 1984), 782–83, 1721, 3503; Paulo Brandi, *Vargas: da vida para a história,* 2nd ed., rev. (Rio de Janeiro: Zahar, 1985), 298; Carlos Lacerda, *Depoimento,* 2nd ed. (Rio de Janeiro: Nova Fronteira, 1978), 147; Stefan Baciu, *Lavradio, 98: Histórias de um jornal de oposição: a Tribuna da Imprensa ao tempo de Carlos Lacerda* (Rio de Janeiro: Nova Fronteira, 1982), 106; *Tribuna da Imprensa* (Rio de Janeiro), August 26, 1954, 14; *Imprensa Popular* (Rio de Janeiro): August 25, 1954, 1; August 26, 1954, 1, 5; August 26

[27], 1954, [9]; *Jornal do Brasil:* August 25, 1954, 9; August 26, 1954, 7; and *Correio da Manhã,* August 26, 1954, sec. 1, 3, 5–6.

3. Robson Gracie, interview, Rio de Janeiro, August 6, 1991; and Nelson Werneck Sodré, *História militar do Brasil* (Rio de Janeiro: Civilização Brasileira, 1965), 278.

4. Centro de Pesquisa e Documentação de História Contemporânea do Brasil (hereafter CPDOC), oral history, "Guilherme Figueiredo," 1977, 62; Dulles, *Brazilian Communism, loc. cit.;* and R. S. Rose, *One of the Forgotten Things: Getúlio Vargas and Brazilian Social Control, 1930–1954* (Westport: Greenwood, 2000), 18.

5. Rose, *Beyond the Pale of Pity,* 143. By 1922, Brazil's political police were called the 4ª Delegacia Auxiliar (police from the 4th Auxiliary Department). Made up of several sectors, the 4ª Delegacia's Seção de Ordem Política e Social (SOPS, the Section of Political and Social Order) came to be called "Delegacia" or "Police Station" instead of the "Seção" or "Section." Until being disbanded, this generic title stuck despite the official name or name changes over the years. In some states, the convention was adopted officially.

6. Eliana Rezende Furtado de Mendonça (dir.), *Os arquivos das polícias políticas: reflexos de nossa história contemporânea* (Rio de Janeiro: FAPERJ, 1994), 16.

7. Aspásia Camargo, "Tenentismo," comments delivered before the seminar "Cenários de 1922," Fundação Getúlio Vargas/CPDOC, Rio de Janeiro, November 19, 1992.

8. With the exception of Vargas' Estado Novo document of 1937, the legal basis for a military intrusion into civilian affairs has been provided in every Brazilian constitution since 1891. *Folha de São Paulo,* September 6, 1987, A-6. The loophole used "made the military obedient to the executive, but significantly stated that they should only be obedient 'within the limits of the law.'" Alfred Stepan, *The Military in Politics: Changing Patterns in Brazil* (Princeton: Princeton University Press, 1971), 75. The *Constitution of 1988* removed the stipulation but, after some haggling between lawmakers and the military, replaced it with an equally porous definition allowing soldiers "in the name of law and order to initiate the defense of the country and guarantees of constitutional power." *Folha de São Paulo,* September 13, 1987, A-11.

9. Thomas Skidmore, *Politics in Brazil, 1930–1964: An Experiment in Democracy* (New York: Oxford University Press, 1967), 103–7, 133, 364n; [Luís Alberto] Moniz Bandeira, *O governo João Goulart: as lutas sociais no Brasil, 1961–1964* (Rio de Janeiro: Civilização Brasileira, 1977), 16; and Beloch and Abreu, 1011–12. Besides his Brazilian army training, Lott studied the art of warfare in France and in 1943 in Kansas at the U.S. army's elite Fort Leaven-

worth Staff College, along with 120 other Brazilians officers. He then did a tour of duty in Italy with the American-supplied Brazilian Expeditionary Force, or FEB. Beloch and Abreu, 1937.

10. *Jornal do Brasil,* August 6, 1955, sec. 1, 6. Besides having shipped out with Góis Monteiro aboard the *USS Nashville,* and in serving on the Brazilian-American mixed commissions guarding Brazil's Northeast, back in the early 1940s Canrobert too went to the Ft. Leavenworth course. Beloch and Abreu, 965. His views represented the pro-American, pro-capitalism, and anti-communism faction within the military, which grew in power and influence in the years ahead—eventually coming to be known as the Sorbonne Group. Jan Knippers Black, *United States Penetration of Brazil* (Philadelphia: University of Pennsylvania Press, 1977), 176–78. The Sorbonne Group would become synonymous with the so-called moderate line and moderate liners surrounding dictator Castelo Branco in the 1960s.

11. Beloch and Abreu, 661, 1508; Bandeira, 33–34; and Victor Civita (ed.), *Nosso século, 1945–1960: a Era dos Partidos* (São Paulo: Abril Cultural, 1985), part II, vol. VIII, 74–75.

12. *Última Hora* (Rio de Janeiro), May 13, 1954, 6; and Carlos Lacerda, *et al., Reportagens que abalaram o Brasil* (Rio de Janeiro: Bloch, 1973), 155.

13. John W. F. Dulles, *Unrest in Brazil: Political-Military Crises, 1955–1964* (Austin: University of Texas Press, 1970), 24–25. For the PCB's support of the two men, see: Political Police Archives, Rio de Janeiro [hereafter PPARJ]: documents: "Reuniões do PCB," August 13, 1960, 1–3, comunismo/pasta [no number]; and "D.P.S. S.I.-S.S.," December 30, 1955, 1–13, comunismo/pasta 48. The charges of election double-dealing would come back to haunt Kubitschek.

14. *Correio da Manhã,* November 2, 1955, sec. 1, 4.

15. Dulles, *Unrest in Brazil,* 31.

16. M. B. Lourenço Filho, "Redução das taxas de analfabetismo no Brasil entre 1900 e 1960: descrição e análise," *Revista Brasileira de Estudos Pedagógicos,* vol. XLIV, no. 100, October-December 1965, 252; Jordan Young, *The Brazilian Revolution of 1930 and the Aftermath* (New Brunswick: Rutgers University Press, 1967), 122n; *Encyclopédia Mirador International* (São Paulo: Encyclopaedia Britannica do Brasil, 1975), 3695–96; Brazil: *Coleção das leis de 1985: atos do poder legislativo e atos legislativos do poder executivo, leis de julho a setembro* (Brasília: Nacional, 1985), vol. V, 10, decree 7332, art. 18; *Constituição [da] República Federativa do Brasil 1988* (Brasília: Centro Gráfico do Senado Federal, 1988), 18, art. 18, no. II, c, par. 2; United States, Central Intelligence Agency [hereafter CIA], document, "Brazil," SR-17, November 30, 1948, 7; and John French, "Industrial Workers and the Birth of the

Populist Republic in Brazil, 1945–1946," *Latin American Perspectives,* vol. XVI, no. 4, Fall 1989, 7.

17. Black, 176–77.

18. Alfred Stepan (ed.), "The New Professionalism of Internal Warfare and Military Role Expansion," *Authoritarian Brazil: Origins, Politics, and Future* (New Haven: Yale University Press, 1973), 54; and Brazil, Escola Superior de Guerra, *Doutrina básica* (Rio de Janeiro: Escola Superior de Guerra, 1979), 64.

19. Brazil, *Doutrina básica,* 63.

20. Stepan, *The Military in Politics,* 178.

21. Café Filho's weak heart may have been of another kind. It has been stated, (CPDOC, oral history, "Renato Archer," 1977–1978, 50–56) that he was not really sick at all, but that he bluffed his malady and stepped aside so that the stronger willed Carlos Luz would become acting president and fire Lott.

22. Dulles, *Unrest in Brazil,* 32–34; Skidmore, *Politics in Brazil,* 151–52; and CPDOC, oral history, "Renato Archer," 49.

23. Skidmore, *Politics in Brazil,* 153; and PPARJ, letter, José Luiz Bettâmino Guimarães to director DPS," September 6, 1955, no. 333/2a/s, administração/pasta 1a. An example of the attempts to keep the inauguration from taking place can be seen in the comments of Col. Nelio Cerqueira. PPARJ, document, "Processo protocolado sob no. 183-S [by hand], informação no. 527," October 7, 1955, administração/pasta 1a.

24. Dulles, *Unrest in Brazil,* 35–40; Skidmore, *Politics in Brazil,* 374n; and Beloch and Abreu, 1962–63.

25. CPDOC, oral history, "Henrique Lott," 1978, 139; Lacerda, 164; and Dulles, *Unrest in Brazil,* 39, 43–58.

26. Arquidiocese de São Paulo, *Brasil: nunca mais,* 6th ed. (Petrópolis: Vozes, 1985), 57; *Jornal do Brasil,* September 19, 1987, sec. 1, 4; Beloch and Abreu, 3157; and José Gomes Talarico in Valentina da Rocha Lima (coord.), *Getúlio: uma história oral* (Rio de Janeiro: Record, 1986), 186.

27. Robert Price, "Rural Unionization in Brazil," University of Wisconsin Land Tenure Center, no. 14, 1964, 66–67; and *Veja* (Rio de Janeiro), June 8, 1988, 49.

28. Bandeira, 31. Col. Amauri Kruel revised Golbery's manuscript to make it less political. Beloch and Abreu, 2071, 3157; and John W. F. Dulles, *Vargas of Brazil: A Political Biography* (Austin: University of Texas Press, 1967), 316.

29. Hélio Silva, *A vez e a voz dos vencidos: militares x militares* (Petrópolis: Vozes, 1988), 79–81; Dulles, *Unrest in Brazil,* 65–66, 79–80, 100; *Folha de São Paulo,* June 18, 1988, 7; and Beloch and Abreu, 159–60, 1631–32.

30. Skidmore, *Politics in Brazil,* 197; Beloch and Abreu, 2851; and *Jornal do Brasil,* August 24, 2001, sec. 1, 5. This last scheme was not put into effect

only because of Quadros' resignation. Beloch and Abreu, 3157–58; *Veja,* September 23, 1987, 22; and "Fantástico," TV Globo, April 18, 1993.

31. Beloch and Abreu, 2850; Skidmore, *Politics in Brazil,* 194–97; and Black, 39.

32. Jânio Quadros, "Brazil's New Foreign Policy," *Foreign Affairs* [hereafter *FA*], vol. XL, no. 1, October 1961, 26.

33. John W. F. Dulles, letter, April 4, 2003 [postmarked]; and Francisco Julião in Dênis de Moraes, *A esquerda e o golpe de 64: vinte e cico anos depois, as forças populares repensam seus mitos, sonhos e ilusões* (Rio de Janeiro: Espaço e Tempo, 1989), 225.

34. Dulles, *Unrest in Brazil,* 124–25, 183; and *Jornal do Brasil,* August 25, 1991, sec. 1, 5. Fidel Castro wanted to start a number of revolutions in Latin America in part to divert U.S. attentions from Cuba. In his view, Brazil was one of the more attractive countries for these activities. Guevara thought so little of the medal that he did not take it with him back to Cuba. Moraes, *loc. cit.;* and *Jornal do Brasil,* August 25, 1991, sec. 1, 5.

35. Adérito Lopes, *O Esquadrão da Morte: São Paulo, 1968–1971* (Lisbon: Prelo, 1973), 32; and *Isto É Senhor* (São Paulo), August 28, 1991, 58. The full speech is given in Carlos Lacerda, *O poder das idéias,* 2nd ed. (Rio de Janeiro: Record, 1963), 327–41. Another reason for Lacerda's outburst was the fact that the governor wanted Quadros' administration to help his financially troubled *Tribuna da Imprensa.* Jânio had ignored the request. *Jornal do Brasil,* August 25, 1991, sec. 1, 4.

36. *Isto É Senhor,* August 28, 1991, 56–59; *Jornal do Brasil,* August 25, 1991, sec. 1, 4; and United Kingdom, Public Record Office [hereafter UKPRO], letter, "R. S. Isaacson to [Robin] E. G. Edmonds," April 19, 1962, FO 371/162132. Unhappy with what in their analysis were his leftist leaning policies, there has been speculation that the military was behind everything. In this regard, see: *Jornal do Brasil,* August 25, 1991, sec. 1, 4; Skidmore, *Politics in Brazil,* 206–7, 391n-392n; and Stepan, *The Military in Politics,* 68n. Jânio's minister of justice, Oscar Pedroso Horta, has also been accused of influencing his chief's decision. Beloch and Abreu, 1595; *Jornal do Brasil,* August 25, 1991, sec. 1, 4; and [Luís Alberto] Moniz Bandeira, *O 24 de agôsto de Jânio Quadros* (Rio de Janeiro: Melso, 1961), 33–34. The navy and air force ministers denied the thesis by Quadros that his act was a move designed to get them to step in and close Congress, and evidently hand the reins of government back to him. *Folha de São Paulo,* May 16, 1989, A-6.

37. John W. F. Dulles, letter, April 4, 2003 [postmarked]; and Skidmore, *Politics in Brazil,* 208.

38. While Denis never studied in the United States, or served with the FEB, he had been the head of the Polícia Militar in the Federal District from

1940 to 1946. Moss took advance training at Ft. Leavenworth in 1942. He was among the Jacareacanga and Aragarças rebels. Heck served as the captain of the submarine *Timbira,* which was under U.S. command from 1943 to just after the end of the war. He was then transferred to Washington, DC, where he worked for the Brazilian navy from January 1946 until April 1948. Back in Brazil, besides being captain of the *Tamandaré,* he was one of the main conspirators in the plot to kidnap Kubitschek when the latter arrived on board the *Barroso* in early 1957. In September 1961, once resigning his post as Minister of the Navy, Heck was imprisoned at the naval stockade in Rio de Janeiro for ten days for making political statements. After a published interview the following January (*O Cruzeiro* [Rio de Janeiro], January 27, 1962, 106–7), he was sentenced to another three days; but beat a hasty retreat to the home of his father-in-law, where he claimed to be too sick with dermatitis to leave his bed. Beloch and Abreu, 1068, 1584, 2296; Mário Victor, *Cinco anos que abalaram o Brasil (de Jânio Quadros ao Marechal Castelo Branco)* (Rio de Janeiro: Civilização Brasileira, 1965), 87 and UKPRO, letter, "P. H. to Assistant Chief of Air Staff (Intelligence)," February 9, 1962, FO 371/162132.

39. *Jornal do Brasil,* September 19, 1987, sec. 1, 4; and Beloch and Abreu, 3158. Golbery had served in the short-lived Quadros government as head of the National Security Council, which was the forerunner of the SNI, the post-1964 dictators' intelligence apparatus. Beloch and Abreu, 3158–59.

40. Victor, 348.

41. John W. F. Dulles, letter, April 4, 2003 [postmarked].

42. *Jornal do Brasil,* August 23, 1991, sec. 1, 2.

43. Skidmore, *Politics in Brazil,* 210; *Jornal do Brasil,* August 20, 2001, sec. 1, 3; Bandeira: *O governo João Goulart,* 47n; *Presença dos Estados Unidos no Brasil: dois séculos de história* (Rio de Janeiro: Civilização Brasileira, 1973), 418; *Los Angeles Times,* August 31, 1961, sec. 1, 30; and Partido Democrático Trabalhista, "Como Kennedy participou da derrubada de João Goulart, "*Gazeta Mercantil* (Rio de Janeiro)," July 21–23, 2000, <http://www.pdt.org.br/jgkencondor.htm>, October 10, 2001.

44. Abelardo Jurema, *Sexta-feira, 13: os últimos dias do governo João Goulart,* 2nd ed. (Rio de Janeiro: Cruzeiro, 1964), 113; Dulles, *Unrest in Brazil,* 156–57; Amir Labaki, *1961: a crise da renúncia e a solução parlamentarista* (São Paulo: Brasiliense, 1986), 124–28; Hélio Silva, *1964: golpe ou contra-golpe?* (Rio de Janeiro: Civilização Brasileira, 1975), 144, 148–49; *Última Hora:* September 5, 1961, 2; September 6, 1961, 1–4; and *Fatos e Fotos* (Rio de Janeiro), September 28, 1963, 14.

45. Beloch and Abreu, 1511. Black (40) adds that "When Goulart took over, concern at the State Department and the Pentagon turned to panic."

46. Bandeira, *O governo João Goulart,* 133–34; *Veja,* December 15, 1976, 33; April 13, 1988, 81; Gileno Dé Carli, *Visão da crise* (Brasília: Universidade de Brasília, 1980), 216–17; John W. F. Dulles: *Carlos Lacerda, Brazilian Crusader, Volume II: The Years 1960–1977* (Austin: University of Texas Press, 1996), 173–74; *Unrest in Brazil,* 237; Raul Ryff, *O fazendeiro Jango no governo* (Rio de Janeiro: Avenir, 1979), 30; PPARJ: documents: "Relatorio: agente A.O.C. de Montevidéu, Uruguai," [no date], pp 3–4, comunismo/pasta 65.; "Montevideo: movimento entre exilados, reuniões," [no date], 7, comunismo/pasta 80; letter, "Matheus de Oliveira Franco to chefe S.I.," February 12, 1960, administração/pasta 3 cont.; *Estado de Minas* (Belo Horizonte), January 8, 1977, 3; Geneton Moraes Neto, *Dossiê Brasil: as histörias por tráis da história recente do país,* 9th ed. (Rio de Janeiro: Objetiva, 1997), 120; "Fantástico," TV Globo, July 21, 1991; *Jornal do Brasil:* April 25, 2000, sec. 1, 10; April 30, 2000, sec. 1, 19; May 9, 2000, sec. 1, 9; September 4, 2001, sec. 1, 5; and João Vicente Goulart, interview, Niterói, December 19, 2000.

47. Victor Civita (ed.), *Nosso século, 1960–1980: sob as ordens de Brasília* (São Paulo: Abril Cultural, 1986), part I, vol. IX, 61; A. J. Langguth, *Hidden Terrors* (New York: Pantheon, 1978), 86–88; and René Armand Dreifuss, *1964: a conquesta do estado: ação política, poder e golpe de classe* (Petrópolis: Vozes, 1981), 183–84, 203–7.

48. Beloch and Abreu, 3158.

49. Dulles, *Unrest in Brazil,* 188. For an important inventory of some of the Instituto de Pesquisas e Estudos Sociais production, see the pioneering work by Dreifuss, Appendix L.

50. Beloch and Abreu, 1610.

51. Brazil, Comissão Especial de Inquérito sôbre atos delituosos da Ditadura, "Depoimento do Luís Carlos Prestes," *Diario do Congresso Nacional,* September 20, 1947, 5905; Dreifuss, 405n; Beloch and Abreu, 699–700, 1235, 1450, 1697, 2157, 2856, 2892; *Folha de São Paulo,* October 24, 1999, sec. 1, 1, 16; and Civita, *Nosso século, 1960–1980,* part I, vol. IX, 60.

52. Beloch and Abreu, 1611, 3158; Norman Blume, "Pressure Groups and Decision-Making in Brazil," *Studies in Comparative International Development,* vol. III, no. 11, 1967–1968, 217; and Dulles, *Unrest in Brazil,* 188–89. IPÊS was not alone. The CIA ran schools that taught union leaders to be procapitalist and anti-anything else. CIA agent William Doherty Jr., headed one of these groups, the Instituto Cultural do Trabalho, or Cultural Labor Institute. *Isto É Senhor,* April 10, 1991, 25.

53. Dulles, *Unrest in Brazil,* 173.

54. Ibid., 181, 184; Dreifuss, 205–7; Leacock, 65; Bandeira: *Presença dos Estados Unidos no Brasil,* 428–30; *O governo João Goulart,* 65; *Jornal do*

Brasil: May 15, 1962, sec. 1, 10; June 15, 1962, sec. 1, 9; July 17, 1962, sec. 1, 9; August 15, 1962, sec. 1, 9; September 15, 1962, sec. 1, 7; and October 17, 1962, sec. 1, 9. For a partial listing of these individuals and companies, see: Dreifuss, Appendices H-I; and Civita, *Nosso século, 1960–1980,* part I, vol. IX, 60.

55. Dulles, *Unrest in Brazil,* 180–81, 188–89; Bandeira, *O governo João Goulart,* 70; and Beloch and Abreu, 12–13, 1010, 1611.

Chapter 2. The Excuse

1. The comments of Gen. Assis Brasil in *O Estado de São Paulo,* July 3, 1964, 5–6; Valério Campos and Flora Maestri, *João Goulart,* 3rd ed. (Porto Alegre: Tchê!, 1985), 12; Bandeira, *O governo João Goulart,* 28, 39–40; and Luís Alberto Moniz Bandeira, interview, Rio de Janeiro, December 16, 1992. Goulart's remarks are from his letter of resignation from the Ministry of Labor in 1954. Arquivo Getúlio Vargas [hereafter AGV], letter, "Goulart to Vargas," February 22, 1954, 02.22/1, 2.

2. Literally "colonel," the word *coronel* was applied liberally to string-pulling, rural potentates up to the 1930s as a sign of respect. The term does not necessarily mean that one served in the military.

3. PPARJ, document, "Planilha de registro," [in file: "João Goulart ou João Belchior Marques Goulart"], prontuário 1305; Campos and Maestri, 10, 16, 17; Pedro Tórtima, interview, Rio de Janeiro, July 13, 1988; Bandeira, *O governo João Goulart,* 25; Samuel Wainer, *Minha razão de viver: memórias de um repórter,* Augusto Nunes (ed.), 4th ed. (Rio de Janeiro: Record, 1988), 235; Beloch and Abreu, 1504; *Jornal do Brasil,* January 12, 1993, sec. 1, 6; and *O Cruzeiro,* September 26, 1964, 9–10.

4. John W. F. Dulles, *Carlos Lacerda, Brazilian Crusader, Volume I,* 121, 387n.

5. Luís Alberto Moniz Bandeira, interview, Rio de Janeiro, December 16, 1992.

6. Ivan Hasslocher: telephone interviews, Fresno/Houston, January 28, 1992; and January 29, 1992.

7. Manuel Pio Corrêa, letter, March 9, 1992.

8. PPARJ, "Relatorio: agente A.O.C. de Montevidéu, Uruguai," 4, comunismo/pasta 65; Beloch and Abreu, 940–41, 1509; Civita, *Nosso século, 1945–1960,* part II, vol. VIII, 87; and Dulles, *Carlos Lacerda, Brazilian Crusader, Volume I,* 224–26, 234–52.

9. William Sweet, "Pandect of My Life," unpublished manuscript, 103, 118, 123.

10. William Sweet, e-mail, May 16, 2003.

11. Sweet, 118, 121.

12. Otti [Otakar O.] Svacina, e-mails: July 15, 2003; and July 16, 2003.

13. João Vicente Goulart, interview, Niterói, December 19, 2000.

14. John W. F. Dulles: telephone interviews: Fresno/Austin, January 24, 1991; April 24, 1991; letters: January 9, 1991; December 20, 1991; and e-mail, June 16, 2003.

15. Arquivo Castelo Branco [hereafter ACB], document, "Investigações especias," part 1, pasta U2.

16. *o Cruzeiro:* August 22, 1964, 20–26; and September 26, 1964, 6–11.

17. John W. F. Dulles, e-mail, April 9, 2003.

18. *Jornal do Brasil,* August 25, 1991, sec. 1, 4; Victor, 158–62; Ruth Leacock, *Requiem for Revolution: The United States and Brazil, 1961–1969* (Kent: Kent State University Press, 1990), 43; Wainer, 237–38; and Rivadavia de Souza, *Botando os pingos nos is: as inverdades nas memórias de Samuel Wainer* (Rio de Janeiro: Record, 1989), 85–88.

19. Rural workers were all but forgotten, and merely given lip service by Vargas in 1951. In April 1954, Jango had just quit as minister of labor; Getúlio sent a bill to Congress that would have made it harder to fire rural workers and would have shortened their working hours. Some benefits would have been offered to their wives and minor children. They would have been allowed to draw a pension. The project was still under discussion when Vargas ended his life. Beloch and Abreu, 1204.

20. *Fatos e Fotos,* September 16, 1961, 30; Carli, 164; Wainer, *loc. cit.;* Dulles, *Unrest in Brazil, loc. cit.;* Bandeira, *O governo João Goulart,* 26; *O Estado de São Paulo,* July 3, 1964, 5–6; Clodesmidt Riani in Dênis de Moraes, 36; Ryff, 11–12; José Gomes Talarico, Hugo de Faria, and Eusébio Rocha in Lima, 184–85; Limeira Tejo, *Jango: debate sôbre a crise dos nossos tempos* (Rio de Janeiro: Andes, 1957), 82; CPDOC: oral histories: "Abelardo Jurema," 1977, 315–16, 430; "Alzira Vargas do Amaral Peixoto," 1979, 120–122; "Osvaldo Lima Filho," 1978–1979, 102–4; Nelson Werneck Sodré, interview, Rio de Janeiro, August 8, 1991; and Luís Alberto Moniz Bandeira, interview, Rio de Janeiro, December 16, 1992. Marco Antonio Villa's one-sided work (*Jango: Um perfil [1945–1964]* [São Paulo: Globo, 2003], 7–241) is a case in point of the ongoing efforts to vilify Jango. The number of twisted and omitted items in Villa's effort is remarkable. A connection between Golbery and IPÊS, for example, is never mentioned.

21. CIA, document, "Memorandum for the United States Intelligence Board," by Joseph Seltzer, NLK-76–199, no. 4, July 2, 1963. 1. Note that this assessment is reiterated in ibid., on 12.

22. Campos and Maestri, 26, 31–32; Beloch and Abreu, 1504, 2599–600; and CPDOC, oral history, "Abelardo Jurema," 179–80.

23. Beloch and Abreu, 1505, 2603; *Folha de São Paulo,* May 21, 2000, A-17; and PPARJ, file, "João Goulart ou João Belchior Marques Goulart," [20 x 14 cm. card listing Goulart's profession as "deputado"], prontuário 1305.

24. Silvio Tendler and Maurício Dias, *Jango,* 2nd ed. (Porto Alegre: L and PM, 1984), 19.

25. Tancredo Neves in Lima, 180; Campos and Maestri, 51; Nelson Werneck Sodré, interview, Rio de Janeiro, August 8, 1991; and João Vicente Goulart, interview, Niterói, December 19, 2000.

26. Beloch and Abreu, 1505–6; and *Folha de São Paulo,* May 21, 2000, A-17.

27. Beloch and Abreu, 2071; and AGV, letter, "Goulart to Vargas," February 22, 1954, 2–3.

28. On February 22, 1954, 1,200 *cruzeiros* was worth $65.36 at the official rate of exchange. *Jornal do Brasil,* February 23, 1954, sec. 1, 14.

29. Beloch and Abreu, 1507; Campos and Maestri, 78; AGV, letter, "Goulart to Vargas," February 22, 1954, *loc. cit.: Jornal do Brasil:* May 4, 1954, sec. 1, 9; and May 5, 1954, sec. 2, 4.

30. Beloch and Abreu, 1521; and Campos and Maestri, 24.

31. Campos and Maestri, 25.

32. Eurides de Sousa Bueno, letter, April 22, 1988. *Dona* Eurides was at one time the governess for João and Maria Tereza Goulart.

33. Dulles, *Unrest in Brazil,* 185–86; Beloch and Abreu, 1515; and *Jornal do Brasil,* January 24, 1963, sec. 1, 1.

34. *Veja,* December 15, 1976, 32. After Jango's March 13, 1964 rally, Tancredo would be one of the ones to turn against Goulart. CPDOC, oral history, "Abelardo Jurema, 327.

35. Beloch and Abreu, 615–16, 2903; E. Bradford Burns, *Nationalism in Brazil: A Historical Survey* (New York: Praeger, 1968), 91; and *Jornal do Brasil,* March 17, 1963, sec. Especial, 5–6.

36. *Novos Rumos* (Rio de Janeiro), September 25, 1962, 2. *O Globo* reporter Ibrahim Sued wrote this report.

37. Brizola was decidedly not a Communist, probably much to the surprise of the CIA. In the years following the 1964 golpe, while Moniz Bandeira was living in Paris, and Brizola in Washington, DC, Luís Carlos Prestes, who was exiled in Moscow, contacted Bandeira to try and arrange a meeting with Brizola. Bandeira relayed the invitation, but Brizola refused it. In fact, the two men *never* met, either before the events of 1964 or in the years following. Only in 1982, during the elections of that year, would Brizola and Prestes meet for the first time. Luís Alberto Moniz Bandeira, interview, Rio de Janeiro, December 16, 1992.

38. Beloch and Abreu, 489, 491, 2845; *Novos Rumos:* July 29-August 4, 1960, 1, 3; August 5–11, 1960, 1, 3; *Diário de Notícias* (Porto Alegre), May 12,

1959, 1, 11; and *Jornal do Brasil,* May 13, 1959, sec. 1, 15. The conversion rate of one nickel is generous. The black market rate would have been below one cent.

39. CPDOC, oral history, "Abelardo Jurema," 344, 500; [Roberto Campos], "Depoimento do Sr. Embaixador Roberto Campos, prestado em 20 e 26–6–63," *Revista Brasileira de Política Internacional,* September-December 1965, 532; Dulles, *Unrest in Brazil,* 169; [Luís Alberto] Moniz Bandeira, *Brizola e o trabalhismo* (Rio de Janeiro: Civilização Brasileiro, 1979), 64; *Jornal do Brasil,* February 17, 1962, sec. 1, 1, 3, 9; and Villa, 91–7. All conversion rates are at the official rate of exchange.

40. Burns, *Nationalism in Brazil,* 108; and Brazil, Ministério do Planejamento e Coordenação Geral, Instituto Brasileiro de Estatística, Departamento de Censos, *Tabulações avançadas do censo demográfico, 1970: resultados preliminares* (Rio de Janeiro: IBGE, 1971), xxix.

41. R. S. Rose, "Slavery in Brazil: Does It Still Exist?" 98–107. A more complete formulation can be seen in R. S. Rose, "Slavery in Brazil: Does it Still Exist Today?" paper presented to the 83rd Annual Meeting of the American Sociological Association, Atlanta, August 26, 1988," 5–11.

42. Burns, *Nationalism in Brazil, loc. cit.;* and Rose, "Slavery in Brazil: Does it Still Exist?" *loc. cit.* .

43. *Jornal do Brasil,* March 14, 1963, sec. 1, 4.

44. Carlos Cortés, *Gaúcho Politics in Brazil: The Politics of Rio Grande do Sul, 1930–1964* (Albuquerque: University of New Mexico Press, 1974), 186; Ryff, 15; and Beloch and Abreu, 2903–4. In respect to the university professors, see the work by Darcy Ribeiro ("Universities and Social Development," *Elites in Latin America,* Seymour Martin Lipset and Aldo Solari [eds.][New York: Oxford University Press, 1967]). Especially relevant are 363–68. Some of Jango's other plans are explained in Ryff, *loc. cit.*

45. Skidmore, *Politics in Brazil,* 244–45.

46. Ibid., 281; CPDOC: oral histories: "Abelardo Jurema," 527; "Alzira Vargas do Amaral Peixoto," 121; Fernando Jorge, *Cale a boca, jornalista: o ódio e a fúria dos mandões contra a imprensa brasileira* (São Paulo: Vozes, 1987), 79–80; Fernando Morais, *Chatô: o rei do Brasil* (São Paulo: Companhia das Letras, 1994), 640; and Affonso Henriques, *Ascensão e queda de Getúlio Vargas: declínio e morte* (Rio de Janeiro: Record, 1966), vol. III, 46–47.

47. Luís Carlos Prestes in Dênis de Moraes, 269. Prestes' exact words were "O Brizola não tinha nada na cabeça naquela época" or "Brizola was empty headed during that period."

48. CPDOC, oral history, "Renato Archer," 385. Another version (Bandeira, *Brizola e o trabalhismo,* 42–44) has it that José Brizola was decapitated for merely being on the losing side of the 1923 gaúcho revolution.

49. CPDOC: oral histories: "Paulo Pinheiro Chagas," 1977, 118–19; "Alzira Vargas do Amaral Peixoto," *loc. cit.;* "Abelardo Jurema," 264–68, 315, 319, 346, 432; "Osvaldo Lima Filho," 100; Luís Carlos Prestes in Dênis de Moraes, *loc. cit.;* and Marcello Cerqueira in Dênis de Moraes, 282.

50. Marcello Cerqueira in Dênis de Moraes, 104–5; and Beloch and Abreu, 214–16.

51. Dulles, *Unrest in Brazil,* 183–84; and PPARJ, document, "Boletim de informações no. 11/62," part 3, [no date], 5, comunismo/pasta 81.

52. CPDOC, oral history, "José Gomes Talarico," 1978–1979, 147; PPARJ, document, "Secretaria da doutrina integalista [*sic*]," March 15, 1935, integralismo/pasta 1; Beloch and Abreu, 1052–53, 1056; and Wainer, 252–53.

53. Skidmore, *Politics in Brazil,* 236–40; *Jornal do Brasil,* March 10, 1963, sec. 1, 3; Bandeira, *O governo João Goulart,* 89–94; Beloch and Abreu, 1515–16; and Dulles, *Unrest in Brazil,* 198–202.

54. Skidmore, *Politics in Brazil,* 241–51; Black, 256; Dulles, *Unrest in Brazil,* 201–2, 214; Bandeira, *O governo João Goulart,* 107; Beloch and Abreu, 64, 322; and *Veja,* March 9, 1977, 4. It is reported that on March 28, 1964, Magalhães Pinto was busy consulting with two generals, Odílio Denis and Mourão Filho, on the overthrow of Goulart. On the eve of the golpe, March 31, Magalhães Pinto assumed the civilian control of the overthrow. *Jornal do Brasil,* "*Jornal do Século*—um produto do *Jornal do Brasil*—1964 Cronologia," <http://jbonline.terra.com.br/jseculo/1964b.html>, January 31, 2002.

55. Black, 47–48, 138–55, 256; Philip Agee, *Inside the Company: CIA Diary* (London: Penguin, 1975), 566; Brazil, *Coleção das leis de 1969: atos do poder executivo, decretos de abril a junho* (Brasília: Nacional, 1969), vol. IV, 88, decree 64416, art. 43; United States, U.S. Senate, Hearings Before the Subcommittee on Western Hemisphere Affairs of the Committee on Foreign Relations, *United States Policies and Programs in Brazil* (Washington, DC: U.S. Government Printing Office, 1971), 7, 10; and Anonymous-1, interview, Rio de Janeiro, April 12, 1994. The actual number of American police advisors given at the U.S. Senate hearings may have been blatantly under reported. The PCB's *Novos Rumos* (June 29-July 5, 1962, 3), citing *A Noite* (Rio de Janeiro), *Jornal do Brasil,* and Federal Congressman José Joffily, who was basing his remarks on conservative newspapers, claimed that the true figure could well have been several thousand by mid-1962. In respect to the Federal Police, although they were named the Polícia Federal on February 25, 1967 (Brazil, *Coleção das leis de 1967: atos do poder legislativo e atos legislativos do poder executivo, leis de janeiro a março* [Brasília: Nacional, 1967], vol. I, 278, decree 200, art. 210), the above-mentioned article. 43 of decree 64416 in 1969 extended their powers nationwide.

56. Skidmore, *Politics in Brazil,* 246.

57. Dulles, *Unrest in Brazil,* 227–30; CPDOC: oral histories: "João Pinheiro Neto," 1977, 85–86; "Paulo Pinheiro Chagas," 120–21; and Beloch and Abreu, 1516–17.

58. Beloch and Abreu, 1204; and Dulles, *Unrest in Brazil,* 220.

59. CPDOC, oral history, "Osvaldo Lima Filho, 107; and Beloch and Abreu, *loc. cit.*

60. Dulles, *Unrest in Brazil,* 220–22; and Bandeira, *O governo João Goulart,* 121–22.

61. Beloch and Abreu, 13, 1605.

62. Langguth, 102.

63. CPDOC, oral history, "Abelardo Jurema," 517; Beloch and Abreu, 1441, 2626, 2933; Dulles, *Unrest in Brazil,* 231; *Fatos e Fotos,* September 28, 1963, 14; José Stacchini, *Março 64: mobilização da audácia* (São Paulo: Nacional, 1965), 54–62; and Bandeira, *O governo João Goulart,* 123.

64. CPDOC: oral histories: "José Gomes Talarico," 150; "Abelardo Jurema," 519, 521–22; Beloch and Abreu, 2934; Dulles, *Unrest in Brazil, loc. cit.;* and Jacob Gorender, *Combate nas trevas: a esquerda brasileira: das ilusões perdidas à luta armada* (São Paulo: Ática, 1987), 57. What happened to Antônio Prestes de Paula is a good example of what the military leaders were talking about in their desire to keep order down below. A Communist since 1946, Paula was arrested once things in the capital were brought under control, but later let go in the amnesty offered by President Goulart. Following the golpe of March 31, 1964, Paula was rearrested, kicked out of the air force, and given a twenty-year prison sentence. He later escaped and left the country. Paula remained in exile until the general amnesty decreed by João Figueiredo in 1979. Beloch and Abreu, 2626; and PPARJ, letter, "Cecil de Macedo Borer to diretor da Seção de Segurança Nacional do M.J.N.I. [Josias de Carvalho Argons]," November 21, 1963, administração/pasta 34.

65. CIA: documents: "TDCS-3/540, 528," March 15, 1963; and "TDCS-3/546, 074," May 4, 1963, 5.

66. *Los Angeles Times,* September 29, 1963, sec. A, 10; and *Brazil Herald* (Rio de Janeiro), October 1, 1963, 12.

67. *Los Angeles Times:* September 29, 1963, sec. A, 1; September 30, 1963, sec 1, 1, 20; and *Brazil Herald,* October 1, 1963, 12.

68. CPDOC, oral history, "Abelardo Jurema," 328.

69. Bandeira, *O governo João Goulart,* 135–36; and *Brazil Herald,* October 1, 1963, 1.

70. CIA: documents: "TDCS-3/546, 074," May 4, 1963, *loc. cit.;* and "TDCS-3/543, 633," April 12, 1963, 1.

71. CIA, document, "Memorandum: Brazil, 3 April 1964," [no number]; and Beloch and Abreu, 2977.

72. CPDOC: oral histories: "Osvaldo Lima Filho," 102–3; "Abelardo Jurema," 330–31; Jurema, *Sexta-feira, 13,* 127; Beloch and Abreu, 2977; and Bandeira, *O governor João Goulart,* 124–25. On April 8, 1970, the São Paulo Força Pública's name was changed to the Polícia Militar. Caco Barcellos, *Rota 66* (São Paulo: Globo, 1992), 67.

73. *Brazil Herald,* October 1, 1963, 1.

74. CPDOC: oral histories: Osvaldo Lima Filho," 102–4; "Abelardo Jurema," 328–31; Jurema, *Sexta-feira, 13,* 130; and Dulles, *Unrest in Brazil,* 238–42. After Jango withdrew the measure, one of his long-time congressional allies, Doutel de Andrade, predicted his own fate, and by implication that of Brazil's president, with the observation that, "this morning, my overthrow began." *Jornal do Brasil,* March 28, 1994, sec. 1, 13.

75. *Pasquim* (Rio de Janeiro), April 28-May 4, 1983, 10. The *Pasquim* account is based on an interview with Amado Ribeiro. Ribeiro traveled to Paraná, Santa Catarina, Rio Grande do Sul, and into parts of Uruguay.

76. PPARJ: documents: "Informe: Grupo dos onze ou comandos nacionalistas," [no date], 1–2, comunismo/pasta 66; "Grupos dos onze de Brizola," [no date], 6, 8–9, comunismo/pasta 66; Dulles, *Unrest in Brazil,* 242–46; Beloch and Abreu, 492; Almino Afonso (in Dênis de Moraes, 322–23); and Arquidiocese de São Paulo, *Perfil dos atingidos* (Petrópolis: Voces, 1988), 109–12. Groups of Eleven were also called "Nationalist Comandos." PPARJ, document, "Informe no. 2533/SFICI (SAS/557/8 Jul 64)," July 8, 1964, 2, comunismo/pasta 120.

77. Araken Távora, *Brasil, 1º de abril,* 2nd ed. (Rio de Janeiro: Buccini, 1964), 54.

78. PPARJ: documents: "Informe no. 574/SFICI," April 13, 1964, 2–3, secreto/pasta 1; "Informe no. 2533/SFICI (SAS/557/8 Jul 64)," July 8, 1964, 2–3, comunismo/pasta 120; "Informe: Grupo dos onze ou comandos nacionalistas," 1–3, comunismo/pasta 66; "Grupos dos onze de Brizola," 10, comunismo/pasta 66; Dulles, *Unrest in Brazil,* 246; and Beloch and Abreu, *loc. cit.* Paulo Schilling said later that the G-11 needed another six to eight months to organize. He counseled Brizola to allow the formation of groups of five. PPARJ, document, "[untitled report on Groups of Eleven]," December 3, 1965 [date received on back of 1], 3, comunismo/pasta 81.

79. Bandeira, *O governo João Goulart,* 144–45; and CPDOC, oral history, "José Gomes Talarico," 146–47.

80. CPDOC: oral histories: "José Gomes Talarico," 146; "Osvaldo Lima Filho," 105; Beloch and Abreu, 492, 1431–32, 1508, 1604, 2749; Skidmore, *Pol-*

itics in Brazil, 268, 409n-410n; and *Jornal do Brasil,* December 20, 1963, sec. 1, 10. The conversion rate, at the official rate of exchange, is taken from the day Pinto left office.

81. John W. F. Dulles, letter, April 4, 2003 [postmarked]; and CPDOC, "Goulart, João," <http://www.cpdoc.fgv.br/dhbb/verbetes_htm/2412_10.asp>, April 6, 2003.

82. Beloch and Abreu, 1518; and Bandeira, *O governo João Goulart,* 148. Until December 1987, only public functionaries were excluded from receiving the 13th Salary. Employees in their first year receive the proportion of the months worked. It is paid out around December 20.

83. Raul Ryff in Dênis de Moraes, 273–74.

84. Bandeira, *O governo João Goulart,* 149–50; *Jornal do Brasil:* January 18, 1964, sec, 1, 1, 3, 13; January 23, 1964, sec. 1, 5; John W. F. Dulles, letter, April 4, 2003 [postmarked]; Dulles, *Unrest in Brazil,* 248–49; Skidmore, *Politics in Brazil,* 271–72; Beloch and Abreu, 1518–19, 2710; and Arquidiocese de São Paulo, *Brasil nunca mais,* 58.

85. Langguth, 104–5. For an example of the documentation, true or otherwise, behind the often rumored plans of Jango to remain in office via his own *coup,* see: CIA, document, "TDCS-3/565, 572," November 22, 1963, 1–3; and Gorender, 60. Note that Gorender's information was provided by a Polícia Militar investigation, evidently conducted after the golpe. For the view that Goulart was not conspiring to bring off a golpe, see: Assis Brasil's remarks in *O Estado de São Paulo,* July 3, 1964, 5; CPDOC: oral histories: "Abelardo Jurema," 318–19, 537; and "Alzira Vargas do Amaral Peixoto," 120–21.

86. Dulles, *Unrest in Brazil,* 256–63; and Blume, *loc. cit.*

87. Skidmore (*Politics in Brazil,* 290) reports that additional meetings were in the works for Belo Horizonte, Bahia, Recife, and São Paulo. Beloch and Abreu (1519) include Porto Alegre but delete Bahia.

88. CPDOC, oral history, "José Gomes Talarico," 152. Jango (*Correio da Manhã,* March 14, 1964, 3) put the number of those present at between 150 and 200 thousand. Brizola's small newspaper (*Panfleto* [Rio de Janeiro], March 16, 1964, 5); Bandeira (*O governo João Goulart,* 163); *Manchete,* March 25, 1989, 16, 19–20; and Talarico (CPDOC, oral history, "José Gomes Talarico," 153) all state that the actual number was in the neighborhood of 200 thousand.

89. Beloch and Abreu, *loc. cit.; Manchete* (Rio de Janeiro), March 25, 1989, 20; Dulles, *Unrest in Brazil,* 268–69; Skidmore, *Politics in Brazil,* 287; Langguth, 104; *Jornal do Brasil,* March 14, 1964, sec. 1, pp 1, 16; and *Correio da Manhã,* March 14, 1964, 1.

90. *Jornal do Brasil,* March 14, 1964, sec. 1, 1, 16; and Távora, 71.

91. *Correio da Manhã,* March 14, 1964, 1.

92. Wainer (250) claims that Brizola re-radicalized his speech together with Arraes. In this regard, see the comments by Talarico, CPDOC, oral history, "José Gomes Talarico," 151–52.

93. *Correio da Manhã,* March 14, 1964, 1.

94. Ibid.

95. Talarico (CPDOC, oral history, "José Gomes Talarico," 154) adds that there were rumors of an attempt to assassinate Goulart.

96. *Jornal do Brasil,* March 14, 1964, sec. 1, 1; Skidmore, *Politics in Brazil,* 287–88. For a picture of the searchlights in action, see *Correio da Manhã,* March 14, 1964, 14.

97. John W. F. Dulles, letter, April 4, 2003 [postmarked].

98. *Correio da Manhã,* March 14, 1964, 3.

99. Vargas most likely committed suicide because he could not deal with being forced to leave office a second time. There is also speculation that he was linked to the attempt to assassinate Carlos Lacerda on August 5, 1954.

100. *Correio da Manhã,* March 14, 1964, 3.

101. Beloch and Abreu, 2903–4, 3284; CPDOC: oral histories: "João Pinheiro Neto," 71–73; "Osvaldo Lima Filho," 98–99; *Jornal do Brasil,* March 16, 1964, sec. 1, 1; *Correio da Manhã,* March 14, 1964, 3; and *Manchete,* March 25, 1989, 20.

102. *Correio da Manhã,* March 14, 1964, 3.

103. Ibid.

104. Ibid.

105. Ibid.

106. Ibid.

107. CPDOC, oral history, "José Gomes Talarico," 154–56.

108. Beloch and Abreu, 2757; *Jornal do Brasil,* March 14, 1964, sec. 1, 5; and *Correio da Manhã,* March 14, 1964, 2.

109. Bandeira, *O governo João Goulart,* 164; and *Jornal do Brasil,* March 16, 1964, sec. 1, 1, 5.

110. *Jornal do Brasil,* March 16, 1964, sec. 1, 1, 5; and *Correio da Manhã,* March 24, 1964, 1, 15.

111. Lacerda later went to have dinner at the São Paulo home of the conservative newspaper owner and anti-government conspirator Assis Chateaubriand. There, dressed as a rural bandit, Lacerda was made a member of a reactionary society of patriots called the Order of the *Jagunço.* John W. F. Dulles: Archive, letter, Napoleão de Carvalho to Fernando Goldgaber, May 12, 1985; letter from John W. F. Dulles, September 16, 1993; "Carlos Lacerda," vol. II, pre-publication manuscript, 328–29; *O Estado de São Paulo,* March 20, 1964, 12; and *Jornal do Brasil,* March 20, 1964, sec. 1, 3.

112. Dulles, *Unrest in Brazil,* 275–77; Bandeira, *O governo João Goulart,* 165–66; and *Correio da Manhã,* March 20, 1964, 12.

113. The name "Green Chickens" comes from one of the many pranks played on Brazil's Fascist party before World War II. Alzira Vargas do Amaral Peixoto recounts (*Jornal do Brasil,* May 8, 1988, sec. 1, 8) that people would paint chickens green, one of the Integralists' colors, and then let them loose on the street as the fascists marched by in order to mock Plínio and his group. Salgado later attempted to use this for his own purposes. Within two weeks after returning to Brazil following his WWII exile, he founded the PRP (Partido de Representação Popular or Popular Representation Party). The PRP took as its symbol a lapel pin with a rendition of a green chicken. Beloch and Abreu, 3059; and PPARJ, physical evidence, "[examples of lapel pins of the] Partido de Representação Popular," [no date], integralismo/pasta 19.

114. Jarbas Passarinho reports (*Playboy* [Brazilian ed.], April 1989, 48) that Castelo Branco was called Tamanco, any of several types of cheap shoes of the clog variety. The sole and heel made of wood usually added height beyond a regular shoe to the wearer. Castelo Branco did not care for the nickname.

115. To this day a good number if not the majority of Brazilians appear to be either afraid to call it what it was, a golpe, or have been educated into not doing so. The word heard time and time again to describe what took place, "revolution," reminded this author of a speech he once listened to by Adolf Hitler. The Nazi dictator used the words "*Nationalsozialistische Revolution*" in his comments, attempting to legitimize his own assumption of power.

116. Távora, 78–79.

117. Ibid., p 80.

118. Ibid.

119. Bandeira, *O governo João Goulart,* 168.

120. The Naval Revolt of 1910 began when seamen—many of them non-White—rebelled aboard two battleships in Guanabara Bay. Directed by a man who would become part of Brazilian history, "The Black Admiral," João Cândido Felisberto, the crews captured their ships and began shelling the capital. Their grievance was over the continued use of a whip studded with nails called the *chibata,* along with bread-and-water punishments. The administration gave in to the demands; but reneged on them later after a bloody second mutiny. Most of the sailors either died in the conflict, or were subsequently murdered, in one way or another, by the government. João Cândido was one of the fortunate few who survived only to be drummed out of the navy.

121. *Jornal do Brasil:* March 27, 1964, sec. 1, 3; March 27, 1994, sec. 1, 7; Wainer, 251; Bandeira, *O governo João Goulart,* 169–70; CPDOC, oral history, "Abelardo Jurema," 528; Civita, *Nosso século, 1960–1980,* part I, vol. IX, 93;

Beloch and Abreu, 147–53, 3292; PPARJ: documents: "Informe no. 850-C/64," November 17, 1964, secreto/pasta 1; "Informe no. SP/015," April 4, 1966, 1, secreto/pasta 21; Marcio Moreira Alves, *Torturas e torturados* (Rio de Janeiro: Novo Idade, 1966), 161–63; *Pasquim,* April 26-May 2, 1984, 8–9; Gorender, 231–32; Thomas Skidmore, *The Politics of Military Rule in Brazil, 1964–1985* (New York: Oxford University Press, 1988), 121, 348n-349n; *O Globo* (Rio de Janeiro), May 18, 2000, 31; and Percival de Souza, *Autópsia do medo: vida e morte do delegado Sérgio Paranhos Fleury* (São Paulo: Globo, 2000), 517. See as well the book by Octávio Ribeiro (*Por que eu traí: confessões de Cabo Anselmo* [São Paulo: Global, 1984]).

122. Civita, *Nosso século, 1960–1980,* part I, vol. IX, 92; *Jornal do Brasil,* March 26, 1964, sec. 1, 5; and Beloch and Abreu, 146–47. Although João Cândido allowed himself to be brought into the meeting on the shoulders of his colleagues, he did have mixed feelings about a naval rebellion on land. For his observations, see Dênis de Moraes, 100.

123. CPDOC, oral history, "Abelardo Jurema," 531–32.

124. Dulles, *Unrest in Brazil,* 281. For more on Aragão and his peculiar personality, see: Ibid., 245; and CPDOC, oral history, "Abelardo Jurema," *loc. cit.*

125. CPDOC, oral history, "Abelardo Jurema," 316–17.

126. Civita, *Nosso século, 1960–1980,* part I, vol. IX, *loc. cit.;* and Távora, 91. Távora (*loc. cit.*) claims that the mutineers were evidently imprisoned in a move to prevent additional outbreaks in the navy that occurred on Friday, March 27.

127. *O Jornal* (Rio de Janeiro), March 31, 1964, sec. 1, 8. Dulles emphasizes that the way the mutiny was settled was of supreme importance to the growing cadre of anti-government officers. John W. F. Dulles, e-mail, April 7, 2003.

128. Beloch and Abreu, 2962; and Dulles, *Unrest in Brazil,* 288–89, 318.

129. Dulles, *Unrest in Brazil,* 289, 300; and John W. F. Dulles, letter, April 4, 2003 [postmarked].

130. Jurema, *Sexta-feira, 13,* 167–68, 173; and Edmar Morél, *O golpe começou em Washington* (Rio de Janeiro: Civilização Brasileira, 1965), 96.

131. *O Jornal,* March 31, 1964, sec. 1, 8.

132. Ibid.

133. Ibid.

134. Ibid.

135. Ibid.

136. Ibid.

137. There are no fewer than three different times cited, all on March 30, for the start of the golpe. Carli (249) states that Carlos Luís Guedes declared

himself in rebellion at 8:30 A.M. Pedro Gomes ("Minas: do diálogo ao 'front,'" *Os idos de março e a queda em abril,* Alberto Dines, *et al.* [eds.], 3rd ed. [Rio de Janeiro: José Alvaro, 1964], 104) puts it at 2:30 in the afternoon. Guedes' account (*Tinha que ser Minas* [Rio de Janeiro: Nova Fronteira, 1979], 202) is the one used here.

138. Arquidiocese de São Paulo, *Brasil nunca mais, loc. cit.*

139. Dulles, *Unrest in Brazil,* 312–13.

140. *Veja,* May 13, 1970, 22.

141. *Jornal do Brasil,* April 7, 1988, sec. 1, 2.

142. Gomes, 108; and Anonymous-1, interview, Rio de Janeiro, March 9, 1989.

143. One of the sick minister's visitors was Juscelino Kubitschek, who hoped to succeed Jango as president in 1965. Kubitschek and Dantas Riberio met alone without aides. Years later, when Juscelino was in the Library of Congress in Washington, DC, he read a CIA report that contained all of the details of this conversation. *Manchete,* April 9, 1989, 26.

144. Ademar de Barros, or persons close to him, sent someone to American Ambassador Lincoln Gordon in an attempt to get Gordon to phone Kruel on the afternoon of March 31. Gordon was to try to talk the 2nd Army general into joining the now unfolding golpe. Later, Gordon categorically denied ever making the call. *Folha de São Paulo,* January 9, 1977, 1.

145. Dulles, *Unrest in Brazil,* 318–20. Dulles (ibid., 320) reports that the officers under Kruel were ready to arrest him and take over if he sided with the president. Luís Carlos Prestes considered Jango to be most at fault for the golpe. After Kruel's ultimatum, Goulart knew he had two options: cave in to the military's demands, and end up being their puppet, or side with the PCB. Luís Carlos Prestes in Dênis de Moraes, 267–68. Amauri Kruel was the younger brother of Gen. Riograndino Kruel, torture ignorer in the 1930s, and momentum behind the coming IPMs in the 1960s.

146. PPARJ, letter, "Olindo Denys to Gonçalves Etchegoyen," July 27, 1943, 1–3, integralismo/pasta 4, cont. i; and Dulles, *Unrest in Brazil,* 322–23.

147. Black, 42–49; *Folha de São Paulo,* January 9, 1977, 1; *Estado de Minas,* January 8, 1977, 3; John W. F. Dulles, letter, April 4, 2003 [postmarked]; and Lyndon B. Johnson Presidential Library [hereafter LBJPL] NSF Co Brazil, box 10, vol. III, 4/64, documents 147–48.

148. *Folha de São Paulo,* January 9, 1977, 1; and LBJPL, NSF Co Brazil, box 10, vol. III 4/64, document 43.

149. Beloch and Abreu, 2961; and Langguth, 107–8, 111.

150. Anonymous-1, interviews: Rio de Janeiro, June 17, 1988; and March 24, 1994. The informant was not sure about Geisel's presence. The author is

aware of plate 32, and caption, in John W. F. Dulles' *Castello Branco: The Making of a Brazilian President* (College Station: Texas A&M Press, 1978).

151. Jurema, *Sexta-feira, 13,* 186–88; and *Folha de São Paulo,* October 24, 1999, sec. 1, 16. Freddie Perdigão Pereira would become a part of the army's intelligence operation. In that capacity he tortured, planted bombs, and plotted the assassination of no less than Ernesto Geisel.

152. Morél, *O golpe começou em Washington,* 108.

153. Dulles, *Unrest in Brazil,* 334–39.

154. Ibid., 339; and CPDOC, oral history, "Osvaldo Lima Filho," 116.

155. Ibid.; Carlos Lacerda, *Depoimento* (Rio de Janeiro: Nova Fronteira, 1977), 384; and *Tribuna da Imprensa,* August 15, 1994, 6.

156. *Jornal do Brasil,* August 10, 2001, sec. 1, 22; and Bandeira, *O governo João Goulart,* 185. Fernando Gabeira adds (*O que é isso companheiro?* 29th ed. [Rio de Janeiro: Nova Fronteira, 1982], 31) that Goulart gave up easily and went into exile because he thought the golpe would bring only a fleeting victory to the military.

157. Gordon claims that his actual comments, delivered before the Escola Superior de Guerra on May 5, 1964, went as follows: "The Brazilian revolution . . . may take its place alongside the initiation of the Marshall Plan, the ending of the Berlin blockade, the defeat of Communist aggression in Korea, and the solution of the Cuban-missile base crisis as one of the critical points of inflection in mid-twentieth century world history." *Commonweal* (New York), August 7, 1970, 379.

158. Darcy Ribeiro in Dênis de Moraes, 299.

159. *Manchete,* December 18, 1976, 18; and João Vicente Goulart, interview, Niterói, December 19, 2000. If Jango had ever made the trip, and been caught, there were orders already issued for his immediate arrest. He was to be taken to the nearest Polícia Militar station and held in strict isolation. In addition, aware that he was later living in Argentina, the Brazilian authorities apparently looked at numerous Aerolineas Argentinas flights, and those of other airlines, landing in Brazil before traveling on to a third country. Had Goulart have been aboard, he would have been removed. PPARJ, telegram, "Sylvio Frota to SSP/RJ," no. 10276, December 13, 1976 [in file: "João Goulart ou João Belchior Marques Goulart"], prontuário 1305.

160. Beloch and Abreu, 1521; *Veja,* December 15, 1976, 31, 33; August 25, 1982, 46; *Jornal do Brasil,* December 7, 1976, sec. 1, 16; *Correio do Povo* (Porto Alegre), August 20, 1982, 2; UKPRO: "R.S. Isaacson to R.E.G. Edmonds;" letter, "C. O. I. Ramsden to [Robin] H. G. Edmonds," April 13, 1962, FO 371/162132; PPARJ, document, "Informe no. 2930/SNI/ARJ (SS 17/676/26 ago 64)," August 26, 1964, secreto/pasta 2; *Jornal do Brasil:* April 26, 2000,

sec. 1, 10; April 27, 2000, 10; May 3, 2000, sec. 1, 13; May 9, 2000, 9; May 13, 2000, 10; and May 15, 2000, 7.

161. *O Globo,* "SNI acampanhou de perto o enterro de Jango," <http://oglobo.globo.com/Ciencia/12421336.htm>, December 16, 2001.

162. *Jornal do Brasil,* April 25, 1994, sec. 1, 11.

163. The term comes from the title of one of Stefan Zweig's books. His *Brasil, país do futuro,* Odilon Gallotti (trans.) (Rio de Janeiro: Guanabara, 1941), was a meager attempt to glorify the country as a land of potential. Among his predictions was one (200–202) that favelas—and indirectly, poverty—would become things of the past. Zweig, an Austrian Jew, and his second wife, Charlotte, committed suicide in Brazil in 1942, afraid that the Nazis were after them. The title of his book caught the attention of persons sharing his wishful thinking and wound its way into their speech and aspirations.

Chapter 3. In Shining Armor

1. Morél, *O golpe començou em Washington, loc. cit.*

2. Carlos Hector Cony, *O ato e o fato: crônicas políticas* (Rio de Janeiro: Civilização Brasileira, 1964), xviii–ixx; and Phyllis Parker, *1964: o papel dos Estados Unidos no golpe de estado de 31 de março,* Carlos Nayfeld (trans.) (Rio de Janeiro: Civilização Brasileira, 1977), 109.

3. Ralph della Cava, "Torture in Brazil," *Commonweal,* April 24, 1970, 140; August 7, 1970, 378; *Jornal do Brasil,* June 26, 1988, sec. B/Especial, 10; and Silva, *A vez e a voz dos vencidos,* 151.

4. Marcio Moreira Alves, *A Grain of Mustard Seed: The Awakening of the Brazilian Revolution* (Garden City: Doubleday Anchor, 1973), 64.

5. Vernon Walters, *Silent Missions* (Garden City: Doubleday, 1978), 376.

6. Jan Knippers Black, *The New Republic* (Washington, DC), September 16–23, 1985, 22.

7. *Newsweek,* November 14, 1966, 56.

8. *The New Republic,* September 16–23, 1985, 23.

9. Ibid.

10. Canada, letter, "James M. Weld to the Under-Secretary of State for External Affairs, Ottawa," January 15, 1962, 2, UKPRO FO 371162132. A picture of the torching of the UNE's literature in front of the student edifice appeared in *Life* ([New York], April 17, 1964, 38b-38c). Two months after the overthrow of Goulart," Costa e Silva affirmed that "No Brazilian was killed [during the golpe]." CIA, document, "TDCS-3/584, 319," June 18, 1964, 2. In opposition to this view by the new war minister, see: Morél, *O golpe começou em Washing-*

ton, 108–9; *Correio da Manhã,* April 7, 1964, sec. 1, 34; and Alves, *Torturas e torturados,* 30.

11. *Jornal do Commercio,* April 2, 1964, sec. 1, 1; and Maria Helena Moreira Alves, *State and Opposition in Military Brazil* (Austin: University of Texas Press, 1985), 32–33.

12. Brazil, *Diário oficial,* April 9, 1964, sec. 1, part 1, 3193, "À Nação."

13. Ibid.

14. Ibid., 3193–94, *Ato Institucional,* arts. 1–4. This time frame was later augmented to forty and then to sixty days. Maria Helena Moreira Alves, 33.

15. Brazil, *Diário oficial,* April 9, 1964, sec. 1, part 1, 3194, arts. 5–8. Maria Helena Moreira Alves, *loc. cit.,* comments on the number jailed.

16. Brazil, *Diário oficial,* April 9, 1964, sec. 1, part 1, 3194, art. 10.

17. Ibid., arts. 10–11.

18. Beloch and Abreu, 2479; and Arquidiocese de São Paulo, *Brasil nunca mais,* 269–70.

19. Brazil, *Diário oficial,* April 10, 1964, sec. 1, part 1, 3217. The first list of one hundred and twenty-two military officers to be placed on the reserve (read: retired) list was published in Brazil, *Diário oficial,* April 11, 1964, sec. 1, part 1, 3258–59.

20. Brazil, *Diário oficial,* April 13, 1964, sec. 1, part 1, 3281, decree 53883, art. 1.

21. Maurio Borges, *O golpe em Goiás: história de uma grande traição* (Rio de Janeiro: Civilização Brasileira, 1965), 110–11. The author of the above volume was the governor of Goiás at the time and one of the individuals at the meeting. Thirty years later, Lincoln Gordon continued to view with favor Brazil's period of military government and to insist that "The five generals who became president did not conduct themselves as dictators." *Jornal do Brasil,* March 27, 1994, sec. 1, 11.

22. *Jornal do Brasil,* February 2, 1985, sec. 1, 13.

23. PPARJ, phamplet [by Neiva Moreira], *O exército e a crise brasileira,* (Montevideo: Diálogo S.R.L., 1968), 34, secreto/pasta 53.

24. Maria Helena Moreira Alves, 34–35.

25. For a similar scenario in Vargas' Brazil, following the events of November 1935, see Rose, *One of the Forgotten Things,* chap. 4.

26. Brazil, *Diário oficial,* April 27, 1964, sec. 1, part 1, 3690, decree 53897.

27. Ibid., art. 1.

28. Maria Helena Moreira Alves, 35.

29. PPARJ, letter, "J.E. Hoover to Brady," April 15, 1964, secreto/pasta 10. The letter turned up in mail of the security section of the Federal Railroad System in Lorena, São Paulo, some 118 miles (nearly 190 km) outside the state capital. PPARJ, letter, "Horácio Pereira (Informação no. 228/65.-)," October

5, 1965, secreto/pasta 10. Note as well the comments on Hoover's unverified letter in Black, (*United States Penetration of Brazil,* 47–48). The communication was published in the Chilean newspaper *Ultima Hora* (Santiago de Chile), July 24, 1964, 1. Agee stated (356), however, that despite its being limited to domestic duties within the U.S., the Federal Bureau of Investigation had an office at the American Embassy in Brazil.

30. ACB, document, "Investigações especias," nos. 1–4, 6–21, pasta U1.

31. Maria Helena Moreira Alves, 35, 39, 57–58.

32. Ibid., 39, 41, 43–47; Cony, 81–82; (Anonymous), "O terrorismo cultural," *Revista Civilização Brasileira,* vol. I, March 1965, 239–97; and Lucia Klein and Marcus Figueiredo, *Legitimidade e coação no Brasil pós-64* (Rio de Janeiro: Forense-Universitária, 1978), 162–63, 169–70. For different figures, many of them based on old or incomplete accountings of either or both the civilian and military sackings, see: the sources listed in Skidmore, *The Politics of Military Rule in Brazil,* 317n.

33. *Veja,* June 15, 1988, 32–33; *Folha de São Paulo,* June 16, 1988, 1, 8; and *O Globo,* June 16, 1988, sec. 1, 1, 3. There are slightly varying tallies on the actual numbers of men affected. Using the somewhat higher numbers presented in *Jornal do Brasil* (August 29, 1989, sec. Cidade, 4) of 1,538 enlisted men, only 136 had been pardoned as of the date of the accounting, and these only after time-consuming and expensive legal appeals.

34. Joseph Page, *The Revolution that Never Was* (New York: Grossman, 1972), 217; ACB, document, "Subversão e IPMs," no. 11, pasta T; Ryff, 46; *Time* (New York), April 17, 1964, 46; *O Globo,* April 6, 1964, 7; *Diário de Notícias* (Rio de Janeiro), April 9, 1964, 1, 8; and PPARJ: document, "Informe no. 323 CH/68," July 26, 1968, secreto/pasta 30; and, letter, "Syseno Sarmento to Gustavo Eugenio Borges," July 2, 1964, secreto/pasta 4. A picture of Gustavo Borges with a set of the despicable clothing is presented here as plate 12.

35. PPARJ, document, "Relação dos esquerdistas e agitadores detidos pelas autoridades revolucionárias em Belo Horizonte, de 1° de abril até a presente data, todos registrados no DOPS," July 30, 1964, 1–7, secreto/pasta 8; *Jornal do Brasil,* April 7, 1964, sec. 1, 4; *Jornal do Commercio,* April 10, 1964, sec. 1, 12; Maria Helena Moreira Alves, 37, 305n; Arquidiocese de São Paulo, *Brasil nunca mais,* 61; Morél, *O golpe começou em Washington,* 109–10, 235–36 and Hemílcio Fróes *Véspera do primeiro de abril: ou nacionalistas x entreguistas* (Rio de Janeiro: Imago, 1993), 23–24. Part of the picture, as well, was the weaponry, and other items, usually planted by DOPS or other agencies of the military government. Fróes, *loc cit.*

36. PPARJ, document, "I.B.G.E," October 7, 1964 [date received], 1–2, comunismo/pasta 64.

37. Luís Carlos Prestes, interview, Rio de Janeiro, August 13, 1987; Fernando Morais, *Olga,* 3rd ed. (São Paulo: Alfa-Omega, 1985), 144–45; Jorge Amado, *A vida de Luís Carlos Prestes: O Cavaleiro da Esperança,* 4th ed. (São Paulo: Martins, 1945), 110–11; Ricardo [Antônio] Silva Seitenfus, *O Brasil de Getúlio Vargas e a formação dos blocos, 1930–1942: o processo do envolvimento brasileiro na II Guerra Mundial* (São Paulo: Nacional, 1985), 415–18; *Jornal do Brasil,* December 7, 1938, 7; *Jornal do Commercio,* April 25, 1925, 10; *Manchete:* April 12, 1958, 75; January 22, 1977, 30; Beloch and Abreu, 2343; CPDOC, oral history, "Augusto do Amaral Peixoto," 1975, 284; and Brazil, *Coleção das leis da República dos Estados Unidos do Brasil de 1933: Atos do Govêrno Provisório, janeiro a março* (Rio de Janeiro: Nacional), 1934, vol. I, 57, decree 22332, art. 18.

38. *État de siège* (State of Siege), directed by Constantin Costa-Gavras, Cinema X/Dieter Geissler Filmproduktion/Euro International Film (EIA) S.p.A./Reggane Films/Unidis, 1973.

39. Christopher Lyon (ed.), *The International Dictionary of Films and Filmmakers: Directors/Filmmakers* (New York: Perigee, 1984), vol. II, 109; *Jornal do Brasil,* October 7, 1989, sec. Cidade, 5; Branca Eloysa, interview, Rio de Janeiro, August 16, 1989; Arquidiocese de São Paulo, *Brasil nunca mais,* 32; *The Nation* (New York), June 24, 1978, 764; Langguth, 43–44, 140; and *Jornal do Brasil,* May 9, 2000, sec. 1, 9.

40. Carlos Wilson, *The Tupamaros: The Unmentionables* (Boston: Branden, 1974), 53.

41. *New Scientist* (London), July 19, 1973, 141; Langguth, 305; Antonio Carlos Fon, *Tortura: a história da repressão política no Brasil,* 7th ed. (São Paulo: Global, 1986), 61; *Jornal do Brasil,* May 1, 2000, sec. 1, 7; Arquidiocese de São Paulo, "O regime militar," Projeto "Brasil: nunca mais," São Paulo: Arquidiocese de São Paulo, 1985, book 1, vol. I, 77; Fernando Gabeira: *Carta sobre a anistia: a entrevista do Pasquim: conversação sobre 1968* (Rio de Janeiro: Codecri, 1979), 29; interview, Rio de Janeiro, November 25, 1992; PPARJ, newspaper article, *Voz Operária* (Rio de Janeiro), November 1971, 2, comunismo/pasta 104; Percival de Souza, 481, 593; and Hélio Bicudo, interview, São Paulo, February 8, 1993. For additional comments on Mitrione, Fleury, and the cooperation between the police forces in the southern part of South America, see *Isto É* (São Paulo), February 14, 1979, 28–34. Pictures of Mitrione were published in several issues of *Última Hora* (beginning on August 1, 1970, 1).

42. Langguth, 15–36.

43. Ibid., 37.

44. *Jornal do Brasil,* October 30, 1966, sec. 1, 19.

45. *Jornal do Brasil,* April 1, 1989, sec. 1, 4. The Crown of Christ (*corôa de cristo*) may have simply been renamed. It was also known as the "Tourniquet," or in the Northeast, where it was used the most, as the *anjinho* ("Thumbscrew"). Fon, 76–77; and Hildérico Oliveira, *Tortura à brasileira* (Brasília: Câmara dos Deputados, 1981), 6. Maria Isabel Pinto Ventura ([ed.], *Dos presos politicos brasileiros: acerca da repressão fascista no Brasil,* [no place: Edições Maria da Fonte, 1976], 48, 172) uses the Crown of Christ and the Tourniquet interchangeably. Luzimar Nogueira Dias ([ed.] *Esquerda armada: testemunho dos presos políticos do presídio Milton Dias Moreira no Rio de Janeiro* [Vitória: Edições do Leitor, 1979], 67), on the other hand, calls it the *corôa de cristo* and the *capacete,* or "Headpiece." Finally, Ayrton Baffa (*Nos porões do SNI: o retrato do monstro de cabeça oca* [Rio de Janeiro: Objetiva, 1969] 70) says it was referred to as the *corda do cristo,* or "Rope of Christ." Whatever name one chooses, this device was being used in Brazil, in Rio Grande do Sul, by at least the 1880s. See in this regard, *Revista Illustrada,* August 31, 1886, 4.

46. Lawrence Weschler, *A Miracle, A Universe: Settling Accounts with Torture* (New York: Pantheon, 1990), 41.

47. Marcio Moreira Alves: *A Grain of Mustard Seed,* 88–89; *Torturas e torturados,* 25–26; Fon, 74, 77–79; North American Congress of Latin America, *NACLA Report on the Americas,* vol. XIII, no. 3, May-June 1979, 28; and Langguth, 125, 164, 193, 220. Americas Watch (*Police Abuse in Brazil: Summary Executions and Torture in Sao [sic] Paulo and Rio de Janeiro,* [no place: Americas Watch, 1987], 5) states that the *pau-de-arara* originated in São Paulo in the 1940s. Americas Watch, appears never to have taken a look at the painting by Jean Debret (*Voyage pittoresque et historique au Brésil* [Paris: Frères, 1835], vol. II, plate 25). Another source reports that the modern version was such an effective technique that the FBI ultimately imported it. *Jornal do Brasil,* March 19, 1967, sec. 1, 24.

48. Weschler, 75.

49. Anita Leocádia Prestes, interview, Rio de Janeiro, August 6, 1994; Lygia Prestes, interview, Rio de Janeiro, August 6, 1994; Togo Meirelles, interview, Rio de Janeiro, August 25, 1994; Luzimar Nogueira Dias, 66; Ventura, 45–47; Gilson Rebello, *A guerrilha de Caparaó* (São Paulo: Alfa-Omega, 1980), 54; Arquidiocese de São Paulo, "O regime militar," Projeto: "Brasil: nunca mais," 71; Baffa, 69; Fon, 72–75; Marcio Moreia Alves, *Torturas e torturados,* 25–27; Langguth, 200; Houaiss, Antônio (ed.), *Grande enciclopédia Delta Larousse,* Rio de Janeiro: Delta, 1978, 1891; Amílcar Lobo, *A hora do lobo, a hora do carneiro* (Petrópolis: Vozes, 1989), 41; *O Estado de São Paulo,* October 26, 1977, 14; *Última Hora,* September 17, 1964, sec. 1, 10; *Jornal do*

Brasil: November 5, 1966, sec. 1, 5; and March 19, 1967, sec. 1. 24. Note that as early as the end of October 1966, one newspaper (*Jornal do Brasil,* October 30, 1966, sec. 1, 19), commented that the police had ways of torturing suspects that did not leave marks. This was misleading because many of the fourteen tortures listed (the story's title claimed there were fifteen methods) leave black-and-blue marks or burnt flesh. That such practices were commonplace is evident in the editorial "Rotina da tortura" ("The Routine of Torture") in the *Jornal do Brasil* two days later (November 1, 1966, sec. 1, 6). Ventura (45) and the *New York Times* (November 4, 1974, 2) claim that the geladeira was an American and not a British invention.

50. PPARJ, phamplet, "*Brasileiros!*" [no place: no publisher, no date (distributed in Rio de Janeiro, April 6, 1970)], comunismo/pasta 90; *Isto É Senhor,* November 7, 1990, 45; and *Jornal do Brasil,* November 22, 1985, sec. 1, 4. *Jornal do Brasil* spells Guimarães' name differently. He was later kicked out of the army for corruption and eventually became a famous numbers-racket don in Rio. *Isto É Senhor,* November 7, 1990, *loc. cit.*

51. Paulo Cavalcanti, *O caso eu conto, como o caso fui: memórias políticas* (Recife: Guararapes, 1980), vol. II, 45; *Correio da Manhã:* September 23, 1964, sec. 1, 14; September 24, 1964, sec. 1, 14; September 30, 1964, sec. 1, 16; *Jornal do Brasil,* November 22, 1985, sec. 1, 4; Marcio Moreira Alves, *Torturas e torturados,* 84, 107–41, 196–97, 213–16; and PPARJ: newspaper articles: *A Luta* (Recife), April 21, 1948, 1–2, comunismo/pasta 4e; and *A Luta,* April 29, 1948, 1–2, comunismo/pasta 4e.

52. Beloch and Abreu, 216; Morél, *O golpe começou em Washington,* 109; Page, 199; Luís Carlos Prestes, interview, Rio de Janeiro, August 13, 1987; and Marcio Moreira Alves, *A Grain of Mustard Seed,* 84–85.

53. Cavalcanti, 59.

54. *Correio da Manhã,* September 20, 1964, sec. 1, 28. The report of a civilian commission set up to investigate charges of torture in Recife stated that Julião remained in his cramped confine for sixty days. The commission's findings are published in Marcio Moreira Alves, *Torturas e torturados,* 65–80.

55. *Veja,* July 25, 1979, 28; Gregório Bezerra in Dênis de Moraes, 237–38; Gregório Bezerra, *Memórias* (Rio de Janeiro: Civilização Brasileira, 1979), vol. II, 189–94; Beloch and Abreu, 289, 387; *Última Hora,* September 17, 1964, 10.; PPARJ, phamplet, "*Eu, Gregório Bezerra, acuso!*" ([no place: no publisher], 1967), 15, comunismo/pasta 82; Brazil, *Diário do Congresso Nacional,* May 11, 1961, sec. 1, 3113; and Marcio Moreira Alves, *A Grain of Mustard Seed,* 87.

56. Marcio Moreira Alves, *A Grain of Mustard Seed, loc. cit.*

57. Bezerra, 194. Page (203) adds, "the military had not forgotten that in 1935 Gregório, then an army sergeant, had played a leading role in the Com-

munist uprising in Recife and had killed a lieutenant. It was now time to even the score." But, naturally, the army forgot the fact that it had had a hand in the torture death of Gregório Bezerra's brother, José Lourenço Bezerra, in August 1936. It was a cold-blooded murder that caused protests in Congress. The responsible parties, police detective Etelvino Lins, and army captain, Frederico Mindelo had homicide charges filed against them. These complaints, however, were later suspended. Beloch and Abreu, 387–88.

58. Ibid., 195; PPARJ, "*Eu, Gregório Bezerra, acuso!*" 14–15, comunismo/pasta 82; and Marcio Moreira Alves, *Torturas e torturados,* 40. There are several spellings of Villocq's names. The ones here are from the list of 251 torturers furnished to the press (*Jornal do Brasil,* November 22, 1985, sec. 1, 4) by the Archdiocese of São Paulo, who were responsible for *Brasil nunca mais.* In Bezerra's own words (196), Villocq was "extremely pathological." He was the cruelest person Bezerra had known in more than forty years of fighting. PPARJ, document, "Extrato das declarações prestadas pelos treze banidos em Cuba," 3, secreto/pasta 61.

59. Ibid.; "*Eu, Gregório Bezerra, acuso!*" 11, 16–17, comunismo/pasta 82; and Cavalcanti, 49.

60. PPARJ, "*Eu, Gregório Bezerra, acuso!*" 16–17, comunismo/pasta 82; Langguth, 181; Page, *loc. cit.;* Fon, 32; and *Correio da Manhã,* September 22, 1964, sec. 1, 18. Cavalcanti (*loc. cit.*) reports that Villocq later had all of the copies of the film rounded up so that he couldn't be charged with torture.

61. Ibid., 196.

62. Ibid.

63. Morél, *O golpe começou em Washington,* 109. Captaincies were vast tracts of land that were handed out to Court favorites in the 1530s while Brazil was still a part of Portugal. Page (196) remarks that "Following the well established Brazilian custom of making fun of all public figures, . . . [the General's] detractors liked to pun on his name to convey the expression 'Justino's full of shit.'" The guilty word was the general's last name, Bastos, which is close to "bosta." In Portuguese, *bosta* is one way of saying excretion.

64. Bezerra, 198; Beloch and Abreu, 388; *Veja,* July 25, 1979, 28; *Correio da Manhã,* September 22, 1964, sec. 1, 18; and PPARJ, "*Eu, Gregório Bezerra, acuso!*" 13, comunismo/pasta 82.

65. Marcio Moreira Alves, *Torturas e torturados,* 50; and *Última Hora,* September 16, 1964, sec. 1, 10.

66. Marcio Moreira Alves, *Torturas e torturados,* 45, 90; Page, 205, 258; Movimento dos Trabalhadores Rurais Sem-Terra, *Assassinatos no campo: crime e impunidade, 1964–1986,* 2nd ed., rev. (São Paulo: Global, 1987), 7, 25–28; and Marcio Moreira Alves, *A Grain of Mustard Seed,* 104.

67. Marcio Moreira Alves, *Torturas e torturados,* 40.

68. Ibid., 88–89; Cavalcanti, 66; *Última Hora,* September 17, 1964, sec. 1, 10; and David Nasser, *Falta alguém em Nuremberg: torturas da polícia de Filinto,* 2nd ed. (Rio de Janeiro: Edições do Povo, [no date]), 33–35. Ventura (54) spells Assis Lima's nickname "Pinoti."

69. *Correio da Manhã,* September 22, 1964, sec. 1, 14, 18; Cavalcanti, 59; and Marcio Moreira Alves, *Torturas e torturados,* 181.

70. The list of 251 torturers made available by the Archdiocese of São Paulo (*Jornal do Brasil,* November 22, 1985, sec. 1, 4) is admittedly incomplete. Church investigators originally began with 1,028 persons but deleted fragmentary names and others where the suspect's official capacity or the place and date of the allegation were omitted. The published article states that it contains 254 complete names. There are, however, three repeats, making the final tally only 251. Marcio Moreira Alves (*Torturas e torturados,* 60 and *Correio da Manhã,* September 22, 1964, sec. 1, 18) accuses the following officers of torture in Pernambuco. These men do not appear on the Archdiocese inventory and probably worked for Costa Lima: Majors Baeri, Amarílo (also spelled Amarillo), Hugo Caetano de Almedia, plus one Captain Haroldo.

71. Marcio Moreira Alves, *Torturas e torturados,* 92, 103.

72. Ibid.; *A Grain of Mustard Seed,* 86; Arquidiocese de São Paulo, "Os funcionários," Projeto "Brasil: nunca mais" (São Paulo: Arquidiocese de São Paulo, 1985), book 2, vol. III, 292; Ventura, 178; and *Jornal do Brasil,* November 22, 1985, sec. 1, 4. Note that some of these sources give slightly different spellings to these names.

73. Marcio Moreira Alves, *A Grain of Mustard Seed, loc. cit.;* and Cavalcanti, 53.

74. Father Hélder was one of those priests who had decidedly right-of-center views back in the 1930s. It went so far in Hélder's case that he became an active member, and even the secretary-general of the Integralists. Margaret Todaro Williams, "Integralism and the Brazilian Catholic Church," *Hispanic American Historical Review,* vol. LIV, no. 3, August 1974, 444–45. Father Hélder later claimed that this earlier Fascist affiliation was an error of his youth. Beloch and Abreu, 551.

75. Marcio Moreira Alves, *Torturas e torturados,* 86–105; *Correio da Manhã:* September 22, 1964, sec. 1, 18; September 26, 1964, sec. 1, 6; Brazil: Comissão Especial de Inquérito sôbre Atos Delituosos da Ditadura, "Depoimento do Paulo Franklin de Souza Elejalde," *Diario do Congresso Nacional,* May 27, 1947, 2005–6; "Depoimento do Samuel Lopes Pereira," *Diario do Congresso Nacional,* May 28, 1947, 2057–59; "Depoimento do Bernardino de Oliveira Carvalho," *Diario do Congresso Nacional,* June 7, 1947, 2370–72;

"Acareação entre os depoentes," *Diario do Congresso Nacional,* June 19, 1947, 2774–77; "Depoimento do Belmiro Valverde," *Diario do Congresso Nacional,* May 27, 1947, 2004; and *Diretrizes* (Rio de Janeiro), April 18, 1947, 1, 2, 5.

76. Marcio Moreira Alves, *Torturas e torturados,* 81.

77. Ibid., 80–81; and Cavalcanti, 63. Cavalcanti (58) claims that the police took the word buque from the German and Portuguesed it. Marcio Moreira Alves (*Torturas e torturados,* 81) adds that the buque was also called "*Brasil Novo,*" or "New Brazil."

78. Marcio Moreira Alves, *Torturas e torturados, loc. cit.;* and Cavalcanti, 66–67.

79. Cavalcanti, 68.

80. *Jornal do Brasil:* October 30, 1966, sec. 1, 19; November 22, 1985, 1, 4; December 2, 1992, sec. 1, 8; January 27, 2000, 16; and Ventura, 55, 59–60, 63, 68, 71–72, 77, 178, 183.

81. Marcio Moreira Alves, *Torturas e torturados,* 25; and *Correio da Manhã,* September 20, 1964, sec. 1, 28.

82. Cavalcanti, 12.

83. Pedro Tórtima, interview, Rio de Janeiro, July 13, 1988.

84. Marcio Moreira Alves, *Torturas e torturados,* 46, 143.

85. Ibid., 31.

86. Ibid., 143–44; and *Correio da Manhã,* September 16, 1964, sec. 1, 16.

87. *Correio da Manhã:* September 18, 1964, sec. 1, 14; September 20, 1964, sec. 1, 28; and *Jornal do Brasil,* November 22, 1985, sec. 1, 4; Percival de Souza, 499; Marcio Moreira Alves, *Torturas e torturados,* 154; Morél, *O golpe começou em Washington,* 122, 161–62, 164; Hélio Silva, *A vez e a voz dos vencidos,* 222; and Gilson Ferreira de Souza, interview, Rio de Janeiro, June 15, 1989. Pictures taken of the *Ari Parreiras* and *Princesa Leopoldina* in Guanabara Bay while they were being used as prison ships were published in *Correio da Manhã,* April 7, 1964, sec. 2, 1.

88. Writing about a case a few years later, Langguth reports (226) on the story of an interesting parallel. "The Brazilian military had set up a camp [also in Niterói] modeled after [the American] . . . Green Berets. The students [recruits] were kept awake, starved, and caged. They were hung on beams in mock crucifixions. As a way of breaking a man, it proved too effective. After eighteen hours, Brazilian soldiers were confessing to crimes they had not committed."

89. Marcio Moreira Alves, *Torturas e torturados,* 200–201, 206–7. Placing prisoners under staircases without toilets or running water and leaving them there for indeterminate periods was long a specialty of the authorities in Rio de Janeiro. Witness the case of Arthur Ernst Ewert, a.k.a. Harry Berger. More on the way Ewert was treated is presented in: Beloch and Abreu, 363–64;

Dulles, *Brazilian Communism,* 79, 84, 109; José Joffily, *Harry Berger* (Rio de Janeiro: Paz e Terra, 1986), 93–94; David Nasser: *A revolução dos covardes: diário decreto de Severo Fournier, reportagens políticas e ordens da censura do ditador* (Rio de Janeiro: O Cruzeiro, 1947), 158; and *Falta alguém em Nuremberg: torturas da polícia de Filinto Strubling Müller,* 4th ed. (Rio de Janeiro: O Cruzeiro, 1966), 72, 74. See also, Brazil, Comissão Especial de Inquérito sôbre Atos Delituosos da Ditadura, "Depoimento do Iguatemi Ramos da Silva," *Diario do Congresso Nacional,* September 9, 1947, 5508.

90. Morél, *O golpe começou em Washington,* 238–39.

91. PPARJ, "Brasileiros!"comunismo/pasta 90; Ventura, 74–6; and *Jornal do Brasil,* November 22, 1985, sec. 1, 4.

92. Marcio Moreira Alves, *Torturas e torturados,* 179–80, 201.

93. *Correio da Manhã,* September 18, 1964, sec. 1, 14.

94. Ibid.; and Marcio Moreira Alves, *A Grain of Mustard Seed,* 81.

95. *Correio da Manhã* (September 18, 1964, sec. 1, 14) states only that there were two foreign powers whose security agents took part in the interrogations of political prisoners. That Portugal was one of the countries involved is evident from Marcio Moreira Alves: *A Grain of Mustard Seed,* 81; *Torturas e torturados,* 39, 184–86; Anita Leocádia Prestes, interview, Rio de Janeiro, August 6, 1994; Lygia Prestes, interview, Rio de Janeiro, August 6, 1994; and *Correio da Manhã,* August 12, 1964, sec. 1, 14. The American presence is deduced from Langguth (162–63) and Moniz Bandeira. Professor Bandeira was arrested twice during the military dictatorship. Following one of his apprehensions he was taken to CENIMAR's Rio headquarters and questioned by two civilians who spoke perfect American English. Luís Alberto Moniz Bandeira, interview, Rio de Janeiro, December 16, 1992.

96. Evarardo Dias, *Bastilhas modernas, 1924–1926* (São Paulo: Obras Sociaes e Literarias, 1926), 31; and Langguth, 162.

97. Langguth, 163; PPARJ, "Brasileiros!"comunismo/pasta 90; *Jornal do Brasil,* November 22, 1985, sec. 1, 4; *Correio da Manhã,* September 18, 1964, sec. 1, 14; *Jornal do Brasil,* May 16, 2000, sec. 1, 12; Ventura, 54, 76; and Marcio Moreira Alves, *Torturas e torturados,* 149. Darcy is reported in these sources as being a lieutenant, captain, or lt. commander. *Correio da Manhã* (September 18, 1964, sec. 1, 14) says that there was also a Perestvello. This is probably a misspelling of Feijó's first name. Boneschi's name was apparently spelled incorrectly in the same accounting as as Bonesqui and Bonesque. Julio Bierrembach denied ever having been a torturer while with CENIMAR. But, he was made a Superior Tribunal Militar (Supreme Military Court) judge. Cavalcanti mentions that by 1980, Francisco de Assis Lima had become one of the powerful chiefs of CENIMAR. He was working as a torturer at least by 1935. Solimar is said to have begun his naval career in 1937. Cavalcanti, 66; and Ventura, 75.

98. Arquidiocese de São Paulo, "Os funcionários," Projeto "Brasil: nunca mais," 51–52; and *Jornal do Brasil,* November 22, 1985, sec. 1, 4. In *Veja,* December 9, 1998, 52, Solimar Adilson Aragão is mentioned as being tied for eighth position on the list of those most often accused of torture during the dictatorship.

99. Langguth, *loc. cit.* In another publication (*The Nation,* June 24, 1978, 762), Langguth remarks that the Bottle Opener's drug of choice was alleged to have been amphetamines.

100. PPARJ, "Brasileiros!"comunismo/pasta 90; Marcio Moreira Alves, *Torturas e torturados,* 150–51; and *Correio da Manhã,* September 18, 1964, sec. 1, 14. As for Fernando Paranhos, was this the incomplete name of the future head of the São Paulo Esquadrão da Morte, Sérgio Fernando Paranhos Fleury?

101. *Correio da Manhã,* September 18, 1964, sec. 1, 14.

102. Morél, *O golpe començou em Washington,* 239, 241; Marcio Moreira Alves, *Torturas e torturados,* 30, 145, 152, 186–88; *Jornal do Brasil:* March 11, 1987, sec. Cidade, 1; August 21, 1966, sec. 1, 5; Paulo Markun and Ernesto Rodrigues, *A máfia manda flores: Mariel, o fim de um mito* (São Paulo: Globo, 1981), 25, 178; and PPARJ, document, "Pedido de busca no. 97/67," July 26, 1966, secreto/pasta 16.

103. *Jornal do Brasil,* March 11, 1987, sec. Cidade, 1.

104. John W. F. Dulles, *Carlos Lacerda, Brazilian Crusader, Volume II,* 297–99; and Marcio Moreira Alves, *Torturas e torturados,* 152–53.

105. Marcio Moreira Alves, *Torturas e torturados,* 91–92; Cony, 83–84; Affonso Henriques, *Ascensão e queda de Getúlio Vargas: o maquiavélico* (Rio de Janeiro: Record, 1966), vol. I, 404; Amado, 269; Nasser, *Falta alguém em Nuremberg,* 4th ed., 50; and Anonymous-4, interview, Rio de Janeiro, February 23, 1988.

106. *Correio da Manhã,* August 12, 1964, sec. 1, 14.

107. Marcio Moreira Alves: *A Grain of Mustard Seed,* 68, 82; *Torturas e torturados,* 39, 45–46, 217–35; *Correio da Manhã,* September 12, 1964, sec. 1, 12; Beloch and Abreu, 951, 2979–80; and Cony, xv.

108. Cony, 46; Skidmore, *The Politics of Military Rule in Brazil,* 316n-317n; *Correio da Manhã,* September 15, 1964, sec. 1, 16; and *Última Hora,* September 17, 1964, sec. 1, 1.

109. Marcio Moreira Alves, *Torturas e torturados,* 49. For some of the evidence against Geisel's truthfulness, see: ibid., 23, 50–51, 55–56, 58–59; *Última Hora:* September 17, 1964, sec. 1, 10; September 19, 1964, sec. 1, 3; *Correio da Manhã:* September 20, 1964, sec. 1, 28; and September 30, 1964, sec. 1, 16.

110. *Última Hora,* September 17, 1964, sec. 1, 1.

111. *Última Hora:* September 18, 1964, sec. 1, 2; and September 19, 1964, sec. 1, 2.

112. Marcio Moreira Alves, *Torturas e torturados,* 40, 59–60, 105–6, 143, 152–54, 166–68, 170, 213–16; and *Última Hora,* September 22, 1964, sec. 1, 2.

113. PPARJ, document, "Informe no. 3211/SNI/ARJ (SS 17/799/06 out 64)," October 6, 1964, secreto/pasta 10.

114. John W. F. Dulles, *President Castello Branco: Brazilian Reformer* (College Station: Texas A&M University Press, 1980), 74–77; and Spartacus, "Charles de Gaulle," <http://www.spartacus.schoolnet.co.uk/2WWdegaulle.htm>, March 2, 2005.

115. Maria Helena Moreira Alves, 44–45. Dulles (*President Castello Branco,* 43) adds that it was an army general who arbitrarily fired the head of the university of Minas Gerais. Castelo Branco reinstated the man.

116. *Jornal do Brasil,* May 2, 1994, sec. 1, 13. Not until 1994 did President Itamar Franco return it to the students. Ibid.

117. Maria Helena Moreira Alves, 45–47, 307n.

118. Brazil: *Diário oficial,* June 3, 1964, sec. 1, part 1, 4713–14, law 4330; July 15, 1964, sec. 1, part 1, 6273–74, degree 54018; September 11, 1964, sec. 1, part 1, 8096–97; law 4390; July 13, 1965, sec. 1, part 1, 6561–62, law 4725; Maria Helena Moreira Alves, 51–53, 55–56; and Daniel Aarão Reis Filho and Pedro de Moraes, *68, a paixão de uma utopia* (Rio de Janeiro: Espaço e Tempo, 1988), 23.

119. Brazil, *Diário oficial,* June 15, 1964, sec. 1, part 1, 5073–74, law 4341; *Jornal do Brasil,* September 19, 1987, sec. 1, 4; and Alfred Stepan, *Rethinking Military Politics: Brazil and the Southern Cone* (Princeton: Princeton University Press, 1988), 15–18.

120. Stepan, *Rethinking Military Politics,* 16, 19; Anonymous-1, interview, Rio de Janeiro, February 24, 1989; and *Jornal do Brasil,* August 5, 1991, sec. 1, 4.

121. Dulles, *President Castello Branco,* 11, 57–58.

122. Maria Helena Moreira Alves, 56–62; and Skidmore, *The Politics of Military Rule in Brazil,* 42–43, 45.

123. Maria Helena Moreira Alves: *State and Opposition in Military Brazil,* 61; and *Estado e oposição no Brasil, 1964–1984,* Clóvis Marques (trad.) (Petrópolis: Vozes, 1984), 89.

124. Maria Helena Moreira Alves, *State and Opposition in Military Brazil,* 62; and Brazil, *Diário oficial,* October 27, 1965, sec. 1, part 1, 11017–19.

125. *Jornal do Commercio,* October 28, 1965, sec. 2, 1

126. Brazil, *Diário oficial,* November 4, 1965, sec. 1, part 1, 11305, Ato Complementar-3, art. 1, sec. A.

127. Maria Helena Moreira Alves, *State and Opposition in Military Brazil,* 63–65; Dulles, *President Castello Branco,* 233; Brazil: *Diário oficial,* October

27, 1965, sec. 1, part 1, 11017–19, "À Nação," AI-2: art. 2, sec. 1; art. 4, parágrafo único; art. 5, secs. 1, 3; art. 6 (arts. 98, 105, sec. 3, no. e); art. 8 (art. 108, sec. 1), sec. 3; art. 9; art. 13, art. 14, parágrafo único; art. 15, parágrafo único; art. 16, secs. 1–4; art. 18, parágrafo único; art. 19, secs. 1–2; art. 31; Ato Complementar-1, art. 1, sec. 2; and November 4, 1965, sec. 1, part 1, 11305, Ato Complementar-3, art. 1, sec. A, 6.

128. Brazil, *Diário oficial,* November 22, 1965, sec. 1, part 1, 11857, Ato Complementar-4; Maria Helena Moreira Alves, *State and Opposition in Military Brazil,* 65; Anonymous-1, interview, Rio de Janeiro, February 29, 1989; and Beloch and Abreu, 2346. Still functioning in his two roles, Müller was among those passengers burned alive on July 11, 1973 when the VARIG flight he was traveling on to Paris crashed while on final approach into Orly Airport. Rose, *One of the Forgotten Things,* 113–14.

129. Maria Helena Moreira Alves, *State and Opposition in Military Brazil,* 70–74; and Brazil: *Diário oficial,* February 7, 1966, sec. 1, part 1, 1435, Ato Institucional-3, arts. 1, 4; October 20, 1966, sec. 1, part 1, 12107, Ato Complementar-23, art. 1; December 7, 1966, sec. 1, part 1, 14187, Ato Institucional-4.

130. Brazil: *Diário oficial,* February 10, 1967, sec. 1, part 1, 1657–62, law 5250; and March 13, 1967, sec. 1, part 1, 2993–95, decree 314.

131. Daniel Drosdoff, *Linha dura no Brasil: o governo Médici, 1969–1974,* Norberto de Paula Lima (trans.) (São Paulo: Global, 1986), 52. In March 1970, Richard Winslow, a USAID operative, suggested that "Funds may not be going for 'economic development,' but 'to increase the efficiency of [Brazil's] oppressive police force.'" *Commonweal,* April 24, 1970, 140–41.

132. Drosdoff, 51.

133. Ibid., 52; Moraes Neto, 240–43; Skidmore, *The Politics of Military Rule in Brazil,* 49–51, 58–60, 328n; Dulles, *President Castello Branco,* 279–314; Beloch and Abreu, 3147; *Jornal do Brasil,* July 26, 1966, sec. 1, 1, 3; *Correio da Manhã,* July 26, 1966, sec. 1, 1, 12; *Última Hora,* July 25, 1966, 2; and PPARJ, document, "Informações atualizadas," June 18, 1964, 1–2, comunismo/pasta 81

134. Peter Flynn, *Brazil: A Political Analysis* (Bolder: Westview, 1978), 376.

135. Ibid., 378; and Beloch and Abreu, *loc. cit.*

136. Beloch and Abreu, 2614, 3304–5, 3148; Skidmore, *The Politics of Military Rule in Brazil,* 67; and Flynn, 379–82.

137. Flynn, 421. At the conclusion of the *golpe,* Gama e Silva was made minister of both justice and education. In these capacities, he was "preparing to have troops close down the University of Brasília and expel those who had turned the university into what he called 'a Communist hotbed.' He favored closing down Congress and instituting a drastic cleanup to put Brazil into a condition that he felt would allow it later to renew democratic ways fully."

Dulles, *Unrest in Brazil,* 355. When Castelo Branco took office, Gama e Silva was replaced. Later, after consulting with his cousin and then-war minister, Costa e Silva, Gama e Silva wrote out a bill that he hoped would be accepted by the government, which, for its part, was in the process of putting together AI-2. His proposal called for the closing of both state and national legislatures, in addition to the installation of what would have amounted to permanent federal intervention in each state. Percival de Souza, 197; Dulles, *President Castello Branco,* 185–86; and Luís Viana Filho, *O governo Castelo Branco* (Rio de Janeiro: José Olympio, 1975), 351.

138. Dickson Grael, *Aventura, corrupção e terrorismo: à sombra da impunidade* (Petrópolis: Vozes, 1986), 23–78.

Chapter 4. The Battle Joined

1. *Pif Paf* (Rio de Janeiro), August 27, 1964, 21

2. Lacerda, *Depoimento,* 386–87; PPARJ, document, "Informe no. 329, SI 66," October 10, 1966, secreto/pasta 12; Beloch and Abreu, 1389; and Zuenir Ventura, *1968: o ano que não terminou* (Rio de Janeiro: Nova Fronteira, 1988), 129.

3. Beloch and Abreu, 1387–89.

4. Ibid.; Skidmore, *The Politics of Military Rule in Brazil,* 68–73; Maria Helena Moreira Alves, *State and Opposition in Military Brazil,* 50–51, 91–93; Flynn, 397–400; and Brazil, *Diário oficial,* April 5, 1968, sec. 1, part 1, 2308, directive 177-GB, arts. 1–2.

5. Issued as Decree-Law 5452 on May 1, 1943, Labor Day—but far from it in *Estado Novo* Brazil—the original measure can be seen it its entirety in Brazil, *Consolidação das leis do trabalho* (Rio de Janeiro: Nacional, 1946).

6. Maria Helena Moreira Alves, *State and Opposition in Military Brazil,* 85–91.

7. According to Ibrahim, the VPR was first formed, although nameless, in March 1968. Arquidiocese de São Paulo, *Perfil dos atingidos,* 57; Gorender, 144; and José Ibrahim in Antônio Caso (ed.), *A esquerda armada no Brasil, 1967–1971,* Thiago de Mello (trans.) (Lisbon: Moraes, 1976), 80.

8. Maria Helena Moreira Alves, *State and Opposition in Military Brazil,* 85–91, 182–91.

9. *Jornal da Tarde* (São Paulo), May 2, 1968, 6–7, 20; and PPARJ, document, "Extra—São Paulo por dentro do Francisco Eugênio Santiago," May 3, 1968, secreto/pasta 19.

10. Brazil, *Diário oficial,* June 14, 1968, sec. 1, part 1, 4857, law 5451, arts. 4, 7.

11. PPARJ, newspaper article, *Unidade Proletária* (Rio de Janeiro), December [no day], 1975, supplement 9, comunismo/pasta 144; *Fatos e Fotos,* May 17, 1968, 8–13; Ibrahim, 63–66, 68–89, 77–78; Gorender, 142–45; Maria Helena Moreira Alves, *State and Opposition in Military Brazil, loc. cit.;* Skidmore, *The Politics of Rule in Military Brazil,* 76–79; and Francisco Correa Weffort, *Participação e conflito industrial: Contagem e Osasco, 1968* (São Paulo: CEBRAP, 1972), 79–80; and *The Nation,* March 17, 1971, 340.

12. *Encyclopædia Britannica,* 15th ed. (Chicago: Encyclopædia Britannica, 1994), Micropædia, vol. XIII, 1809. Later encyclicals, such as *Humanae Vitae* (1968), would show a different kind of Pope Paul VI.

13. PPARJ, identity card, "*Dom* Adherbal Franco Moraes," March 14, 1966, secreto/pasta 46.

14. Beloch and Abreu, 552; Thomas Bruneau, "Conflict and Change in the Brazilian Catholic Church," unpublished Ph.D. diss., Department of Political Science, University of California, Berkeley, 1970, 319; and Kevin Neuhouser, "The Radicalization of the Brazilian Catholic Church in Comparative Perspective," *American Sociological Review,* vol. LIV, no. 2, April 1989, 237.

15. (Anonymous), "Nova questão religiosa?" *Paz e Terra,* vol. I, no. 2, September 1966, 248–49. This important article is really a collection of commentaries beginning with the communiqué of the Catholic Workers Action Organization, the bishops' agreement with this declaration, a message from Northeastern bishops after their remarks were banned, part of the condemnation of Dom Hélder by the commander of the 4th Army, and other related statements. Included (269–72) is Câmara's reply to Gilberto Freyre. Freyre had insinuated that the archbishop was a Fascist and a tool of the Communists. Bruneau, 321. For the full text of the eminent sociologist's invective, see *Diario de Pernambuco* (Recife), August 21, 1966, 4. It should be added that Freyre was on good terms with at least the first of the post-1964 military dictators. Page, 218.

16. Bruneau, 315–18.

17. Bruneau, 319–20; and Beloch and Abreu, 887.

18. Leonardo Boff and Clodovis Boff, *Da libertação: o sentido teológico das libertações sócio-históricas* (Petrópolis: Vozes, 1979), 26–27.

19. Flynn, 409. No one was injured.

20. Ibid., 407, 409, 465n; and *Jornal do Brasil,* May 21, 1989, sec. 1, 1, 15.

21. Marcio Moreira Alves, *A Grain of Mustard Seed,* 145.

22. Reis Filho and Moraes, 21.

23. Flynn, 408.

24. PPARJ: documents: "Encaminhamento no. 102/ARSI/GB/DSI/MEC/71," December 29, 1971, 1–2, comunismo/pasta 137; "Infiltração no meio artís-

tico," August 28, 1967, 2, secreto/pasta 15; Percival de Souza, 26; Maria Isabel Pinto Ventura, 77; Anonymous-1, interview, Rio de Janeiro, April 2, 1993; and Anonymous-3, interview, Rio de Janeiro, August 1, 2001.

25. Maria Isabel Pinto Ventura, 73, 180; Percival de Souza, 370; Beloch and Abreu, 842, 2319; *O Estado de São Paulo,* February 24, 1988, 7; Canada, "James M. Weld to the Under-Secretary of State for External Affairs, Ottawa;" and Arquidiocese de São Paulo, "O regime militar," Projeto "Brasil: nunca mais," 77. For a partial list of other productions the military did not care for once they took over, see Zuenir Ventura, 94–96. One of the plays that were blacklisted, Tennessee Williams's *A Streetcar Named Desire,* helped to provoke a strike by intellectuals of various stripes. The names of these people are given in Zuenir Ventura, 95.

26. Maria Isabel Pinto Ventura, 59–60; Zuenir Ventura, 90–92, 229–37; Percival de Souza, 380; Reis Filho and Moraes, 20; Carlos A. L. Salum, "Chico Barque: uma história em 4 tempos: poeta, ídolo, vilão, profeta," *Vilão & Guitarra MPB,* vol. I, no. 7, 1981, 10–11; *Correio da Manhã,* July 20, 1968, sec. 1, 5; and *O Estado de São Paulo,* July 19, 1968, 11. An interesting accounting of the censorship process of *Roda viva* is presented in *Jornal do Brasil,* June 9, 1990, sec. Caderno B, 5.

27. Regina Zappa, *Chico Buarque: para todos,* 4th ed. (Rio de Janeiro: Relume Dumará, 1999), 82.

28. PPARJ, letter, "Joaquim Miguel Vieira Ferreira to Adauto Esmeraldo," March 24, 1955, comunismo/pasta 70.

29. "Para não dizer que não falei das flores," composed by Geraldo Vandré [Geraldo Pedrosa de Araújo Dias], 1968. Vandré's own story on what really happened is given in *News from Brazil* (Los Angeles), June 16–30, 1992, 14.

30. *O Cruzeiro,* October 19, 1968, 24.

31. Zuenir Ventura, 206.

32. PPARJ: documents: "DSIEC/SEP/Ofício confidencial no. 6/circular," September 8, 1969, 1–2, secreto/pasta 50; "Informação no. 541," October 1, 1968, 1–2, secreto/pasta 31; and letter, "Mario Borges to José Pereira de Vasconcellos," October 7, 1968, 1–2, comunismo/pasta 87. The handbills can be found in PPARJ, document, "CARIOCAS," [no date], comunismo/pasta 87.

33. Skidmore, *The Politics of Military Rule in Brazil,* 74.

34. Brazil, *Diário oficial,* November 11, 1964, sec. 1, part 1, 10169–71.

35. PPARJ, document, "Informe no. 3322/SNI/ARJ (SS 17/853/20 out 64)," October 20, 1964, 1, secreto/pasta 5; and *New York Times,* October 21, 1964, 73. Note that the official rate of exchange was used to convert the salary figure.

36. PPARJ, "Informe no. 3322/SNI/ARJ (SS 17/853/20 out 64)," October 20, 1964, 2.

37. Reis Filho and Moraes, 12.

38. Beloch and Abreu, 708; Reis Filho and Moraes, 13; and Gabeira, *O que é isso companheiro?*, 60.

39. PPARJ, document, "Centro de Informações da Marinha, Informe no. 0686," May 20, 1966, secreto/pasta 8; John W. F. Dulles, "The Case Against the Vargas Regime (1930–1945): Adventures of Sobral Pinto, the Conscience of Brazil," pre-publication manuscript, ii; and Beloch and Abreu, 712. Within a month, still more graffiti appeared. PPARJ, letter, "Luiz Guimenez Neves to chief of S.O.P. [Secção Ordem Política]," June 13, 1966, secreto/pasta 8.

40. Anonymous-1, interview, Rio de Janeiro, June 9, 1989; and Zuenir Ventura, 216.

41. LBJPL, NSF Co Brazil, boxes 11–12, vol. VI, 12/65–3/67, document 61, sec. 3, no. 18.

42. Beloch and Abreu, 23; Skidmore, *The Politics of Military Rule in Brazil*, 75; and Elinor Brito, Vladimir Palmeira, and José Dirceu de Oliveira in Reis Filho and Moraes, 109, 134–35, 158. Note the interesting comments of student leader Jean Marc van der Weid (Reis Filho and Moraes, 119–20) concerning MEC-USAID plans. The idea was to start the privatization process with small fees, which would no doubt have been raised later. Only 1 percent of all children who had begun elementary school were entering Brazil's universities by 1968. Langguth, 150.

43. Reis Filho and Moraes, 50, 201–4; Vladimir Palmeira and Elinor Brito in Reis Filho and Moraes, 106, 155–57; and Zuenir Ventura, 43, 134.

44. PPARJ, letter, "Deuteronomio Rocha dos Santos to José Pereira de Vasconcellos," July 1, 1968, 2, secreto/pasta 24; and Elinor Brito in Reis Filho and Moraes, 156–57.

45. PPARJ, document, "Centro de Informações da Marinha, Informe no. 0566," May 9, 1967, secreto/pasta 8.

46. PPARJ: documents: "Pedido de busca no. 56/SP," January 22, 1968, secreto/pasta 28; "Operação Limpeza," September 13, 1967, secreto/pasta 14; "Pichamento de muro," September 19–20, 1967, secreto/pasta 14; "Detidos—F.M.I.," [no date], secreto/pasta 14; "Estudantes detidos,"[no date], secreto/pasta 14; letter, "Darcy Schettino Rocha to José Pombo Pereira Filho," September 30, 1967, 1, secreto/pasta 14; *Jornal do Brasil:* September 21, 1967, sec. 1, 16; and September 22, 1967, sec. 1, 5.

47. Vladimir Palmeira in Reis Filho and Moraes, 99–101; Skidmore, *The Politics of Military Rule in Brazil*, 74; and Luiz Henrique Romagnoli and Tânia Gonçalves (eds.), "Das ruas, com o povo, à clandestinidade," *História imediata: a volta da UNE: de Ibiúna a Salvador* (São Paulo: Alfa-Omega, 1979), vol. V, 8. A slightly different reason in the student's refusal to give up

the body of their fallen colleague (i.e., that they decided to keep it so that no one could claim that he was merely missing) is given in Gabeira, *O que é isso companheiro?,* 76.

48. Elinor Brito in Reis Filho and Moraes, 163.

49. Reis Filho and Moraes, 14; Vladimir Palmeira in Reis Filho and Moraes, 103–4; Zuenir Ventura, 103–5; *Jornal do Brasil:* March 30, 1968, sec. 1, 1; March 30, 1968, sec. 1, 5, PPARJ: document, "Ministério da Marinha, Centro de Informações da Marinha, Informação no. 0345," May 29, 1968, 2, secreto/pasta 27; and letter, "Airton José Guimarães Gouget to diretor Departamento de Ordem Política [e] Social," April 9, 1968, administração/pasta 42.

50. PPARJ: identity card, "Administração Estudantes Calabouço: no. 994—Ocimar Modesto Gonçalves," December 30, 1967, secreto/pasta 24; and document, "Inqueirto no. 09/68," March 31, 1968, secreto/pasta 18.

51. Romagnoli and Gonçalves, 8–9; Maria Helena Moreira Alves, *State and Opposition in Military Brazil,* 84; *Jornal do Brasil,* March 30, 1968, sec. 1, 1–2, 16; Reis Filho and Moraes, 203; and Zuenir Ventura, 102.

52. For a day-by-day rendition of the events in the metropolitan areas involved in this cavalcade, see: Reis Filho and Moraes, 203–4; and *Jornal do Brasil,* March 30, 1968, sec. 1, 17.

53. Reis Filho and Moraes, 151–52, 203; and Zuenir Ventura, 111. Zuenir Ventura (ibid.) lists five other students as having gun shot wounds: three in Minas and two in Goiânia.

54. At least one batch of DOPS police beat a participant from the crowd in the back of their Volkswagen bus. Zuenir Ventura, 119.

55. Some 300 of these individuals—basically students—were meeting at the Metro Cinema in Copacabana. *Jornal do Brasil,* May 5, 1968, sec. 1, 1. The authorities later claimed that a total of 374 students were detained. PPARJ, document, "DI/SP/SAS—Informação no. 887," November 8, 1968, 1–2, secreto/pasta 34. Besides the Candelária service, there were masses for Édson Luís in several churches in Rio's South Zone. The people from DOPS kept everyone under observation. PPARJ, "DI/SP/SAS—Informação no. 887," 2, secreto/pasta 34.

56. Ibid., 1–3; Reis Filho and Moraes, 14–15, 203–4; and Zuenir Ventura, 115–23.

57. *Jornal do Brasil,* September 17, 1991, sec. 1, 7; and *O Globo,* September 15, 1992, sec. 1, 15.

58. Zuenir Ventura, 138–42; *Jornal do Brasil,* June 21, 1968, sec. 1, 1, 4–5, 14–15; and *Correio da Manhã,* June 21, 1968, sec. 1, 1–4.

59. Anonymous-1: interviews, Rio de Janeiro, April 26, 1989; and July 29, 1989.

60. PPARJ: documents: "Informe no. 210," August 19, 1968, secreto/pasta 28; "DI/SP/SAS—Informação no. 631," August 20, 1968, secreto/pasta 28; Reis Filho and Moraes, 16–17, 207; "Informe no. 279 CH/68," July 15, 1968, secreto/pasta 29; "DI/SP/SAS—Informação no. 701," September 6, 1968, secreto/pasta 29; letter, "Darcy Schettino Rocha to Hennio Corrêia da Silva," July 12, 1968, secreto/pasta 25; *Correio da Manhã,* June 22, 1968, sec. 1, 2–3, 5; Beloch and Abreu, 2618; Romagnoli and Gonçalves, 9; and Zuenir Ventura, 85, 133–42.

61. Zuenir Ventura, 179–80.

62. *Manchete,* April 8, 1989, 30; and Reis Filho and Moraes, 208.

63. PPARJ, document, "DI/SP/SA—Informe no. 464," June 24, 1968, secreto/pasta 26; Reis Filho and Moraes, 208–10; Marcio Moreira Alves, *A Grain of Mustard Seed,* 11; and Zuenir Ventura, 193–200.

64. Brazil, *Diario do Congresso Nacional,* September 4, 1968, sec. 1, supplement, 9.

65. Reis Filho and Moraes, 211; Skidmore, *The Politics of Military Rule in Brazil,* 79–80; Maria Helena Moreira Alves, *State and Opposition in Military Brazil,* 93–94; and Marcio Moreira Alves, *A Grain of Mustard Seed,* 11–14.

66. Beloch and Abreu, 506–7, 2318; Zuenir Ventura, 209–19; Hélio Silva, *A vez e a voz dos vencidos,* 171–83; *Jornal do Brasil:* June 27, 1991, sec. 1, 7; September 5, 1991, sec. 1, 7; Fon, 35; *Manchete,* November 28, 1992, 36–39; "Jornal da Manchete," TV Manchete, September 5, 1991; and João Luiz de Moraes, *O Calvário de Sônia Angel: uma história de terror nos porões da ditadura* (Rio de Janeiro: MEC, 1994), 10, 40. Note that Burnier went to court to ban the sale of João Luiz de Moraes's book.

67. Percival de Souza (387) points out that São Paulo's shady governor, Ademar de Barros, gave the CCC its machine guns.

68. Reis Filho and Moraes, 139–41; Zuenir Ventura, 221–25; Percival de Souza, 415; Romagnoli and Gonçalves, 10–11; *Correio da Manhã,* October 3, 1968, sec. 1, 9; *Folha de São Paulo:* October 3, 1968, sec. 1, 17; October 4, 1968, sec. 1, 12–13; *O Cruzeiro,* October 19, 1968, 120; and *Jornal do Brasil,* May 27, 1993, sec. 1, 14.

69. Gabeira, *O que é isso companheiro?,* 110; and José Dirceu de Oliveira in Reis Filho and Moraes, 139.

70. Zuenir Ventura, 185, 189, 239, 251; and PPARJ, deposition, "Saulo Garroux," April 3, 1968, secreto/pasta 15.

71. Estimates vary as to the numbers of police who invaded the UNE gathering and the exact time they commenced operations. The size of the Força Pública detachment has been placed at between 120 and 400, while those of the political police at no less than thirty and no more than eighty. As for the

hour the combined force charged in, 7 A.M. to 7:45 A.M., and a few times in between, have all be given. Zuenir Ventura, 248–49; Romagnoli and Gonçalves, 12; *Jornal do Brasil,* October 13–14, 1968, sec. 1, 1; *Correio da Manhã,* October 13, 1968, sec. 1, 1, 24; *O Cruzeiro,* October 26, 1968, 26, 31; and *Manchete,* October 26, 1968, 15.

72. PPARJ, document, "Participantes 30° congresso da UNE," [no date], comunismo/pasta 127a. The foregoing document lists 103 arrests. Names number 71 and 72, however, are duplicates. DOPS admitted that between five and ten students did escape. *Correio da Manhã,* October 13, 1968, sec. 1, 24; and *O Cruzeiro,* October 26, 1968, 29. The students clamed that around thirty of their members fled. Romagnoli and Gonçalves, 12.

73. Zuenir Ventura, 239–55; José Dirceu de Oliveira in Reis Filho and Moraes, 144–46; Romagnoli and Gonçalves, 11–12; and Percival de Souza, 100.

74. Maria Helena Moreira Alves, *State and Opposition in Military Brazil,* 94–95; Marcio Moreira Alves, *A Grain of Mustard Seed,* 22–25; *Jornal do Brasil,* April 21, 2004, B2; and Skidmore, *The Politics of Military Rule in Brazil,* 80–81. Skidmore (*The Politics of Military Rule in Brazil,* 80) points out that the Costa e Silva was not merely trying to lift Márcio Moreira Alves' immunity, but also those of another deputy, Hermano Alves (no relation), who had similar views.

75. Maria Helena Moreira Alves, *State and Opposition in Military Brazil,* 95.

76. Brazil, *Diário oficial,* December 13, 1968, sec. 1, part 1, 10801, Ato Institucional No. 5, de 13 dezembro de 1968.

77. Brazil, *Diário oficial,* December 13, 1968, sec. 1, part 1, 10801–2, Ato Institucional No. 5, arts. 1–11, Ato Complementar No. 38, art. 1.

78. John W. F. Dulles, e-mails: August 16, 2000; and April 7, 2003.

79. PPARJ, letter, "Maria Cristina Lacerda to Arthur da Costa e Silva," December 20, 1968, secreto/pasta 39; John W. F. Dulles: e-mail, August 16, 2000; and "The Case Against the Vargas Regime," 266.

80. Skidmore, *The Politics of Military Rule in Brazil,* 82.

81. Beloch and Abreu, 950–51; Gabeira, *O que é isso companheiro?,* 40; Cícero Sandroni in *I seminário do grupo tortura nunca mais: depoimentos e debates,* Branca Eloysa (org.) (Petrópolis: Vozes, 1987), 38, 41–42; and Drosdoff, 82–83.

82. PPARJ, "DSIEC/SEP/Ofício confidencial no. 6/circular," *loc. cit.,* secreto/pasta 50; Maria Helena Moreira Alves, *State and Opposition in Military Brazil,* 96–100; and Skidmore, *The Politics of Military Rule in Brazil,* 82–83.

83. *The Nation,* March 15, 1971, 338.

84. PPARJ: documents: "Pedido de busca no. [408]," October 4, 1967, secreto/pasta 19; "Pedido de busca no. 2280/SNI/ARJ/1967," September 26,

1967, secreto/pasta 34; "Refª: Prot° no. DO-359/68—Informação: no. MR-2/194/68," October 8, 1968, secreto/pasta 34; newspaper article, *Última Hora,* September 25, 1967, secreto/pasta 19; Skidmore, *The Politics of Military Rule in Brazil,* 86; and João Quartim, *Dictator and Armed Struggle in Brazil,* David Fernbach (trans.) (New York: New Left Review, 1971), 162.

85. PPARJ, document, "As Ligas Camponesas (Servico Cubano de Informação) (Carlos Todd, Red.), Coral Gables, Fla., especialmente os nos. 118, 119, 120 e 121," [no date], 1–2, comunismo/pasta 50.

86. PPARJ: documents: "As Ligas Camponesas (Servico Cubano de Informação) (Carlos Todd, Red.), Coral Gables, Fla., especialmente os nos. 118, 119, 120 e 121)," [no date], 1–2, comunismo/pasta 50; "Acción Cubana en el Brasil," June 1–15, 1963, 9–10, comunismo/pasta 79; "Cursos realizados em Cuba," November 21, 1972, 2–3, 5–21, 38–105 comunismo/pasta 115; letter, "Gerardo to Petronio," October [no day], 1962, 1–5, comunismo/pasta 50;

87. CIA, document, "TDCS-314/12799–67," August 31, 1967, 2; Skidmore, *The Politics of Military Rule in Brazil,* 121; Percival de Souza, 384–85; and *Jornal do Brasil,* July 11, 1993, sec. 1, 4. Anselmo claimed, however, that Algeria was the center for support to Brazilian revolutionary groups and not Cuba. *Jornal do Brasil,* March 27, 1994, sec. 1, 7.

88. The date pays homage to the day of Ché Guevara's death.

89. VAR-Palmares was named after the largest and most famous community of escaped slaves in colonial Brazil. Palmares existed as a semi-nation state in what is now Alagoas from about 1605 to 1694 before being crushed. R. K. Kent, "Palmares: An African State in Brazil," *Journal of African History,* vol. VI, no. 2, 1965, 165, 174; and Renato Mocellin, *A história crítica da nação brasileira,* 5th ed. (São Paulo: Editora do Brasil, 1987), 49. Other works claim slightly different dates. See for example, Abdias do Nascimento, *O quilombismo* (Petrópolis: Vozes, 1980), 47.

90. PPARJ, document, "Informe no. 25-B/73," June 27, 1973, 1–3, comunismo/pasta 119; and Percival de Souza, 99–100, 256–57.

91. LBJPL, NSF Co Brazil, boxes 11–12, vol. VII, 3/67–11/68, document 2, 2; and Moraes Neto, 219. For the Brizola tie in, see Rebello, 47, 161–65.

92. Beloch and Abreu, 2094; Brazil, Comissão Especial de Inquérito sôbre Atos Delituosos da Ditadura, "Depoimento do Carlos Marighella," *Diario do Congresso Nacional,* August 28, 1947, 5203–4; and PPARJ, document, "Histórico das atividades políticas dos parlamentares comunistas," [no date], 9, comunismo/pasta 23.

93. *Frei* Betto [Carlos Alberto Libanio Christo], *Batismo de sangue: os dominicanos e a morte de Carlos Marighella,* 2nd ed. (Rio de Janeiro: Civilização Brasileiro, 1982), 11–16; Skidmore, *The Politics of Military Rule in Brazil,*

84–86; Maria Helena Moreira Alves, *State and Opposition in Military Brazil,* 104–5; Beloch and Abreu, pp 2094–96; Carlos Marighela, *Escritos de Carlos Marighella* (São Paulo: Livramento, 1979), 5, 11; Quartim, 155–62; PPARJ, document, "[Apelidos dos dirigentes do P.C.B.]," [no date], 3, comunismo/ pasta 69; and *Correio da Manhã,* May 13, 1964, sec. 1, 14. One of these pictures is reproduced here as plate 15.

94. Arquidiocese de São Paulo, *Perfil dos atingidos,* 117.

95. An armored car robbery in Rio's Bento Ribeiro suburb, allegedly led by Carlos Marighella, is outlined in PPARJ: documents: "Assalto ao carro pagador do IPEG," November 19, 1968, secreto/pasta 34; and "DI/SP/SAS—Informação no. 893," November 11, 1968, secreto/pasta 34. A list of 23 cleared up cases attributed to leftists as of January 1969, including the quantities of money stolen in robberies, can be found in PPARJ, document, "Inquérito de subversão e terrorismo: casos esclarecidos no presente inquérito, com o consequente estabelecimento das respectivas autorais," January 23, 1969, comunismo/pasta 141.

96. *Veja,* February 4, 1970, 19–20; and *Jornal do Brasil,* July 23, 1989, sec. 1, 4. Jornal do Brasil (July 23, 1989, sec. 1, 4) spells Capriglione's name Capligioni. As for the rest of the money, see the interesting comments by Chizuo Osawa, one of the leaders of the allied VPR, in *Jornal do Brasil,* November 3, 1992, sec. 1, 4.

97. *O Globo,* July 21, 1993, sec. 2, 1; *Lamarca,* directed by Sérgio Rezende, Morena Filmes/Produção da Cinema Filmes, 1994; and Skidmore, *The Politics of Military Rule in Brazil,* 88.

98. Percival de Souza, 187, 190; Pedro Lobo de Oliveira in Caso, 160–61; Fon, 61; and PPARJ, document, "A nova téchnica da subversão," February [no day], 1969, secreto/pasta 40.

99. *Jornal do Brasil,* September 3, 1989, sec. 1, 8–9; Skidmore, *The Politics of Military Rule in Brazil,* 86–88; and Quartim, 162–67. One of the best narratives, from the perspective of one of the twelve revolutionaries who had a role in the kidnapping, can be found in Gabeira, *O que é isso companheiro?,* 137–71. Another good accounting is in *Jornal do Brasil,* September 3, 1989, sec. 1, 8–9. There's also the interesting description in Langguth (166–96).

100. Carlos Marighela, *For the Liberation of Brazil,* John Butt and Rosemary Sheed (trans.) (Middlesex: Penguin, 1971), 14. The full text of the abductors' remarks can be found in ibid., 25–27.

101. Ibid., 27.

102. *Jornal do Brasil:* September 3, 1989, sec. 1, 9; and September 17, 1989, sec. 1, 15.

103. Fernando Gabeira, interview, Rio de Janeiro, November 25, 1992.

104. Flynn, 443; *Time,* July 27, 1970, 27; Emiliano José, and Oldack Miranda, *Lamarca: o capitão da guerrilha,* 10th ed. (São Paulo: Global, 1986),

99–105; *Jornal do Brasil,* September 15, 1991, sec. 1, 16; and Lester Sobel (ed.), *Political Terrorism* (New York: Facts on File, 1975), 117.

105. Maria Helena Moreira Alves, *State and Opposition in Military Brazil,* 120. Maria Helena Moreira Alves' observations on these points are most interesting.

106. Ibid., 117.

107. Maria Helena Moreira Alves, "The Formation of the National Security State: The State and the Opposition in Military Brazil," Ph.D. diss., Department of Political Science, Massachusetts Institute of Technology, 1982, 404–10; and Percival de Souza, 18.

108. Beloch and Abreu, 509–10; and *Isto É Senhor,* July 17, 1991, 20–21.

109. *Isto É,* March 1, 1978, 6, 9.

110. Betto, 159; Gorender, 175; Gene Hanrahan, Carlos Marighella, *The Terrorist Classic: Manual of the Urban Guerrilla,* Gene Hanrahan (ed.) (Chapel Hill: Documentary, 1985), 14–15; Percival de Souza, 93–94; and *Veja,* May 9, 1979, 31–32. The accounts in *Época* (March 13, 2000, 39) and Betto (167–83), on the other hand, are at odds with these descriptions. The latter goes so far as to say that Carlos Marighella was killed elsewhere and transported to the ambush site. Percival de Souza (92–93) spells Stella's name as "Estela."

111. Beloch and Abreu, 2907; Betto, 145–53; Percival de Souza, 93–94, 245–49; and Victor Marchetti and John Marks, *The CIA and the Cult of Intelligence* (New York: Alvred Knopf, 1974), 250–51. The torture of the Dominican priests is recounted in Betto, *loc. cit.* See also the story of Frei Tito in Tortura Nunca Mais, "Tito de Alencar Lima (Frei)," <http://www.torturanuncamais.org.br/mtnm_mor/mor_mortes_exilio/mor_tito_lima.htm>, March 2, 2005.

112. *O Estado de São Paulo,* October 25, 1970, 36; and Lopes, 140.

113. PPARJ: document, "Terroristas/assaltantes," June 24, 1969 [date received], 1, secreto/pasta 46; newspaper article, *Jornal da Tarde,* June 4, 1970, 16, secreto/pasta 52; José and Miranda, 165–66; Beloch and Abreu, 1743; *Isto É,* March 1, 1978, 8; *Jornal do Brasil:* September 15, 1991, sec. 1, 16; June 17, 1993, 2nd ed., sec. Cidade, 16; June 18, 1993, sec. B, 5; *Veja,* May 9, 1979, 32; *Pasquim,* February 18–24, 1982, 5; *O Dia* (Rio de Janeiro), March 25, 1998, 15; *O Globo:* September 15, 1992, sec. 1, 15; and July 21, 1993, sec. 2, 1.

114. Percival de Souza, 237–38.

115. The only exception was a September 1972 article in *O Estado de São Paulo.*

116. Accounts vary as to the exact number. *Jornal do Brasil* (December 8, 1985, sec. 1, 29) claims that there were forty-seven rebels. *Veja* (September 6, 1978, 52) increases this number to sixty-three, while Maria Helena Moreira

Alves (*State and Opposition in Military Brazil,* 121) states that the entire group had no more than sixty-nine members.

117. Again, specialists list different numbers. The ten-thousand-man statistic comes from *Veja* (September 6, 1978, 52). In Maria Helena Moreira Alves's (*State and Opposition in Military Brazil, loc. cit.*) view, a total of 20,000 military personnel were part of the effort. Her source appears to have been one of the campaign's commanders, General Viana Moog, who commented as follows, "It was the biggest troop mobilization that the army has conducted. In fact, it was similar to the mobilization of the FEB, which fought fascism in Europe [Italy] during the Second World War." The number of fighting men in the FEB that were actually sent to Italy was 25,334. Frank McCann, *The Brazilian-American Alliance, 1937–1945* (Princeton: Princeton University Press, 1973), 430; and Dulles, *Vargas of Brazil,* 241. The twenty-six-thousand estimate comes from the Comitê Brasileiro pela Anista (*Desaparecidos políticos: artigos, entrevistas, documentos, reportagens, depoimentos, fotografias* [Rio de Janeiro: Opção, 1979], 261).

118. Maria Isabel Pinto Ventura, 52, 66; *Jornal do Brasil:* November 22, 1985, sec. 1, 4; December 8, 1985, sec. 1, 29; September 7, 2001, sec. 1, 4; and PPARJ, document, "Comunicado no. 8 das forças guerrilheiras do Araguaia," [July 1974], comunismo/pasta 140.

119. *Veja,* September 6, 1978, 52–58; Clóvis Moura, *Diário da guerrilha do Araguaia* (São Paulo: Alfa-Omega, 1979), 50, 59–60; Percival de Souza, 158; and Comitê Brasileiro pela Anista, 262.

120. The political police in São Paulo had their name changed to DEOPS (Departamento Estadual de Ordem Política e Social, or the State Department of Political and Social Order) through state decree 52213 on July 24, 1969. Guedo Fonseca, "DOPS: pouco do seu história," *Revista da associação dos delagados da polícia,* ano X, no. 28, December 1989, 79.

121. Rebello, 54.

122. Ibid.

123. Fon, 54–55; Arquidiocese de São Paulo, "O regime militar," Projeto "Brasil: nunca mais," 72; Langguth, 160, 122–23; Percival de Souza, pp 7–14, 163, 172, 215, 388; and Maria Isabel Pinto Ventura, 41, 57, 179. Boilesen is spelled Boilensen by some authors.

124. Arquidiocese de São Paulo, "O regime militar," Projeto "Brasil: nunca mais," 71–72.

125. *Folha de São Paulo,* October 24, 1999, sec. 1, 16; and *Veja,* November 18, 1992, 22–32. The material cited in *Veja* was made available by one of the first members of a torture unit to break ranks. Former sergeant Marival Dias Chaves do Canto's job was to analyze and compare the information collected in torture sessions.

126. *Veja,* November 18, 1992, 22–32; and Percival de Souza, 179–93, 409.

127. The São Paulo Força Pública changed its name to the Polícia Militar on April 8, 1970.

128. *Veja,* February 21, 1979, 62, 68; and *Jornal do Brasil,* December 16, 1992, sec. 1, 6.

129. *Veja,* November 18, 1992, 27–28.

130. Beloch and Abreu, 1459–60; and *Folha de São Paulo,* March 12, 2000, sec. 1, 10.

131. How a large part of this grim accounting came to be available, it was condensed into the *Brasil nunca mais* volumes, is explained in the first part of Weschler. Were it not for such brave individuals as the Archbishop of São Paulo, Cardinal Dom Paulo Evaristo Arns, Minister Jaime Wright, and a host of others, much of this material would still be locked in military archives if not destroyed completely.

132. Note especially the comments on this presented in Juan de Onis, "Brazil on the Tightrope toward Democracy," *FA,* vol. LXVIII, no. 4, Fall 1989, 137–42.

133. PPARJ, "Brasileiros!"comunismo/pasta 90; Maria Isabel Pinto Ventura, 56, 65; Beloch and Abreu, 2479; *Jornal do Brasil:* November 22, 1985, sec. 1, 4; and October 10, 1994, sec. Cidade, 14. Luiz Lima's middle name is given as Timóteo, Timote, and Timotheo, respectively, in the first three sources cited. He is listed (*Veja,* December 9, 1998, 52) as being tied for seventh position on the list of those most accused of torture during the dictatorship. Francisco Moacyr Mayer Fontinelli is placed in a tie for fourteenth on this same accounting. Juvenal Antunes Pereira also tortured at the Vila Militar in Rio.

134. This was the location of one of the most detested DOI-Codi torture centers in Rio during the military dictatorship. It was known by a number of names, such as "*Casa do medo,*" ("House of Fear"), "*Casa do terror,*" ("House of Terror"), and "*Usina do terror*" ("Factory of Terror"). *Jornal do Brasil,* November 11, 1992, 2nd ed., sec. 1, 16.

135. Lobo, 27–28.

136. *Veja,* November 18, 1992, 29; and *Jornal do Brasil,* April 24, 1987, sec. B, 1. The revelation of what happened to Paiva's body was made by Amílcar Lobo on the radio ("Encontro com a imprensa," Radio Jornal do Brasil [Rio de Janeiro], April 23, 1987) and confirmed by Marival Dias Chaves do Canto in *Veja.*

137. Skidmore, *The Politics of Military Rule in Brazil,* 130; and *Veja,* October 30, 1991, 22.

138. Maria Helena Moreira Alves, *State and Opposition in Military Brazil,* 241.

139. Elio Gaspari, *A ditadura derrotada: o sacerdote e o feiticeiro* (São Paulo: Companhia das Letras, 2003), 324.

140. Maria Helena Moreira Alves, *State and Opposition in Military Brazil,* 142–47.

141. Kenneth Serbin, "The Anatomy of a Death: Repression, Human Rights and the Case of Alexandre Vannucchi Leme in Authoritarian Brazil," *Journal of Latin American Studies* [hereafter *JLAS*], vol. XXX, part I, February 1998, 2–3; Fernando Jordão, *Dossiê Herzog: prisão, tortura e morte no Brasil,* 3rd ed. (São Paulo: Global, 1979), 185; *Jornal do Brasil:* November 22, 1985, sec. 1, 4; August 13, 1992, sec. 1, 8; *Veja,* November 18, 1992, 29, 31; and *Isto É Senhor,* March 25, 1992, 20–26. The 2nd Army tried to pass off a fake confession by Herzog to the effect that he had been a PCB militant since 1971 or 1972. Jordão, 184. Note as well the remarks (Jordão, *loc. cit.*) by Maurício Azedo concerning his experiences with the Dragon's Chair. Strapped into one in the neighboring state of Rio de Janeiro, Azedo had heard his torturers joke among themselves, "Let's Herzog him," before turning on the current. The device, obviously, had been given the expression by those in the know.

142. For the government's version, see: *Folha de São Paulo:* October 27, 1975, 3; October 28, 1975, 3; *O Estado de São Paulo,* October 28, 1975, 21–23; and *Ex-15* (São Paulo), November 1975, 33–40. The essay in *Ex-* also presents the story of Vladimir's execution from the point of view of his colleagues. Observe that one month later, the entire issue of *Ex-16* (the numbers indicate the issue) was confiscated because it contained a story on the Herzog murder that the dictators' censors found insulting. PPARJ: document, "Informação no. 0738/75," December 2, 1975, comunismo/pasta 144; and newspaper article, *Jornal do Brasil,* December 2, 1975, [no page], comunismo/pasta 144.

143. Weschler, 26.

144. Maria Helena Moreira Alves, *State and Opposition in Military Brazil,* 157–58.

145. Skidmore, *The Politics of Military Rule in Brazil,* 177–78.

146. Carlos Alberto Luppi, *Manoel Fiel Filho: quem vai pagar por este crime?* (São Paulo: Escrita, 1980), 22. He was said to be distributing the party's newspaper, *Voz Operária,* to fellow workers at his Metal Arte job.

147. Ibid., 64, 111.

148. Ibid., 111; and Percival de Souza, 209.

149. Luppi, 111–12.

150. Ibid., 65–67, 111–12.

151. Ibid., 16; PPARJ: letter, "Alex Polari de Alverga, *et al.,* to conselho federal da Ordem dos Advogados do Brasil," November 24, 1976, comunismo/pasta 149; and document, "Informação no. S-072/76/JSPDN," December 12, 1976, 6, comunismo/pasta 149. Percival de Souza comments

(202, 205) on the torture and suicide of a left-leaning member of the Polícia Militar, Lieutenant José Ferreira de Almeida, on July 8, 1975. According to Percival de Souza, Ferreira de Almeida's death kicked off a virtual witch-hunt for progressives within the Polícia Militar.

152. Skidmore, *The Politics of Military Rule in Brazil,* 177–78; and Stepan, *Rethinking Military Politics,* 39.

153. Skidmore, *The Politics of Military Rule in Brazil,* 183–84. Dom Adriano was noted for his liberationist views. See, as example, the comments of a government agent who witnessed a mass given by the bishop in PPARJ, document, "Informação no. 02213 DARQ/DGIE," June 23, 1976, comunismo/ pasta 146. A one-time member of the group that abducted Dom Adriano and touched off the bomb was Freddie Perdigão Pereira. *Jornal do Brasil,* May 25, 2000, sec. 1, 10.

154. *Folha de São Paulo,* October 24, 1999, sec. 1, 16; and *Jornal do Brasil,* May 25, 2000, sec. 1, 10.

155. *Movimento* (São Paulo): May 19–25, 1980, 12–13; May 26-June 1, 1980, 4–5; *Em Tempo* (São Paulo): March 20-April 2, 1980, 13; April 3–16, 1980, 11; May 1–14, 1980, 13; *Companheiro* (São Paulo), April 23-May 6, 1980, 8; Partido dos Trabalhadores, Comunicado à imprensa da Secretaria Nacional de Imprensa e Propaganda do PT, August 14, 1980; and Vito Giannotti, e-mail, February 6, 2004.

156. *New York Times:* March 30, 1978, A1, A3; April 1, 1978, 3; and Albert Fishlow, "Flying Down to Rio: Perspectives on U.S.-Brazil Relations," *FA,* vol. LVII, no. 2, Winter 1978/79, 387.

157. Lobo, 39–40.

158. Ibid. Figueiredo denied everything. "Jornal Nacional," TV Globo, May 19, 1988. But see in this regard, *Veja,* November 25, 1987, 8. Rubens Paim Sampaio recounted for Lobo that he personally murdered at least one person in the Petrópolis death house. *Folha de São Paulo,* March 12, 2000, sec. 1, 10. Later promoted to the rank of general, José Luís Coelho Neto was said to have been the mastermind behind the bombing at Riocentro. Freddie Perdigão Pereira was implicated in the plot. *Folha de São Paulo,* October 24, 1999, sec. 1, 16. Other sources (*Jornal do Brasil,* May 5, 2000, sec. 1, 6) claim that Freddie Perdigão was the author of the bombing.

159. Victor Civita (ed.), *Nosso século, 1960–1980: sob as ordens de Brasília* (São Paulo: Abril Cultural, 1986), part II. vol. X, 158; *Veja,* May 1, 1991, 60, 66; and "Jaguar," interview [via Maria Tereza Viana de Freitas Corujo], Rio de Janeiro, July 26, 1991. There were, of course, other bombs in earlier years, twenty in 1968 alone just in Rio de Janeiro. *Folha de São Paulo,* October 24, 1999, sec. 1, 16.

160. *Veja,* May 1, 1991, 62; *Jornal do Brasil:* September 24, 1985, sec. 1, 7; September 7, 1987, sec. 1, 4; and *Folha de São Paulo,* September 28, 1987, A-5. Probably the two best descriptions of all the kidnappings and bombings, especially Riocentro and its immediate aftermath, are given in *Veja* (May 1, 1991, 60–73) and by Maria Helena Moreira Alves (*State and Opposition in Military Brazil,* 221–23). In 1999, then-colonel Wilson Machado was finally indicted for the crime. *O Globo,* September 19, 1999, 1, 3. As of this writing, the case is still pending.

161. As Maria Helena Moreira Alves (*State and Opposition in Military Brazil,* 211–12) points out, the Amnesty Bill of 1979 was a compromise measure, granting amnesty to political opponents who were not involved in so-called blood crimes. Other categories of offenders were excluded or slowed up in the judicial process, as were future prisoners of conscience.

162. Luís Carlos Prestes, interview, Rio de Janeiro, Aug. 13, 1987; and Anita Leocadia Prestes and Lygia Prestes, interview, Rio de Janeiro, April 17, 2004.

Chapter 5. The Real Rural Bandits

1. Federico Pernambucano de Mello, *Guerreiros do sol: o banditismo no nordeste do Brasil* (Recife: Massangana, 1985), 222–24; Júlio J. Chiavenato, *Cangaço: a força do coronel* (São Paulo: Brasiliense, 1990), 30–31; Chandler, 233; and *Jornal do Brasil,* May 11, 1986, B/Especial, 8.

2. Candance Slater, "Messianism and the Padre Cicero Stories," *Luso-Brazilian Review* [hereafter *LBR*], vol. XXVIII, no. 1, Summer 1991, 118; Henry Keith, "Soldiers as Saviors: the Brazilian Military Revolts of 1922 and 1924 in Historical Perspective," unpublished PhD thesis, Department of History, University of California, Berkeley, 1970, 231; and Levine, Robert, "Mud-Hut Jerusalem: Canudos Revisited," *Hispanic American Historical Review,* vol. LXVIII, no. 3, August 1988, 564. This chapter is an extension of the thinking presented in Rose, *Beyond the Pale of Pity,* chapters 2 and 3.

3. One might make the exact opposite case for the absence of Sebastianism in the official form of Brazilian Catholicism.

4. Maria Isaura Pereira de Queiroz, *O messianismo: no Brasil e no mundo* (São Paulo: Dominus, 1965), 139–364; Robert Levine, "Editor's Introduction: The Millenarian and Messianic Legacy," *LBR,* vol. XXVIII, no. 1, Summer 1991, 1–3; Patricia Pessar, "Three Moments in Brazilian Millenarianism: The Interrelationship between Politics and Religion," *LBR,* vol. XXVIII, no. 1, Summer 1991, 95; Carole Myscofski, "Messianic Themes in Portuguese and Brazilian Literature in the Sixteenth and Seventeenth Centuries," *LBR,* vol.

XXVIII, no. 1, Summer 1991, 77–91; and *Folha de São Paulo,* October 25, 1999, sec. 8, 6.

5. Sources: Lopes, *loc. cit.;* Brazil: Secretaria de Planejamento, *Anuuário estatístico do Brasil, 1982* (Rio de Janeiro: IBGE, 1986), 121; and Secretaria de Planejamento, *Anuário estatístico do Brasil, 1985* (Rio de Janeiro, IBGE, 1986) 121.

6. A beato is a religiously active layperson who has made vows of chastity and who has no profession. *Beatos* (*beatas* for women) lived off of charity. Xavier de Oliveira, *Beatos e cangaceiros* (Rio de Janeiro: Revista dos Tribunais, 1920), 39.

7. *Veja,* April 24, 1996, 40.

8. Ibid.

9. Mino Carta and Raimundo Rodrigues Pereira (dirs.), *Retrado do Brasil (da monarquia ao estado militar)* (São Paulo: Política Editora, 1984), vol. I, 92; and Beloch and Abreu, 3244–47.

10. Gilberto Freyre, *The Masters and the Slaves: A Study in the Development of Brazilian Civilization,* Samuel Putnam (trans.), 2nd ed. (New York: Alfred Knopf, 1966), 48n, 66n-67n; Henriques, vol. I, 53; Francisco Julião, "The Practice and Preaching of Revolution," *Revolution in Brazil: Politics and Society in a Developing Nation,* Irving Horowitz (ed.) (New York: E. P. Dutton, 1964), 35n; Peter Singelmann, "Political Structure and Social Banditry in Northeastern Brazil," *JLAS,* vol. VII, no. 1, May 1975, 61; and Jorge Amado, *The Violent Land,* Samuel Putnam (trans.), 4th ed. (New York: Avon, 1979), 189, 220, 275–76.

11. Americas Watch, *Rural Violence in Brazil* (New York and Washington, DC: Human Rights Watch, 1991), 23; Sebastião Barbosa, *Brasil: o país da impunidade* (São Paulo: Siciliano, 1991), 160; and *Veja,* May 21, 1986, 32.

12. Alex Shoumatoff, *The World is Burning* (Boston: Little, Brown, 1990), 94.

13. Ibid., 95.

14. Arquivo Filinto Müller, biography, "Lindolfo Collor," 1937, CPDOC, 1–3, 5–6; and *Fresno Bee* (Fresno, CA), May 8, 1999, A-7.

15. Sebastião Barbosa, *loc. cit.* Winners of the 1991 Alternative Nobel Prize, the Comissão Pastoral da Terra is connected to the Catholic Church's CNBB. Ecumenical, its members come from a number of different religions. It was created in 1975 to deal with land conflicts in Brazil.

16. Sebastião Barbosa, 162.

17. *Veja,* May 21, 1986, 31; and "The Decade of Destruction," directed by Adrian Cowell, "Killing for Land," episode 2, PBS TV, September 22, 1990.

18. Shoumatoff, 95–96.

19. *Jornal do Brasil,* August 29, 1999, sec. 1, 12. Of the five incarcerated mandantes, at least two escaped from detention. This included Darli Alves da

Silva. Comissão Pastoral da Terra [hereafter CPT], *Relação dos julgamentos—Tribunal do júri de assassinatos de trabalhadores rurais, índios, advogados e agentes pastorais de 01 de janeiro de 1964 a 31 de dezembro de 1993* (Goiânia: CPT, 1994), 6–8.

20. CPT, *Relação dos julgamentos—Tribunal do júri de assassinatos de trabalhadores rurais, índios, advogados e agentes pastorais de 01 de janeiro de 1964 a 31 de dezembro de 1993*, 1–9.

21. Ibid., 31–32; and *O Globo*, January 15, 1989, 18. *Veja* (May 21, 1986, 31–32) reports that some assassins were themselves murdered following a job so they would not give their employers problems later.

22. *O Globo:* January 14, 1989, 22; and January 15, 1989, 18.

23. Sources: *Ciência Hoje* (Rio de Janeiro), January-February 1987, supplement, 8; CPT: *Conflitos no campo Brasil/85* ([no place: no publisher, no date]), quadro 11; *Conflitos no campo Brasil/86* ([no place: no publisher, no date]), 32–37; *Conflitos no campo Brasil/87* ([no place]: Comsaude, 1988), 34–40; *Conflitos no campo Brasil/88* (Goiânia: CPT, 1989), 50–52; *Conflitos no campo Brasil/89* (Goiânia: CPT, 1990), 44–47; *Espinhoso caminho para a liberdade: conlitos no campo Brasil—1990* (Goiânia: CPT, 1991), quadro 6; *Conflitos no campo—Brasil/1991* (Goiânia: CPT, 1992), quadro 6; *Conflitos no campo Brasil' 92* (Goiânia: CPT, 1993), [80–81]; *Conflitos no campo Brasil 93* (Goiânia: CPT, 1994), 43–44; *Conflitos no campo Brasil 94* (Goiânia: CPT, 1995), 47–48; *Conflitos no campo Brasil 95* (Goiânia: CPT, 1996), 35–36; *Conflitos no campo Brasil 96* (Goiânia: CPT, 1997), 45–46; *Conflitos no campo Brasil 97* (Goiânia: CPT, 1998), 68; *Conflitos no campo Brasil 98* (Goiânia: CPT, 1999), 66–67; and *Conflitos no campo Brasil 99* (Goiânia: CPT, 2000), 68, 70.

24. *Jornal do Brasil,* April 24, 1994, sec. 1, 14; and "The Decade of Destruction."

25. *Jornal do Brasil,* December 8, 1985, sec. 1, 28.

26. *Jornal do Brasil:* "Religioso foi mártir," <http://jbonline.terra.com.br/destaques/campo/campo_1412b.html>, December 22, 2001; "Mandante de assassinato é localizado," <http://jbonline.terra.com.br/destaques/campo/campo_1412.html>, December 22, 2001; "Denúncia do JB põe acusado na prisão," <http://jbonline.terra.com.br/destaques/campo/campo_1512.html>, December 22, 2001; and "Acusado nega ser mandante," <http://jbonline.terra.com.br/destaques/campo/campo_1712.html>, December 22, 2001.

27. *Jornal do Brasil,* December 8, 1985, sec. 1, 28.

28. A check of the "Indícios de autoria" columns of the CPT's *Conflitos no campo Brasil,* for the three crimes in question, corroborates the joint actions of the police, the elite, and other enforcers.

29. Sources: CPT: *Conflitos no campo* [all editions], *loc. cit.*

30. A photograph of one Polícia Militar in action in rural Rio de Janeiro can be seen here in plate 28. It is contrasted with slaves and police in the 1820s in Rio de Janeiro depicted by Jean Debret (here plate 27). The latter can be found in Debret, vol. II, 140 and plate 45.

31. Sources: CPT: *Conflitos no campo* [all editions], *loc. cit.;* Movimento dos Trabalhadores Rurais Sem-Terra, 23–487, 505–15, 525–30, 547–53; *Ciência Hoje,* January-February 1987, supplement, 7; Amnesty International, *Brazil: Authorized Violence in Rural Areas* (London: Amnesty International, 1988), 6; and Arquidiocese de São Paulo, *Brasil: nunca mais,* 291–93.

32. There are several books in English about the death of Mendes. In addition to Shoumatoff, two good sources are Andrew Revkin, *The Burning Season: The Murder of Chico Mendes and the Fight for the Amazon Rain Forest* (Boston: Houghton Mifflin, 1990); and Adrian Cowell, *The Decade of Destruction: The Crusade to Save the Amazon Rain Forest* (New York: Holt, 1990). This last work was made into a TV production. Also useful is Duncan Green (ed.), *Fight for the Forest: Chico Mendes in His Own Words,* Chris Whitehouse (trans.) (London: Latin America Bureau, 1989). There are a multitude of reports in Portuguese. One of the best summations, which came out just before the judgment in the case, can be found in *Jornal do Brasil,* December 9, 1990, sec. Especial, 1–8.

33. Shoumatoff, 103–4; *Veja,* December 12, 1990, 34; and Brazil, Senado, "A morte anunciada," <http://www.senado.gov.br/web/senador/marinasi/chmende4.htm>, March 21, 2002. Shoumatoff goes on to suggest (147, 151, 247) a broader plot in Mendes' death.

34. Americas Watch, *Rural Violence in Brazil,* 44.

35. Shoumatoff, 107; and *Veja,* December 12, 1990, 35.

36. *Veja,* December 12, 1990, 32–33; and *Jornal do Brasil,* November 22, 1985, sec. 1, 4.

37. *Jornal do Brasil,* December 15, 1990, sec .1, 1, 5.

38. Francisco Alves Filho, interview, Rio de Janeiro, December 23, 1992; Malu Maranhão, telephone interview, Rio de Janeiro/Goiânia, October 15, 1999; *Folha de São Paulo,* August, 9, 1995, sec. 1, 9; *Jornal do Brasil:* February 17, 1993, sec. 1, 7; February 18, 1993, sec. 1, 7; March 17, 1993, sec. 1, 8; March 24, 1993, sec. 1, 7; *New York Times,* February 29, 1992, 4; *Los Angeles Times,* November 26, 1996, A10; CPT-Acre Archives [hereafter CPTAA]: newspaper articles: *A Gazeta* (Rio Branco), January 1, 1994; January 13, 1994; March 2, 1994; July 7, 1995; November 26, 1996; *O Rio Branco* (Rio Branco), January 11, 1995; January 20, 1995; July 5, 1995; July 2, 1996; July 14, 1999; *Página 20* (Rio Branco), October 1, 1995; August 18, 1996; July 14, 1999; November 26, 1996; and *Jornal do Brasil,* February 18, 1993, sec. 1, 7.

39. Sources: CPT: *Conflitos no campo* [all editions], *loc. cit.*

40. Amnesty International evidently got their data from an earlier Movimento dos Trabalhadores Rurais Sem-Terra work. *Ciência Hoje* acquired their figures in part from Movimento dos Trabalhadores Rurais Sem-Terra as well. The data for each of the four sources were as follows:

	1985	1986
Amnesty International	222	
Ciência Hoje	226	
Comissão Pastoral da Terra	139	122
Movimento dos Trabalhadores Rurais Sem-Terra	170	150

41. Sources: CPT: *Conflitos no campo* [all editions], *loc. cit.*

42. One estimate (*Jornal do Brasil,* October 17, 1991, sec. 1, 1, 4) puts the number of Native Brazilians at the time of the discovery at around five million. By the time of the report, a mere 5 percent, or two hundred fifty thousand, remained. Slavery and the sicknesses brought from Europe account for this dramatic decline.

43. For some examples that made it into print see Neill Macaulay, *The Prestes Column: Revolution in Brazil* (New York: New Viewpoints, 1974), 172. Note as well Macaulay's comments (130) on a landowner who received moral support from a federal senator after he castrated a runaway ranch hand. Other cases, including the continued enslavement of selected native Brazilians, are reported in Zoroastro Artiaga, *História de Goiás,* 2nd ed. (Goiânia: Estado de Goiás, 1959), 267; Ferrera de Castro, *A selva,* 15th ed. (Lisboa: Gulmarães, 1954), 224–25; Herman James, *Brazil after a Century of Independence* (New York: Macmillian, 1925), 454, 458, 461, 464; Bernardo Élis, *A enxada veranico de janeiro,* 6th ed. (Rio de Janeiro: José Olympio, 1987), 37–61; Jorge Amado, *São Jorge dos Ilheus,* 20th ed. (São Paulo: Martins, 1970), 71–72, 96, 105–11, 115, 169, 254–55; José Audrin: *Os sertanejos que eu conheci* (Rio de Janeiro: José Olympio, 1963), 181–91; *Entre sertanejos e índios do norte* (Rio de Janeiro: Púgil and Agir, [1947]), 88; CPDOC, oral history, "Osvaldo Lima Filho," 104; and *O Globo,* April 19, 1928, 2nd ed., 1.

44. Brazil, Comissão Especial de Inquérito sôbre Atos Delituosos da Ditadura, "Depoimento do João Alves de Mota," *Diario do Congresso Nacional,* August 28, 1947, 5206; and PPARJ, document, "Atividades particulares do atual interventor de Mato Grosso," [no date], alemão/pasta 17. In May 1941, the U.S. military attaché in Rio remarked that Mato Grosso was "the worst hotbed of Naziism in Brazil—probably with Mueller's [former Polícia Civil Chief Filinto Müller's] co-operation." United States, National Archives, letter, "Sibert to A.C. of S., G-2," May 2, 1941, MID 2657-K-128/5, no. 2703, 2.

45. Beloch and Abreu, 2342–43, 2347–48.

46. Brazil, Comissão Especial de Inquérito sôbre Atos Delituosos da Ditadura, "Depoimento de João Alves de Mota," *loc. cit.*

47. United States, Department of State, document, "Strategic Survey of Amazonas, Acre, Matto Grosso, and Goyaz," April 1, 1942, 097.3/Z1092/no. 724, 8, 51. The 9.7-cent figure is the black-market rate.

48. United States, Office of Strategic Services, Latin America Section, document, "Survey of Interior Brazil," October 21, 1942, 097.3/Z1092/no. 784c, 12.

49. See chapter 2.

50. This information excludes persons in the rural portions of Acre, Amapá, Amazonas, Goiás, Pará, Rondônia, and Roraima where wages are even lower.

51. Defined as at least ten years of age and employed.

52. Brazil, Ministério da Economia, Fazenda e Planejamento, *Anuário estatístico do Brasil* (Rio de Janeiro: IBGE, 1990), 97.

53. Americas Watch, "Forced Labor in Brazil," December 30, 1990, 2–5; *New York Times,* May 29, 1977, 1, 38.

54. Rose, "Slavery in Brazil: Does it Still Exist?" 100–107. A more recent effort at summarizing the debt-peonage situation in Brazil can be seen in the work sponsored by the CPT, VV.AA., *Trabalho escravo no Brasil contemporâneo* (São Paulo: Edições Loyola, 1999). The publications surveyed from Rio de Janeiro were *Jornal do Brasil, O Dia,* and *O Globo,* and from São Paulo *Folha de São Paulo, Jornal da Tarde,* and *O Estado de São Paulo.*

55. *Folha de São Paulo:* March 8, 1979, 18; August 5, 1979, 14; May 3, 1980, 5; March 1, 1983, 14; October 3, 1984, 20; October 4, 1985, 1, 11; April 15, 1986, 4; December 27, 1986, A-1, A-11; June 14, 1987, A-4; *Jornal da Tarde:* July 17, 1981, 2; August 26, 1986, 7; *Jornal do Brasil:* February 17, 1979, sec. 1, 8; May 26, 1979, sec. 1, 9; June 26, 1979, sec. 1, 18; August 24, 1979, sec. 1, 7; September 15, 1979, sec. 1, 15; September 27, 1979, sec. 1, 28; November 26, 1979, sec. 1, 16; April 26, 1980, sec. 1, 20; May 30, 1980, sec. 1, 14; February 6, 1981, sec. 1, 8; May 30, 1984, sec. 1, 13; November 7, 1984, sec. 1, 5; May 8, 1985, sec. 1, 13; June 27, 1985, sec. 1, 8; October 13, 1985, sec. 1, 8; April 29, 1986, sec. 1, 9; June 28, 1986, sec. 1, 9; July 11, 1986, sec. 1, 17; August 8, 1986, sec. 1, 9; August 9, 1986, sec. 1, 13; August 11, 1986, sec. 1, 13; January 8, 1987, sec. 1, 14; February 11, 1987, sec. 1, 7; June 19, 1987, sec. 1, 8; July 8, 1987, sec. 1, 5; *O Dia,* March 1, 1979, 7; *O Estado de São Paulo:* March 14, 1979, sec. 1, 21; June 21, 1979, 19; June 18, 1981, 12; October 9, 1981, 12; December 3, 1981, 15; May 8, 1982, 16; May 25, 1983, 11; June 24, 1983, 14; March 7, 1985, 24; July 19, 1986, 10; August 2, 1986, 9; August 20, 1986, sec. 1, 10; *O Globo:* November 29, 1979, sec. 1, 6; January 11, 1981, sec. 1, 7; September 25, 1981, sec. 1, 16; March 7,

1983, sec. 1, 5; May 7, 1983, sec. 1, 6; September 19, 1983, sec. 1, 10; January 28, 1984, sec. 1, 1, 5; November 10, 1984, sec. 12; November 14, 1984, sec. 1, 7; February 8, 1985, sec. 1, 11; February 9, 1985, sec. 1, 6; December 17, 1985, sec. 1, 5; and April 19, 1987, sec. 1, 7. In situations where a duplication of individual accountings in different newspapers was suspected, or even possible, only one report was recorded.

56. The 177 cases are presented in "Trabalho escravo," prepared by the government agency Coordenadoria de Conflitos Agrários of the Ministério da Reforma e Desenvolvimento Agrário. A copy of this document was obtained by and published in part in *Folha de São Paulo* (December 27, 1986, A-11). The newspaper's commentary does not list instances by year (other than that they occurred between May 1985 and November 1986), or the sex, age, and race of the victims. The only material provided are the state and municipality in which the alleged offense occurred, and the type of business involved in the charge. In a different report, listing 167 rural entities involved in contemporary slavery (Arquivo, *Jornal do Brasil, Retrato do Brasil* [January 22, 1987] in "Trabalho Escravidão" file, 11–13), several concerns are identified by name.

57. Eucaflora, a subsidiary of Eucatex, used children five to fifteen years of age to plant pine trees in rural Mato Grosso do Sul. *O Estado de São Paulo,* May 25, 1983, 11. For other instances of child-slave labor, see *Folha de São Paulo,* March 8, 1979, 18; *Jornal da Tarde,* July 17, 1981, 2; and *O Globo,* November 29, 1979, sec. 1, 6. One article (*Jornal do Brazil,* May 26, 1979, sec. 1, 9) states that some children were even tortured.

58. *Jornal do Brasil:* August 8, 1986, sec. 1, 9; August 9, 1986, sec. 1, 13; *Jornal da Tarde,* August 26, 1986, 7; Beloch and Abreu, 2052; and *Folha de São Paulo,* "Maluf troca imóveis por empresas, indica IR," <http://www1.folha.uol.com.br/folha/brasil/ult96u24828.shl>, March 2, 2004.

59. *Jornal do Brasil,* October 13, 1985, sec. 1, 8.

60. Arquivo *Jornal do Brasil* [hereafter A*JB*], *Retrato do Brasil,* [January 22, 1987], 12, trabalho escravidão/pasta.

61. *O Globo,* March 7, 1983, sec. 1, 5.

62. *O Globo,* January 28, 1984, sec. 1, 1, 5, 20.

63. *O Estado de São Paulo,* May 8, 1982, 16.

64. *Jornal do Brasil,* October 13, 1985, sec. 1, 8.

65. *Jornal do Brasil,* June 19, 1987, sec. 1, 8. Remember that the conversion figures use the official rate of exchange.

66. "Pega corrupto!" <http://www.pegacorrupto.hpg.com.br/maluf.html>, May 27, 2001.

67. *Visão* (Rio de Janeiro), September 1987, 30, 47, 52, 62, 100, 124, 126, 146, 183, 186, 188, 202, 218, 228, 298, 356, 364; A*JB:* newspaper articles: *Jor-*

nal do Brasil, September 15, 1979, sec. 1, 15, trabalho escravidão/pasta; July 11, 1986, sec. 1, 17, trabalho escravidão/pasta; August 8, 1986, sec. 1, 9, trabalho escravidão/pasta; August 9, 1986, sec. 1, 13, trabalho escravidão/pasta; *O Globo,* May 7, 1983, sec. 1, 6, trabalho escravidão/pasta; April 19, 1987, sec. 1, 7, trabalho escravidão/pasta; *O Estado de São Paulo,* August 2, 1986, 9, trabalho escravidão/pasta; *Jornal da Tarde,* August 26, 1986, 7, trabalho escravidão/pasta: and *Retrato do Brasil,* [January 22, 1987], 11–13, trabalho escravidão/pasta.

68. Nancy Cardia, *Pesquisa sobre atitudes, normas culturais e valores em relação a violência em 10 capitais brasileiras* (Brasília: Ministério da Justiça, Secretaria de Estado dos Direitos Humanos, 1999), 95. Under the column "Atrir," or shoot over the heads of the MST targets, 11 percent (176 persons) of 1,600 respondents from Belém answered in the affirmative. While this same percentage was given by those asked in Recife, Belém led the nation with 4 percent (64 individuals) who felt the police should shoot to kill.

69. This quote is from João Pedro Stédile, the leader of the MST. *Jornal do Brasil,* "Sem-terra continuarão presos," <http://jbonline.terra.com.br/jb/papel/brasil/2002/03/28/jorbra20020328013.html>, March 29, 2002.

70. *Veja,* April 24, 1996, 34–39; *Isto É,* April 24, 1996, 20–24; *O Globo,* August 20, 1999, 1–3; and *Jornal do Brasil,* August 4, 2001, sec. 1, 1, 5.

71. At one point, Cardoso insisted oddly that the overall economy, under his stewardship, was not going from bad to worse. "You can't say that it's going from bad to better [either]. It's going at least from bad to less bad." *Jornal do Brasil,* May 16, 2000, sec. 1, 3.

72. *Folha de São Paulo,* September 2, 2001, A-5.

73. *O Globo,* April 20, 2003, 1–14.

74. *Isto É,* April 3, 2002, 30; and *Veja,* April 3, 2002, 46–48.

75. Besides the MST, the others are: the MLT (Movimento de Luta pela Terra—Fight for Land Movement), the MLST (Movimento de Libertação dos Sem-Terra—Liberty for the Landless Movement), and the MAST (Movimento dos Agricultores Sem-Terra—Landless Agricultural Workers Movement). *Época,* May 8, 2000, 40.

76. *Jornal do Brasil:* May 5, 2000, 5; May 8, 2000, 3; and *Veja,* May 10, 2000, 42–49.

77. *Jornal do Brasil,* May 15, 2000, sec. 1, 5.

78. Ibid.

79. One should remember that while only about five hundred thousand slaves entered the United States, some four million were taken to Brazil. *Newsweek,* December 8, 1997, 62.

80. *Veja,* April 19, 2000, 31.

81. *Folha de São Paulo,* May 7, 2000, 8, 10. The UDR denied that it hired guards to act as gunmen. Ibid.

82. *Jornal do Brasil,* December 15, 2002, A2.

83. James Joyce, *Ulysses* (New York: Modern Library, 1934), 34. The remark by the character Stephen Dedalus in *Ulysses* goes, "History is a nightmare from which I am trying to awake."

Chapter 6. Urbancide

1. PPARJ: newspaper articles: *O Globo,* August 10, 1951, n.p., administração/pasta 22; *Diario Popular* (Rio de Janeiro), August 10, 1951, n.p., administração/pasta 22; *Diario Carioca* (Rio de Janeiro), August 11, 1951, n.p., administração/pasta 22; *Última Hora,* August 13, 1951, n.p., administração/pasta 22; *Última Hora,* August 15, 1951, n.p., administração/pasta 22; and *Correio da Noite,* August 15, 1951, n.p., administração/pasta 22.

2. *Pixote: a lei do mais fraco,* directed by Hector Babenco, Embrafilme/HB Filmes, 1981; *Notícias Populares,* August 25, 1997, 5; *Notícias Populares,* September 17, 1995, 14; and *Época* (Rio de Janeiro), October 6, 2003, 110.

3. Thomas Holloway: *Policing Rio de Janeiro: Repression and Resistance in a 19th-Century City* (Stanford: Stanford University Press, 1993), 22, 55–57, 204; "The Brazilian 'Judicial Police' in Florianópolis, Santa Catarina, 1841–1871," *Journal of Social History,* vol. XX, no. 4, Summer 1987, 737, 745, 75; Karasch, 156–58; Henry Chamberlain, *Views and Costumes of the City and Neighbourhood of Rio de Janeiro, Brazil: from Drawings Taken by Lieutenant Chamberlain, Royal Artillery, during the Years 1819 and 1820 with Descriptive Explanations* (London: Thomas McLean, 1822), comments following plate 35; Daniel Kidder and James Fletcher, 131; Daniel Kidder, *Sketches of Residence and Travels in Brazil: Embracing Historical and Geographical Notices of the Empire and its Several Provinces* (Philadelphia: Sorin and Ball; London: Wiley and Putnam, 1845), vol. I, 100; Moreira de Azevedo, *O Rio de Janeiro: sua história, monumentos, homens notáveis, usos e curiosidades,* 3rd ed. (Rio de Janeiro: Brasiliana, 1969), vol. II, 437–59; George Gardner, *Travels in the Interior of Brazil: Principally through the Northern Provinces and the Gold and Diamond Districts, during the Years 1836–1841* (London: Reeve, 1846), 18; [José Gabriel de] Lemos Britto, *Os systemas penitenciarios do Brasil* (Rio de Janeiro: Nacional, 1925), vol. II, 148; and Robert Conrad, "Nineteenth-Century Brazilian Slavery," *Slavery and Race Relations in Latin America,* Robert Toplin (ed.)(Westport: Greenwood, 1974), 160.

4. Ibid., 160–183; Rose, *One of the Forgotten Things,* 42–69, 87–91.

5. *Época,* July 16, 2001, 8–9; *Folha de São Paulo,* December 3, 1992, sec. 1, 14; and Joanna Weschler, "Massacre na casa de detenção," Aryeh Neier (ed.), Beatriz Castelo and Armanda Morris (trad.), *Os diretos humanos no Brasil* (São Paulo: Núcleo de Estudos da Violência, Universidade de São Paulo, 1993), 64–71. For a graphic description, in color, of life at Carandiru, South America's largest prison, see Drauzio Varella, *Estação Carandiru* (São Paulo: Companhia das Letras, 1999). A largely accurate summary of the situation in Brazil's jails and prisons, is given in Amnesty International, *Brazil: "No One Here Sleeps Safely," Human Rights Violations against Detainees* (New York: Amnesty International, 1999).

6. Eduardo Barbosa, *loc. cit.*

7. PPARJ, miscellaneous documents, "Sindicancia para apurar como o jornal *O Mundo* obteve fotografias idênticas do prontuário de Cecil Borer," 1947, administração/pasta 1e; Cecil Borer, interview, Rio de Janeiro, May 28, 1998; Solomão Malina, interview, São Paulo, July 28, 1994; Jose Luiz Del Roio, telephone interview, Rio de Janeiro/São Paulo, July 31, 1994; and Thomé Amado, interview, Rio de Janeiro, August 21, 1994.

8. In 1960, when the federal capital was moved to Brasília, this section of the Polícia Civil, along with the uniforms, was done away with. Anonymous-1, interview, Rio de Janeiro, September 17, 1992.

9. PPARJ: miscellaneous documents, "Sindicancia para apurar como o jornal *O Mundo* obteve fotografias idênticas do prontuário de Cecil Borer," 1947, administração/pasta 1e; and Thomé Amado, interview, Rio de Janeiro, September 21, 1994.

10. PPARJ, letter, "Chefe do setor [unsigned] to D.P.S.," relação de investigadores ns° 1 a 87, July 31, 1947, administração/pasta 15.

11. *Folha de São Paulo,* March 5, 1978, 32; *Jornal da Tarde,* November 6, 1981, 11; and *Pasquim,* April 28–May 4, 1983, 10.

12. José Monteiro and Adriano Barbosa, *Do Esquadrão ao Mão Branca* (Rio de Janeiro: Jaguaribe, 1980), 86; and Rose, *Beyond the Pale of Pity,* 35–37.

13. *Pasquim,* April 28–May 4, 1983, 10.

14. Sodré, *História militar do Brasil, loc. cit.*

15. The nickname was an invention of Le Cocq's. The reflexive verb "se invocar" (meaning "Hot Head") was shortened, because it was easier to pronounce, to "se vocar," which became with time, "Sivuca." Octávio Ribeiro, *Barra Pesada* (Rio de Janeiro: Codecri [Coleção Edições do *Pasquim,* vol. XII], [no date]), 154.

16. José Guilherme Godinho Ferreira "Sivuca," telephone interview, Rio de Janeiro, May 25, 2000; Anonymous-3, interview, Rio de Janeiro, July 27, 1993; Octávio Ribeiro, *Barra Pesada,* 155, 161; *Jornal do Brasil,* November 11,

1989, sec. Cidade, 5; and *O Fluminense* (Niterói), September 2, 1976, 7. The first four men, Sivuca, Guaíba, Jacaré, and Lincoln Monteiro, went on to help found the Scuderie. Euclides Nascimento, Sivuca, Guaíba, Lincoln Monteiro, and Aníbal Beckman became members of the Twelve Golden Men.

17. *Status* (Rio de Janeiro), March 1986, 35. One could conclude from this that these things had been done in the past.

18. José Guilherme Godinho Ferreira "Sivuca," telephone interview, Rio de Janeiro, May 25, 2000.

19. *Jornal do Brasil:* June 7, 1971, sec. 1, 26; May 2, 1988, sec. Cidade, 5; *Jornal da Tarde,* November 6, 1981, 11; *O Cruzeiro,* September 19, 1964, 12; Percival de Souza, *A maior violência do mundo: Baixada Fluminense, Rio de Janeiro, Brasil* (São Paulo: Traço, 1980), 118; and *Status,* March 1986, 31, 35.

20. *Folha de São Paulo,* March 5, 1978, 32; *Jornal do Brasil,* May 2, 1988, sec. Cidade, 5; *Status,* March 1986, 35; and *Fatos e Fotos,* July 1, 1971, 15.

21. When data is released, it is often contradictory. For example, official statistics on killings by the police in the line of duty—provided by the police themselves—for São Paulo for the year 1991 show three different figures: 1074, 1140, and 1171. Paul Chevigny, "Urban Police Violence in Brazil: Torture and Police Killings in São Paulo and Rio de Janeiro after Five Years," (Paulo Sérgio Pinheiro and Cynthia Arnson eds.), *Americas Watch,* vol. V, no. 5, May 31, 1993, 4; *Folha de São Paulo:* November 14, 1992, sec. 3, 1; December 3, 1992, sec. 1, 14; and January 21, 1993, sec. 3, 4.

22. An illustration of this change of focus can be noted by comparing the crime coverage in the first three months of 1999 by *O Dia* and a newer blood-drenched journal, *Povo do Rio* (Rio de Janeiro). While *O Dia* reported 80 killings that fit the methods used by extermination groups, *Povo do Rio* recounted 202 murders of this type during the same period and a total of 758 for the year. *Povo do Rio* began circulating in 1983 as *Povo da Rua.* It changed its name to *Povo do Rio* in 1995.

23. Anonymous-3, interview, Rio de Janeiro, November 6, 1999.

24. Marcio Luiz Donnici, interview, Rio de Janeiro, February 28, 1982. This methodology was also used in Caco Barcellos's work.

25. As an example, an analysis of 1,091 victims in São Paulo portion of the study revealed that each corpse had an average of just over eleven bullets (11.02) fired into it.

26. A member of Fleury's team, Alberto Barbour, carried out this role in São Paulo. Percival de Souza, *Autópsia do medo,* 17.

27. Anonymous-3: interviews, Rio de Janeiro, January 19, 1982; February 12, 1982; and February 27, 1982.

28. In order to simplify the process, the research workers were given but five options: Asian, white, indigenous, mulatto, and black. Please see the Note

on Racial Types on page xvii. Since Brazilians tend to classify people as whiter than would Americans or Europeans, the figures presented for white victims are probably overrepresented by the standards of these non-Brazilian areas.

29. Again, in order to streamline the procedure, a three-part class universe was chosen: high, middle, and low. Yet even with this typology, a placement decision had to be deduced from the other variables. Such things as profession, residence, photographs of the victim, the clothing found on the body, plus the commentary of the news article were used to assign social class. The author is aware of the limitations discussed in Harold Kerbo, *Social Stratification and Inequality: Class Conflict in Historical, Comparative, and Global Perspective,* 5th ed. (New York: McGraw-Hill, 2003), 142–49.

30. This study used the *barrio* or suburb plan for both cities from 1990.

31. Larger Rio de Janeiro is divided into a number of zones, which are often indicative of an individual's social class. In order of wealth, they are: South Zone, Center, North Zone, West Zone, and the district to the north of the city known collectively as the Baixada Fluminense. One should keep in mind that the difference between the Baixada, North, and West Zones is sometimes minimal at best.

32. Beloch and Abreu, 754, 1724; "Favela Tem Memória," <http://www.favelatemmemoria.com.br/publique/cgi/cgilua.exe/sys/start.htm?sid=7&infoid=109>, February 16, 2005.

33. One is presented here as plate 18.

34. *Última Hora:* January 23, 1963, 1; January 25, 1963, 1; January 28, 1963, 1, 8; January 30, 1963, 1–2; January 31, 1963, 3, 9; February 1, 1963, 9; February 4, 1963, 8; February 8, 1963, 9; March 4, 1963, 1, 12; March 11, 1963, 1–2; March 12, 1963, 1, 8; March 22, 1963, 1, 5; *Correio da Manhã,* February 3, 1963, 5; *O Dia,* March 23, 1974, 7; *Jornal do Brasil,* August 31, 1982, sec. 1, 2; *Isto É,* September 8, 1982, 26; Wainer, 236–37; Rivadavia de Souza, 112–15; and Monteiro and Barbosa, 77–78.

35. *Isto É,* May 20, 1992, 18–19; *O Globo:* April 15, 1999, O País, 9; October 20, 1999, 1, March 10, 2000, O País, 5; *Folha de São Paulo,* October 24, 1999, sec. 1, 16; and *Jornal do Brasil,* May 5, 2000, sec. 1, 6.

36. The week of his death, Le Cocq was planning to start a vacation in order to prepare his defense. Accusations had been brought against him in the killing of Mino. *Última Hora,* August 29, 1964, 3.

37. *Jornal do Brasil:* August 29, 1964, sec. 1, 13; June 7, 1971, sec. 1, 26; April 25, 1989, sec. Cidade, 1; *Fatos e Fotos,* July 1, 1971, 15; *Folha de São Paulo,* March 3, 1978, 32; *Jornal da Tarde,* November 6, 1981, 11; *Correio da Manhã,* August 29, 1964, 10; and Octávio Ribeiro, *Barra Pesada,* 179–80.

38. *O Cruzeiro,* September 19, 1964, 12; and *Jornal do Brasil,* August 29, 1964, sec. 1, 10, 13. The exchange rate used is the black-market rate.

39. *O Cruzeiro,* September 19, 1964, 14; *Última Hora,* August 29, 1964, 8; and Beloch and Abreu, 1695.

40. *Jornal do Brasil,* August 29, 1964, sec. 1, 13.

41. Octávio Ribeiro, *Barra Pesada,* 180. Percival de Souza (*A maior violência do mundo,* 118–19) is of a different opinion. He states that this killing took place because the two peace officers were arguing, face-to-face, over who would identify himself to the other first.

42. *Correio da Manhã:* September 4, 1964, 10; October 4, 1964, 19; and Percival de Souza, *A maior violência do mundo,* 119–20.

43. Octávio Ribeiro, *Barra Pesada, loc. cit.;* and *Fatos e Fotos,* October 17, 1964, 17. The latter also presents a grizzly picture of the dead Horse Face.

44. *Fatos e Fotos,* October 17, 1964, *loc. cit.;* Percival de Souza, *A maior violência do mundo,* 119–20; *Autópsia do Medo,* 70; *Correio da Manhã,* October 4, 1964, 19; and Octávio Ribeiro, *Barra Pesada,* 181–82.

45. *Jornal do Brasil,* October 4–5, 1964, sec. 1, 1, 10.

46. Percival de Souza, *A maior violência do mundo,* 120–21; and *Status,* March 1986, 32.

47. *Jornal do Brasil,* October 4–5, 1964, sec. 1, 10.

48. Ibid.

49. *O Dia,* August 29, 1964, 2.

50. *Jornal do Brasil,* June 7, 1971, sec. 1, 26; and Monteiro and Barbosa, 89.

51. Scuderie Detetive Le Cocq [hereafter SDLC], reciepts nos.1 19883–84, November 11, 1992; Octávio Ribeiro, *Barra Pesada,* 173; Brazil, Arquivo Nacional, document PH/FOT/2086, 1–2; and *Status,* March 1986, 31–32. Note that there are several different spellings and combinations of Mariel's complete name. The one used here is from the headstone of his grave.

52. *Jornal do Brasil:* May 2, 1988, sec. Cidade, 5; August 19, 2001, 25; *Jornal da Tarde,* November 6, 1981, 11; and *Status,* March 1986, 31. Some earlier versions of the logo did not have the E.M.

53. SDLC, document, "Informativo social," November-December 1992; and *Jornal do Brasil,* July 13, 1986, sec. 1, 14.

54. Sivuca, in the interview he gave to *Status* (March 1986), asserted that there were three thousand members, of whom twelve hundred were active police. Sivuca was president of the Scuderie at the time. Four months later, in a statement to *Jornal do Brasil* (July 13, 1986, sec. 1, 14), he claimed that the Scuderie had about fifty thousand members, five thousand of whom were from the police.

55. *Jornal do Brasil,* July 13, 1986, sec. 1, 14; and *Status,* March 1986, 31. Amin was one of the military dictator's governors of Santa Catarina, and a loosing presidential candidate in 1994.

56. *Status,* March 1986, 31.

57. Telecomunicações do Rio de Janeiro, "Serviços & negócios 1997," *Rio listas,* Rio de Janeiro: TELERJ, 1997, 890.

58. Rio de Janeiro, Secretaria de Estado de Justiça, Departamento Geral de Documentação, *Legislação do estado do Rio de Janeiro: lei complementar, leis, decreto legislativo, decretos,* Rio de Janeiro: Oficial, 1982, vol. VIII, no. 12, December 23, 1982, 1326, law 638. The Scuderie's affiliate in the state of Santa Catarina was likewise declared a state public utility. In that case, the authorities in the city of Itajaí went so far as to donate the land on which the Scuderie built its branch headquarters. There was enough property for about five homes. SDLC, document, "Informativo social," November-December 1992.

59. *Status,* March 1986, 32.

60. Anonymous-1, interview, October 28, 1992, Rio de Janeiro.

61. The newsletter was free and had a circulation of 3,000 in 1974. *Veja,* September 11, 1974, 27.

62. "Hino da Scuderie Detetive Le Cocq," by Hugo Bellard and Nelson de Carvalho, 1974.

63. The group was also known as "Anjos da guarda" (Guardian Angels) and "Esquadrão da vida" (Squadron of Life). *Jornal do Brasil,* August 19, 2001, sec. 1, 25. Mariel said (*Pasquim,* September 17–23, 1981, 13) that the reporters from *Última Hora* came up with the name Men of Gold.

64. Markun and Rodrigues, 49; and *Pasquim,* September 17–23, 1981, 13.

65. Octávio Ribeiro, *Barra Pesada,* 221.

66. Ibid.; Monteiro and Barbosa, 3; *Jornal do Brasil,* August 19, 2001, sec. 1, 25; and *Jornal da Tarde,* November 6, 1981, 11. Note again that José Guilherme Godinho Ferreira, Hélio Jamie de Lima, Lincoln Monteiro, Euclides Nascimento, Hélio Guaíba Nunes, and the sometimes participant, Aníbal Beckman dos Santos, had been among the original members of Le Cocq's group.

67. Monteiro and Barbosa, 87–88; and Markun and Rodrigues, 50–51.

68. Sivuca, in the long interview in Octávio Ribeiro (*Barra Pesada,* 220) pointed out, "The group was created solely to calm the press, [and thus] to give society some satisfaction."

69. Sivuca also claimed (ibid.) that the Twelve Golden Men killed a mere twelve people.

70. Only Elinto Pires and Vigmar Riberio Gonçalves escaped serious charges. *Jornal da Tarde,* November 6, 1981, 11.

71. *Jornal do Brasil:* April 25, 1989, sec. Cidade, 1; September 23, 1993, sec. Cidade, 16; April 1, 1994, sec. 1, 12; April 2, 1994, sec. 1, 12; April 3, 1994, sec. 1, 15; April 5, 1994, sec. 1, 13; *O Globo:* September 23, 1993, sec. 2, 9; September 24, 1993, sec. 2. 11; October 6, 1993, sec. 2, 17; and *O Estado de São Paulo,* August 28, 1994, C4.

72. *Pasquim,* September 17–23, 1981, 11.

73. Markun and Rodrigues, 25, 41–49; *Pasquim,* October 28-November 3, 1981, 10; and R. S. Rose, "The Man of Gold," *Today* [Academy of Criminal Justice Sciences], September 1989, 5–6.

74. *Pasquim,* September 17–23, 1981, 11.

75. *O Dia:* May 21, 1971, 1,7; May 30–31, 1971, 1, 13; *Notícias Populares* (São Paulo): April 9, 1969, 10; and October 12, 1969, 15.

76. Anonymous-5, interview, Rio de Janeiro, December 20, 1992.

77. *Jornal do Brasil,* November 6, 1981, sec. 1, 11.

78. Markun and Rodrigues, 73.

79. *Veja,* March 21, 1973, 31; and Markun and Rodrigues, 64–65, 70, 72–73.

80. Markun and Rodrigues, 74.

81. Ibid., 81, 86.

82. *Veja,* February 5, 1975, 25; and *Jornal do Brasil,* March 19, 1980, sec. B, 1.

83. Octávio Ribeiro, *Barra Pesada,* 196.

84. *Lúcio Flávio: o passageiro da agonia,* directed by Hector Babenco, Embrafilme/HB Filmes/Unifilme, 1977; and Lopes, 26n.

85. *Lúcio Flávio,* directed by Hector Babenco.

86. *Veja,* October 14, 1981, 34.

87. Such may well have been true, even if it is confirmed only in the film by Babenco, which is based on the book by José Louzeiro (*Lúcio Flávio: o passageiro da agonia,* 9th ed. [Rio de Janeiro: Nova Fronteira, 1985]).

88. Markun and Rodrigues, 86–87, 183; and Louzeiro, 13, 110–11 (caption on the last picture). See also the different version for Lúcio Flávio's death by one of Mariel's friends, Sivuca, in Octávio Ribeiro (*Barra Pesada,* 198).

89. Markun and Rodrigues, 87, 90. In August 1975, Mariel's lawyer got the 16 plus 1 sentence reduced to nine years. Ibid., 89.

90. See as examples: *Veja,* March 3, 1976, 27; and Markun and Rodrigues, 101–2.

91. Markun and Rodrigues, p 100; and *Pasquim,* September 17–23, 1981, 14.

92. Markun and Rodrigues, 105–17.

93. Ibid.

94. Ibid., 34; *Veja,* October 14, 1981, 32, 34; *Eu matei Lúcio Flávio,* directed by Antônio Calmon, Atlântida Cinematográfica/Magnus Filmes, 1979; *República dos assassinos,* directed by Miguel Faria Jr., Roma Filmes do Brasil, 1979; and *Reporter* (Rio de Janeiro), October 1981, 2. *Reporter* puts the time of the first shots fifteen minutes later. For some of the theories as to who did it, see: *Pasquim:* October 28-November 3, 1981, 13; November 5–11, 1981, 15; December 3–9, 1981, 20; *Jornal do Brasil,* September 22, 1987, sec. B, 1; and Markun and Rodrigues, 121–47.

95. Markun and Rodrigues, 29.

96. Ibid., 24–29; and *Veja,* October 14, 1981, 34.

97. *Veja,* March 26, 1980, 26. That this *Veja* article was conjecture is evident from the month of the report. The Mão Branca killings were still taking place in March 1980.

98. See as examples the material presented in *Jornal do Brasil,* March 19, 1980, sec. B, 1; *O Globo:* March 31, 1980, 11; April 1, 1980, 17; *Veja:* March 26, 1980, 26; and May 28, 1980, 70.

99. Anonymous-3, interview, Rio de Janeiro, January 19, 1982.

100. Monteiro and Barbosa, 89.

101. Marcio Luiz Donnici: interviews, Rio de Janeiro, February 28, 1982; December 10, 1992; Monteiro and Barbosa, *loc. cit.;* and R. S. Rose, "Vigilantism and the Police in Brazil: The State of Rio de Janeiro," paper presented at the World Congress of Sociology, Mexico City, August 18, 1982, 5n.

102. Someone even tried to cash in by making a compact disc about Mão Branca. *Veja,* May 28, 1980, 70.

103. Lopes, 41–46; and Percival de Souza, *Autópsia do medo,* 71.

104. Lopes, 46–47.

105. Ibid., 47. There was possibly one earlier paulistano Esquadrão da Morte victim: a 34 year-old working-class Black male whose death appeared in *Notícias Populares,* January 20, 1966, 1, 12.

106. Hélio Pereira Bicudo, *Meu depoimento sobre o Esquadrão da Morte,* 3rd ed., rev. (São Paulo: Pontifícia Comissão de Justiça e Paz, 1976), 46; Percival de Souza, *Autópsia do medo,* 301; and Lopes, 48–49.

107. See the problem faced in this respect by Barcellos (120–22).

108. The São Paulo cases did not include a zone of residence or a zone for the location of the body.

109. Percival de Souza, *Autópsia do medo,* 71–72; and *Jornal do Brasil,* November 5, 2000, sec. 1, 8. Note the different number of days in these two sources as to how long it took the police to locate Saponga. Correinha claims 70 days in the *Jornal do Brasil* article, while Percival de Souza states that it was fifty-three.

110. *Jornal do Brasil,* October 24, 1973, sec. 1, 30; Percival de Souza, *Autópsia do medo,* 297; and São Paulo, Polícia Militar, GARRA, "Grupo Armado de Repressão a Roubos e Assaltos," <http://www.seguranca.sp.br/garra/pagina2.html>, June 20, 2001. *Frei* Betto, (144) mistakenly places Fleury's entrance into the police at age nineteen.

111. Percival de Souza, *Autópsia do medo,* 29.

112. Ibid., 29–32, 44; and Rose, *One of the Forgotten Things,* 61.

113. Percival de Souza, *Autópsia do medo,* 31.

114. Ibid., 32.

115. Hélio Bicudo, interview, São Paulo, February 8, 1993.

116. Percival de Souza, *Autópsia do medo,* 74–75; and *O Estado de São Paulo,* "Livro revela a polêmica trajetória do delegado Fleury," <http://www.jt.estadao.com.br/editorias/2000/11/27/ger432.html>, June 30, 2001.

117. Percival de Souza, *Autópsia do medo,* 18, 298.

118. Ibid., 40

119. Ibid., 12, 98–99, 173, 501; and *Jornal do Brasil,* October 24, 1973, sec. 1, 30.

120. *Jornal do Brasil,* October 24, 1973, sec. 1, 30. A similar version is presented in *Isto É,* March 1, 1978, 7.

121. Percival de Souza, *Autópsia do medo,* 105–7, 393; Bicudo: *Meu depoimento sobre o Esquadrão da Morte,* 38–39, 147–50; and e-mail, October 29, 2001. It would be interesting indeed to look at the link, Percival de Souza does not do so, between Fleury's understanding of religion and his practice of it, his use of the nickname "The Pope," the fact that he often dressed as a member of the cloth when going on stake out near a church, and his friendship with an individual such as Padre Agostinho since childhood.

122. Bicudo, *Meu depoimento sobre o Esquadrão da Morte,* 149, 274–78; Maria Isabel Pinto Ventura, 51–56, 60–63, 70–75, 176–77, 181; and Tortura Nunca Mais, "Olavo Hansen," <http://www.torturanuncamais.org.br/mtnm_mor/mor_mortes_oficiais/mor_1970_olavo_hans>, June 29, 2001.

123. Hélio Bicudo, interview, São Paulo, February 8, 1993; *Veja,* May 23, 1973, 26; and Maria Isabel Pinto Ventura, 61.

124. The brother of Fininho-I, Antonio Augusto de Oliveira, was called Fininho-II. Bicudo, *Meu depoimento sobre o Esquadrão da Morte,* 144.

125. *Veja,* May 23, 1973, 26; Lopes, 78; Maria Isabel Pinto Ventura, 186; and Percival de Souza, *Autópsia do medo,* 76, 397;

126. *Veja,* May 23, 1973, 26; and *Jornal do Brasil,* November 5, 2000, sec. 1, 8.

127. Bicudo: *Meu depoimento sobre o Esquadrão da Morte,* 15–18, 28–34; and Percival de Souza, *Autópsia do medo,* 77–89.

128. "Jornal da Globo," TV Globo, February 5, 1985. An article on this episode can be seen in *Última Hora,* February 5, 1985. 1.

129. Percival de Souza, *Autópsia do medo,* 318–19; and Bicudo: *Meu depoimento sobre o Esquadrão da Morte,* 32, 36–53, 153–56, 161–63, 165–66, 177–80, 185–89, 207–213.

130. Hélio Bicudo, e-mails: September 11, 2001; October 29, 2001; October 31, 2001; and December 12, 2001. The guilty parties were freed owing to the Lei Fleury.

131. Bicudo: *Meu depoimento sobre o Esquadrão da Morte,* 96–105, 155–56, 215; interview, São Paulo, February 8, 1993; e-mails: July 11, 2001; July 16, 2001; and Tulio Kahn, interview, São Paulo, July 28, 1994. Kahn goes on to

note, in his overall analysis of vigilantism in Brazil, that taxi-driver police instigate numerous lynchings.

132. Percival de Souza, *Autópsia do medo,* 319, 360, 363; and Brazil, *Diário oficial,* November 23, 1973, sec. 1, part 1, 12009, decree 5941.

133. Percival de Souza, *Autópsia do medo,* 487–89, 584–85, 591–604, 619–20; and Gaspari, 398–99. Hélio Bicudo and Vladimir Sacchetta independently agreed to the thesis that the government was the executioner in separate interviews. Hélio Bicudo, interview, São Paulo, February 8, 1993; and Vladimir Sacchetta, interview, São Paulo, August 17, 1994.

134. Rose, *Beyond the Pale of Pity,* 51–54; and "Beast of Burden," *Some Girls,* composed by Mick Jagger and Keith Richards, 1977.

135. As but a starting point in the reoccurring literature, see: Gilberto Dimenstein, author of the chilling monograph, *A guerra dos meninos: assassinatos de menores no Brasil* (São Paulo; Brasiliense, 1990), 16, 18, 21–22, 31–33, 35–37, 44, 53–66, 84, 86, 88–89, 93–94, 96–97 (this work is now available in English as *Brazil: War on Children.* Jan Rocha [intro.], Chris Whitehorse [trans.] [London: Latin America Bureau, 1991]); *San Francisco Chronicle,* July 18, 1990, 3; *Jornal do Brasil:* June 19, 1991, 2nd ed., sec. 1, 5; December 6, 1991, sec. 1, 4; September 21, 1991, sec. 1, 6; September 28, 1991, sec. Cidade, 5; June 2, 1994, 2nd ed., 13; *O Globo,* February 23, 1993, sec. 1, 10; and *Folha de São Paulo,* December 5, 1992, sec. 3, 7.

136. For Chi-square and its application see Herman Loether and Donald McTavish, *Descriptive and Inferential Statistics: An Introduction* (Boston: Allyn and Bacon, 1976), 528–50.

137. Brazil: Fundação IBGE—Instituto Brasileiro de Estatística, Serviço Nacional de Recenseamento, *Distrito Federal, censo demográfico [1950]* (Rio de Janeiro: IBGE, 1955), vol. XXIV, tomo I, 5; Fundação IBGE—Instituto Brasileiro de Estatística, Serviço Nacional de Recenseamento, *Estado do Rio de Janeiro, censo demográfico [1950]* (Rio de Janeiro: IBGE, 1955), vol. XXIII, tomo I, 5; Fundação IBGE—Instituto Brasileiro de Estatística, Serviço Nacional de Recenseamento, *Estado de São Paulo, censo demográfico [1950]* (Rio de Janeiro: IBGE, 1954), 5; Fundação IBGE—Instituto Brasileiro de Estatística, Serviço Nacional de Recenseamento, *Censo demográfico de 1960, Guanabara* (Rio de Janeiro: IBGE, 1968), vol. I, tomo XII, 1ª parte, 8; Fundação Instituto Brasileiro de Geografia e Estatística, Departamento de Estatísticas de População, *Censo demográfico de 1960, Rio de Janeiro* (Rio de Janeiro: IBGE, n.d.), vol. I, tomo XI, 8; Fundação Instituto Brasileiro de Geografia e Estatística, Departamento de Estatísticas de População, *Censo demográfico de 1960, São Paulo* (Rio de Janeiro: IBGE, n.d.), vol. I, tomo XIII, 10; Secretaria de Planejamento da Presidência da República, Fundação Instituto Brasileiro

de Geografia e Estatística, *Censo demográfico [1980], dados gerais—migração—instrução—fecundidade—mortalidade, Rio de Janeiro* (Rio de Janeiro: IBGE, 1983), vol. I, tomo 4, número 18, 10–11; and Secretaria de Planejamento da Presidência da República, Fundação Instituto Brasileiro de Geografia e Estatística, *Censo demográfico [1980], dados gerais—migração—instrução—fecundidade—mortalidade, São Paulo* (Rio de Janeiro: IBGE, 1982), vol. I, tomo 4, número 19, 10–11.

138. *Veja*, January 23, 2002, 92.

139. Brazil: *Distrito Federal, censo demográfico [1950], loc. cit.; Estado do Rio de Janeiro, censo demográfico [1950], loc. cit.; Estado de São Paulo, censo demográfico [1950], loc. cit.; Censo demográfico de 1960, Guanabara, loc. cit.; Censo demográfico de 1960, Rio de Janeiro, loc. cit.; Censo demográfico de 1960, São Paulo, loc. cit.; Censo demográfico [1980], dados gerais—migração—instrução—fecundidade—mortalidade, Rio de Janeiro, loc. cit.; Censo demográfico [1980], dados gerais—migração—instrução—fecundidade—mortalidade, São Paulo, loc. cit.;* Instituto Brasileiro de Geografia e Estatística: "Tabela 200—População residente por sexo, situação e grupos de idade, 1970 [Guanabara]," <http://www.sidra.ibge.gov.br/bda/tabela/protabl.asp?z=t&o=1&i=P> March 2, 2005; Instituto Brasileiro de Geografia e Estatística: "Tabela 200—População residente por sexo, situação e grupos de idade, 1970 [Rio de Janeiro]," <http://www.sidra.ibge.gov.br/bda/tabela/protabl.asp?z=t&o=1&i=P> March 2, 2005; Instituto Brasileiro de Geografia e Estatística: "Tabela 200—População residente por sexo, situação e grupos de idade, 1970 [São Paulo]," <http://www.sidra.ibge.gov.br/bda/tabela/protabl.asp?z=t&o=1&i=P> March 1, 2005; "Censo demográfico 1991, População residente por situação (urbana e rural), segundo o sexo," <http://www.ibge.gov.br/ibge/estatistica/populacao/censodem/tab202.shtm>, December 2, 2001; "Censo demográfico 2000—Sinopse preliminar, População residente, em valores absolutos e relativos, total, em situação urbana e em situação urbana na sede municipal, área total e densidade demográfica, segundo as unidades da federação e municípos, [Rio de Janeiro]," <http://www.ibge.gov.br/ibge/estatistica/populacao/censo2000/sinopse.php?tipo=21&uf=33>, December 2, 2001; and "Censo demográfico 2000—Sinopse preliminar, População residente, em valores absolutos e relativos, total, em situação urbana e em situação urbana na sede municipal, área total e densidade demográfica, segundo as unidades da federação e municípos, [São Paulo]," <http://www.ibge.gov.br/ibge/estatistica/populacao/censo2000/sinopse.php?tipo=21&uf=35>, December 2, 2001.

140. Hélio Bicudo, interview, São Paulo, February 8, 1993.

141. Anonymous-3, telephone interview, Bakersfield/São Paulo, November 29, 2001.

142. *Tira* (São Paulo), July 1990, 19.

143. *Folha de São Paulo,* August 23, 1981, sec. 2, 25.

144. *O Estado de São Paulo,* December 14, 1991, 3; and *Folha de São Paulo,* May 31, 1993, sec. 3, 1. The credible source was Dimenstein, author of *A guerra dos meninos.*

145. Gunnar Myrdal's classic *An American Dilemma* (New York: Harper and Brothers, 1944) served as both an inspiration for and a measure of this tragedy.

Epilogue

1. Paulo Sérgio Pinheiro, "The Legacy of Authoritarianism: Violence and the Limits of Democratic Transitions," comments delivered during the presentation of his paper presented to the 16th Conference of the Latin American Studies Association, Washington, DC, April 4–6, 1991. Paulo Sérgio was the founder of the Center for the Study of Violence at the University of São Paulo.

2. *Folha de São Paulo,* December 3, 2000, A24.

3. *O Globo:* December 4, 2003, 1, 8; December 29, 2003, 1, 3–5; July 28, 2004, 1, 3–4; *Jornal do Brasil:* December 30, 2002, C1; April 17, 2004, A5; and *O Globo,* "Homicídios dolosos caem 7,5% no estado, mas PM mata 60% a mais em 2003," <http://oglobo.globo.com/online/sp/133722908.asp>, February 1, 2004.

4. Richard Quinney, "The Way of Peace: On Crime, Suffering, and Service," *Criminology as Peacemaking,* Harold Pepinsky and Richard Quinney (eds.) (Bloomington: University of Indiana Press, 1991), 9.

5. Robert K. Merton, "Social Structure and Anomie," *American Sociological Review,* vol. III, October 1938, 672–82.

6. *O Globo,* April 12, 2004, 2nd ed., 8. Rio de Janeiro's Minister of the Environment, Luiz Paulo Conde, made the original suggestion.

7. Paulo Apulcro Fonseca, e-mail, June 4, 2004.

8. *Jornal do Brasil,* May 2, 2004, A1, A3.

9. See *Jornal do Brasil,* April 16, 2004, A3; and *O Globo,* April 16, 2004, Economia—29.

10. Charles Darwin, *The Voyage of the Beagle* (New York: Collier), 1909, 35.

Selected Glossary

AI-1—(see Abbreviations)

AI-2—(see Abbreviations)

AI-5—(see Abbreviations)

Alvorada—The presidential palace in Brasília.

arrocho salarial—"Salary squeeze." The slow economic strangulation of the Brazilian worker by not increasing his/her salary to keep pace with inflation.

banqueiro—(lit., banker) The ruler of a *jogo do bicho* territory.

boletin de ocorrência—Notice of an incident. A written police report detailing a potential criminal event. Boletins are required police paper work.

buque—(lit., bunker) The buque was nothing more than several different cubicle-like receptacles located at the headquarters of the Secretary for Public Security in Recife. Each was dark, humid, and without bathing facilities. They ranged in size from one person crypts, to those a bit larger that could be packed with up to fifteen bodies.

cachaça—Sugarcane brandy.

cangaço—The period of rural banditry that existed mainly in the Northeast until 1940.

capanga—Privately hired bodyguards who intimidated/murdered when so ordered by their masters/employers.

carioca—A person or thing from the city of Rio de Janeiro.

cassações—The process under AI-1 whereby an individual's political rights (i.e., to vote, to run for office, to belong to a political party, etc.) were suspended for ten years.

Catete—The former presidential palace in Rio de Janeiro. Also a suburb in that city.

coronel (pl., *coronéis*)—Literally "colonel," the word was applied liberally to string-pulling rural potentates up to the 1930s as a sign of respect. The term does not necessarily mean that the person served in the military.

dedo-duro—(lit., a hard finger) A finger-pointer or stool pigeon.

Dom—An honorific form of address, equivalent to "Sir."

Esquadrão da Morte—Precisely translated, "Squadron of Death." The name used in various states for Brazil's death squads. These groups are not necessarily interconnected.

Estado Novo—The dictatorial "New State," initiated by Getúlio Vargas on November 10, 1937.

favela—A shantytown.

favelado—A shantytown dweller.

fazenda—A farm.

fazendeiro—The owner of a farm.

fluminense—A person or thing from the state of Rio de Janeiro.

foco theory—By Régis Debray, from the Cuban Revolution, proposing that a small team of dedicated rural guerrillas could bring off a national uprising if they could incite a rebellion among poor peasants.

gato—(lit., "cat") A dishonest middleman who offers seasonal or temporary jobs, at appealing salaries on fazendas in other states, to the unemployed poor, often in Brazil's Northeast. The gato thus functions as a labor agent in contemporary debt-peonage operations.

gaúcho—A person or thing from the state of Rio Grande do Sul.

Gegê—A nickname for Getúlio Vargas.

golpe—(lit., a "strike") A coup, often by an armed force, to overthrow a functioning government or some other entity.

Integralists—Brazil's Fascist party in the 1930s and beyond. Initially called the Ação Integralísta Brasileira (AIB—Brazilian Integralist Movement), it was led by Plínio Salgado.

jagunço—An individual retained to supervise the slaves on large estates in times of peace who also did the killing for his boss(es) when called upon to do so.

Jango—An epithet for João Goulart since childhood.

jogo do bicho—(lit., "Game of the Animals") A tacitly legal numbers racket that uses numbers and simple animal symbols. It is very popular all over the country, but particularly among Brazil's working-class.

justiceiro(s)—Civilian vigilante(s).

latifundiário—Large landed estate owner.

mandante—The hirer of an assassin.

mendigo—A beggar.

mineiro—A person or thing from the state of Minas Gerais.

Minimum Salary—Brazil's equivalent of a minimum monthly wage. Salaries are expressed in number of Minimum Salaries.

pasta—(used in the bibliography) A folder.

pau-de-arara—"Parrot's Perch." A torture where a victim is made to sit on the floor with bound wrists. Their knees are forced together and bent upward in between their arms. A pole is slid through the gap just under the knees and on top of the individual's elbows. Thus constrained, the rod and attached victim are lifted off the ground. Both ends of the pole are placed on two independent but secure positions, such as on two stacks of old tires. While dangling, sufferers are raped, beaten, burned with cigarettes, drowned, or shocked. The pau-de-arara is reportedly still in use in many Brazilian police stations.

paulista—A person or thing from the state of São Paulo.

paulistano—A person or thing from the city of São Paulo.

Polícia Civil—"Civilian Police." The main function of this plainclothes group is to carry out detective work. They are a separate entity from the Polícia Militar.

Polícia Especial—"Special Police." An offensive police unit until 1960 in selected metropolitan areas, especially Rio de Janeiro. Known in street vernacular as the "Tomato Heads" because of their khaki uniforms and red caps, they were generally not popular with the public.

Polícia Federal—"Federal Police." Formed with American help in the late 1960s, the Polícia Federal operates in areas of interstate and international crime. They often provide technical help to the country's other police forces, control its borders, and even safeguard its judicial process.

Polícia Militar—"Military Police." Called "military" because they use uniforms and live together in barracks, these constables have nothing to do with the Brazilian armed forces or the Polícia Civil. They are supposed to provide the services of a regular, visable police force protecting the civilian population.

polish corridor—A method of torture involving two lines of individuals with Billy clubs who beat detainees scampering between the lines from one end to the other.

povão—Common people in both rural and urban settings.

presunto—(lit., a "ham") A murder victim in the argot of extermination groups. The term comes from the reality that Brazilians usually eat their ham cold, coupled to the fact that a corpse turns cold.

queimando o arquivo—(lit., "burning the archive") In police parlance, the expression is used to describe the murder of potential witnesses.

subelites—Situational and transitory muscle providers, examples of which include the police, conscripted members of the military, guards, and all types of bullies in the employ of some higher authority. Note that the Brazilian lower classes (including trustworthy non-Whites) are easily fitted into the fleeting roles of subelites.

tenentes—"lieutenants." Often used in connection with *tenentismo* or the movement of idealistic lieutenants in the 1920s. These officers often felt that only they knew what was best for the country.

tenentismo—See above under tenentes.

Bibliography

In 1988, the bulk of material from Rio de Janeiro's DOPS files was given to the Arquivo Público do Estado do Rio de Janeiro (APERJ). Sadly, over the years, the document classification systems used for this material by the many variations of Rio's political police have been inconsistent. Objects from this source are thus cited here by headline, date (when given), and identifying topic, plus the *pasta* (or folder) in which each can be located.

Moreover, APERJ divided the bequest into items from DESPS (the Delegacia Especial de Segurança Política e Social) and objects from DOPS. Another division is in the planning stages. Because such groupings and their implementation are beyond the scope of this project, and since every object can be located by the above method, the generic acronym PPARJ (for Political Police Archives, Rio de Janeiro) is used in this volume before each entry to signify *all* political police items housed at APERJ.

In respect to the rest of the references, the names of authors, titles of works, places of publication, and publishers are given exactly as they appeared at the time of publication on the entries listed below. Orthographic reforms between Portugal and Brazil have resulted in slightly different spellings of some Portuguese words in the text. Except where specifically noted, all archival entries are from Brazil.

Archives

Arquivo Castelo Branco [ACB], document, "Investigações especias," nos. 1–4, 6–21, pasta U1.

———, document, "Investigações especias," part 1, pasta U2.

———, document, "Subversão e IPMs," no. 11, pasta T.

Arquivo Filinto Müller, biography, "Lindolfo Collor," 1937, CPDOC.

Arquivo Getúlio Vargas [AGV], letter, "Goulart to Vargas," February 22, 1954, 02.22/1.

Arquivo *Jornal do Brasil* [*AJB*], *Retrato do Brasil* [January 22, 1987], trabalho escravidão/pasta.

———, newspaper article, *Jornal do Brasil,* September 15, 1979, escravidão/pasta.

———, newspaper article, *Jornal do Brasil,* July 11, 1986, escravidão/pasta.

———, newspaper article, *Jornal do Brasil,* August 8, 1986, escravidão/pasta.

———, newspaper article, *Jornal do Brasil,* August 9, 1986, escravidão/pasta.

———, newspaper article, *O Globo,* May 7, 1983, escravidão/pasta.

———, newspaper article, *O Globo,* April 19, 1987, escravidão/pasta.

———, newspaper article, *Estado de São Paulo,* August 2, 1986, escravidão/pasta.

———, newspaper article, *Jornal da Tarde,* August 26, 1986, escravidão/pasta.

Arquivo Nacional, document PH/FOT/2086.

Canada, letter, "James M. Weld to the Under-Secretary of State for External Affairs, Ottawa," January 15, 1962, UKPRO FO 371162132.

Centro de Pesquisa e Documentação de História Contemporânea do Brasil [CPDOC], oral history, "Abelardo Jurema," 1977.

———, oral history, "Alzira Vargas do Amaral Peixoto," 1979.

———, oral history, "Augusto do Amaral Peixoto," 1975.

———, oral history, "Guilherme Figueiredo," 1977.

———, oral history, "Henrique Lott," 1978.

———, oral history, "João Pinheiro Neto," 1977.

———, oral history, "José Gomes Talarico," 1978–79.

———, oral history, "Osvaldo Lima Filho," 1978–79.

———, oral history, "Paulo Pinheiro Chagas," 1977.

———, oral history, "Renato Archer," 1977–78.

Comissão Pastoral da Terra [CPT]-Acre Archives: newspaper article, *A Gazeta* (Rio Branco). January 1, 1994.

———, newspaper article, *A Gazeta.* January 13, 1994.

———, newspaper article, *A Gazeta.* March 2, 1994.

———, newspaper article, *A Gazeta.* July 7, 1995.

———, newspaper article, *A Gazeta.* November 26, 1996.

———, newspaper article, *O Rio Branco* (Rio Branco). January 11, 1995.

———, newspaper article, *O Rio Branco.* January 20, 1995.

———, newspaper article, *O Rio Branco.* July 5, 1995.

———, newspaper article, *O Rio Branco.* July 2, 1996.

———, newspaper article, *O Rio Branco.* July 14, 1999.

———, newspaper article, *Página 20* (Rio Branco). October 1, 1995.

———, newspaper article, *Página 20.* August 18, 1996.

———, newspaper article, *Página 20.* July 14, 1999.

John W.F. Dulles Archive, letter, Napoleão de Carvalho to Fernando Goldgaber, May 12, 1985.

Lyndon B. Johnson Presidential Library [LBJPL] NSF Co Brazil, box 10, vol. III, 4/64, documents 147–48.

———, NSF Co Brazil, boxes 11–12, vol. VI, 12/65–3/67, document 61.

———, NSF Co Brazil, boxes 11–12, vol. VII, 3/67–11/68, document 2.

Political Police Archives, Rio de Janeiro [PPARJ], deposition, "Saulo Garroux," April 3, 1968, secreto/pasta 15.

———, document, "Acción Cubana en el Brasil," June 1–15, 1963, comunismo/pasta 79.

———, document, "A nova téchnica da subversão," February [no day], 1969, secreto/pasta 40.

———, document, "[Apelidos dos dirigentes do P.C.B.]," [no date], comunismo/pasta 69.

———, document, "As Ligas Camponesas (Servico Cubano de Informação) (Carlos Todd, Red.), Coral Gables, Fla., especialmente os nos. 118, 119, 120 e 121," [no date], comunismo/pasta 50.

———, document, "Assalto ao carro pagador do IPEG," November 19, 1968, secreto/pasta 34.

———, document, "Atividades particulares do atual interventor de Mato Grosso," [no date], alemão/pasta 17.

———, document, "Boletim de informações no. 11/62," part 3, [no date], comunismo/pasta 81.

———, document, "CARIOCAS," [no date], comunismo/pasta 87.

———, document, "Centro de Informações da Marinha, Informe no. 0566," May 9, 1967, secreto/pasta 8.

———, document, "Centro de Informações da Marinha, Informe no. 0686," May 20, 1966, secreto/pasta 8.

———, document, "Comunicado no. 8 das forças guerrilheiras do Araguaia," [July 1974], comunismo/pasta 140.

———, document, "Cursos realizados em Cuba," November 21, 1972, comunismo/pasta 115.

———, document, "Detidos—F.M.I," [no date], secreto/pasta 14.

———, document, "DI/SP/SA—Informe no. 464," June 24, 1968, secreto/pasta 26.

———, document, "DI/SP/SAS—Informação no. 631," August 20, 1968, secreto/pasta 28.

———, document, "DI/SP/SAS—Informação no. 701," September 6, 1968, secreto/pasta 29.

———, document, "DI/SP/SAS—Informação no. 887," November 8, 1968, secreto/pasta 34.

———, document, "DI/SP/SAS—Informação no. 893," November 11, 1968, secreto/pasta 34.

———, document, "D.P.S. S.I.-S.S," December 30, 1955, comunismo/pasta 48.

———, document, "DSIEC/SEP/Ofício confidencial no. 6/circular," September 8, 1969, secreto/pasta 50.

———, document, "Encaminhamento no. 102/ARSI/GB/DSI/MEC/71," December 29, 1971, comunismo/pasta 137.

———, document, "Estudantes detidos,"[no date], secreto/pasta 14.

———, document, "Extra—São Paulo por dentro do Francisco Eugênio Santiago," May 3, 1968, secreto/pasta 19.

———, document, "Extrato das declarações prestadas pelos treze banidos em Cuba," secreto/pasta 61.

———, document, "Grupos dos onze de Brizola," [no date], comunismo/pasta 66.

———, document, "Histórico das atividades políticas dos parlamentares comunistas," n.d., comunismo/pasta 23.

———, document, "I.B.G.E," October 7, 1964 [date received], comunismo/pasta 64.

———, document, "Infiltração no meio artístico," August 28, 1967, secreto/pasta 15.

———, document, "Informação no. 541," October 1, 1968, secreto/pasta 31.

———, document, "Informação no. 0738/75," December 2, 1975, comunismo/ pasta 144.

———, document, "Informação no. 02213 DARQ/DGIE," June 23, 1976, comunismo/pasta 146.

———, document, "Informação no. S-072/76/JSPDN," December 12, 1976, comunismo/pasta 149.

———, document, "Informações atualizadas," June 18, 1964, comunismo/pasta 81.

———, document, "Informe: Grupo dos onze ou comandos nacionalistas," [no date], comunismo/pasta 66.

———, document, "Informe no. 25-B/73," June 27, 1973, comunismo/pasta 119.

———, document, "Informe no. 210," August 19, 1968, secreto/pasta 28.

———, document, "Informe no. 279 CH/68," July 15, 1968, secreto/pasta 29.

———, document, "Informe no. 323 CH/68," July 26, 1968, secreto/pasta 30.

———, document, "Informe no. 329, SI 66," October 10, 1966, secreto/pasta 12.

———, document, "Informe no. 574/SFICI," April 13, 1964, secreto/pasta 1.

———, document, "Informe no. 850-C/64," November 17, 1964, secreto/pasta 1.

———, document, "Informe no. 2533/SFICI (SAS/557/8 Jul 64)," July 8, 1964, comunismo/pasta 120.

———, document, "Informe no. 2930/SNI/ARJ (SS 17/676/26 ago 64)," August 26, 1964, secreto/pasta 2.

———, document, "Informe no. 3211/SNI/ARJ (SS 17/799/06 out 64)," October 6, 1964, secreto/pasta 10.

———, document, "Informe no. 3322/SNI/ARJ (SS 17/853/20 out 64)," October 20, 1964, secreto/pasta 5.

———, document, "Informe no. SP/015," April 4, 1966, secreto/pasta 21.

———, document, "Inquérito de subversão e terrorismo: casos esclarecidos no presente inquérito, com o consequente estabelecimento das respectivas autorais," January 23, 1969, comunismo/pasta 141.

———, document, "Inqueirto no. 09/68," March 31, 1968, secreto/pasta 18.

———, document, "Ministério da Marinha, Centro de Informações da Marinha, Informação no. 0345," May 29, 1968, secreto/pasta 27.

———, document, "Montevideo: movimento entre exilados, reuniões," [no date], comunismo/pasta 80.

———, document, "Operação Limpeza," September 13, 1967, secreto/pasta 14.

———, document, "Participantes 300 congresso da UNE," [no date], comunismo/pasta 127a.

———, document, "Pedido de busca no. 56/SP," January 22, 1968, secreto/pasta 28.

———, document, "Pedido de busca no. 97/67," July 26, 1966, secreto/pasta 16.

———, document, "Pedido de busca no. [408]," October 4, 1967, secreto/pasta 19.

———, document, "Pedido de busca no. 2280/SNI/ARJ/1967," September 26, 1967, secreto/pasta 34.

———, document, "Pichamento de muro," September 19–20, 1967, secreto/pasta 14.

———, document, "Planilha de registro," [in file: "João Goulart ou João Belchior Marques Goulart"], prontuário 1305.

———, document, "Processo protocolado sob no. 183-S [by hand], informação no. 527," October 7, 1955, administração/pasta 1a.

———, document, "Refª: Prot° no. DO-359/68—Informação: no. MR-2/194/68," October 8, 1968, secreto/pasta 34.

———, document, "Relação dos esquerdistas e agitadores detidos pelas autoridades revolucionárias em Belo Horizonte, de 1° de abril até a presente data, todos registrados no DOPS," July 30, 1964, secreto/pasta 8.

———, document, "Relatorio: agente A.O.C. de Montevidéu, Uruguai," [no date], comunismo/pasta 65

———, document, "Reuniões do PCB," August 13, 1960, comunismo/pasta [no number].

———, document, "Secretaria da doutrina integalista [*sic*]," March 15, 1935, integralismo/pasta 1.

———, document, "Terroristas/assaltantes," June 24, 1969 [date received], secreto/pasta 46.

———, document, "[untitled report on Groups of Eleven]," December 3, 1965, comunismo/pasta 81.

———, file, "João Goulart ou João Belchior Marques Goulart," prontuário 1305.

———, identity card, "Administração Estudantes Calabouço: no. 994—Ocimar Modesto Gonçalves," December 30, 1967, secreto/pasta 24.

———, identity card, "*Dom* Adherbal Franco Moraes," March 14, 1966, secreto/pasta 46.

———, letter, "Airton José Guimarães Gouget to diretor Departamento de Ordem Política [e] Social," April 9, 1968, administração/pasta 42.

———, letter, "Alex Polari de Alverga, *et al.*, to conselho federal da Ordem dos Advogados do Brasil," November 24, 1976, comunismo/pasta 149.

———, letter, "Cecil de Macedo Borer to diretor da Seção de Segurança Nacional do M.J.N.I. [Josias de Carvalho Argons]," November 21, 1963, administração/pasta 34.

———, letter, "Chefe do setor [unsigned] to D.P.S," relação de investigadores ns° 1 a 87, July 31, 1947, administração/pasta 15.

———, letter, "Darcy Schettino Rocha to Hennio Corrêia da Silva," July 12, 1968, secreto/pasta 25.

———, letter, "Darcy Schettino Rocha to José Pombo Pereira Filho," September 30, 1967, secreto/pasta 14.

———, letter, "Deuteronomio Rocha dos Santos to José Pereira de Vasconcellos," July 1, 1968, secreto/pasta 24.

———, letter, "Gerardo to Petronio," October [no day], 1962, comunismo/pasta 50.

———, letter, "Horácio Pereira (Informação no. 228/65.-)," October 5, 1965, secreto/pasta 10.

———, letter, "J.E. Hoover to Brady," April 15, 1964, secreto/pasta 10.

———, letter, "Joaquim Miguel Vieira Ferreira to Adauto Esmeraldo," March 24, 1955, comunismo/pasta 70.

———, letter, "José Luiz Bettâmino Guimarães to director DPS," September 6, 1955, no. 333/2a/s, administração/pasta 1a.

———, letter, "Luiz Guimenez Neves to chief of S.O.P. [Secção Ordem Política]," June 13, 1966, secreto/pasta 8.

———, letter, "Maria Cristina Lacerda to Arthur da Costa e Silva," December 20, 1968, secreto/pasta 39.

———, letter, "Mario Borges to José Pereira de Vasconcellos," October 7, 1968, comunismo/pasta 87.

———, letter, "Matheus de Oliveira Franco to chefe of S.I," February 12, 1960, administração/pasta 3 cont.

———, letter, "Olindo Denys to Gonçalves Etchegoyen," July 27, 1943, integralismo/pasta 4, cont. i.

———, letter, "Syseno Sarmento to Gustavo Eugenio Borges," July 2, 1964, secreto/pasta 4.

———, miscellaneous documents, "Sindicancia para apurar como o jornal *O Mundo* obteve fotografias idênticas do prontuário de Cecil Borer," 1947, administração/pasta 1e.

———, newspaper article, *A Luta,* April 21, 1948, comunismo/pasta 4.

———, newspaper article, *A Luta,* April 29, 1948, comunismo/pasta 4e.

———, newspaper article, *Correio da Noite,* August 15, 1951, administração/pasta 22.

———, newspaper article, *Diario Carioca,* August 11, 1951, administração/pasta 22.

———, newspaper article, *Diario Popular,* August 10, 1951, administração/pasta 22.

———, newspaper article, *Jornal da Tarde,* June 4, 1970, secreto/pasta 52.

———, newspaper article, *Jornal do Brasil,* December 2, 1975, comunismo/pasta 144.

———, newspaper article, *O Globo,* August 10, 1951, n.p., administração/pasta 22.

———, newspaper article, *Última Hora,* August 13, 1951, administração/pasta 22.

———, newspaper article, *Última Hora,* August 15, 1951, administração/pasta 22.

———, newspaper article, *Última Hora,* September 25, 1967, secreto/pasta 19.

———, newspaper article, *Unidade Proletária,* December [no day], 1975, supplement, comunismo/pasta 144.

———, newspaper article, *Voz Operária,* November 1971, comunismo/pasta 104.

———, phamplet, "*Brasileiros!*" [no place: no publisher, no date (distributed in Rio de Janeiro, April 6, 1970)], comunismo/pasta 90.

———, phamplet, "*Eu, Gregório Bezerra, acuso!*" ([no place: no publisher], 1967), comunismo/pasta 82.

———, phamplet [by Neiva Moreira], *O exército e a crise brasileira.* (Montevideo: Diálogo S.R.L., 1968), secreto/pasta 53.

———, physical evidence, "[examples of lapel pins of the] Partido de Representação Popular," [no date], integralismo/pasta 19.

———, telegram, "Sylvio Frota to SSP/RJ," no. 10276, December 13, 1976 [in file: "João Goulart ou João Belchior Marques Goulart"], prontuário 1305.

Scuderie Detetive Le Cocq [SDLC], document, "Informativo social," November–December 1992.

———, reciepts, nos.1 19883–84, November 11, 1992.

United Kingdom, Public Record Office [UKPRO], letter, "C. O. I. Ramsden to [Robin] H. G. Edmonds," April 13, 1962, FO 371/162132.

———, letter, "P. H. Baldwin to Assistant Chief of Air Staff (Intelligence)," February 9, 1962, FO 371/162132.

———, letter, "R. S. Isaacson to [Robin] E. G. Edmonds," April 19, 1962, FO 371/162132.

United States, Central Intelligence Agency [CIA], document, "Brazil," SR-17, November 30, 1948.

———, document, "Memorandum: Brazil, 3 April 1964," [no number].

———, document, "Memorandum for the United States Intelligence Board," by Joseph Seltzer, NLK-76–199, no. 4, July 2, 1963.

———, document, "TDCS-3/540, 528," March 15, 1963.

———, document, "TDCS-3/543, 633," April 12, 1963.

———, document, "TDCS-3/546, 074," May 4, 1963.

———, document, "TDCS-3/565, 572," November 22, 1963.

———, document, "TDCS-3/584, 319," June 18, 1964.

———, document, "TDCS-314/12799–67," August 31, 1967.

———, Department of State, document, "Strategic Survey of Amazonas, Acre, Matto Grosso, and Goyaz," April 1, 1942, 097.3/Z1092/no. 724.

———, National Archives, letter, "Sibert to A.C. of S., G-2," May 2, 1941, MID 2657-K-128/5, no. 2703.

———, Office of Strategic Services, Latin America Section, document, "Survey of Interior Brazil," October 21, 1942, 097.3/Z1092/no. 784c.

Books, Journal Articles, Manuscripts, and Dissertations

Agee, Philip. *Inside the Company: CIA Diary.* London: Penguin, 1975.

Alves, Marcio Moreira. *A Grain of Mustard Seed: The Awakening of the Brazilian Revolution.* Garden City: Doubleday Anchor, 1973.

———. *Torturas e torturados.* Rio de Janeiro: Novo Idade, 1966.

Alves, Maria Helena Moreira. *Estado e oposição no Brasil, 1964–1984.* Clóvis Marques (trad.). Petrópolis: Vozes, 1984.

———. *State and Opposition in Military Brazil.* Austin: University of Texas Press, 1985.

———. "The Formation of the National Security State: The State and the Opposition in Military Brazil." Ph.D. diss., Department of Political Science, Massachusetts Institute of Technology, 1982.

Amado, Jorge. *A vida de Luís Carlos Prestes: O Cavaleiro da Esperança.* 4th ed. São Paulo: Martins, 1945.

———. *São Jorge dos Ilheus.* 20th ed. São Paulo: Martins, 1970.

———. *The Violent Land.* Samuel Putnam (trans.). 4th ed. New York: Avon, 1979.

Americas Watch. "Forced Labor in Brazil," December 30, 1990.

———. *Police Abuse in Brazil: Summary Executions and Torture in Sao* [*sic*] *Paulo and Rio de Janeiro.* [no place] Americas Watch, 1987.

———. *Rural Violence in Brazil.* New York and Washington DC: Human Rights Watch, 1991.

Amnesty International. *Brazil: Authorized Violence in Rural Areas.* London: Amnesty International, 1988.

———. *Brazil: "No One Here Sleeps Safely," Human Rights Violations against Detainees.* New York: Amnesty International, 1999.

Anderson, Kevin and Richard Quinney (eds.). *Erich Fromm and Critical Criminology: Beyond the Punitive Society.* Heinz Osterle and Kevin Anderson (trans.). Urbana: University of Illinois Press, 2000.

(Anonymous). "Nova questão religiosa?" *Paz e Terra.* vol. I, no. 2, September 1966.

(Anonymous). "O terrorismo cultural," *Revista Civilização Brasileira.* vol. I, March 1965.

Arquidiocese de São Paulo. *Brasil: nunca mais.* 6th ed. Petrópolis: Vozes, 1985.

———. "O regime militar," Projeto "Brasil: nunca mais." São Paulo: Arquidiocese de São Paulo, 1985, book 1, vol. I.

———. "Os funcionários," Projeto "Brasil: nunca mais." São Paulo: Arquidiocese de São Paulo, 1985, book 2, vol. III.

———. *Perfil dos atingidos.* Petrópolis: Voces, 1988.

Arruda, Marcos, *et al. The Multinational Corporations and Brazil: the Impact of Multinational Corporations in the Contemporary Brazilian Economy.* Toronto: Latin American Research Unit, 1975.

Artiaga, Zoroastro. *História de Goiás.* 2nd ed. Goiânia: Estado de Goiás, 1959.

Audrin, José. *Entre sertanejos e índios do norte.* Rio de Janeiro: Púgil and Agir, 1947.

———. *Os sertanejos que eu conheci.* Rio de Janeiro: José Olympio, 1963.

Azevedo, Moreira de. *O Rio de Janeiro: sua história, monumentos, homens notáveis, usos e curiosidades,* 3rd ed. Rio de Janeiro: Brasiliana, 1969, vol. II.

Baciu, Stefan. *Lavradio, 98: Histórias de um jornal de oposição: a Tribuna da Imprensa ao tempo de Carlos Lacerda.* Rio de Janeiro: Nova Fronteira, 1982.

Baffa, Ayrton. *Nos porões do SNI: o retrato do monstro de cabeça oca.* Rio de Janeiro: Objetiva, 1969.

Bandeira, [Luís Alberto] Moniz. *Brizola e o trabalhismo.* Rio de Janeiro: Civilização Brasileira, 1979.

———. *O governo João Goulart: as lutas sociais no Brasil, 1961–1964.* Rio de Janeiro: Civilização Brasileira, 1977.

———. *O 24 de agôsto de Jânio Quadros.* Rio de Janeiro: Melso, 1961.

———. *Presença dos Estados Unidos no Brasil: dois séculos de história.* Rio de Janeiro: Civilização Brasileira, 1973.

Barbosa, Adriano. *Esquadrão da Morte: um mal necessário?* Rio de Janeiro: Mandarino, 1971.

Barbosa, Eduardo. "As 1200 mortes do Esquadrão da Morte," *Violência.* June 1–14, 1973.

Barbosa, Sebastião. *Brasil: o país da impunidade.* São Paulo: Siciliano, 1991.

Barcellos, Caco. *Rota 66.* São Paulo: Globo, 1992.

Beloch, Israel and Alzira Alves de Abreu (coords.). *Dicionário histórico-biográfico brasileiro, 1930–1983.* Rio de Janeiro: Forense-Universitária, 1984.

Benci, Jorge. *Economia Cristã dos senhores no governo de escravos: livro brasileiro de 1700.* 2nd ed., Serafim Leite (ed.), Porto: Apostolado, 1954.

Betto, *Frei* [Carlos Alberto Libanio Christo]. *Batismo de sangue: os dominicanos e a morte de Carlos Marighella.* 2nd ed. Rio de Janeiro: Civilização Brasileira, 1982.

Bezerra, Gregório. *Memórias.* Rio de Janeiro: Civilização Brasileira, 1979, vol. II.

Bicudo, Hélio Pereira. *Meu depoimento sobre o Esquadrão da Morte.* 3rd ed., rev. São Paulo: Pontifícia Comissão de Justiça e Paz, 1976.

Biocca, Ettore. *Estratégia do terror: a face oculta e repressiva do Brasil.* Maria de Carvalho (trans.). Lisbon: Iniciativas, [no date].

Black, Jan Knippers. *United States Penetration of Brazil.* Philadelphia: University of Pennsylvania Press, 1977.

Blume, Norman. "Pressure Groups and Decision-Making in Brazil," *Studies in Comparative International Development.* vol. III, no. 11, 1967–68.

Boff, Leonardo and Clodovis Boff. *Da libertação: o sentido teológico das libertações sócio-históricas.* Petrópolis: Vozes, 1979.

Borges, Maurio. *O golpe em Goiás: história de uma grande traição.* Rio de Janeiro: Civilização Brasileira, 1965.

Boxer, Charles. *Race Relations in the Portuguese Colonial Empire, 1415–1825,* Oxford: Clarendon, 1963.

———. *The Golden Age of Brazil, 1695–1750: Growing Pains of a Colonial Society.* Berkeley: University of California Press, 1962.

Brandi, Paulo. *Vargas: da vida para a história.* 2nd ed., rev. Rio de Janeiro: Zahar, 1985.

Britto, Lemos. *Os systemas penitenciarios do Brasil.* Rio de Janeiro: Nacional, 1925, vol. II.

Bruneau, Thomas. "Conflict and Change in the Brazilian Catholic Church." unpublished Ph.D. diss., Department of Political Science, University of California, Berkeley, 1970.

Burns, E. Bradford. *Nationalism in Brazil: A Historical Survey.* New York: Praeger, 1968.

Calhoun, Craig. "Why Historical Sociology?" *Handbook of Historical Sociology.* Geard Delanty and Engin Isin (eds.). London: Sage, 2003.

Camargo, Aspásia. "Tenentismo," comments delivered before the seminar "Cenários de 1922." Fundação Getúlio Vargas/CPDOC, Rio de Janeiro, November 19, 1992.

[Campos, Roberto]. "Depoimento do Sr. Embaixador Roberto Campos, prestado em 20 e 26–6-63," *Revista Brasileira de Política Internacional.* September–December 1965.

Campos, Valério and Flora Maestri. *João Goulart.* 3rd ed. Porto Alegre: Tchê!, 1985.

Cardia, Nancy. *Pesquisa sobre atitudes, normas culturais e valores em relação a violência em 10 capitais brasileiras.* Brasília: Ministério da Justiça, Secretaria de Estado dos Direitos Humanos, 1999.

Carli, Gileno Dé. *Visão da crise.* Brasília: Universidade de Brasília, 1980.

Carneiro, Maria Luiza Tucci. *O anti-semitismo na era Vargas: fantasmas de uma geração, 1930–1945.* São Paulo: Brasiliense, 1988.

Carta, Mino and Raimundo Rodrigues Pereira (dirs.). *Retrado do Brasil (da monarquia ao estado militar).* São Paulo: Política Editora, 1984, vol. I.

Caso, Antônio (ed.). *A esquerda armada no Brasil, 1967–1971.* Thiago de Mello (trans.). Lisbon: Moraes, 1976.

Castro, Ferrera de. *A selva.* 15th ed. Lisboa: Gulmarães, 1954.

Cava, Ralph della. "Torture in Brazil," *Commonweal.* April 24, 1970.

Cavalcanti, Paulo. *O caso eu conto, como o caso fui: memórias políticas.* Recife: Guararapes, 1980, vol. II.

Chamberlain, Henry. *Views and Costumes of the City and Neighbourhood of Rio de Janeiro, Brazil: from Drawings Taken by Lieutenant Chamberlain, Royal Artillery, during the Years 1819 and 1820 with Descriptive Explanations.* London: Thomas McLean, 1822.

Chandler, Billy Jaynes. *The Bandit King: Lampião of Brazil.* College Station: Texas A&M University Press, 1978.

Chevigny, Paul. "Urban Police Violence in Brazil: Torture and Police Killings in São Paulo and Rio de Janeiro after Five Years," (Paulo Sérgio Pinheiro and Cynthia Arnson eds.). *Americas Watch,* vol. V, no. 5, May 31, 1993.

Chiavenato, Júlio J. *Cangaço: a força do coronel.* São Paulo: Brasiliense, 1990.

Civita, Victor (ed.), *Nosso século, 1945–1960: a Era dos Partidos.* São Paulo: Abril Cultural, 1985, part II, vol. VIII.

———. *Nosso século, 1960–1980: sob as ordens de Brasília.* São Paulo: Abril Cultural, 1986, part I, vol. IX.

———. *Nosso século, 1960–1980: sob as ordens de Brasília.* São Paulo: Abril Cultural, 1986, part II. vol. X.

Comissão Pastoral da Terra. *Conflitos no campo Brasil/85.* [no place: no publisher, no date].

———. *Conflitos no campo Brasil/86.* [no place: no publisher, no date].

———. *Conflitos no campo Brasil/87.* [no place]: Comsaude, 1988.

———. *Conflitos no campo Brasil/88.* Goiânia: CPT, 1989.

———. *Conflitos no campo Brasil/89.* Goiânia: CPT, 1990.

———. *Conflitos no campo—Brasil/1991.* Goiânia: CPT, 1992.

———. *Conflitos no campo Brasil' 92.* Goiânia: CPT, 1993.

———. *Conflitos no campo Brasil 93.* Goiânia: CPT, 1994.

———. *Conflitos no campo Brasil 94.* Goiânia: CPT, 1995.

———. *Conflitos no campo Brasil 95.* Goiânia: CPT, 1996.

———. *Conflitos no campo Brasil 96.* Goiânia: CPT, 1997.

———. *Conflitos no campo Brasil 97.* Goiânia: CPT, 1998.

———. *Conflitos no campo Brasil 98.* Goiânia: CPT, 1999.

———. *Conflitos no campo Brasil 99*. Goiânia: CPT, 2000.

———. *Espinhoso caminho para a liberdade: conlitos no campo Brasil—1990*. Goiânia: CPT, 1991.

———. *Relação dos julgamentos—Tribunal do júri de assassinatos de trabalhadores rurais, índios, advogados e agentes pastorais de 01 de janeiro de 1964 a 31 de dezembro de 1993*. Goiânia: CPT, 1994.

———. VV.AA. *Trabalho escravo no Brasil contemporâneo*. São Paulo: Edições Loyola, 1999.

Comitê Brasileiro pela Anista. *Desaparecidos políticos: artigos, entrevistas, documentos, reportagens, depoimentos, fotografias*. Rio de Janeiro: Opção, 1979.

Conrad, Robert. *Children of God's Fire: A Documentary History of Black Slavery in Brazil*. Princeton: Princeton University Press, 1983.

———. "Nineteenth-Century Brazilian Slavery," *Slavery and Race Relations in Latin America*, Robert Toplin (ed.), Westport: Greenwood, 1974.

Cony, Carlos Hector. *O ato e o fato: crônicas políticas*. Rio de Janeiro: Civilização Brasileira, 1964.

Cortés, Carlos. *Gaúcho Politics in Brazil: The Politics of Rio Grande do Sul, 1930–1964*. Albuquerque: University of New Mexico Press, 1974.

Cowell, Adrian. *The Decade of Destruction: The Crusade to Save the Amazon Rain Forest*. New York: Holt, 1990.

Dallari, Dalmo de Abreu. "The *Força Pública* of São Paulo in State and National Politics," *Perspectives on Armed Politics in Brazil*. Henry Keith and Robert Hayes (eds.). Tempe: Arizona State University Press, 1976.

Darwin, Charles. *The Voyage of the Beagle*. New York: Collier, 1909.

Debret, Jean. *Voyage pittoresque et historique au Brésil*. Paris: Frères, 1835, vol. II.

Dias, Evarardo. *Bastilhas modernas, 1924–1926*. São Paulo: Obras Sociaes e Literarias, 1926.

Dias, Luzimar Nogueira (ed.). *Esquerda armada: testemunho dos presos políticos do presídio Milton Dias Moreira no Rio de Janeiro*. Vitória: Edições do Leitor, 1979.

Dimenstein, Gilberto. *A guerra dos meninos: assassinatos de menores no Brasil*. São Paulo; Brasiliense, 1990.

———. *Brazil: War on Children*. Jan Rocha (intro.). Chris Whitehorse (trans.). London: Latin America Bureau, 1991.

Dreifuss, René Armand. *1964: a conquesta do estado: ação política, poder e golpe de classe*. Petrópolis: Vozes, 1981.

Drosdoff, Daniel. *Linha dura no Brasil: o governo Médici, 1969–1974.* Norberto de Paula Lima (trans.). São Paulo: Global, 1986.

Dulles, John W. F. *Brazilian Communism, 1935–1945: Repression during World Upheaval.* Austin: University of Texas Press, 1983.

———. *Carlos Lacerda, Brazilian Crusader, Volume I: The Years 1914–1960.* Austin: University of Texas Press, 1991.

———. *Carlos Lacerda, Brazilian Crusader, Volume II: The Years 1960–1977.* Austin: University of Texas Press, 1996.

———. "Carlos Lacerda." vol. II, pre-publication manuscript.

———. *Castello Branco: The Making of a Brazilian President.* College Station: Texas A&M Press, 1978.

———. *President Castello Branco: Brazilian Reformer.* College Station: Texas A&M University Press, 1980.

———. "The Case Against the Vargas Regime (1930–1945): Adventures of Sobral Pinto, the Conscience of Brazil." pre-publication manuscript.

———. *Unrest in Brazil: Political-Military Crises, 1955–1964.* Austin: University of Texas Press, 1970.

———. *Vargas of Brazil: A Political Biography.* Austin: University of Texas Press, 1967.

Edmundo, Luiz. *O Rio de Janeiro no tempo dos vice-reis,* 4th ed. Rio de Janeiro: Conquista, 1956, vol. I.

Élis, Bernardo. *A enxada veranico de janeiro.* 6th ed. Rio de Janeiro: José Olympio, 1987.

Encyclopædia Britannica. 15th ed. Chicago: Encyclopædia Britannica, 1994, Micropædia, vol. XIII.

Encyclopédia Mirador International. São Paulo: Encyclopaedia Britannica do Brasil, 1975.

Ewbank, Thomas. *Life in Brazil: Or a Visit to the Land of the Cocoa and the Palm.* New York: Harper, 1856.

Faulkner, William. *Requiem for a Nun.* adapted to the stage by Ruth Ford, New York: Random House, 1959.

Fishlow, Albert. "Flying Down to Rio: Perspectives on U.S.-Brazil Relations," *Foreign Affairs,* vol. LVII, no. 2, Winter 1978/79.

Flynn, Peter. *Brazil: A Political Analysis.* Bolder: Westview, 1978.

Fon, Antonio Carlos. *Tortura: a história da repressão política no Brasil.* 7th ed. São Paulo: Global, 1986.

Fonseca, Guedo. "DOPS: pouco do seu história," *Revista da associação dos delagados da polícia.* ano X, no. 28, December 1989.

Foucault, Michel. *Discipline and Punish: The Birth of the Prison.* Alan Sheridan (trans.), 2nd ed., New York: Vintage Books, 1997.

French, John. "Industrial Workers and the Birth of the Populist Republic in Brazil, 1945–1946," *Latin American Perspectives.* vol. XVI, no. 4, Fall 1989.

Freyre, Gilberto. *The Masters and the Slaves: A Study in the Development of Brazilian Civilization.* Samuel Putnam (trans.). 2nd ed. New York: Alfred Knopf, 1966.

Fróes, Hemílcio. *Véspera do primeiro de abril: ou nacionalistas x entreguistas.* Rio de Janeiro: Imago, 1993.

Gabeira, Fernando. *Carta sobre a anistia: a entrevista do Pasquim: conversação sobre 1968.* Rio de Janeiro: Codecri, 1979.

———. *O que é isso companheiro?* 29th ed. Rio de Janeiro: Nova Fronteira, 1982.

Gardner, George. *Travels in the Interior of Brazil: Principally through the Northern Provinces and the Gold and Diamond Districts, during the Years 1836–1841.* London: Reeve, 1846.

Gaspari, Elio. *A ditadura derrotada: o sacerdote e o feiticeiro.* São Paulo: Companhia das Letras, 2003.

Gomes, Pedro. "Minas: do diálogo ao 'front,'" *Os idos de março e a queda em abril.* Alberto Dines, *et al.* (eds.), 3rd ed. Rio de Janeiro: José Alvaro, 1964.

Gorender, Jacob. *Combate nas trevas: a esquerda brasileira: das ilusões perdidas à luta armada.* São Paulo: Ática, 1987.

Grael, Dickson. *Aventura, corrupção e terrorismo: à sombra da impunidade.* Petrópolis: Vozes, 1986.

Green, Duncan (ed.). *Fight for the Forest: Chico Mendes in His Own Words.* Chris Whitehouse (trans.). London: Latin America Bureau, 1989.

Guedes, Carlos Luís. *Tinha que ser Minas.* Rio de Janeiro: Nova Fronteira, 1979.

Hahner, June. *Poverty and Politics: the Urban Poor in Brazil, 1870–1920.* Albuquerque: University of New Mexico Press, 1986.

Hall, Michael and Paulo Sérgio Pinheiro. "The Control and Policing of the Working Class in Brazil." paper presented to the Conference on the History of Law, Labor and Crime, University of Warwick, September 15–18, 1983.

Heine, Heinrich. *Almansor: Eine Tragödie.* Berlin: Duemmler, 1823.

Henriques, Affonso. *Ascensão e queda de Getúlio Vargas: declínio e morte.* Rio de Janeiro: Record, 1966, vol. III.

———. *Ascensão e queda de Getúlio Vargas: o maquiavélico.* Rio de Janeiro: Record, 1966, vol. I.

Hobsbawm, Eric. *Bandits.* New York: Delacorte, 1969.

Holloway, Thomas. *Policing Rio de Janeiro: Repression and Resistance in a 19th-Century City.* Stanford: Stanford University Press, 1993.

———. "The Brazilian 'Judicial Police' in Florianópolis, Santa Catarina, 1841–1871," *Journal of Social History,* vol. XX, no. 4, Summer 1987.

Houaiss, Antônio (ed.). *Grande enciclopédia Delta Larousse.* Rio de Janeiro: Delta, 1978.

James, Herman. *Brazil after a Century of Independence.* New York: Macmillian, 1925.

Joffily, José. *Harry Berger.* Rio de Janeiro: Paz e Terra, 1986.

Jordão, Fernando. *Dossiê Herzog: prisão, tortura e morte no Brasil.* 3rd ed. São Paulo: Global, 1979.

Jorge, Fernando. *Cale a boca, jornalista: o ódio e a fúria dos mandões contra a imprensa brasileira.* São Paulo: Vozes, 1987.

José, Emiliano and Oldack Miranda. *Lamarca: o capitão da guerrilha.* 10th ed. São Paulo: Global, 1986.

Joyce, James. *Ulysses.* New York: Modern Library, 1934.

Julião, Francisco. "The Practice and Preaching of Revolution," *Revolution in Brazil: Politics and Society in a Developing Nation.* Irving Horowitz (ed.). New York: E. P. Dutton, 1964.

Jurema, Abelardo. *Sexta-feira, 13: os últimos dias do governo João Goulart.* 2nd ed. Rio de Janeiro: Cruzeiro, 1964.

Karasch, Mary. "Slave Life in Rio de Janeiro, 1808–1850." Ph.D. diss., Department of History, University of Wisconsin, 1972.

Henry Keith. "Soldiers as Saviors: the Brazilian Military Revolts of 1922 and 1924 in Historical Perspective," unpublished PhD thesis, Department of History, University of California, Berkeley, 1970.

Kent, R. K. "Palmares: An African State in Brazil," *Journal of African History.* vol. VI, no. 2, 1965.

Kerbo, Harold. *Social Stratification and Inequality: Class Conflict in Historical, Comparative, and Global Perspective.* 5th ed. New York: McGraw-Hill, 2003.

Kidder, Daniel and James Fletcher. *Brazil and the Brazilians: Portrayed in Historical and Descriptive Sketches.* Philadelphia: Childs and Peterson, 1857.

Kidder, Daniel. *Sketches of Residence and Travels in Brazil: Embracing Historical and Geographical Notices of the Empire and its Several Provinces.* Philadelphia: Sorin and Ball, London: Wiley and Putnam, 1845, vol. I.

Klein, Lucia and Marcus Figueiredo. *Legitimidade e coação no Brasil pós-64.* Rio de Janeiro: Forense-Universitária, 1978.

Labaki, Amir. *1961: a crise da renúncia e a solução parlamentarista.* São Paulo: Brasiliense, 1986.

Lacerda, Carlos. *Depoimento.* Rio de Janeiro: Nova Fronteira, 1977.

———. *Depoimento.* 2nd ed. Rio de Janeiro: Nova Fronteira, 1978.

———. *et al. Reportagens que abalaram o Brasil.* Rio de Janeiro: Bloch, 1973.

———. *O poder das idéias.* 2nd ed. Rio de Janeiro: Record, 1963.

Landes, Ruth. *The City of Women.* New York: Macmillian, 1947.

Langguth, A. J. *Hidden Terrors.* New York: Pantheon, 1978.

Leacock, Ruth. *Requiem for Revolution: The United States and Brazil, 1961–1969.* Kent: Kent State University Press, 1990.

Levine, Robert. "Editor's Introduction: The Millenarian and Messianic Legacy," *Luso-Brazilian Review.* vol. XXVIII, no. 1, Summer 1991.

———. "'Mud-Hut Jerusalem': Canudos Revisited," *Hispanic American Historical Review.* vol. LXVIII, no. 3, August 1988.

Lewin, Linda. "The Oligarchical Limitations of Social Banditry in Brazil: the Case of the 'Good' Thief Antonio Silvino," *Past and Present.* no. 82, 1979.

Lima, Valentina da Rocha (coord.). *Getúlio: uma história oral.* Rio de Janeiro: Record, 1986.

Lobo, Amílcar. *A hora do lobo, a hora do carneiro.* Petrópolis: Vozes, 1989.

Loether, Herman and Donald McTavish. *Descriptive and Inferential Statistics: An Introduction.* Boston: Allyn and Bacon, 1976.

Lopes, Adérito. *O Esquadrão da Morte: São Paulo, 1968–1971.* Lisbon: Prelo, 1973.

Lourenço Filho, M. B. "Redução das taxas de analfabetismo no Brasil entre 1900 e 1960: descrição e análise," *Revista Brasileira de Estudos Pedagógicos.* vol. XLIV, no. 100, October-December 1965.

Louzerio, José. *Lúcio Flávio: o passageiro da agonia.* 9th ed. Rio de Janeiro: Nova Fronteira, 1985.

Luppi, Carlos Alberto. *Manoel Fiel Filho: quem vai pagar por este crime?* São Paulo: Escrita, 1980.

Lyon, Christopher (ed.). *The International Dictionary of Films and Filmmakers: Directors/Filmmakers.* New York: Perigee, 1984, vol. II.

Macaulay, Neill. *The Prestes Column: Revolution in Brazil.* New York: New Viewpoints, 1974.

Marchetti, Victor and John Marks. *The CIA and the Cult of Intelligence.* New York: Alfred Knopf, 1974.

Marighela, Carlos. *Escritos de Carlos Marighella.* São Paulo: Livramento, 1979.

———. *For the Liberation of Brazil.* John Butt and Rosemary Sheed (trans.). Middlesex: Penguin, 1971.

———. *The Terrorist Classic: Manual of the Urban Guerrilla.* Gene Hanrahan (ed.). Chapel Hill: Documentary, 1985.

Markun, Paulo, and Ernesto Rodrigues. *A máfia manda flores: Mariel, o fim de um mito.* São Paulo: Globo, 1981.

Marx, Karl and Frederick Engels. *Manifesto of the Communist Party: A Modern Edition.* London and New York: Verso, 1998.

McCann, Frank. *The Brazilian-American Alliance, 1937–1945.* Princeton: Princeton University Press, 1973.

Mello, Federico Pernambucano de. *Guerreiros do sol: o banditismo no nordeste do Brasil.* Recife: Massangana, 1985.

Mendonça, Eliana Rezende Furtado de (dir.). *Os arquivos das polícias políticas: reflexos de nossa história contemporânea.* Rio de Janeiro: FAPERJ, 1994.

Merton, Robert K. "Social Stucture and Anomie," *American Sociological Review,* vol. III, October 1938.

Mocellin, Renato. *A história crítica da nação brasileira.* 5th ed. São Paulo: Editora do Brasil, 1987.

Monteiro, José and Adriano Barbosa. *Do Esquadrão ao Mão Branca.* Rio de Janeiro: Jaguaribe, 1980.

Moraes, Dênis de. *A esquerda e o golpe de 64: vinte e cico anos depois, as forças populares repensam seus mitos, sonhos e ilusões.* Rio de Janeiro: Espaço e Tempo, 1989.

Moraes, João Luiz de. *O Calvário de Sônia Angel: uma história de terror nos porões da ditadura.* Rio de Janeiro: MEC, 1994.

Moraes Neto, Geneton. *Dossiê Brasil: as histörias por tráis da história recente do país.* 9th ed. Rio de Janeiro: Objetiva, 1997.

Morais, Fernando. *Chatô: o rei do Brasil.* São Paulo: Companhia das Letras, 1994.

———. *Olga,* 3rd ed. São Paulo: Alfa-Omega, 1985.

Morél, Edmar. *O golpe começou em Washington.* Rio de Janeiro: Civilização Brasileira, 1965.

Moura, Clóvis. *Diário da guerrilha do Araguaia.* São Paulo: Alfa-Omega, 1979.

Movimento dos Trabalhadores Rurais Sem-Terra. *Assassinatos no campo: crime e impunidade, 1964–1986.* 2nd ed., rev. São Paulo: Global, 1987.

Myrdal, Gunnar. *An American Dilemma.* New York: Harper and Brothers, 1944.

Myscofski, Carole. "Messianic Themes in Portuguese and Brazilian Literature in the Sixteenth and Seventeenth Centuries," *Luso-Brazilian Review.* vol. XXVIII, no. 1, Summer 1991.

Nascimento, Abdias do. *O quilombismo.* Petrópolis: Vozes, 1980.

Nasser, David. *A revolução dos covardes: diário decreto de Severo Fournier, reportagens políticas e ordens da censura do ditador.* Rio de Janeiro: O Cruzeiro, 1947.

———. *Falta alguém em Nuremberg: torturas da polícia de Filinto.* 2nd ed. Rio de Janeiro: Edições do Povo, [no date].

———. *Falta alguém em Nuremberg: torturas da polícia de Filinto Strubling Müller.* 4th ed. Rio de Janeiro: O Cruzeiro, 1966.

Neuhouser, Kevin. "The Radicalization of the Brazilian Catholic Church in Comparative Perspective," *American Sociological Review.* vol. LIV, no. 2, April 1989.

North American Congress on Latin America. *NACLA Report on the Americas.* vol. XIII, no. 3, May–June 1979.

Oliveira, Hildérico. *Tortura à brasileira.* Brasília: Câmara dos Deputados, 1981.

Oliveira, Xavier de. *Beatos e cangaceiros.* Rio de Janeiro: Revista dos Tribunais, 1920.

Onis, Juan de. "Brazil on the Tightrope toward Democracy," *Foreign Affairs.* vol. LXVIII, no. 4, Fall 1989.

Page, Joseph. *The Revolution that Never Was.* New York: Grossman, 1972.

Parker, Phyllis. *1964: o papel dos Estados Unidos no golpe de estado de 31 de março.* Carlos Nayfeld (trans.). Rio de Janeiro: Civilização Brasileira, 1977.

Pessar, Patricia. "Three Moments in Brazilian Millenarianism: The Interrelationship between Politics and Religion," *Luso-Brazilian Review.* vol. XXVIII, no. 1, Summer 1991.

Pinheiro, Paulo Sérgio. "The Legacy of Authoritarianism: Violence and the Limits of Democratic Transitions." comments delivered during the presentation of his paper presented to the 16th Conference of the Latin American Studies Association, Washington, DC, April 4–6, 1991.

———. "The Legacy of Authoritarianism: Violence and the Limits of Democratic Transitions." paper presented to the 16th Conference of the Latin American Studies Association, Washington, DC, April 4–6, 1991.

Price, Robert. "Rural Unionization in Brazil." University of Wisconsin Land Tenure Center, no. 14, 1964.

Quadros, Jânio. "Brazil's New Foreign Policy," *Foreign Affairs.* vol. XL, no. 1, October 1961.

Quartim, João. *Dictator and Armed Struggle in Brazil.* David Fernbach (trans.). New York: New Left Review, 1971.

Queiroz, Maria Isaura Pereira de. *O messianismo: no Brasil e no mundo.* São Paulo: Dominus, 1965.

Quinney, Richard. *Class, State and Crime: On the Theory and Practice of Criminal Justice.* New York: David McKay, 1977.

———. *Critique of Legal Order: Crime Control in Capitalist Society.* New York: Little, Brown, 1974.

———. "The Existential Question, What is Real," *The Critical Criminologist.* vol. VI, no. 2, Summer-Fall, 1994.

———. *The Problem of Crime.* New York: New York University Press, 1970.

———. "The Way of Peace: On Crime, Suffering, and Service," *Criminology as Peacemaking.* Harold Pepinsky and Richard Quinney (eds.). Bloomington: University of Indiana Press, 1991.

Rebello, Gilson. *A guerrilha de Caparaó.* São Paulo: Alfa-Omega, 1980.

Reis Filho, Daniel Aarão and Pedro de Moraes. *68, a paixão de uma utopia.* Rio de Janeiro: Espaço e Tempo, 1988.

Revkin, Andrew. *The Burning Season: The Murder of Chico Mendes and the Fight for the Amazon Rain Forest.* Boston: Houghton Mifflin, 1990.

Ribeiro, Darcy. "Universities and Social Development," *Elites in Latin America.* Seymour Martin Lipset and Aldo Solari (eds.). New York: Oxford University Press, 1967.

Ribeiro, Octávio. *Barra Pesada.* Rio de Janeiro: Codecri [Coleção Edições do *Pasquim.* vol. XII], [no date].

———. *Por que eu traí: confessões de Cabo Anselmo.* São Paulo: Global, 1984.

Romagnoli, Luiz Henrique and Tânia Gonçalves (eds.). "Das ruas, com o povo, à clandestinidade," *História imediata: a volta da UNE: de Ibiúna a Salvador.* São Paulo: Alfa-Omega, 1979, vol. V.

Rose, R. S. *Beyond the Pale of Pity: Key Episodes of Elite Violence in Brazil to 1930*. Bethesda: Austin and Winfield, 1998.

———. *One of the Forgotten Things: Getúlio Vargas and Brazilian Social Control, 1930–1954*. Westport: Greenwood, 2000.

———. "Slavery in Brazil: Does It Still Exist?" *Review of Latin American Studies*. vol. IV, no. 1, 1991.

———. "Slavery in Brazil: Does it Still Exist Today?" paper presented to the 83rd Annual Meeting of the American Sociological Association, Atlanta, August 26, 1988.

———. "The Man of Gold," *Today* [Academy of Criminal Justice Sciences]. September 1989.

———. "Vigilantism and the Police in Brazil: The State of Rio de Janeiro." Paper presented at the World Congress of Sociology, Mexico City, August 18, 1982.

Ryff, Raul. *O fazendeiro Jango no governo*. Rio de Janeiro: Avenir, 1979.

Salum, Carlos A. L. "Chico Barque: uma história em 4 tempos: poeta, ídolo, vilão, profeta," *Vilão & Guitarra MPB*. vol. I, no. 7, 1981.

Sandroni, Cícero. *I seminário do grupo tortura nunca mais: depoimentos e debates*. Branca Eloysa (org.). Petrópolis: Vozes, 1987.

Schlichthorst, Carl. *O Rio de Janeiro como é, 1824–1826: huma vez e nunca mais*. Rio de Janeiro: Getulio Costa, 1943.

Seitenfus, Ricardo [Antônio] Silva. *O Brasil de Getúlio Vargas e a formação dos blocos, 1930–1942: o processo do envolvimento brasileiro na II Guerra Mundial*. São Paulo: Nacional, 1985.

Serbin, Kenneth. "The Anatomy of a Death: Repression, Human Rights and the Case of Alexandre Vannucchi Leme in Authoritarian Brazil," *Journal of Latin American Studies*. vol. XXX, part I, February 1998.

Sevcenko, Nicolau. *Literatura como missão: tensões sociais e criação cultural na Primeira República*. São Paulo: Brasiliense, 1983.

Shoumatoff, Alex. *The World is Burning*. Boston: Little, Brown, 1990.

Silva, Hélio. *A vez e a voz dos vencidos: militares x militares*. Petrópolis: Vozes, 1988.

———. *1964: golpe ou contra-golpe?* Rio de Janeiro: Civilização Brasileira, 1975.

Singelmann, Peter. "Political Structure and Social Banditry in Northeastern Brazil," *Journal of Latin American Studies*. vol. VII, no. 1, May 1975.

Skidmore, Thomas. *Black into White: Race and Nationality in Brazilian Thought*. New York: Oxford University Press, 1974.

———. *Politics in Brazil, 1930–1964: An Experiment in Democracy*. New York: Oxford University Press, 1967.

———. *The Politics of Military Rule in Brazil, 1964–1985*. New York: Oxford University Press, 1988.

Slater, Candance. "Messianism and the Padre Cicero Stories," *Luso-Brazilian Review*, vol. XXVIII, no. 1, Summer 1991.

Sobel, Lester (ed.). *Political Terrorism*. New York: Facts on File, 1975.

Sodré, Nelson Werneck. *História militar do Brasil*. Rio de Janeiro: Civilização Brasileira, 1965.

Souza, Percival de. *A maior violência do mundo: Baixada Fluminense, Rio de Janeiro, Brasil*. São Paulo: Traço, 1980.

____. *Autópsia do medo: vida e morte do delegado Sérgio Paranhos Fleury*. São Paulo: Globo, 2000.

Souza, Rivadavia de. *Botando os pingos nos is: as inverdades nas memórias de Samuel Wainer*. Rio de Janeiro: Record, 1989.

Stacchini, José. *Março 64: mobilização da audácia*. São Paulo: Nacional, 1965.

Stepan, Alfred. *Rethinking Military Politics: Brazil and the Southern Cone*. Princeton: Princeton University Press, 1988.

———. *The Military in Politics: Changing Patterns in Brazil*. Princeton: Princeton University Press, 1971.

———. "The New Professionalism of Internal Warfare and Military Role Expansion," *Authoritarian Brazil: Origins, Politics, and Future*, Alfred Stepan (ed.). New Haven: Yale University Press, 1973.

Sweet, William. "Pandect of My Life." unpublished manuscript.

Távora, Araken. *Brasil, 1° de abril*. 2nd ed. Rio de Janeiro: Buccini, 1964.

Tejo, Limeira. *Jango: debate sôbre a crise dos nossos tempos*. Rio de Janeiro: Andes, 1957.

Telecomunicações do Rio de Janeiro. "serviços & negócios 1997," *Rio listas*. Rio de Janeiro: TELERJ, 1997.

Tendler, Silvio and Maurício Dias. *Jango*. 2nd ed. Porto Alegre: L and PM, 1984.

Varella, Drauzio. *Estação Carandiru*. São Paulo: Companhia das Letras, 1999.

Ventura, Maria Isabel Pinto (ed.). *Dos presos politicos brasileiros: acerca da repressão fascista no Brasil*. no place: Edições Maria da Fonte, 1976.

Ventura, Zuenir. *1968: o ano que não terminou*. Rio de Janeiro: Nova Fronteira, 1988.

Viana Filho, Luís. *O governo Castelo Branco.* Rio de Janeiro: José Olympio, 1975.

Victor, Mário. *Cinco anos que abalaram o Brasil (de Jânio Quadros ao Marechal Castelo Branco).* Rio de Janeiro: Civilização Brasileira, 1965.

Wainer, Samuel. *Minha razão de viver: memórias de um repórter.* Augusto Nunes (ed.), 4th ed. Rio de Janeiro: Record, 1988.

Walsh, Robert. *Notices of Brazil in 1828 and 1829.* London: Westly and Davis, 1830, vol. II.

Walters, Vernon. *Silent Missions.* Garden City: Doubleday, 1978.

Weffort, Francisco Correa. *Participação e conflito industrial: Contagem e Osasco, 1968.* São Paulo: CEBRAP, 1972.

Weschler, Joanna. "Massacre na casa de detenção," Aryeh Neier (ed.), Beatriz Castelo and Armanda Morris (trad.), *Os diretos humanos no Brasil.* São Paulo: Núcleo de Estudos da Violência, Universidade de São Paulo, 1993.

Weschler, Lawrence. *A Miracle, A Universe: Settling Accounts with Torture.* New York: Pantheon, 1990.

Williams, Margaret Todaro. "Integralism and the Brazilian Catholic Church," *Hispanic American Historical Review.* vol. LIV, no. 3, August 1974.

Wilson, Carlos. *The Tupamaros: The Unmentionables.* Boston: Branden, 1974.

Young, Jordan. *The Brazilian Revolution of 1930 and the Aftermath.* New Brunswick: Rutgers University Press, 1967.

Zappa, Regina. *Chico Buarque: para todos.* 4th ed. Rio de Janeiro: Relume Dumará, 1999.

Zweig, Stefan. *Brasil, país do futuro.* Odilon Gallotti (trans.). Rio de Janeiro: Guanabara, 1941.

Films, Musical Recordings, Radio, and Television Programs

"Beast of Burden," *Some Girls,* composed by Mick Jagger and Keith Richards, 1977.

"Encontro com a imprensa," Radio Jornal do Brasil, April 23, 1987.

État de siège (State of Siege). Directed by Constantin Costa-Gavras, Cinema X/Dieter Geissler Filmproduktion /Euro International Film (EIA) S.p.A./Reggane Films/Unidis, 1973.

Eu matei Lúcio Flávio, directed by Antônio Calmon, Atlântida Cinematográfica/Magnus Filmes, 1979.

"Fantástico," TV Globo, July 21, 1991.

"Fantástico," TV Globo, April 18, 1993.

"Hino da Scuderie Detetive Le Cocq," by Hugo Bellard and Nelson de Carvalho, 1974.

"Jornal da Globo," TV Globo, February 5, 1985.

"Jornal da Manchete," TV Manchete, September 5, 1991.

"Jornal Nacional," TV Globo, May 19, 1988.

Lamarca. directed by Sérgio Rezende, Morena Filmes/Produção da Cinema Filmes, 1994.

Lúcio Flávio: o passageiro da agonia. directed by Hector Babenco, Embrafilme/HB Filmes/Unifilme, 1977.

"Para não dizer que não falei das flores," composed by Geraldo Vandré [Geraldo Pedrosa de Araújo Dias], 1968.

Pixote: a lei do mais fraco. directed by Hector Babenco, Embrafilme/HB Filmes, 1981.

República dos assassinos, directed by Miguel Faria Jr., Roma Filmes do Brasil, 1979.

"The Decade of Destruction," directed by Adrian Cowell, "Killing for Land," episode 2, PBS TV, September 22, 1990.

Government and Official Publications

Brazil. *Coleção das leis da República dos Estados Unidos do Brasil de 1933: atos do Govêrno Provisório, janeiro a março.* Rio de Janeiro: Nacional, 1934, vol. I.

———. *Coleção das leis de 1967: atos do poder legislativo e atos legislativos do poder executivo, leis de janeiro a março.* Brasília: Nacional, 1967, vol. I.

———. *Coleção das leis de 1969: atos do poder executivo, decretos de abril a junho.* Brasília: Nacional, 1969, vol. IV.

———. *Coleção das leis de 1985: atos do poder legislativo e atos legislativos do poder executivo, leis de julho a setembro.* Brasília: Nacional, 1985, vol. V.

———. *Constituição [da] República Federativa do Brasil 1988.* Brasília: Centro Gráfico do Senado Federal, 1988.

———. Comissão Especial de Inquérito sôbre Atos Delituosos da Ditadura, "Acareação entre os depoentes," *Diario do Congresso Nacional.* June 19, 1947.

———. Comissão Especial de Inquérito sôbre Atos Delituosos da Ditadura, "Depoimento do Belmiro Valverde," *Diario do Congresso Nacional.* May 27, 1947.

———. Comissão Especial de Inquérito sôbre Atos Delituosos da Ditadura, "Depoimento do Bernardino de Oliveira Carvalho," *Diario do Congresso Nacional.* June 7, 1947.

———. Comissão Especial de Inquérito sôbre Atos Delituosos da Ditadura, "Depoimento do Carlos Marighella," *Diario do Congresso Nacional.* August 28, 1947.

———. Comissão Especial de Inquérito sôbre Atos Delituosos da Ditadura, "Depoimento do Iguatemi Ramos da Silva," *Diario do Congresso Nacional.* September 9, 1947.

———. Comissão Especial de Inquérito sôbre Atos Delituosos da Ditadura, "Depoimento do João Alves de Mota," *Diario do Congresso Nacional.* August 28, 1947.

———. Comissão Especial de Inquérito sôbre Atos Delituosos da Ditadura, "Depoimento do Luís Carlos Prestes," *Diario do Congresso Nacional.* September 20, 1947.

———. Comissão Especial de Inquérito sôbre Atos Delituosos da Ditadura, "Depoimento do Paulo Franklin de Souza Elejalde," *Diario do Congresso Nacional.* May 27, 1947.

———. Comissão Especial de Inquérito sôbre Atos Delituosos da Ditadura, "Depoimento do Samuel Lopes Pereira," *Diario do Congresso Nacional.* May 28, 1947.

———. *Consolidação das leis do trabalho.* Rio de Janeiro: Nacional, 1946.

———. *Diário do Congresso Nacional.* May 11, 1961, sec. 1.

———. *Diario do Congresso Nacional.* September 4, 1968, sec. 1, supplement.

———. *Diário oficial.* April 9, 1964, sec. 1, part 1.

———. *Diário oficial.* April 11, 1964, sec. 1, part 1.

———. *Diário oficial.* April 13, 1964, sec. 1, part 1.

———. *Diário oficial.* April 27, 1964, sec. 1, part 1.

———. *Diário oficial.* June 3, 1964, sec. 1, part 1.

———. *Diário oficial.* June 15, 1964, sec. 1, part 1.

———. *Diário oficial.* July 15, 1964, sec. 1, part 1.

———. *Diário oficial.* September 11, 1964, sec. 1, part 1.

———. *Diário oficial.* November 11, 1964, sec. 1, part 1.

———. *Diário oficial.* July 13, 1965, sec. 1, part 1.

———. *Diário oficial.* October 27, 1965, sec. 1, part 1.

———. *Diário oficial.* November 4, 1965, sec. 1, part 1.

———. *Diário oficial.* November 22, 1965, sec. 1, part 1.

———. *Diário oficial.* February 7, 1966, sec. 1, part 1.

———. *Diário oficial.* October 20, 1966, sec. 1, part 1.

———. *Diário oficial.* December 7, 1966, sec. 1, part 1.

———. *Diário oficial.* February 10, 1967, sec. 1, part 1.

———. *Diário oficial.* March 13, 1967, sec. 1, part 1.

———. *Diário oficial.* April 5, 1968, sec. 1, part 1.

———. *Diário oficial.* June 14, 1968, sec. 1, part 1.

———. *Diário oficial.* December 13, 1968, sec. 1, part 1.

———. *Diário oficial.* November 23, 1973, sec. 1, part 1.

———. Escola Superior de Guerra. *Doutrina básica.* Rio de Janeiro: Escola Superior de Guerra, 1979.

———. Fundação IBGE—Instituto Brasileiro de Estatística, Serviço Nacional de Recenseamento, *Censo demográfico de 1960, Brasil.* Rio de Janeiro: IBGE, n.d., vol. I.

———. Fundação IBGE—Instituto Brasileiro de Estatística, Serviço Nacional de Recenseamento, *Censo demográfico de 1960, Guanabara.* Rio de Janeiro: IBGE, 1968, vol. I, tomo XII, 1ª parte.

———. Fundação IBGE—Instituto Brasileiro de Estatística, Serviço Nacional de Recenseamento, *Distrito Federal, censo demográfico [1950].* Rio de Janeiro: IBGE, 1955, vol. XXIV, tomo I.

———. Fundação IBGE—Instituto Brasileiro de Estatística, Serviço Nacional de Recenseamento, *Estado do Rio de Janeiro, censo demográfico [1950].* Rio de Janeiro: IBGE, 1955, vol. XXIII, tomo I.

———. Fundação IBGE—Instituto Brasileiro de Estatística, Serviço Nacional de Recenseamento, *Estado de São Paulo, censo demográfico [1950].* Rio de Janeiro: IBGE, 1954.

———. Fundação Instituto Brasileiro de Geografia e Estatística, Departamento de Estatísticas de População, *Censo demográfico de 1960, Rio de Janeiro.* Rio de Janeiro: IBGE, n.d., vol. I, tomo XI.

———. Fundação Instituto Brasileiro de Geografia e Estatística, Departamento de Estatísticas de População, *Censo demográfico de 1960, São Paulo.* Rio de Janeiro: IBGE, n.d., vol. I, tomo XIII.

———. Ministério da Economia, Fazenda e Planejamento, *Anuário estatístico do Brasil.* Rio de Janeiro: IBGE, 1990.

———. Ministério da Reforma e Desenvolvimento Agrário, Coordenadoria de Conflitos Agrários, "Trabalho escravo," 1986.

———. Ministério do Planejamento e Coordenação Geral, Instituto Brasileiro de Estatística, Departamento de Censos, *Tabulações avançadas do censo demográfico, 1970: resultados preliminares.* Rio de Janeiro: IBGE, 1971.

———. Secretaria de Planejamento, *Anuuário estatístico do Brasil, 1982.* Rio de Janeiro: IBGE, 1986.

———. Secretaria de Planejamento, *Anuário estatístico do Brasil, 1985.* Rio de Janeiro, IBGE, 1986.

———. Secretaria de Planejamento da Presidência da República, Fundação Instituto Brasileiro de Geografia e Estatística, *Censo demográfico [1980], dados gerais—migração—instrução—fecundidade—mortalidade, Rio de Janeiro.* Rio de Janeiro: IBGE, 1983, vol. I, tomo 4, número 18.

———. Secretaria de Planejamento da Presidência da República, Fundação Instituto Brasileiro de Geografia e Estatística, *Censo demográfico [1980], dados gerais—migração—instrução—fecundidade—mortalidade, São Paulo.* Rio de Janeiro: IBGE, 1982, vol. I, tomo 4, número 19.

Partido dos Trabalhadores, Comunicado à imprensa da Secretaria Nacional de Imprensa e Propaganda do PT, August 14, 1980.

Rio de Janeiro. Secretaria de Estado de Justiça, Departamento Geral de Documentação, *Legislação do estado do Rio de Janeiro: lei complementar, leis, decreto legislativo, decretos.* Rio de Janeiro: Oficial, 1982, vol. VIII.

United States. Department of Commerce, *Statistical Abstract of the United States, 1961.* Washington, DC: U.S. Government Printing Office, 1961.

———. U.S. Senate, Hearings Before the Subcommittee on Western Hemisphere Affairs of the Committee on Foreign Relations, *United States Policies and Programs in Brazil.* Washington, DC: U.S. Government Printing Office, 1971.

Internet Articles

Brazil. Senado. "A morte anunciada." <http://www.senado.gov.br/web/senador/marinasi/chmende4.htm>, March 21, 2002.

———. Instituto Brasileiro de Geografia e Estatística. "Censo demográfico 1991, População residente por situação (urbana e rural), segundo o sexo."

<http://www.ibge.gov.br/ibge/estatistica/populacao/censodem/tab202.shtm>, December 2, 2001.

———. Instituto Brasileiro de Geografia e Estatística. "Censo demográfico 2000—Sinopse preliminar, População residente, em valores absolutos e relativos, total, em situação urbana e em situação urbana na sede municipal, áre a total e densidade demográfica, segundo as unidades da federação e municípos, [Rio de Janeiro]." <http://www.ibge.gov.br/ibge/estatistica/populacao/censo2000/sinopse.php?tipo=21&uf=33>, December 2, 2001.

———. Instituto Brasileiro de Geografia e Estatística. "Censo demográfico 2000—Sinopse preliminar, População residente, em valores absolutos e relativos, total, em situação urbana e em situação urbana na sede municipal, área total e densidade demográfica, segundo as unidades da federação e municípos, [São Paulo]." <http://www.ibge.gov.br/ibge/estatistica/populacao/censo2000/sinopse.php?tipo=21&uf=35>, December 2, 2001.

———. Instituto Brasileiro de Geografia e Estatística. "Tabela 200—População residente por sexo, situação e grupos de idade, 1970 [Guanabara]." <http://www.sidra.ibge.gov.br/bda/tabela/protabl.asp?z=t&o=1&i=P>, March 2, 2005.

———. Instituto Brasileiro de Geografia e Estatística. "Tabela 200—População residente por sexo, situação e grupos de idade, 1970 [Rio de Janeiro]." <http://www.sidra.ibge.gov.br/bda/tabela/protabl.asp?z=t&o=1&i=P>, March 2, 2005.

———. Instituto Brasileiro de Geografia e Estatística. "Tabela 200—População residente por sexo, situação e grupos de idade, 1970 [São Paulo]." <http://www.sidra.ibge.gov.br/bda/tabela/protabl.asp?z=t&o=1&i=P>, March 1, 2005.

CPDOC. "Goulart, João." <http://www.cpdoc.fgv.br/dhbb/verbetes_htm/2412_10.asp>, April 6, 2003.

"Favela Tem Memória," <http://www.favelatemmemoria.com.br/publique/cgi/cgilua.exe/sys/start.htm?sid=7&infoid=109>, February 16, 2005.

Folha de São Paulo. "Maluf troca imóveis por empresas, indica IR." <http://www1.folha.uol.com.br/folha/brasil/ult96u24828.shl>, March 2, 2004.

Jornal do Brasil. "Acusado nega ser mandante." <http://jbonline.terra.com.br/destaques/campo/campo_1712.html>, December 22, 2001.

———. "Denúncia do JB põe acusado na prisão." <http://jbonline.terra.com.br/destaques/campo/campo_1512.html>, December 22, 2001.

———. "*Jornal do Século*—um produto do *Jornal do Brasil*—1964 Cronologia." <http://jbonline.terra.com.br/jseculo/1964b.html>, January 31, 2002.

———. "Mandante de assassinato é localizado." <http://jbonline.terra.com.br/destaques/campo/campo_1412.html>, December 22, 2001.

———. "Religioso foi mártir." <http://jbonline.terra.com.br/destaques/campo/campo_1412b.html>, December 22, 2001.

———. "Sem-terra continuarão presos." <http://jbonline.terra.com.br/jb/papel/brasil/2002/03/28/jorbra20020328013.html>, March 29, 2002.

O Estado de São Paulo. "Livro revela a polêmica trajetória do delegado Fleury." <http://www.jt.estadao.com.br/editorias/2000/11/27/ger432.html>, June 30, 2001.

O Globo. "Homicídios dolosos caem 7,5% no estado, mas PM mata 60% a mais em 2003." <http://oglobo.globo.com/online/sp/133722908.asp>, February 1, 2004.

———. "SNI acampanhou de perto o enterro de Jango." <http://oglobo.globo.com/Ciencia/12421336.htm>, December 16, 2001.

Partido Democrático Trabalhista. "Como Kennedy participou da derrubada de João Goulart. "*Gazeta Mercantil* (Rio de Janeiro)," July 21–23, 2000. <http://www.pdt.org.br/jgkencondor.htm>, October 10, 2001.

São Paulo. Polícia Militar. GARRA. "Grupo Armado de Repressão a Roubos e Assaltos." <http://www.seguranca.sp.br/garra/pagina2.html>, June 20, 2001.

Spartacus. "Charles de Gaulle." <http://www.spartacus.schoolnet.co.uk/2WWdegaulle.htm>, March 2, 2005.

Tortura Nunca Mais. "Olavo Hansen." <http://www.torturanuncamais.org.br/mtnm_mor/mor_mortes_oficiais/mor_1970_olavo_hans>, June 29, 2001.

———. "Tito de Alencar Lima (Frei)." <http://www.torturanuncamais.org.br/mtnm_mor/mor_mortes_exilio/mor_tito_lima.htm>, March 2, 2005.

Interviews

Alves Filho, Francisco. Interview, Rio de Janeiro, December 23, 1992.

Amado, Thomé. Interview, Rio de Janeiro, August 21, 1994.

Anonymous-1: Interviews: Rio de Janeiro, June 17, 1988; February 24, 1989; February 29, 1989; March 9, 1989; April 26, 1989; June 9, 1989; July 29, 1989; September 17, 1992; October 28, 1992; April 2, 1993; March 24, 1994; and April 12, 1994.

Anonymous-3: Interviews: Rio de Janeiro, January 19, 1982; February 12, 1982; February 27, 1982; February 5, 1989; July 27, 1993; November 6, 1999; August 1, 2001; December 10, 2002; and telephone interview, Bakersfield/São Paulo, November 29, 2001.

Anonymous-4. Interview, Rio de Janeiro, February 23, 1988.

Bandeira, Luís Alberto Moniz. Interview, Rio de Janeiro, December 16, 1992.

Bicudo, Hélio. Interview, São Paulo, February 8, 1993.

Borer, Cecil. Interview, Rio de Janeiro, May 28, 1998.

Del Roio, Jose Luiz. Telephone interview, Rio de Janeiro/São Paulo, July 31, 1994.

Donnici, Marcio Luiz: Interviews: Rio de Janeiro, February 28, 1982; and December 10, 1992.

Dulles, John W.F.: Telephone interviews, Fresno/Austin, January 24, 1991; and April 24, 1991.

Eloysa, Branca. Interview, Rio de Janeiro, August 16, 1989.

Gabeira, Fernando. Interview, Rio de Janeiro, November 25, 1992.

Goulart, João Vicente. Interview, Niterói, December 19, 2000.

Gracie, Robson. Interview, Rio de Janeiro, August 6, 1991.

Hasslocher, Ivan: Telephone interviews: Fresno/Houston, January 28, 1992; and January 29, 1992.

"Jaguar" [Sérgio de Magalhães Gomes Jaguaribe]. Interview [via Maria Tereza Viana de Freitas Corujo], Rio de Janeiro, July 26, 1991.

Kahn, Tulio. Interview, São Paulo, July 28, 1994.

Cássio, Loredano [Cássio Loredano]. Telephone interview, Rio de Janeiro, January 13, 2003.

Malina, Solomão. Interview, São Paulo, July 28, 1994.

Maranhão, Malu. Telephone interview, Rio de Janeiro/Goiânia, October 15, 1999.

Meirelles, Togo. Interview, Rio de Janeiro, August 25, 1994.

Prestes, Anita Leocádia. Interviews: Rio de Janeiro, August 6, 1994; and April 17, 2004.

Prestes, Luís Carlos. Interview, Rio de Janeiro, August 13, 1987.

Prestes, Lygia. Interviews: Rio de Janeiro, August 6, 1994; and April 17, 2004.

Sacchetta, Vladimir. Interview, São Paulo, August 17, 1994.

"Sivuca" [José Guilherme Godinho Ferreira]. Telephone interview, Rio de Janeiro, May 25, 2000.

Sodré, Nelson Werneck. Interview, Rio de Janeiro, August 8, 1991.

Souza, Gilson Ferreira de. Interview, Rio de Janeiro, June 15, 1989.

Tórtima, Pedro. Interview, Rio de Janeiro, July 13, 1988.

Letters and E-mails

Bicudo, Hélio: e-mails: July 11, 2001; July 16, 2001; September 11, 2001; October 29, 2001; October 31, 2001; and December 12, 2001.

Bueno, Eurides de Sousa, letter, April 22, 1988.

Dulles, John W. F.: e-mails: August 16, 2000; April 7, 2003; April 9, 2003; June 16, 2003; letters: January 9, 1991; December 20, 1991; September 16, 1993; and April 4, 2003 [postmarked].

Fonseca, Paulo Apulcro, e-mail, June 4, 2004.

Giannotti, Vito, e-mail, February 6, 2004.

Svacina, Otti [Otakar O.], e-mails: July 15, 2003; and July 16, 2003.

Sweet, William, e-mail, May 16, 2003.

Newspapers and Periodicals

A Gazeta (Rio Branco), 1994–96.

A Luta (Recife), 1948.

Brazil Herald (Rio de Janeiro), 1963.

Ciência Hoje (Rio de Janeiro), 1987.

Commonweal (New York), 1970.

Companheiro (São Paulo), 1980.

Correio da Manhã (Rio de Janeiro), 1954–68.

Correio da Noite (Rio de Janeiro), 1951.

Correio do Povo (Porto Alegre), 1982.

Diario Carioca (Rio de Janeiro), 1951.

Diário de Notícias (Porto Alegre), 1959.

Diário de Notícias (Rio de Janeiro), 1964.
Diario de Pernambuco (Recife), 1966.
Diario Popular (Rio de Janeiro), 1951.
Diretrizes (Rio de Janeiro), 1947.
Em Tempo (São Paulo), 1980.
Época (Rio de Janeiro), 2000–2003.
Estado de Minas (Belo Horizonte), 1977.
Ex-15 (São Paulo), 1975.
Fatos e Fotos (Rio de Janeiro), 1961–71.
Folha de São Paulo, 1977–2001.
Fresno Bee (Fresno, CA), 1999.
Gazeta Mercantil (Rio de Janeiro), 2000.
Harper's (New York), 1999.
Imprensa Popular (Rio de Janeiro), 1954.
Isto É (São Paulo), 1978–2002.
Isto É Senhor (São Paulo), 1990–1992.
Jornal da Tarde (São Paulo), 1968–86.
Jornal do Brasil (Rio de Janeiro), 1938–2004.
Jornal do Commercio (Rio de Janeiro), 1907–65.
Life (New York), 1964.
Los Angeles Times, 1961–96.
Manchete (Rio de Janeiro), 1958–92.
Movimento (São Paulo), 1980.
New Scientist (London), 1973.
Newsweek (New York), 1966–97.
New York Times, 1964–99.
News from Brazil (Los Angeles), 1992.
Notícias Populares (São Paulo), 1963–99.
Novos Rumos (Rio de Janeiro), 1960–62.
O Cruzeiro (Rio de Janeiro), 1962–68.
O Dia (Rio de Janeiro), 1951–99.
O Estado de São Paulo, 1964–94.
O Fluminense (Niterói), 1976.
O Globo (Rio de Janeiro), 1951–2004.

O Jornal (Rio de Janeiro), 1964.
O Mundo (Rio de Janeiro), 1947.
O Rio Branco (Rio Branco), 1995–99.
O Tira (São Paulo), 1990.
Página 20 (Rio Branco), 1995–99.
Panfleto (Rio de Janeiro), 1964.
Pasquim (Rio de Janeiro), 1981–84.
Pif Paf (Rio de Janeiro), 1964.
Playboy (Brazilian ed.), 1989.
Povo do Rio (Rio de Janeiro), 1983–99.
Revista Illustrada (Rio de Janeiro), 1886.
San Francisco Chronicle, 1990.
Status (Rio de Janeiro), 1986.
The Nation (New York), 1971–78.
The New Republic (Washington, DC), 1985.
Time (New York), 1964–70.
Tribuna da Imprensa (Rio de Janeiro), 1951–94.
Última Hora (Rio de Janeiro), 1951–85.
Ultima Hora (Santiago de Chile), 1964.
Unidade Proletária (Rio de Janeiro), 1975.
Veja (Rio de Janeiro), 1970–2002.
Visão (Rio de Janeiro), 1987.
Voz Operária (Rio de Janeiro), 1971.

Index

* = extermination group in 1951–99 Rio/São Paulo death squad killings